Winner of the Jules and Frances Landry Award for 1987

Southern Biography Series
William J. Cooper, Jr., Editor

John C. Calhoun and the Price of Union

John Niven

John C. Calhoun

nd the Price of Union

A Biography

Louisiana State University Press
Baton Rouge and London

97   96   95   94   93   92   91   90   89   88   5   4   3   2   1

Designer: Laura Roubique Gleason
Typeface: Baskerville
Typesetter: The Composing Room of Michigan, Inc.
Printer: Thomson-Shore, Inc.
Binder: John H. Dekker & Sons, Inc.

Library of Congress Cataloging-in-Publication Data
Niven, John.
    John C. Calhoun and the price of union: a biography / John Niven.
        p.   cm.—(Southern biography series)
    Bibliography: p.
    Includes index.
    ISBN 0-8071-1451-0 (alk. paper)
        1. Calhoun, John C. (John Caldwell), 1782–1850. 2. United States—
Politics and government—1815–1861. 3. Legislators—United States—
Biography. 4. United States. Congress. Senate—Biography.
I. Title. II. Series.
E340.C15N58   1988
328.73'092'4—dc19
[B]   88-11775
                                                                CIP

To the memory of my mother,
Marian Fredricks Niven

Contents

Preface   xv

Abbreviations and Short Titles   xvii

    I   A Frontier Heritage   1

   II   Self-Imposed Exile   13

  III   Hawk   26

  IV   Not a Moment to Lose   43

    V   Erecting Defenses   58

  VI   Panic, Politics, and Personality   78

  VII   Vice-President   102

VIII   Reluctant Jacksonian   122

  IX   "Exposition" and "Protest"   154

    X   Nullification, 1831–1833   179

  XI   An Unlikely Cause   200

  XII   A Cautious Return   219

XIII   Hope Springs Eternal   239

XIV   Texas   264

XV   Oregon and Mexico   283

XVI   A Southern Man and a Slaveholder   306

XVII   The Price of Union   322

On the Sources   347

Index   355

Illustrations

following page 137

John C. Calhoun, late 1840s
Charleston, South Carolina, late 1840s
Floride Calhoun
Andrew Pickens Calhoun
Anna Maria Clemson
Thomas Green Clemson
Francis Wilkinson Pickens
Joel Roberts Poinsett
Robert Barnwell Rhett
Franklin Harper Elmore
Dixon Lewis
George McDuffie
Henry Clay
Daniel Webster
Cartoon of the presidential campaign, 1844
Fort Hill, Calhoun's home
John Quincy Adams
Martin Van Buren
James K. Polk

Preface

When I was asked if I would be willing to write a biography of John C. Calhoun for the Southern Biography Series, I had several reservations before I finally agreed to undertake the project. As a northerner, born and bred in New York and Connecticut, I wondered whether I could do justice to this epitome of antebellum southernism. Although I have always sought to avoid the historical sin of present-mindedness, I could never bring myself to consider objectively Calhoun's position on slavery and the nature of the Union. Could I then do justice to the man and his career? Could I say anything about him that had not already been well said by others?

After renewing my acquaintance with the literature on Calhoun and studying some of his speeches and more revealing correspondence, I formed an opinion of him that differed somewhat from conventional views. I must confess, however, that my negative opinions on Calhoun's defense of slavery and his ideas on the nature of the Union were reinforced by my close study of the man and his writing.

I found Calhoun to be more consistent in his political career than his contemporaries or his previous biographers have given him credit. I also detected a defensive posture on public policy that controlled his reaction to the rapidly changing political, social, and economic environment of the United States after the War of 1812. The war itself, of which he was a leading instigator and which nearly resulted in the ruin of the nation, I came to believe made a lasting impression on his mind and personality, which were cast in a defensive mode. I have tried throughout this work to bolster these impressions of Calhoun's character and policies with his own remarks in speeches, debates, and correspondence. My assessment of Calhoun's own writings on political theory, "The Discourse on the Constitution" and "The Disquisition on Government," differs markedly from current interpretations, in that these works are considered as contemporary political documents, almost in a pamphleteering sense, rather than as treatises in political philosophy. I have also pointed out their originality and their impact on American thought.

Finally, I was motivated to do this traditional biography because I felt that there still remains a place in historical scholarship for writing about leaders without denigrating the followers who have so captivated some modern historians. In short, I believe there remains a place for scholarly biography outside of popular treatments for popular markets that are increasingly entrusted to journalists. In writing about Calhoun, I have simply composed a biography based largely on primary sources. I have not engaged in psychic analysis of my subject, nor have I tried to utilize Calhoun as a means of assessing the mind or the sociology of the antebellum South.

Many friends and associates have helped me with this work. William J. Cooper, dean of the graduate school at Louisiana State University and editor of the Southern Biography Series, has been a source of never-failing encouragement. I have benefited much from his incomparable knowledge of antebellum politics in the South. Ernest M. Lander, Jr., of Clemson University, an authority on Calhoun and on the Old South, has read and criticized the entire manuscript. As a Yankee, I would never have dared venture into the very special territory of southern history without Lander's expert criticism. Robert V. Remini of the University of Illinois, Chicago Circle, and Hans Trefousse of City University of New York have also read the manuscript, and I have profited much from their insightful comments. I reserve a special word of thanks for Les Phillabaum, Beverly Jarrett, Catherine Silvia, and Catherine Landry of Louisiana State University Press. In addition, my colleagues Alfred Louch, Henry Gibbons, Ralph Ross, John H. Kemble, Charles Lofgren, and William Evans have reviewed all or a part of this work. Clyde Wilson, editor of *The Papers of John C. Calhoun,* supplied me with valuable copies of Calhoun's correspondence that have not as yet been published. Lelah Mullican typed and retyped the manuscript through its many revisions. John Walsh checked the footnotes. I thank them all for their help; and for any errors that may appear, I take full responsibility.

Abbreviations and Short Titles

Adams Memoirs   Charles Francis Adams, ed. *Memoirs of John Quincy Adams*. 12 vols. Philadelphia, 1874–77.

Calhoun Correspondence   J. Franklin Jameson, ed. *Correspondence of John C. Calhoun*. Washington, D.C., 1900.

Calhoun Papers   W. Edwin Hemphill, Robert L. Meriwether, and Clyde Wilson, eds. *The Papers of John C. Calhoun*. 16 vols. Columbia, S.C., 1959–84.

Calhoun Works   Richard Crallé, ed. *The Works of John C. Calhoun*. 6 vols. New York, 1854–57.

FNYPL   A. C. Flagg Papers, New York Public Library, New York City.

Jackson Correspondence   John S. Bassett, ed. *Correspondence of Andrew Jackson*. 7 vols. Washington, D.C., 1926–35.

JHLC   James H. Hammond Papers, Division of Manuscripts, Library of Congress, Washington, D.C.

Life of JCC   William M. Meigs. *The Life of John C. Calhoun*. 2 vols. New York, 1917.

Polk Correspondence   Herbert Weaver *et al.*, eds. *The Correspondence of James K. Polk*. 6 vols. Nashville, 1969–83.

VBLC   Martin Van Buren Papers, Division of Manuscripts, Library of Congress, Washington, D.C.

Webster Papers   Charles M. Wiltse, ed. *The Papers of Daniel Webster: Correspondence*. 7 vols. Hanover, N.H., 1974–86.

John C. Calhoun and the Price of Union

I

A Frontier Heritage

It was obvious to those who visited John C. Calhoun during the second week of March, 1850, that the sixty-eight-year-old southern statesman was extremely ill. Since his last visit to the Senate on March 13, when he responded to the criticisms of the pugnacious senator from Mississippi, Henry S. Foote, he had been confined to his room on the second floor of H. V. Hill's boardinghouse near the Capitol. Calhoun, feverish, breathless, and frequently wracked with coughing, still thought that the disease would run its course and his health could be restored. He had had many similar bouts with what he called his "catarrhal weakness" and had managed to recover. But the tuberculosis from which he suffered had indeed reached a critical stage. With this insidious disease, the patient suffered bouts of acute pulmonary and cardiac distress that were followed by comparative relief, even a sense of returning health. After one such attack, so severe that his kinsman Armistead Burt had telegraphed Calhoun's wife Floride in South Carolina to hasten to Washington, Calhoun had suddenly seemed to recover. He had walked about his chamber and resumed dictation to his volunteer secretary, the young New York journalist Joseph A. Scoville.

At this time Calhoun with uncanny clarity prophesied almost the exact order of events over the next decade or so that he thought would bring about the destruction of the Union. "I fix its probable occurrence within twelve years or three presidential terms," he told Senator James M. Mason of Virginia. "You and others of your age will probably live to see it; I shall not. The mode by which it will be done is not so clear; it may be brought about in a manner that no one now foresees. But the probability is, it will explode in a presidential election."[1] Calhoun was responding to the hostile northern reaction that greeted his speech delivered for him by Mason in the Senate on March 4, 1850, and to Daniel Webster's strenuous effort three days later to appease the South. Yet he continued even in these last days of his life to hope that a South

1. Virginia Mason (ed.), *Public Life and Diplomatic Correspondence of James M. Mason* (Roanoke, Va., 1903), 72, 73.

united on the slavery issue would force the North to make the concessions he deemed essential.

Calhoun had spent considerable time since the commencement of the Thirty-first Congress helping to organize a convention of the slaveholding states that would meet at Nashville, Tennessee, on June 3. He believed that the gesture would force a practical solution to what was undoubtedly a dangerous state of affairs for the nation, and was willing to risk secession to gain it. More importantly, he saw the convention as a powerful impulse toward southern unification, a process he had been cultivating in speeches and debates, and through correspondence and spirited conversation, during the past twenty years.

Despite the acute sensitivity Calhoun had exhibited on the slavery issue, and the constant adumbration of southern weakness and of northern exploitation he had seen, he still shrank from the consequences of disunion. And when Henry Foote implied that Calhoun favored separation of the states, he hotly denied it.[2] He had, after all, spent his adult life under the Union as established by the Constitution. No budding politician had voiced more patriotic sentiments than he at the beginning of his career. Nor had any member of Congress pressed more eloquently and passionately for nationhood—for war with Great Britain to settle once and for all the question of national independence.

Even when economic and moral pressure against southern society and its "peculiar institution" began to temper his stand, Calhoun saw clearly the dread consequence of disunion. At the height of abolitionist agitation in the 1830s, he wrote his beloved daughter Anna Maria, who had suggested peaceful separation of the sections, that though such a condition was "a natural and common conclusion . . . those who make it up, do not think of the difficulty involved . . . how many bleeding pours [sic] must be taken up in passing the knife of seperation [sic] through a body politick, (in order to make two of one) which has been so long bound together by so many ties, political, social and commercial."[3]

Throughout a lengthy, contentious political career, Calhoun had been charged with inconsistency, with starting out in Congress as a nationalist of broadest stripe and then in midpassage switching to the narrowest sort of sectionalism as expressed in nullification. Calhoun indignantly denied the charge. He had always been, he maintained, a staunch supporter of the interests of his state, his class, and his region.

2. *Calhoun Works*, IV, 577.
3. *Calhoun Correspondence*, II, 391.

What had been right for South Carolina and the South as a whole in 1816 had been right for the nation. A protective tariff could help in developing industry in his state as a complement to its agriculture. The same formula applied to the North and the West. Internal improvements at public expense and a sound currency system benefited all regions. By 1824, however, dominance of the slave-cotton culture in the South, as opposed to emergent industry in the North, had struck an imbalance. Calhoun decided that special consideration for industrial development at the expense of agricultural and commercial interests was wrong for South Carolina, the South, and the Union, and for the next ten years he battled for tariff reform with the entrepreneurs of the free states. Slavery by now had become not just essential to his state's and his region's economies but, as Calhoun saw it, an intrinsic part of the South's social order. To a South Carolinian first and a southerner second, the northern and northwestern states with their manufacturing interests and antislavery bias were threatening the Union, not the South. To Calhoun there was no question of morality in the tariff controversy; the tariff was a violation of "the natural order of things," and it had to be reversed.

But during those last days of his life—his logical mind at times sharpened by the fever of his illness—Calhoun was obsessed with the issue of slavery. When he was not dictating resolutions to be offered at the forthcoming Nashville convention or revising the as yet incomplete manuscript of "The Discourse on the Constitution," he was wrestling with that problem which he knew was the fundamental issue facing the nation and which in his darker moments he decided was insoluble. Yet he had not always believed so. As his memory, always acute, went back to his boyhood in southwestern South Carolina, he realized that he had taken slavery for granted—like family, like the red soil of his father's farm that he had plowed with help of an ox team and his slave companion, Sawney. Farming was not just an aspect of one's existence; it had always been and would always be the basic structure of any region.

When Calhoun surveyed the situation in the society and the economy of the world he knew, he was of two minds—one deeply rooted in eighteenth-century thought, the other strikingly modern even for the nineteenth century. His analysis of politics was in the vanguard of modern thinkers, his perception of interests and class conflict predated Karl Marx and John Stuart Mill. Yet his conclusions were single-minded and reactionary.

In thinking about the history of organized society, Calhoun had early decided that agriculture was the fundamental activity of so-

4

cialized man. Agriculture reinforced republican virtue and democratic government. As early as 1820, he wrote his friend Micah Sterling that "nothing can be more congenial to our excellent political institutions, than the habits produced by agricultural pursuits."[4] Commerce, service industries like banking, and such manufacturing as existed in the mid-1830s were simply ancillary to agriculture and subservient to it. A nation's wealth must be measured, as Adam Smith and the Physiocrats before him had argued, in its agricultural output. Agriculture was first, Smith declared, "in the natural order of things." Calhoun would have added that agriculture also formed a nation's society and its moral purpose. Again following Smith's dictum, any different ranking would be "unnatural and retrograde."[5]

Political parties in the United States and in Europe existed, Calhoun felt, to settle political differences, not economic ones. The issues had been liberty versus tyranny, virtue versus power. His interpretation of English history ruled out any economic conflict between the major parties and factions. The English civil war saw gentlemen of landed property on both sides, the issue being not one of class conflict but a political contest of power between an absolute monarchy and an oligarchy. He considered the Glorious Revolution in the same light. The spirit of the French Revolution left Calhoun's thinking untouched except for its insistence on reason and inquiry, which he assimilated as instruments for his probings of the body politic. Natural rights, the equality of man, the social contract—all those notions dear to Jefferson and to the men of the Enlightenment—became simply political effusions that had little grounding in fact or experience when he subjected them to his own careful scrutiny. As for slavery, it was simply a practical application of labor under certain rules to agricultural production in certain areas. He avoided the moral implications of slavery and refused to consider the institution in abstract terms.

Like most men of his time and station, Calhoun had accepted the rhetoric of the American Revolution without much thought until a

4. *Calhoun Papers*, V, 42. See also the stimulating essay of Theodore R. Marmor, "Anti-Industrialism and the Old South: The Agrarian Perspective of John C. Calhoun," *Comparative Studies in Society and History*, IX (1966–67), 377–406.

5. Adam Smith, *The Wealth of Nations* (Chicago, 1972), Book III, 405. Calhoun's position was similar to prevailing thought in South Carolina during the antebellum years. Drew Gilpin Faust, in her close study of agricultural rhetoric, has shown that most Carolinian orators extolled agriculture as the cornerstone of society ("The Rhetoric and Ritual of Agriculture in Antebellum South Carolina," *Journal of Southern History*, XLV, No. 4 [November, 1979], 544, 545).

political division over divergent economic interests became apparent to him in the tariff debates of 1824. It was not a question of agrarianism versus capitalism. Neither the word *agrarianism* nor the word *capitalism,* as expressing a principle or a concept, was invented until after Calhoun's death. If the words had been in common use, however, the thrust of Calhoun's thought would have followed capitalist lines. His conclusions about wealth, community, and social stability were all expressed through private ownership and the working of land. The idea of organizing and directing a labor force with the assistance of machine technology was appropriate so long as it provided support for dominant agriculture. But when this system of economic activity with its ever-increasing division of free labor began to assert its dominance over farm society, when it threatened to bend all to its value system, Calhoun clearly recognized the implications for his region and saw its menace to what for him was the established order of things. His protest became ever more vehement, his analysis ever more penetrating. For his was a mind superior to those of most of his colleagues and peculiarly concentrated through the conditions of his family, his youth, and his education.

There was another factor in Calhoun's stance, however, a personal one, that was deeply rooted in his past and enhanced by a succession of events. Although Calhoun radiated confidence in his manner, his speech, and his personal affairs, he was a deeply insecure man. The Indian menace and the social upheaval in the backcountry during the last years of the revolutionary war, when Tory families engaged in blood feuds with their Whig neighbors, were still very much present during his childhood. The loss of both parents and a beloved only sister while Calhoun was an adolescent had left him not only grief stricken but lonely and disturbed. He compensated for these personal fears through unyielding industry and such an emphatic display of self-reliance that friends, neighbors, and teachers marked him as an impressively gifted and independent young man.

But Calhoun's experience as a thoughtless advocate of war in 1811 and 1812 exaggerated his latent fears. He felt keenly his own responsibility for nearly bringing everything he held dear down in ruins as his unprepared nation came close to dissolution. In his tireless quest for security after the debacle of 1812, he supported manufacturing as contributing to national self-sufficiency. From then until the end of his life, Calhoun sought protection first from the western Indians and the British while he was secretary of war, then from what he regarded as the North's exploitation of southern resources through its manipulation of public policy when he was vice-president and a senator from his home state. And finally, once the nation seemed safe, he sought security for his community and his region, with its slave-plantation system of economic and social values. He sought security for a section that he freely admitted was weaker in population and material resources, and he defended a position that he knew was morally inferior.

Calhoun was a driven man and a tragic figure. His ambition, his personal desire to achieve leadership, was often thwarted by lesser men than he. The life he made for himself, the security he felt on his plantation with his dependent retainers, and the agricultural pursuits that represented to him and to his neighbors stability in a rapidly changing environment were beyond price. Any menace to the southern institutions he valued was to be resisted with all the force of his character and his intellect. In this struggle, as he perceived it, he would overcompensate and in the end would more than any other individual destroy the culture he sought to preserve, perpetuating for several generations the very insecurity that had shaped his public career.

John Caldwell Calhoun was born on March 18, 1782, on his father's large farm at what was then called the district of Ninety-Six in southwestern South Carolina. Only twenty-six years before his birth, his father, Patrick Calhoun, together with his widowed mother, his brothers, and their families, had settled in the region. The Calhouns, a Scotch-Irish family, had a tradition of emigration. Originally from the highlands of Scotland, they had crossed the Irish Sea in the early years of the eighteenth century to settle in County Donegal on lands the British government had set aside to establish a Protestant enclave in what had formerly been an overwhelmingly Roman Catholic country.[6]

Tough and acquisitive, the family endured but one generation of farming under an increasingly restrictive land ownership system. In the mid-1730s the Calhouns left Ireland, attracted by land grants from the proprietors of Pennsylvania, who were seeking to stabilize the frontier from incursions of the French and the aggressive Indians of the Six Nations. They settled in southwestern Pennsylvania near what is now the Maryland line.

Although the Calhouns had to hack their farmlands and homesteads out of virgin wilderness, they enjoyed a modest prosperity for that time and place. When Patrick Calhoun died in 1741, he left an estate of £150, as well as his stock and land. Like so many of their neighbors, the Calhouns were a restless lot. Three or four years after

6. *Calhoun Papers*, XV, 774.

old Patrick Calhoun's death, they learned of land opportunities in southwestern Virginia, where again the provincial government was trying to secure the frontiers of the colony. The Calhouns moved south and west with their animals, wagons, and implements, finally taking up land near present-day Wytheville in Augusta County, about 15 miles from the North Carolina line. As in Pennsylvania, the family prospered. By the 1750s, the Calhouns owned 3,000 acres of land, more than 200 acres of which they had rendered tillable at the cost of unrelenting labor.[7]

7

No doubt the Calhouns and many other sturdy Scotch-Irish who had emigrated into the region would have remained had not the French and Indian War intervened. In the late summer of 1755, after General Braddock's defeat at Fort Duquesne (now Pittsburgh), the Calhouns and their neighbors were faced with the savage fury of a wide-scale Indian attack as war parties of the Six Nations began to assemble. But providentially, a refuge had just opened to the south.

One week before the British defeat, the royal governor of South Carolina concluded a treaty with the Cherokee nation in the western reaches of the colony, reaffirming the purchase of all lands east of a line running south from Waxhaw, a settlement on the North Carolina line, and east of Long Canes Creek. The line bisected present-day Laurens, Spartanburg, and Abbeville counties. The most important section of the treaty was Cherokee agreement to support the English rather than the French in the war, thus opening for settlement several hundred thousand acres of fertile lands. The colony promised to build a fort and a trading post at what was called Ninety-Six. About fifteen miles west of that point and running north and south, the territory was deemed to be Cherokee land. Royal governor William Henry Lyttelton, as anxious as his colleagues in Virginia and Pennsylvania to stabilize the frontier, inaugurated a liberal policy for disposal of these lands.[8]

Twenty-nine-year-old Patrick Calhoun, the only unmarried son in the family (he was a widower), happened to be at Waxhaw, South Carolina, at the time of the new Cherokee treaty. It is probable that he traveled south to inspect the lands around the new fort at Ninety-Six.[9]

7. Lyman Chalkley (comp.), *Chronicles of the Scotch Irish Settlement in Virginia; Extracted from the original Court Records of Augusta County, 1745–1800* (3 vols.; Rosslyn, Va., 1912–13), I, 5.

8. Charles M. Wiltse, *John C. Calhoun, Nationalist: 1782–1828* (Indianapolis, 1944), 11–16; David Duncan Wallace, *South Carolina: A Short History* (Columbia, S.C., 1961), 173–76.

9. W. Pinkney Starke, *Account of Calhoun's Early Life* (Washington, D.C., 1900), 66.

There were thousands of acres of rich soil on rolling hills. An enormous canebrake, much of it standing as high as twenty feet, covered the land. Prudent and observant frontier farmer that Calhoun was, he would have concluded that canes were much easier to clear than virgin forest. He would also have noted that the numerous fast-flowing streams of the region could be harnessed for water power that could turn sawmills and gristmills. And three rivers, navigable for small boats and rafts, flowed through the lands, providing access to the populous, long-settled coast. Abundance of game for food and peltry was additional incentive. Patrick Calhoun must have been impressed with what he saw because when he returned home, he urged the family to dispose of its holdings and move to the South Carolina frontier. It took little persuasion, because the Indian war, long threatened, was already driving frontier families to the east. Although hostilities had not as yet reached the Calhouns and other Scotch-Irish settlers in their valley, many were already on the move.

The four Calhoun brothers; their widowed sister, Mary Noble; their families; and their elderly mother, Catherine Montgomery Calhoun, left their Virginia homes in midwinter, 1756. They were part of a larger body of immigrants who had also decided to try their luck in the newly opened region. Their progress was slow but steady, dictated by the gait of the ox teams that drew their heavily laden wagons. Unquestionably, Patrick Calhoun acted as leader of the group, not just because he had an air of command, but because he had traversed the route and, as a self-taught surveyor of no mean skill, was able to find the easiest trail.

The main party reached Long Canes Creek a few miles to the west of the Ninety-Six fort in February, 1756, and there established what became known as the Long Canes settlement. But Patrick Calhoun had already prospected the area, and on his advice the family pushed several miles farther to the west, where they took up parcels of land along a small river and its tributary stream, which became known as Little River and Calhoun's Creek, respectively. Patrick staked out for himself an acreage just below the lands of his brothers where the creek divided into two forks. Here he cleared the land, and cutting logs from stands of virgin timber along the south fork, he built his cabin.[10]

Technically squatters on the land, the Calhouns soon regularized their holdings and secured additional acreage. Although he had only six months of formal schooling, Patrick Calhoun had somehow over-

10. *Ibid.*, 66–67.

come his educational limitations and had sufficiently impressed the authorities in Charleston with his surveying skill to be appointed a deputy surveyor for the region. He used his new post to reap advantages for himself and his family in securing the choicest plots. But he also worked diligently, and by 1758 he had surveyed and laid out the plots for the Calhouns as well as the families of Long Canes settlement, reserving for himself and his family 1,750 acres in the first distribution. Eventually, the Calhouns' individual holdings were far larger and far more fertile than the average grants in the frontier region of the colony.

9

The Calhouns and their neighbors paid a heavy price for their land hunger. Having already encroached on Indian land, they were the victims of a sudden foray of Cherokees in early 1760. The settlers had decided to move back from what was an imminent attack, but as they prepared to cross Long Canes Creek, a large war party ambushed them. Before the men could reach their guns, the Cherokees had killed or mortally wounded dozens of settlers, seized a number of others for hostages, and driven the remainder into flight. The Indians scalped the dead and wounded, and pillaged the abandoned wagons before they disappeared into the forest. Among those killed and mutilated were James Calhoun, Patrick's older brother; two of Patrick's nieces; and his aged mother, Catherine. Another niece was carried off into captivity. Patrick and two of his brothers managed to escape the first onslaught. While the remainder of the party fled south to Augusta in the Georgia Colony, he and a small group of armed men returned to the scene of the massacre, determined to recover the wounded, bury the dead, and salvage what they could of their possessions.

The scene was one of horror, even to those who had witnessed massacres on the frontiers of Virginia and Pennsylvania. To Patrick Calhoun, personal tragedy compounded the frightful butchery. But stifling his remorse, he helped bury the dead and later marked his mother's grave with a crude stone monument. He was active in securing military support for a reckoning with the Cherokees, and he participated in the successful expedition of 1761 that broke Cherokee military power in the area. The treaty of Paris in 1763 that ended the French and Indian War brought peace to the South Carolina frontier, though there were occasional raids for the next twenty years. The near presence of the powerful Cherokee and Creek nations brought a sense of distant but impending peril and even impermanence to the backcountry, not entirely dispelled until the early years of the nineteenth century.

During the late 1760s and through the revolutionary war, Patrick Calhoun added to his acres and his standing in what was now called the up-country. He took a prominent part in the Regulator movement that dealt severely with the lawlessness of immigrants, many of them free-booters, who crowded into the up-country after the defeat of the Cherokees. As a Regulator, he opposed the system of representation and taxation that favored the rich tidewater planters and merchants at the expense of up-country farmers.[11] By 1768, he had become one of the more prominent political leaders in his section, and he served in the legislature of the colony until 1774. He tirelessly fought for equitable representation of the more-populous up-country in the government of the colony, but his efforts and those of other frontier representatives were unavailing. The royal governor and his council, together with the planter-dominated legislature, managed to block all efforts at reform.

In 1770, Patrick Calhoun married for the second time. The tall, dark-eyed, dark-haired Martha Caldwell, like her husband, was of Scotch-Irish descent, and she seems to have shared her husband's managerial talents. She was also of a studious temperament—a quality she would bequeath to all of her children, though none more so than her fourth child, John, who bore her family name.[12]

At the outbreak of the revolutionary war, Patrick Calhoun was elected to the first and second provincial legislatures that declared independence from Great Britain and formed the first state constitution. Although an outspoken Whig, he did not enter the field against the Tories and the British who rampaged much of the up-country during the war. Unlike his brother-in-law Major John Caldwell, whom the Tories murdered after burning down his house, Patrick Calhoun maintained a low profile while internecine warfare raged through the up-country.[13] He retained his property though he did not conceal his loyalties, and remained a member of the South Carolina legislature. Moreover, Patrick Calhoun prospered during the war, which saw many other South Carolinians driven into poverty. A spacious eight-room, two-story frame dwelling had replaced the log cabin he had built with his own hands.

Patrick Calhoun may have held the rich rice planters of the coast in contempt, but he emulated them in engaging a slave labor force that

11. William A. Schaper, *Sectionalism and Representation in South Carolina* (1916; rpr. New York, 1968), 42, 43.

12. Margaret L. Coit, *John C. Calhoun: An American Portrait* (New York, 1950), 11; *Calhoun Papers*, XV, 122; Starke, *Calhoun's Early Life*, 69.

13. *Life of JCC*, 4.

would cultivate his acres of corn, wheat, and oats, and would husband his herds of cattle, swine, and sheep. By 1790, when his third son, John Caldwell Calhoun, was eight years old, Patrick Calhoun owned thirty-one slaves. As he was one of the largest slave owners in the entire up-country, he was also one of the richest farmers in the region. His wealth, however, could not be compared to that of the Charleston nabobs. And since most of it derived from diversified farming, his living standard did not differ markedly from that of his neighbors. Everyone on the plantation, black and white, worked together in the fields, on the farm, and in the slaughtering pens and the smokehouses; and the women, slave and free, devoted long hours to spinning and weaving the homespun that clothed the master and the bondservant.

During John Calhoun's youth, monumental changes were taking place in the social and economic order of South Carolina. He could only have been aware of them through the conversations of his father and his father's friends around the great fireplace that served all of the first-floor rooms. The slave population, while still centered in the coastal counties, was moving steadily westward. Whereas the Calhoun plantation had been one of few in the up-country to have depended on a slave labor force in 1790, eight years later, most of the planters in the Ninety-Six district who owned 500 acres or more were slaveholders. But whites in the up-country were more than four times as numerous as blacks—a situation almost exactly the reverse in the three coastal counties of Beaufort, Charleston, and Georgetown. In the low country, there were 28,644 whites to 79,716 blacks, while in the up-country there were 111,534 whites to 26,679 blacks, who were evenly distributed over more than two-thirds of the land area of the state. Calhoun listened as his father criticized the discriminatory apportionment between the tidewater counties and the up-country.[14]

Even after heated debate in the Constitutional Convention of 1790, the rich rice and long-staple cotton planters of the coast managed to continue their political hold on the state by insisting that taxable property including slaves be used as a base along with population for representation in the state legislature. As was stipulated in the new federal constitution, slaves in South Carolina would be counted in apportioning political control. The result was that one-fifth of South Carolina's white population ruled the state.

Removal of the state capital to Columbia in the up-country, a conces-

14. Wallace, *South Carolina*, 341, 342.

sion the tidewater interests made, was small consolation to planters like Patrick Calhoun who saw the resources of the entire state being diverted to furthering the wealth of the coastal regions through the political manipulation of a numerical minority. In the relatively isolated farm country of Ninety-Six and other up-country counties, improved transportation for moving produce to market was a compelling need. Yet Patrick Calhoun recognized that appropriations for internal improvements would be hard to obtain under the new constitution. While he fumed about the injustice of the situation, the progressive establishment of planter hegemony over the entire up-country soon made such arguments sound quaint and old-fashioned. The steady march of cotton planting into Calhoun's region was fastening slave labor inexorably, it seemed, on the up-country. World markets for the staple were expanding dramatically through technological change in the cotton textile industry and population growth in Europe and in the northern and new western states of the Union.

All that this meant to the growing boy John was that his elders talked as much about slave labor as they did about corn and wheat and hogs, and there was less criticism of coastal planters. His father, who had opposed the Constitution with much the same arguments he had leveled at the state constitution, seemed to have reconciled himself to that instrument of government after Jefferson attached to it the Bill of Rights. These amendments satisfied him that individual liberties were not to be jeopardized by a remote authority over which local government and opinion would have little or no control.[15]

15. James Parton, *Famous Americans of Recent Times* (Boston, 1867), 118.

II

Self-Imposed Exile

Young John Calhoun absorbed Jeffersonian principles without really comprehending why they were either true or just. His education had been virtually nonexistent. There were no schools within one hundred miles, no resident schoolteachers, in fact no villages that might support a teacher, and no formal churches whose ministers might hold classes or lend books on a regular basis. Like his brothers and sister, Calhoun learned the rudiments of reading and writing by attending whenever available a so-called field school, where for a few months an itinerant teacher drilled farm boys and girls in rote exercises. Beyond the family Bible, there were no books in the Calhoun household. Only an occasional newspaper from Charleston found its way into that part of Ninety-Six. What religious needs were served in the community, now aspiring to the more refined name of Abbeville, came from an occasional traveling preacher. And, of course, Patrick conducted family devotions from remembered Calvinist teaching.

One of the visiting preachers, Moses Waddel, was to make a lasting impression on young Calhoun and, surprisingly, on an entire generation of southern statesmen. When Waddel first preached at Abbeville, he was twenty-four years old. An earnest, rather stout young man of middle height and serious bearing, he, like the Calhouns, was of Scotch-Irish descent. Born in the North Carolina up-country, he had received a sketchy education before he moved with his family to the Georgia frontier, where at eighteen he had tried to support himself by establishing a school. When it failed, as it was bound to, considering the sparse population of the area, he traveled to Virginia, where he studied theology at the newly established Hampden-Sydney College. Ordained a Presbyterian minister, Waddel took up the arduous life of a circuit rider and part-time schoolmaster. In what time he could wrench from his duties, he studied a Greek and a Latin grammar and built on a rudimentary knowledge of those classic languages that he had gained at Hampden-Sydney. His training in theology and the classics was elementary, yet Waddel made up for his educational shortcomings with his passion for learning, his indefatigable industry, and the singularly compressed mind of the autodidact. The labored religiosity that burdens the pages of his one book, *The Memoirs of the Life of Miss Caroline Elizabeth Smelt*, produced in his mature years, is a sobering example of how the gospel of work can overwhelm all inspiration. Yet Waddel's transparent sincerity made a strong impression on the Calhouns, especially on John's older sister, Catherine—an attraction that proved mutual. With family encouragement, Waddel paid court to Catherine, and after a brief period, another circuit-riding minister married them.[1]

Before his marriage, Waddel had already decided again to set up a school in his home environment. Probably at Martha Caldwell Calhoun's request, he agreed to take John as a pupil at his new school near Appling, Georgia, which he named, appropriately enough, Carmel Academy because it seemed to him a sanctuary in the wilderness. Neither Carmel Academy nor John's formal education lasted long. He began his studies under Waddel's tutelage late in 1795 and ended them a few months later when his sister Catherine died. A bereaved Waddel closed the school and sought to assuage his grief by riding off on a round of circuit preaching.[2]

John, too, was grief stricken, and left alone for over three months. The gloomy forest that encircled Waddel's rude dwelling seemed to enhance his helplessness. He sought a refuge from his fears in ransacking the slender stocks of his brother-in-law's library. Besides some theological works, Waddel had managed to collect a few historical and philosophical volumes. Young John avoided the religious books but seized upon the English translation of the French historian Charles Rollin's eight-volume *Ancient History*—more a compilation than a history, but a work that stimulated the boy's imagination about vanished civilizations that had been mere names he remembered from his reading of the Bible. After the sterile pages of Rollin, he must have enjoyed Voltaire's more spritely *History of Charles XII* and even William Robertson's *History of the Reign of Emperor Charles V* or his *History of America* and Captain James Cook's *Narrative of the Voyages*. The thirteen-year-old lad then set himself to studying John Locke's dense "Essay Concerning Human Understanding," which he worked over so diligently that he suffered from eye strain, lack of exercise, and bad eating habits. On Waddel's return, the minister found his charge in such poor physical

---

1. Ralph M. Lyon, "Moses Waddel and the Willington Academy," *North Carolina Historical Review*, VIII, No. 3 (July, 1931), 286–90.

2. *Ibid.*, 293.

and mental health that he immediately sent the boy home to his mother's care.[3]

Patrick Calhoun had died in the meantime, and thus, in the space of a few months, John had lost his sister and his father, a heavy blow to the sensitive boy. But he had also gained from this short period of enforced self-tutelage and loneliness. He discovered that he had a taste for history and, through his fumbling attempts to penetrate the difficulties of Locke, a decided interest in philosophical speculation. His father's death brought about a sudden change in family responsibilities. John's two older brothers were just beginning business careers, James in Augusta, Georgia, William in Charleston; his younger brother Patrick was still a child.

Although a stripling, John slipped into the management not just of the home farm but of five other adjoining farms his father had acquired. For the next four years, he worked in the fields and acted as overseer. But he continued his reading of whatever came his way— occasional issues of the Charleston *Gazette* and other newspapers, odd volumes of the *Annals of Congress* that found their way to Abbeville, the spare book or two his brothers sent from Charleston and Augusta. Yet much of the time he had left over from taxing farm labor he divided between hunting and fishing, healthful and useful diversions.[4]

Despite the limitations on his education, Calhoun's natural abilities for learning and an ambition to improve his situation in life became apparent to the family. On a trip home, his brother James broached the idea that he should prepare himself for one of the learned professions—the law, medicine, or the ministry. John was willing but made two stipulations: his mother's consent and support for the seven years he estimated it would take to complete his education.[5] Since his brother Patrick was now old enough to take over the management of the farms, Martha Calhoun agreed to John's absence. James Calhoun thought that the family could afford the costs for his education. His conditions met, John, it was decided, should return to the tutelage of Waddel, who had remarried and reopened his school at Appling.

In June, 1800, seventeen-year-old Calhoun once again made the fifty-mile journey to Appling. He was six feet two inches tall. His stiff, brown hair stood up straight on his head, adding to his angular appearance. Thin and awkward, he was strong and limber from farm work and outdoor exercise. He was square jawed, and his deep-set

3. W. Pinkney Starke, *Account of Calhoun's Early Life* (Washington, D.C., 1900), 72, 73.
4. *Life of JCC*, 5.
5. *Ibid.*, 6.

hazel eyes under heavy brows were clear and bright. He was handsome in a rugged way, and his conversation bespoke self-confidence as well as a seriousness unusual for a farm lad of his age.

16   Waddel was a disciplinarian who, however, was in advance of his time in the latitude he gave his students once he was convinced that they followed the rules he had set down. He never had to worry about young Calhoun, who was so anxious to fill in the huge gap in his education that Waddel cautioned him on excessive application. Calhoun absorbed as much Latin, Greek, mathematics, and philosophy as Waddel could provide. In the spring of 1801, Calhoun was stricken again with sudden, deep grief, for the third time in his young life. His mother had died after a brief illness. "I never experienced so sever [*sic*] and unexpect[ed] shock," he wrote his cousin Andrew Pickens, Jr., who was a student at Providence College, now Brown University.[6]

But this bereavement, while it deepened a latent insecurity, stimulated Calhoun to even greater efforts. By September, he had advanced in New Testament Greek "as far as the Acts of the Apostles." In Latin and in all other academic subjects of Waddel's competency, he had progressed as far as he could. By the fall of 1802, Waddel thought that Calhoun was sufficiently well prepared to pass college entrance examinations. Calhoun had decided upon Yale College. Its new president, Timothy Dwight, had gained a reputation as an educator and a teacher that had reached even the remote hamlets of Appling and Abbeville. Moreover, Dwight, who was then engaged in a fund-raising and building program, was anxious to increase enrollment. He was willing to admit older prospective students to advanced standing if they could pass the requisite examinations. From all accounts, the examinations even for advanced standing were not that difficult for someone like Calhoun, who had almost two years of Waddel's instruction added to his years of self-study. Zedekiah Barstow, for instance, a nineteen-year-old farmer from Canterbury, Connecticut, who entered Yale in 1809, passed his examination in the classics after only twenty-six weeks of study with his pastor.[7]

Confident that he would gain both admission and upper-class standing, Calhoun left home in August, 1802, and reached New York City probably on November 16. By November 23, he had passed his examinations and was renting a room in Yale's new dormitory, Union Hall.

6. William J. Grayson, *James Louis Petigru: A Biographical Sketch* (New York, 1866), 34–35; *Calhoun Papers*, I, 4.

7. *Calhoun Papers*, I, 3; Charles E. Cunningham, *Timothy Dwight, 1752–1817* (New York, 1942), 232–36.

His roommate was Christopher Gadsden of the rich Charleston family, acquaintances of Calhoun's brothers. Although Calhoun found his studies "very pleasant and not very difficult," he was not quick at making friends. Nor was he impressed by his fellow students. "We board in Commons," he wrote, "and here you have an opportunity to see human life in all its phases of incivility and selfishness . . . not at all flattering to the good quality of mankind."[8]

Yale may have had its weaknesses, but for the time it offered one of the best collegiate educations in the nation. With a faculty of twenty instructors, including President Dwight (six tutors and nine resident graduate teachers), the institution had broadened its curriculum over the past seven years. A professor of law and another of chemistry had been added to the faculty. While still required to study Greek and Latin for four years, students could now take such practical courses as chemistry, geography, English grammar, surveying, navigation, and modern European languages. Chapel, over which Dwight officiated, was of course compulsory. The president also lectured to seniors on the prescribed courses of history of civil society, rhetoric, logic, and metaphysics. Yet even Dwight found it difficult to prepare his students adequately during Calhoun's years at Yale because of the state of the college library, which contained a scant 2,500 volumes, with perhaps another 500 volumes divided between the two student societies, Linonian and Brothers in Unity.

To a young man whose mind had been so long fettered by the constraints of an isolated rural society where books were a rarity that one treasured, the Yale library seemed incredibly rich. In addition, Calhoun was chosen a member of the Linonian student society and thus had access to its collection of books. He did not begrudge the considerable expense of paying from three cents to nine cents a month for each volume borrowed, depending upon size.[9] In fact, everything about Yale and the town of New Haven seemed quite splendid to a boy accustomed to hamlets in the wilderness. The original buildings of the college, together with those built since Dwight's accession to the presidency, presented a handsome, even imposing appearance with their two matching cupolas and weather vanes, and their five-story brick façades extending for an entire block along what was prosaically named College Street. The college buildings faced a green on which stood two brick Congregational churches and the colonial statehouse

8. *Calhoun Papers*, I, 5.

9. *The Laws of Yale College, in New Haven in Connecticut Enacted by the President and Fellows, the Sixth Day of October, 1795* (New Haven, 1795), Chapter IX.

18

where the Connecticut legislature met in alternate years. A row of young elms that James Hillhouse, a public-spirited New Haven merchant, had had planted along College Street separated Yale's buildings from the green on which New Haven residents, including the college faculty, pastured their cattle and sheep. Swine roamed about on the green and in the streets as they always had—a rustic intrusion that young Calhoun would have found familiar and appropriate.

New Haven itself was a busy little city of four thousand whose economic life centered on its wharves as its social life centered on the college. Just now, its trade with the West Indies and its re-export trade to Europe were booming as a result of the brief peace of Amiens between Great Britain and France. The tall, spare Carolinian was impressed by the commercial activity along Water Street, even though the port could not compare with Charleston for size and diversity of goods on the docks and in the warehouses.

But the city and the college seemed simply adjuncts to that splendid figure Timothy Dwight, now in his fiftieth year. At the full flood of his powers, this revolutionary war veteran, poet, preacher, and educator, was a massive, majestic person. Smooth-faced and balding, with large, nearsighted eyes, Dwight had become almost a national institution in a country where notables were scarce. Like all the other students, Calhoun admired Dwight's extemporaneous sermons, his seemingly encyclopedic knowledge, and his awesome mastery of the classics, of the tenets of Calvinism, and of metaphysics. No one, he thought, could explicate the language of John Locke with such clarity.

Vehemently outspoken on the perils of Unitarianism, Dwight denounced French Jacobinism, which he variously defined as the politics of Thomas Jefferson and the Deism of Voltaire and Condorcet. A Federalist of purpose and conviction, Dwight condemned unsparingly the purported excesses of the Republicans, who included his first cousin, Aaron Burr.[10] But Dwight, for all his presence and his systematic argument, could not make a Federalist of Calhoun. Here was a mind as fixed in theory as Dwight's and whose natural powers of logical discourse stood up well even against such a formidable adversary. Family training and background had anchored Calhoun's political inclinations. What his father and Moses Waddel had taught about Jefferson's principles of limited government and individual liberty not only seemed to square with actual social conditions he had observed at home and in his limited travels but breathed the spirit of youth and progress.

10. Cunningham, *Timothy Dwight*, 293, 299–301; Timothy Dwight, *Travels in New England and New York* (4 vols.; New Haven, 1821–22), IV, 301, 372–92; Samuel G. Goodrich, *Recollections of a Lifetime* (New York, 1856), 347–49.

Calhoun must have found Dwight's discourses on races disturbing. Environment, according to Dwight, not genetic inheritance, accounted for racial differences. Negroes in the temperate climate of the United States would eventually take on the color and the lineaments of the whites, and everyone, Negro slaves included, had the same moral attributes and predestined depravity. For a young southerner accustomed to the notion that black slaves were mentally and morally inferior, Dwight's lectures must have contributed to his sense of being an alien in a world of sharp contrast to what he had known and believed.[11] Calhoun did share with his learned and persuasive mentor his passion for geography, especially where it emphasized the physical features of the nation, its enormous distances, its varied climate, and its great promise as the land of the future. Dwight's ideas about size and diversity of nations and their impact on human behavior, which he advanced at every opportunity and under many guises, awakened a sympathetic response in Calhoun.

The other teacher whom Calhoun found interesting and instructive was young Benjamin Silliman, the professor of chemistry. Only three years Calhoun's senior and a Yale graduate, Silliman had received his postcollegiate training in the law, but Dwight, with his usual disregard for specialized education, had chosen Silliman for the chemistry post, assuming that intelligence and application would provide the necessary background. His choice was sound. Silliman would gain an international reputation in chemistry. Calhoun, then in his senior year, was fortunate to be a student in Silliman's first course of lectures and to share his enthusiasm for his new calling.[12]

Although Calhoun applied himself diligently and proved a superior scholar, like most students then and now, he found the college routine tedious. On more than one occasion, he longed for the time when he could be free to pursue his own career. "Books, Books, Books engross our whole time and attention" he wrote. "Let it be a winter's day. Begin when the morning bell, ere yet the sun has dispeled the darkness, summons him to chapel. . . . He spends the day in pouring over long and abstruse mathimatical demonstrations. . . . He studies till the clock striks twelve. Pale and meager, with a shattred constitution, he retires to bed. His sleep is short and interupted. Again the bell rings, he rises again and again goes the same round."[13]

Although scarcely a gregarious individual, Calhoun made some life-

11. Dwight, *Travels*, I, 124–30, III, 183–87.
12. George P. Fisher, *Life of Benjamin Silliman, MD. LL.D* (2 vols.; New York, 1866), I, 91–95, 288, II, 97, 98.
13. *Calhoun Papers*, I, 7, 8.

long friends at Yale. Micah Sterling and his brother Ansel, both Connecticut Yankees, and fellow South Carolinians James MacBride, John Felder, and Christopher Gadsden formed the small circle in which he moved. Among the faculty, Silliman and Jeremiah Day, professor of mathematics and later president of Yale, were closest to Calhoun. He spent some carefree hours at the Roger Sherman home near the college, where he enjoyed the company of the three attractive Sherman sisters. Calhoun also was elected to Phi Beta Kappa, which then combined social functions with scholarly achievement.[14]

But Calhoun felt estranged from the New England atmosphere of the college. As he commented to his cousin Andrew, there existed "a considerable prejudice here against both the southern states and students. However I have found a considerable number of New England students, young men of information and worth, free of prejudice. With these I associate. As to those of local prejudice I contemn [*sic*] and avoid." Yankees he thought were "more penurious, more contracted in their sentiments, and less social, than the Carolinians. But as to morality we must yield."[15]

The Yale faculty voted that as one of the few outstanding students in the class of 1804, Calhoun was to be honored by giving an address at commencement day on September 12. Typically, he worked long hours in preparing a discourse, which he entitled "The Qualifications Necessary for a Statesman." He never delivered it, however, and was absent from commencement exercises. Unusually healthy during most of his two years in New Haven, Calhoun had come down with a severe attack of dysentery in August, 1804, that almost killed him. He was still convalescing when he received a letter from his cousin John E. Colhoun's widow, Floride Bonneau Colhoun (this branch of the family spelled the name differently), who was spending the summer in Newport, Rhode Island. She had heard that Calhoun was sick, and suggested that when he recovered sufficiently he recuperate at her summer home.[16]

Mrs. Colhoun was rich and lived in the high style of the tidewater planters. When she made her summer trips with her family to escape Charleston's fevers and heat, she traveled in a carriage drawn by four

14. Fisher, *Silliman*, II, 98; George F. Hoar, *Autobiography of Seventy Years* (New York, 1903), 7, 8.

15. *Calhoun Papers*, I, 10.

16. *Ibid.*, 11. In a letter to his son Patrick written years later, on September 17, 1840, Calhoun recalled his illness. "The fall that I graduated," he wrote, "I was attacked by it, in its most malignant form, and did not recover from it for five, or six weeks, and remained puny during the succeeding winter" (*Ibid.*, XV, 358).

matched horses managed by an English coachman. Behind this splendid equipage came wagons with provisions for the road, clothes, and a retinue of black house servants. An heiress before her marriage, Floride Colhoun had enabled her late husband to devote himself to politics **21** and public service. When he died in 1802, he was a United States senator from South Carolina after having served several years in the state legislature.

Calhoun admired his cousin, whose career he hoped to follow. He was delighted to accept Floride Colhoun's invitation, and spent a month in her hospitable household, which included her three children: thirteen-year-old John Ewing; Floride, dark-eyed, dark-haired, and a year younger; and James Edward, a six-year-old. Calhoun enjoyed himself at Newport, which he thought "quite a pleasant place" though its old buildings "give some-what a melancholy aspect." Ever the observant farmer, he noted that Rhode Island soil was fertile and the climate temperate. Otherwise, he found that the city's Baptist religion, its customs, and its morals were of a low order. He made no comment in a letter home about Floride and her family, though he seems to have been attracted to the shapely, dark-haired, wealthy widow.[17] In her household he found the security of home surroundings he had missed for the past three years.

No doubt Floride Colhoun drew out her young cousin-in-law on his career plans. Long ago at a family council, it had been decided that he was to be educated for a profession. A year before his graduation from college, he specifically avowed to his cousin Andrew Pickens, Jr., that the law was his chosen field, though he was under no illusions about the hard work and tedious study that would be involved.[18]

Entirely recovered from his illness, Calhoun returned to South Carolina with Floride and her children. It is likely that he visited his cousin Andrew and other relatives in the vicinity of Pendleton, a small village some fifty miles northwest of Abbeville. In late December he was in Charleston, where he began to study law with Henry William De-Saussure, a Federalist and a judge whose firm was the most prestigious in that prosperous, highly social city. DeSaussure was a busy man who found little time to instruct his ambitious pupil. He had Calhoun study law books like Thomas Chitty's bulky and distressingly dull volume *Notes and Bills* and, as all law students before him, copy legal instruments.

17. *Ibid.,* I, 8, 9, 12, 13; Coit, *John C. Calhoun,* 33, 34.
18. Coit, *John C. Calhoun,* 9, 10.

After a few months of this tiresome occupation, Calhoun, for the first and perhaps the only time in his life, realized that he was not grasping the fundamentals of the subject matter. This prompted him to seek a course of formal training. Characteristically, he wanted to understand thoroughly the basic concepts of any subject he was study-ing, whether it be chemistry or natural rights philosophy or, in this case, the law. His friend and college classmate John Felder was likewise dissatisfied with his law apprenticeship. From another friend, Eldred Simkins of nearby Edgefield, they had heard of Tapping Reeve's law school in Litchfield, Connecticut. Simkins was completing his course of study there and provided a testimonial for the school. Calhoun quite probably received recommendations from the Yale faculty. Although Reeves himself was a graduate of Princeton University, his assistant and principal instructor, James Gould, was a Yale graduate, and most of the school's graduates and students had attended Yale.[19]

After Felder and Calhoun agreed to enroll in the school, Felder went on ahead to engage lodgings, while Calhoun spent some weeks in Newport visiting Floride Colhoun. In early July he began his journey to Litchfield. By chance, he found that his fellow passenger on the stage from Hartford was Tapping Reeve himself. Reeve was sixty years old at the time, his portly frame clothed in long coat, waistcoat, knee breeches, and silk stockings of the revolutionary war generation to which he belonged. He was an engaging person with large, soft eyes and gray hair that fell to his shoulders. As befit a former tutor of James Madison at Princeton, his conversation was serious and pointed when he learned that one of his fellow passengers was from the South and that he was enrolling as a student in his school. Although his voice was so low as to be barely above a whisper, so clear was Reeve's articulation that Calhoun had no difficulty in following his line of thought. "I delivered my letters to him," he wrote Floride Colhoun, "and found him on the passage open and agreeable."[20]

Litchfield was a quiet, prosperous city of five thousand inhabitants, enfolded in the foothills of the Berkshires. It derived some income from being the county seat and more from being the principal market town for the farms of northwestern Connecticut. But its major source of wealth was that it was a focal point for the great inland route from New York to Boston and from Hartford to the rich and populous

19. Alain C. White, *The History of the Town of Litchfield, Conn., 1720–1920* (Litchfield, Conn., 1920), 100–104.

20. Charles Beecher (ed.), *Autobiography of Lyman Beecher* (2 vols.; New York, 1864), I, 224; *Calhoun Papers*, I, 15.

Hudson River Valley south of West Point. The town had escaped the ravages of the Revolution. Local entrepreneurs, like Julius Deming and Colonel Benjamin Tallmadge, had made money from the war, as the stately dwellings along South and East streets testified.

Felder had rented a room for himself and Calhoun in one of these homes at the corner of Spencer and West streets. After some months, they found a more suitable lodging in the home of Reuben Webster on Prospect Street.[21] From their quarters they walked to Reeve's school, a small, one-room, clapboarded building behind his imposing two-story dwelling with its colonnaded front porch. Gould, Reeve's assistant, handled most of the instruction, for Reeve, who had been appointed a superior court judge in 1798, found that his judicial duties and his large law practice left little time for lectures. Yet he managed to cover twenty-one distinct areas of equity, admiralty, and criminal law.

Gould, a master of common law, lectured on subjects that would be of particular use to a practicing lawyer, such as contracts, pleadings, writs of error, and municipal law. He also presided at moot courts that were held weekly. When Calhoun and Felder attended his classes, Gould was thirty-five years old and in his prime as a teacher and a lawyer. Of average height and extremely nearsighted, he peered at his class through tortoiseshell spectacles. He lectured so slowly and distinctly that the students were able to copy down everything he said. It was not unusual for one's lecture notes to fill five good-sized volumes. In contrast to Reeve's rambling and sometimes confused style, Gould's lectures were simple, clear, and eminently logical. He, too, dressed in the conventional garb of an eighteenth-century gentleman and shared with Reeve a passionate devotion to the Federalist party.[22]

Unquestionably, Gould's lectures made a lasting impact on Calhoun, not so much for the material covered as for the spare language and the always logical argument from first principles. Gould's politics, however, made absolutely no impression. Although both Reeve and Gould were friendly to the young Carolinian and entertained him at their homes, they were unable, as Dwight had been before them, to convert him to orthodox Federalism. Calhoun found party feeling so intense that he and Felder decided it was best "to form few connections in town."[23]

Calhoun was fortunate in having his friend Felder as a roommate and companion, and his Yale classmate Micah Sterling paid several

21. Coit, *John C. Calhoun,* 37.
22. White, *History of the Town of Litchfield,* 103, 104.
23. *Calhoun Papers,* I, 25.

visits. But he was quite lonely. "This is rather an out of the way place," he wrote Floride, "and, unless, it is now and then a Southerner from college, we rarely see any one from our end of [the] Union." Eventually, Calhoun came to accept Litchfield despite its political and religious intolerance, its harsh winter climate, and his increasing aversion to the law that the best efforts of Reeve and Gould could not dispel. Not that Calhoun neglected his studies, quite the reverse: as he explained to Andrew Pickens, Jr., he drew "a motive of industry" from his intense dislike. If the work must be done, he said, "the sooner the better is often my logick."[24]

After completing his law studies, Calhoun left Litchfield in the early fall of 1806 for the long journey home. He rode in a stage to Philadelphia, where he purchased a horse and completed his trip alone on horseback. As he "experienced many solitary hours," he could not help but reflect on his four-year residence in New England and especially his sojourn in Litchfield. In both New Haven and Litchfield, he had lived and worked among some of the most passionate, well-informed, and powerful Federalists in the nation. Yet he had emerged from this environment with his Jeffersonianism intact. He had been a witness to an incident that showed him how seriously the New England public took its politics—the jailing of the young Jeffersonian editor in Litchfield, Selleck Osborne, for his caustic attacks on local Federalists. Calhoun had defied the warnings of Reeve and Gould and the town elders. He had marched with a small group of Jeffersonians to the jail where Osborne was confined to protest the arrest as an infringement on freedom of speech and the press.[25]

Despite his nonconformity in politics, faith, and morals, the lanky Carolinian had been treated well and had made some firm friends. He was satisfied that his decision to seek his education in the North had been a wise one. Calhoun had seen how the people of another section of his vast country lived, how their society operated, what was unique in their customs and morals, and what was similar to his own section. Exposed to New England separatism, even in its nascent stage, Calhoun's sense of regional and national identity was strengthened as he sought to defend southern institutions against such powerful detractors as Tapping Reeve and even the genial Oliver Wolcott, John Adams' secretary of the treasury and a leading member of Litchfield society.[26]

Calhoun himself, the half-educated farmboy who had gone north in

24. *Ibid.*, 18, 23.
25. *Ibid.*, 32; New York *Patriot*, November 1, 1823.
26. White, *History of the Town of Litchfield*, 137.

1802, was now a cultivated gentleman with what might be described as a cosmopolitan outlook. His quest for personal security and social stability had quickened immeasurably. He was looking forward to completing his apprenticeship in DeSaussure's law office, but only in order to pass the bar examination and gain sufficient funds from a law practice so that he would be free to enter politics like Floride's late husband, John E. Colhoun, who had combined a prosperous law practice with a political career.[27] Calhoun desperately wanted to make a mark in the public life of his state and nation. The law, however distasteful to him, was the means to that end.

27. *Calhoun Papers,* I, 33n, 41.

III

Hawk

After remaining at Abbeville for a few weeks, Calhoun made his way to Charleston to continue his legal apprenticeship with DeSaussure, who had extensive connections with Charleston society and its business community. His cousin-in-law Floride, to whom he was now devoted, lived part of the year at her rice plantation, Bonneau Ferry, a scant twenty miles from the city. And Calhoun's two older brothers had at one time engaged in business that involved the family with Charleston's mercantile community. Ezekiel Pickens, Calhoun's second cousin and the grandson of the revolutionary war hero General Andrew Pickens, who had married Rebecca Calhoun, was a rice planter in the marshy meadows near Charleston. Pickens had just been elected to the state senate from the parishes of St. Thomas and St. Dennis, which bordered the northeastern outskirts of the city.

Charleston at the time was the fifth-largest city in the United States, with a population of almost 28,000.[1] It was a colorful, compact town of crooked streets, Georgian houses painted in pastel colors, and slave markets. The wharves, warehouses, ships, and shipyards that bespoke its commercial importance were all within walking distance of its busy center. Palmettos, hibiscuses, oleanders, and other semitropical flowering trees and plants adorned the back and side gardens of its townhouses. Charleston's unpaved, sandy streets were littered and filthy, and jammed with horse-drawn traffic as in other American cities. Slaves and free blacks mingled with seafaring men, merchants, and clerks. Prosperous rice planters dressed in the latest English fashion and their ladies in imported taffetas were easily distinguished from the up-country people in gray or brown homespun, who were visiting town to conduct business or to purchase some luxury articles for home. In the summer, or the "sickly season," as it was called, the whole city seemed deserted. Only those who had to be there—slaves, sailors, and merchants' apprentices, for the most part—were to be seen in the

---

1. Adam Seybart, *Statistical Annals, Embracing Views of the Population, Commerce of the United States of America, Navigation, Fisheries, Public Lands* (Philadelphia, 1818), 2.

harbor areas, and even they would disappear during the torrid heat of midday.[2]

Charleston was a place of startling contrasts and movement, yet as many travelers remarked, it was the most European in appearance and in society of any American city. Rich planters and their wives set a social tone that would scarcely comport with vaunted American principles of equality. Well-educated professionals and businessmen were frequently excluded from the soirees of the arrogant, status-conscious planters. And many scions of these families, especially the males, led lives of pointless luxury that all too frequently degenerated into drunkenness, gambling, and licentious behavior. Yet there had been considerable leveling of classes as population streamed into the state after the Revolution. Up-country farmers were even now beginning to make fortunes in cotton culture, and like the Calhouns and their wide network of kin, the Pickenses, the Nobles, the Ewings, the Caldwells, and the Burts were moving aggressively up the social scale.[3]

To Calhoun, Charleston had always been an "extremely corrupt" place. He was as blind to its attractions and its boisterous, vibrant lifestyle as he was to its social pretensions, none of which squared with his rather strait-laced, Calvinist outlook. For one so extremely ambitious and work-haunted as Calhoun, the idle life of inherited wealth was blasphemy. He would endure Charleston only as long as he felt clerking in DeSaussure's office was essential to his training for his future law practice and his political career. "Since my arrival here," he wrote, "I have been very much of a recluse. I board with the French prodestant [*sic*] minister Mr. Detargney in Church Street. It is a quiet house and answers my purpose well." In June, with the approach of the "sickly season," Calhoun left Charleston with no regrets to complete his required apprenticeship with yet another relative by marriage, George Bowie of Abbeville. He was admitted to the bar in December, 1807, and to practice before the chancery court three months later.[4]

By then Calhoun had already begun his practice, which at first was confined to the rural up-country counties near his home but soon extended to Columbia and Charleston. Calhoun was not by temperament or training the kind of advocate that country folk admired. In-

2. Captain Basil Hall, *Travels in North America in the Years 1827 and 1828* (3 vols.; London, 1829), III, 138–42; Raymond A. Mohl (ed.), "The Grand Fabric of Republicanism: A Scotsman Describes South Carolina, 1810–1811," *South Carolina Historical Magazine*, LXXI (July, 1970), 171–73, 182.

3. Wallace, *South Carolina*, 350–52.

4. *Calhoun Papers*, I, 28, 33, 39 n25.

stead of the florid, declamatory rhetoric that often swayed country juries and judges, Calhoun relied on calm, dispassionate, eminently logical discourse much better suited to a reasoned argument in a judge's chambers than to the hurly-burly of the county assizes. Yet his family connections, his superior education, his ability to marshal evidence in a matter-of-fact way, and his unerring sense of detecting and exploiting the weakness of his opponents' arguments all combined to provide him with considerable business from the beginning of his career. Calhoun's experiences as a lawyer, while pointing to a prosperous future, also confirmed absolutely his dislike for the legal profession as his means of livelihood. He had been receiving some income from his share of the family plantations, and he yearned for a time when he could devote himself to farming and, he hoped, a career in public life that would supply both the esteem and the security his introspective nature craved.

Calhoun's chance for gaining a rung towards his objective came shortly after he began to practice law. Since the brief peace of Amiens between France and England, the war in Europe had not only heightened in intensity but become a world war, especially on the high seas. Napoleon sought to cripple Britain economically through his Berlin and Milan decrees, which interdicted its trade with the Continent and wherever else his power reached. Great Britain retaliated with its orders-in-council that blocked neutral trade with France and its allies. The United States, as the largest neutral power, and second only to Great Britain as a maritime nation, was caught between these two adversaries. Events that menaced American shipping on the high seas were set in motion just as Calhoun began his law practice.

The Royal Navy was virtually unopposed on world shipping lanes. Thus it was the British rather than the French who first engaged in overt action against American shipping. This took the form of an unprovoked attack by a British frigate, the *Leopard*, on the American frigate *Chesapeake* off the Virginia Capes. After the *Chesapeake* surrendered with twenty-one of its sailors either killed or wounded, officers of the *Leopard* boarded the stricken ship and impressed four of her crew for service in the Royal Navy.

Since American independence, tension had been building between the two powers in three major areas of conflict. The British still maintained frontier posts on what the United States claimed was its territory in the Northwest. American trade with British possessions was subject to vexing limitations. And finally, with the rise of French power in Europe, the Royal Navy, always short of men, had begun boarding

American vessels and removing seamen, some of whom were not of British nationality. The Jefferson administration hoped to avoid hostilities even after the attack on the *Chesapeake*. Refusing to be stampeded by the public clamor, it merely ordered the expulsion of armed British vessels from American ports while awaiting an expected disavowal from the Canning ministry for the *Leopard*'s attack and the abandonment of the impressment policy. But public outrage ran strong and deep. The national mood, stimulated by colorful newspaper accounts and exaggerated word of mouth, promised rich returns for the aspiring politician alert enough to exploit the issue.

Already a confirmed nationalist and from family tutelage an anglophobe, Calhoun was personally outraged at the news of the unprovoked attack and alert enough to capitalize upon it. He was a prime mover in the convening of a protest meeting held at the new courthouse in Abbeville on the sultry afternoon of August 3, 1807. So well organized was the meeting that a large group of planters, local professionals, and businessmen crowded into the courthouse despite the fact that it was a Monday and that most of them had to give up a day's work as well as endure the inconvenience of travel through wilderness paths to attend. Calhoun, who had prepared himself carefully for the event, made an imposing appearance.[5]

In his high, flat voice that carried to the outer reaches of the milling crowd, Calhoun moved that his cousin Colonel Joseph E. Calhoun, member of Congress from the district, be named chairman of the meeting. The motion was carried by acclamation, as was Colonel Calhoun's appointment of a twenty-one member committee to draw up resolutions. He appointed another Calhoun relative, George C. Bowie, chairman and his young cousin John a member of the committee. The meeting adjourned until three in the afternoon; during the interval, John Calhoun prepared a sharp indictment of British policy on impressment and a series of eleven resolutions specifically condemning the *Leopard* attack, while calling for preparedness and an embargo against British goods. The mass meeting was then called to order, and the audience listened to the secretary read the resolutions. Raised to a high pitch of exuberance perhaps as much from the abundant supplies of liquor as from the emotional impact of Calhoun's resolutions, the audience was stirred even more when the young lawyer, at the committee's request, summed up the arguments for a united stand against further British encroachments on American sovereignty, ending his

5. James Parton, *Famous Americans of Recent Times* (Boston, 1867), 124.

short speech by calling for approval of the resolutions. Both speech and resolutions, which were accepted with enthusiasm, were applauded roundly. Calhoun's first public speech had earned him instant popularity.[6]

With his family connections, his seizure of a popular issue, and the wide visibility he had gained among local opinion makers by his performance at the mass meeting, Calhoun experienced no difficulty in having himself nominated and elected to the state legislature, "at the head of the ticket," as he proudly explained later, "and at a time when the prejudice against lawyers was strong in the district."[7] He approached his legislative duties as he had his study of the law, diligently and earnestly, but as he had anticipated, he found committee work and political discussion much more congenial than attendance at the regular sessions. Calhoun was appointed to eight committees during the two sessions he served in the legislature. Most of these assignments were concerned with constitutional and judicial reforms, but one committee he chaired was responsible for a law that eventually fixed white manhood suffrage in the South Carolina constitution. He gained most acclaim, however, in the political rather than the legislative forum.

When the Republican party legislative caucus assembled to nominate electors for president and vice-president of the United States, Calhoun showed an independent spirit that would characterize his political career and that was also well calculated to exhibit him as one who was conversant with men and measures outside of South Carolina. The Republican ticket presented to the legislature consisted of James Madison for president and George Clinton for vice-president. Madison's nomination gained approval by acclamation. When Clinton's name was presented, most assumed he would be likewise nominated without opposition. After all, it had been Republican party policy for the past twelve years to choose the president from Virginia and the vice-president from New York.

As soon as the motion was put, Calhoun was on his feet protesting. His theme was a familiar one, harking back to the resolutions he had prepared for the Abbeville meeting. He spoke of the European war and how the belligerents were violating American rights on the high seas with impunity. He doubted whether Jefferson's embargo of trade with Europe would work. "War, with Great Britain," he declared, "would be unavoidable." It was therefore absolutely essential that the

6. *Life of JCC*, 7; *Calhoun Papers*, I, 34–37, 37n.
7. *Life of JCC*, 7.

Republican party preserve its unity. Clinton was an estimable man, but if elected, he would unquestionably precipitate factional movements that would divide the party. Clinton's nephew, De Witt, whom Calhoun characterized as a politician "with an aspiring disposition," would widen the cleavage his uncle George's election had started. Calhoun then proposed the relatively obscure John Langdon of New Hampshire in place of Clinton. Calhoun's earnestness and the logical case he made carried the caucus with him. Langdon received the electoral vote of South Carolina, but Clinton was elected to a second term. As Calhoun had hoped, however, Langdon's nomination gained considerable support in several other states whose pretensions for national recognition, like those of South Carolina, had been ignored by the Virginia-New York alliance.[8]

What Calhoun was saying and what appealed to his fellow legislators was that South Carolina should have a share in national decision making, whether it be in party councils or in policy. And they did not miss Calhoun's criticism of the embargo that even then was ruining Charleston's commerce and impoverishing the planters who had been shipping their rice and cotton to the booming overseas markets. Obviously the young, articulate lawyer from Abbeville was the right person to represent South Carolina in Congress as a vigorous spokesman for public opinion that demanded a vigorous stand against Great Britain. His cousin Joseph was so impressed with what he heard of Calhoun's influence in the state legislature and especially among the planters of the Abbeville district that he indicated his wish to retire from Congress in Calhoun's favor. This move virtually assured the latter's nomination and election to the Twelfth Congress.[9]

That Calhoun had made an instant mark is also borne out by his election as a trustee of the newly established South Carolina College and the recognition his old mentor Moses Waddel accorded him. In June, 1810, Calhoun attended the commencement of Waddel's school as he had done several times previously. On this occasion, he occupied the platform with the huge, handsome senator from Georgia, William H. Crawford, like Calhoun an alumnus of the school. Crawford at this stage in his career had a far wider reputation than Calhoun, yet Waddel made sure that Calhoun gave out the prizes, probably to Crawford's annoyance.

8. *Ibid.*

9. Charles Wiltse, *John C. Calhoun, Nationalist: 1782–1828* (Indianapolis, 1944), 46–48, 51; *Calhoun Papers*, I, 50.

Calhoun had gotten a later start in politics than most of his contemporaries. His years on the farm, at Waddel's school, Yale, and Litchfield, and in legal apprenticeship had been well spent; yet at the advanced age of twenty-seven, he was just beginning the career he had so carefully planned. He had still to acquire a plantation and, above all, a wife if he were to take his place in community, state, and nation. Moreover, he was drawn to marriage by his passionate temperament, which his ambition and his Calvinist training had inhibited.

For the past two years he had been in love with his eighteen-year-old second cousin, Floride Colhoun, namesake and daughter of the much-beloved woman who was virtually his foster mother, Floride Bonneau Colhoun. Practical as well as emotional, Calhoun was aware that a marriage with a rich tidewater heiress would provide an income that would supplement whatever he might derive from his own investments and release him from the drudgery of law practice. He could then pursue the congenial and highly acceptable career of a South Carolina gentleman—planting and public service. Family ties meant much to Calhoun, and the fact that young Floride was also a blood relative, though distant enough, counted in his romantic quest.

Young Floride was a small, shapely, black-haired beauty whose appearance favored the French side of her family rather than the tall, loose-limbed Calhouns. Besides her physical attributes, which Calhoun found most attractive, Floride's musical ability was notable. She had acted as organist on occasion in church at Newport and sung the plaintive ballads of the day, accompanying herself on the spinnet. To a country lawyer whose education in New England and residence in such a cosmopolitan city as Charleston had never quite compensated for a certain rusticity, Floride's vivacious personality was infinitely charming. His marriage into the Charleston social circle, though never appealing to Calhoun's sense of work and duty, did satisfy his craving for status and security. Floride's mother, who had long cherished Calhoun, approved of the courtship. Floride herself found her ruggedly handsome, magnetic cousin quite overwhelming, with his air of self-assurance and his increasing popularity among the older members of her social circle and her mother's generation.

In an approach that had now become habitual, Calhoun planned his courtship step by step. During a visit to Bonneau Ferry in June, 1809, he broached the subject to Mrs. Colhoun. She neither encouraged nor discouraged him, prompting him to write a careful letter aimed at extracting a commitment. "It will be useless for me to conceal from you my increased anxiety on the subject," he wrote. "If, I should finally be disappointed by any adverse circumstance, which heaven forbid, it will be by far the most unlucky accident in my life." His letter had the desired effect. Mrs. Colhoun, evidently speaking for herself and her daughter, replied promptly from Newport giving her permission for the courtship. During the next eighteen months, the two were much in each other's company when Mrs. Colhoun and her family were at Bonneau Ferry. Towards the end of the engagement, Calhoun could hardly restrain the outpouring of his emotions. "What pleasure I have experienced in your company," he wrote Floride, "what delight in the exchange of sentiment, what transport in the testimonies of mutual love."[10]

Calhoun also dealt with the practical aspects of his impending marriage. He began prospecting for land that would be near the plantations of his relatives. Eventually he purchased an 800-acre plantation near Willington, one of the outlying hamlets in the Abbeville area, on a bluff along the Savannah River, a dozen miles south of his boyhood home. The plantation house, called Bath, was a modest one, even for the up-country. Floride would begin her married life in a more primitive, more isolated setting than she had ever known. But the land was fertile, much of it cleared. There were substantial barns and well-built slave quarters.

Calhoun opposed marriage settlements, which were customary among the wealthy planter families, but he certainly approved of the law in most states, including his own, that placed all property of the wife in her husband's hands. He had a ready moral argument to justify this apparent paradox. "That entire confidence, which is reposed by a female in the object of her choice," he said, "in placing both honor and property in his custody gives rise to the most sacred and tender regard." He had no objection, therefore, when Mrs. Colhoun divided much of her property among her three children and left lands she owned in the Pendleton district near the Pickens plantation in the foothills of the southern Appalachian range to Floride and hence to Calhoun.[11]

Calhoun married Floride on January 8, 1811, at Bonneau Ferry. It was a lavish affair, as befit the marriage of a low country heiress to a successful lawyer of a prominent up-country family who had just been elected to Congress. The newly married couple began housekeeping at Bath, but they did not stay long. They went to Bonneau Ferry in the early spring to await Mrs. Colhoun's return from Newport, for Floride,

10. *Calhoun Papers*, I, 42, 57.
11. *Ibid.*, 55; Wiltse, *Calhoun, Nationalist*, 50, 51.

who was now pregnant, wanted to be near her mother while Calhoun was much on the road during these months, closing up his law practice.[12]

Although Calhoun had not as yet taken his seat in Congress, he had already aroused concerted political opposition, which, as he soon discovered, also had a personal dimension. William Smith, a self-important, middle-aged lawyer, resented the younger man's popularity and his rapid rise in prestige. Resolved to check Calhoun's growing influence at the outset, Smith accused him of devoting himself to national affairs while neglecting those of his state and locality. Beyond referring to Smith as "a weak political intriguer," Calhoun dismissed all criticism as so much "factious interest" and looked forward to participation in the Twelfth Congress, which was due to convene on November 4, 1811. There was, of course, the problem of Floride's confinement, but she obliged by giving birth to a son on October 15. Calhoun had just enough time to satisfy himself that the mother and child were doing well before he left for Washington, D.C. He and Floride named their son Andrew Pickens after the revolutionary war hero and a Calhoun relative by marriage, General Pickens.[13]

Calhoun arrived in Washington, D.C., on November 6. Congress had already convened, and Henry Clay, whom John Randolph had contemptuously dubbed the "Western Star," was the new Speaker of the House. The tall, lean congressman from Kentucky, though only five years older than Calhoun, had already enjoyed a distinguished political career. Twice elected United States senator, he was now the leading power in the House and perhaps the most popular figure in the small community of social Washington. Shrewd, and facile in speech and wit, he was immensely attractive to both men and women. He, in his turn, was adept at recognizing those of political talent who would rally behind his leadership in pushing a reluctant administration to a more forceful, if not warlike, posture against Great Britain.

Like Calhoun, Clay was not only responding to the restless land hunger of his frontier region, its chafing against the restraints imposed by British power in the West, but guiding and directing what he perceived as a popular issue to promote his own bid for power. That Clay was instantly attracted to Calhoun is evident by his invitation, gratefully accepted, that the Carolinian join his mess. Two other Carolinians, Langdon Cheves and William Lowndes, who oddly enough

12. *Calhoun Papers,* I, 58, 59.
13. *Ibid.,* 62, 86, 87.

had never met Calhoun, were already members. Dr. William Bibb, the Virginia-born, Pennsylvania-educated congressman from Georgia, and Felix Grundy, the portly former Kentucky judge and expert politician who was now representing the Nashville district of Tennessee, completed the mess. Cheves's wife and two children and Grundy's wife, Calhoun's second cousin, brought a family atmosphere to the Washington boardinghouse. From the beginning of their association, Calhoun found Lowndes the most interesting and compatible of his messmates. This odd-looking, soft-spoken planter from the low country of South Carolina seemed to fit Calhoun's ideal of the gentleman statesman.

Lowndes was six feet six inches tall, narrow chested, painfully thin, and delicate. His features were large, his nose uncommonly so; his heavy-lidded eyes gave him an air of languid detachment. His mind, however, was quick and well disciplined. Although privately educated, he was a fine classics scholar, equal to if not superior to that other contemporary savant, John Quincy Adams, in Greek and Latin. Calhoun found these intellectual attributes most congenial. Also attractive was the fact that Lowndes was almost the same age as he while Clay, Cheves, and Grundy were from five to six years older. The attraction was mutual. After only one day's acquaintance, Lowndes found Calhoun "well informed, easy in his manners and I think admirable in his disposition. I like him already better than any member of our mess and I give his politics the same preference."[14]

With the exception of Lowndes, all the members of the mess were westerners and reflected the expansive, highly individualistic outlook of their region. And all members including Lowndes were ardent nationalists, at least in their attitudes towards internal development and foreign policy. Otherwise, they shared Jeffersonian tenets of states' rights and personal liberty in the abstract sense; for they were all slave owners, and slavery to them was part of the accepted order of things. It was neither practical nor even believable to consider slaves as sharing the liberty Jefferson spoke of in the Declaration of Independence. Clay stood alone in being an active member of the American Colonization Society. But slavery as a political or moral issue did not concern any of the messmates at this time. Their chief interest was foreign policy, and their objective was twofold: to drive Britain out of North America and to force that imperious, imperial nation to respect the American flag

14. Harriott Horry Ravenel, *Life and Times of William Lowndes of South Carolina* (Boston, 1901), 86.

on the high seas. Their boardinghouse became known as the "war mess," and the members of their group, which also included Richard M. Johnson of Kentucky, Peter B. Porter of New York, and David Williams, another of Calhoun's colleagues from South Carolina, were dubbed war hawks by their persistent antagonist, the eccentric, wraith-like congressman from Virginia, John Randolph of Roanoke.[15]

Clay set the tone of the Twelfth Congress with his major committee assignments. Peter B. Porter, a square-jawed, dashing figure who sat a horse well and was equally adept as a trial lawyer and frontier developer, was named chairman of the all-important foreign affairs committee. For second place on that committee, Clay chose Calhoun, probably at Porter's suggestion. The New Yorker was a graduate of Yale and of Tapping Reeve's law school. Southerners, particularly those who had gone north for their education, were particularly noted in the network of alumni that Benjamin Silliman and Timothy Dwight kept active and current. Calhoun's close friend and classmate Micah Sterling, who served in the New York legislature with Porter, must certainly have reinforced that connection.[16]

Clay put Calhoun on Porter's committee before he arrived in Washington, D.C. Langdon Cheves, the bespectacled lawyer whom Calhoun had met when both were members of the South Carolina legislature, became chairman of the naval affairs committee. David Williams was assigned chairmanship of military affairs. William Lowndes chaired the key committee of commerce and manufactures. Three of South Carolina's eight congressmen, then, either chaired or claimed second place on the most important committees of the House, though they represented a relatively small state that ranked sixth in population and wealth. Only ways and means went to a non-Carolinian, Ezekiel Bacon of Massachusetts, who represented a district in the more radical western part of that state. Like Porter and Calhoun, Bacon was a Yale graduate and an alumnus of Reeve's law school. He sympathized with the war hawks and relied on the counsel of Cheves, who, in addition to his naval committee assignment, held second place on the ways and means committee.

A week after being sworn in, Calhoun had met twice with his committee to consider that part of President Madison's message relating to foreign affairs. Besides his regular attendance at the House sessions and conferences with his colleagues, he was hard at work on the com-

15. Ravenel, *Lowndes*, 86.
16. Samuel Eliot Morison, *The Life and Letters of Harrison Gray Otis, Federalist* (2 vols.; Boston, 1913), II, 32.

mittee report that would shape the government's policy toward Great Britain and France. "This place is quite gay, during the session," he said, "but I do not participate in it much myself."[17] When Calhoun spoke thus of Washington society, he had already written most of Porter's report from the foreign relations committee and had made two speeches. His first effort, a comparatively short address on apportionment for representation according to the census of 1810, was an earnest argument for popular representation, the exclusive powers of the House, and the division of sovereignty between state and federal power. There was nothing particularly novel or startling about this inaugural address, but it did show a thorough understanding of *The Federalist Papers* and the nature of the national government. Those who were curious about the young man from South Carolina heard his remarks delivered extemporaneously in a conversational voice that relied on logic and organization rather than rhetorical flourish.

Far more important to Calhoun's career and the future of the nation was his speech on the report from the committee of foreign relations. Three days before he rose to address his colleagues, the cavernous chamber of the House had resounded to the shrill voice of John Randolph, who had launched a bitter attack on the report. He had charged that the hawks were clearly moving towards war with Great Britain. Ridiculing the pretensions of these young men, Randolph in a more sober vein had pointed out the defenseless state of the nation, particularly its vulnerable coastline, and raised the dread issue of a slave revolt in the event of war. How could an English-speaking country that owed its law, many of its customs and values, and its very heritage to Britain, he asked, become an ally of the French tyrant, Napoleon?

Calhoun had already sparred with Randolph, who was a minority member of the foreign relations committee. Each man had taken the other's measure, and each knew in general terms what the other would say in public debate on the report. Thus, Calhoun's defense of the committee's report was a point-by-point rebuttal that dovetailed neatly with what previous defenders had said. But it differed in its concise argument, its careful organization, and its persuasive power couched in logical terms that went directly to the heart of the matter. Candidly, Calhoun admitted the warlike tenor of the committee's report and then gave his reasons why war was to be preferred to a pusillanimous submission. He countered Randolph's point about a gross lack of preparedness with statistics that demonstrated the intrinsic strength of the

17. *Calhoun Papers*, I, 87.

country in population and resources. Turning to the argument that France was as hostile to American interests as Great Britain, Calhoun agreed that "we have still causes of complaint" but said that he was willing to accept the French foreign ministry's statement that the Berlin and Milan decrees had been repealed; the British orders-in-council, he noted, remained in effect. He alluded to impressment, noting that "the evil still grows," but he reserved his most telling point to counter Randolph's argument that war would bring slave revolts.[18]

His eyes flashing with indignation and his voice scornful, Calhoun turned away from Speaker Clay and addressed Randolph directly. He voiced his doubt that there was any danger of a slave uprising. The presence of a militia on alert, as it would be in a war situation, made any such disturbance most unlikely. As to Randolph's contention that the slaves would become rebellious because of the leveling principles of the French Revolution, Calhoun ridiculed the notion. "I cannot think our ignorant blacks have felt much of their baneful influence," he said. "I dare say more than half of them never heard of the French Revolution." He could have applied this ratio to the white population, too, but like others in Congress and among the upper strata of society, he sincerely believed that on matters of topical interest most citizens had some awareness.[19]

That Calhoun, fresh from the backwoods of South Carolina, had had the temerity to engage Randolph in a public debate commended him to his colleagues as a man confident of his own abilities. The Republican press was extravagant in its praise for his speech, many papers declaring flatly that Calhoun must take his place with Clay as a leading figure in Congress, to the annoyance of the "Western Star."

Calhoun had satisfied himself that war with Great Britain was inevitable before he left South Carolina, but like Lady Macbeth, he was not above becoming an active agent in a self-fulfilling prophecy. His reasons were both personal and public. He had grown up in a home and community where the death and destruction the British and their Tory allies had brought to the up-country in the last years of the revolutionary war were still vividly remembered. Scarcely a family in Calhoun's home region had escaped without some loss in that conflict. Anglophobia had taken on the proportions of blood feuds among the clannish Scotch-Irish, and Calhoun was not immune to prevailing attitudes toward the British.

18. *Ibid.*, 78, 79, 83, 76.
19. *Ibid.*, 75–85.

Of course, as a careful student of history and philosophy, Calhoun drew a distinction between such Whig heroes as Lord Shaftesbury, John Locke, and the elder William Pitt, and arrogant military figures like Banastre Tarleton and Lord Rawdon, whose forces had ravaged his native state. It was the oligarchic government, commercial pretensions, and assumed imperialist aims of Great Britain in North America that he hated and feared, not the English people or many of their leading intellectuals.

Calhoun had traveled enough in the United States to appreciate its strength and diversity. Ambitious for himself, he was also ambitious for his state and his nation. Britain he saw as a barrier to expansion westward, to the commercial prosperity of the country's seaports, Charleston among them, and to the maintenance and spread of democratic institutions, which he firmly believed were the only guarantors of personal liberty and the most nearly perfect form of government yet conceived. And one cannot ignore even at this early date Calhoun's sense of his own worth, which had been nurtured by such diverse individuals as his mother, Moses Waddel, Andrew Pickens, Jr., Timothy Dwight, Benjamin Silliman, and James Gould. Calhoun and Clay especially among the war hawks' leadership fit well this comment by John Randolph: "They have entered this House with their eye on the Presidency and mark my words sir, we shall have war before the end of the session."[20]

Calhoun also subscribed to the romantic notion that war brings out the best in a people, especially a people grown careless about its fundamental interests. As he remarked in a speech on nonimportation: "The difference is great between the passive and active state of mind. Tie down a hero, and he feels the puncture of a pin; but throw him into battle, and he is scarcely sensible of vital gashes. So in war; impelled alternately by hope and fear, stimulated with revenge, depressed with shame, or elevated with victory, the people become invincible."[21]

It was quite in keeping, therefore, that Calhoun should find President Madison lacking in decisiveness—"those commanding talents, which are necessary to controul [*sic*] those around him"—and that he should decide James Monroe, the stoop-shouldered secretary of state with whom he and other members of the foreign relations committee had frequent conferences, was more sympathetic to his belligerent views. Monroe, very much the courtly Virginian, had never forgotten

20. William Cabell Bruce, *John Randolph of Roanoke* (2 vols.; New York, 1922), I, 370.
21. *Calhoun Papers*, I, 132.

his wartime service with George Washington and his exposure to British arrogance and intransigence when, as American minister to the Court of St. James, he had failed to settle any of the outstanding differences between the two countries. Although judicious by nature, Monroe could not help being impressed by the spirit and the arguments of the war hawks. His considerable influence with President Madison tended more and more to bring that reluctant executive behind a war policy.[22]

Besides enlisting Monroe in the cause, Calhoun took every opportunity under the wary but approving eye of Speaker Clay to push Congress towards war. Randolph was Calhoun's principal opponent in the verbal exchange, but the Federalist minority was more to be feared because it was an organized political opposition. The Virginia congressman represented only himself and occasionally a few ultra-Jeffersonians. There is no doubt that the leadership of the Republican party was slipping away from the White House and into the eager hands of Calhoun and Clay.

They and their colleagues knew that Randolph was right when he said the nation was unprepared. Its standing army numbered a mere 4,000 men, almost all of them scattered among more than a dozen frontier posts along thousands of miles of ill-defended border wilderness. The navy, because of Jeffersonian policy and congressional parsimony, was almost nonexistent—six frigates, six brigs, two sloops, and several flotillas of gunboats scarcely suitable even for coastal defense. The Royal Navy at this time had over 200 ships at sea and another 500 in reserve. Yet to the brash war hawks, these limitations counted for little. Calhoun pointed out that the country was capable of raising 30,000 troops and as many as a half-million militiamen. He, like other war hawks, emphasized the population and resources of the country. These advocates of war were not so expansive when it came to the means that would be required for an adequate armed force to fight the most powerful nation in the world.[23]

When the president asked for authority to raise 10,000 men for the regular army, Calhoun and his colleagues increased the number to 25,000 without proper consideration of all the logistics required for such a force—uniforms, arms, equipment, barracks, and the like, as well as a system for recruitment. As Calhoun explained, he voted for

22. *Ibid.*, 100; Thomas Hart Benton, *Thirty Years' View* (2 vols.; New York, 1854–56), I, 680; Harry Ammon, *James Monroe: The Quest for National Identity* (New York, 1971), 301.
23. *Calhoun Papers*, I, 79, 80, 91.

the larger number because he wanted to sustain the momentum of preparation. A bill for enlargement of the regular army and of the militia passed both houses of Congress, though not without fierce resistance from the Federalists, from Randolph, and from within the Republican party itself, whose ideology and policy had long opposed military power as a threat to internal freedom. Cheves's bill to increase the navy by twelve ships of the line and twenty frigates was defeated, notwithstanding Clay's impassioned advocacy. Not until 1813, after a year of war, did Congress approve an enlargement of the navy. The war hawks were more successful with their financial measures. They managed to get congressional approval for the doubling of customs duties, a direct levy on the states, excise taxes on a number of consumer articles, and a bond issue for eleven million dollars.[24]

Despite internal and partisan opposition, and despite slow, fitful steps to prepare the nation, a majority in the Congress pushed on with its demands for war against Great Britain. Impressment had become a major target for the war hawks. "Our Commerce," said Calhoun at a later date, "was reduced to a state of dependence as complete as when we were her colonies, and our ships were converted at the same time, into recruiting grounds to man her Navy. Not a vessel of ours was permitted to reach Europe but through her ports, and more than 3,000 of our hardy seaman were impressed into her services, to fight battles in which they had no interest."[25]

When news reached Washington, D.C., that Great Britain would not rescind its orders-in-council and refused even to discuss impressment or other issues between the two nations, the administration announced a sixty-day embargo, which was tantamount to an ultimatum. During this period, events in London did move toward a repeal, but at such a glacial rate that nothing had been resolved when the embargo expired on May 1, 1812. Calhoun, Clay, and others of the war party knew that the prime reason for conflict would be settled within a relatively short time. Yet neither they nor President Madison, who had come round to their position, was willing to hold back, especially since they sensed war had popular support. And other issues besides impressment and commercial rivalry, issues like western posts and British Indian policy, were

24. *Ibid.*, 90; Henry Adams, *History of the United States of America During the First Administration of James Madison* (2 vols.; New York, 1890), II, 435–58, and *History of the United States of America During the Second Administration of James Madison* (2 vols.; New York, 1904), II, 193, 194, 238–67; Reginald Horsman, *The Causes of the War of 1812* (New York, 1962), 242.

25. *Life of JCC*, 9.

at stake. As Calhoun remarked, this would be "the second struggle for our liberty."[26]

On May 19, 1812, dispatches from London indicated a continuing stalemate in the British Parliament. Madison accordingly prepared a war message, which he sent to Congress on June 1. For the diminutive president who, together with his predecessor, had striven to keep America neutral in a world war, the message represented a radical change in policy. In its analysis of the causes for war, it followed closely the speeches of Clay, Calhoun, Porter, and others of the war party.[27]

Calhoun had been chairman of the foreign relations committee since early April, replacing Porter, who had been granted a leave of absence. Calhoun took it upon himself to prepare the report of the committee on the president's war message, and he provided an outline of the grievances against Britain. Impressment was a major issue, along with the alleged effort on the part of the British to arm and incite the Indian tribes on the western borders to attack American settlements.

The report, unlike Calhoun's speeches and other writings thus far, was short on facts and examples, and dismissed with a cavalier disregard the French decrees. These became in his hands merely a pretext for Britain to wage a commercial war against the United States. Calhoun closed his report with a bill to declare war. Clay referred the report immediately to a committee of the whole, which reported favorably the next day, and after a third reading it passed the House, though there was significant resistance. In the Senate, antagonism was even more vehement, but the bill passed 19 to 13. President Madison signed it on June 18, 1812.

Calhoun had his war, but he knew that opposition was widespread. "The distrust of the people," he wrote his close friend Virgil Maxcy, "at that trying period . . . extended to many in our ranks, of whom not a few openly left us." Unknown to the administration and Congress, Parliament had rescinded the orders-in-council five days after the declaration of war, thus removing a major issue of the conflict. An ill-prepared, divided nation had been pushed into a war that, in Calhoun's words, "will prove to the enemy and to the World, that we have not only inherited that liberty which our Fathers gave us, but also the will and power to maintain it."[28]

26. *Calhoun Papers*, I, 107.

27. James D. Richardson (ed.), *A Compilation of the Messages and State Papers of the Presidents, 1789–1897* (20 vols.; Washington, D.C., 1900), II, 484–90.

28. *Calhoun Papers*, X, 42, I, 122.

IV

Not a Moment to Lose

During the first year and a half of the War of 1812, the nation suffered, it seemed, almost continuous disaster. Unreliable, ill-equipped militia troops, superannuated commanders, ill-trained officers, an acute scarcity of regulars, overly ambitious strategic plans, and inept leadership from the administration resulted in a series of reverses. British and Canadian forces captured Detroit, drove the American forces back from the New York frontier, and controlled both Lake Erie and Lake Ontario. Finances were in complete disarray, as the central bank had ceased to function after Congress refused to renew its charter. War aims remained cloudy when evidence multiplied that the French government had duped the Madison administration on the repeal of the Berlin and Milan decrees. Although the administration had proposed an armistice shortly after the declaration of war, neither the American nor the British government pushed negotiations to that end. Napoleon's retreat from Russia and his crushing defeat at Leipzig in October, 1813, followed by his abdication, allowed Britain to devote her entire military and naval strength to the war with the United States.

In this somber period, Madison nearly failed reelection, and a number of service secretaries and incompetent general officers were removed. Among the few incidents that cheered the drooping spirits of party leaders were the naval victories of American frigates on the high seas. Republican party leaders made the most of them in Congress. The restive Federalists mounted an attack against not just the conduct of the war but the war itself. The Thirteenth Congress was not as malleable as its predecessor. The Republicans maintained their ascendancy though they lost several key figures in the House, like Ezekial Bacon, Richard M. Johnson, David Williams, and Peter B. Porter. Early in the second session, Henry Clay accepted nomination as a peace commissioner and resigned his seat as Speaker of the House. Cheves was chosen in his place after Calhoun refused to be considered. The hawks could take some comfort in the absence of the rasping criticism from John Randolph and Josiah Quincy; the one had been defeated for reelection, the other had resigned in disgust. But they had to face a much more incisive critic in Daniel Webster, the deep-browed lawyer from New Hampshire whose oratorical gifts were evident from his first appearance in the House. Webster was joined on the Federalist side by the gifted, sardonic partisan Timothy Pickering, on whom age (he was sixty-five years old) and experience seem to have had a permanently souring effect. A third member of the opposition in the House whose polemics was to be respected was Thomas P. Grosvenor from New York, whom Calhoun had known at Yale and whose opinions on the war and on the war hawks were hostile to the nether point of intransigence.[1]

In the face of these merciless critics, Calhoun found himself increasingly drawn into the defense of an administration that did not command his respect. Before the second session was many months old, Webster had become his principal antagonist. As chairman of the foreign relations committee, Calhoun defended with skill the administration's bungling policy towards France by shifting his argument to what he claimed was Britain's insistence on dominating the world's commerce. While American arms lurched from one setback to another, the Federalist opposition, claiming its constitutional right of free speech and asserting also the rights of states, began threatening the very existence of the Union. Felix Grundy, in a powerful indictment, charged the Federalists with "moral treason." Calhoun did not use such intemperate language, but in a speech on what he called "factious opposition," he neatly removed the constitutional grounds from the Federalist argument and issued a warning that their tactics would lead to "national ruin," which the people would prevent at all costs.[2]

In a later speech Calhoun posed the question of to what extent a minority during wartime might oppose the conflict. He supported an individual's right to his opinion if he believed the war unjust, but claimed that no upright citizen, however adverse his opinions on the war, had the right to act in such a manner as to "put his country in the power of the enemy."[3] Clearly Calhoun was shaken. His brash overconfidence at the beginning of the conflict had worn thin. Federalist arguments that squared with the facts of utter unpreparedness and dwindling morale even in his own section were undermining his veneer of self-assurance.

This changing posture was evident in Calhoun's explanations for

1. *Webster Papers,* I, 147.
2. *Calhoun Papers,* I, 169–74, 424; Joseph Howard Sparks, *Felix Grundy, Champion of Democracy* (Baton Rouge, 1940), 80, 81; *Calhoun Papers,* I, 189–200.
3. *Calhoun Papers,* I, 234.

joining Cheves and Lowndes in their independent stand opposing the administration's policy of trade restriction. Calhoun had believed trade restrictions to be unworkable before the war. Now that war had not only come but threatened to divide the Union, he found the policy to be both impractical and divisive. In taking this position, Calhoun was speaking to a larger audience than Congress—the merchants and bankers of Charleston; the potent commercial communities of Baltimore, Philadelphia, New York, and Boston; the smaller river ports and seaports like Albany and New Haven; and the agricultural interests whose surplus cotton and grains had mouldered in the warehouses during the long period of the Embargo and the Nonintercourse acts. More personally compelling than this pragmatic stand was Calhoun's search for political stability. Through his opposition he would restore, among other things, his own sense of security, and above all, he would justify his role in precipitating the war.

When Albert Gallatin, secretary of the treasury, proposed a tax on part of the profits of cargoes that had been shipped after the orders-in-council were repealed, but before news of the war reached Britain, Calhoun had fought the policy vehemently and successfully.[4] A few months after hostilities opened, the British began blockading the American coast from Long Island Sound south, hoping to foster a disaffection in New England and to ensure supplies from that region for British dependencies in Canada and the West Indies. To that end the British government issued licenses to New England shippers for trade under certain specifications. Yankee merchants saw nothing wrong in trading with the enemy, but the Madison administration certainly did. It aimed to reimpose the embargo and outlaw licensing.

Calhoun opposed this policy. Heeding partisan opposition in Congress and sectional movements in New England, he argued that the proper course was to raise duties on imports rather than promote further divisive forces with a renewal of trade restrictions. His motives were not without their political side. Commercial and agricultural interests at home as well as in New England were important, he felt, to his own future. And it seemed impractical to him, given the present condition of public opinion in New England, to pass restrictive legislation that could not be enforced. Considering the state of the treasury, higher duties would provide additional funds for the war effort, while smuggling would become less attractive if most of these import taxes were passed on to the consumer. Exports, of course, would be un-

4. *Ibid.*, 136–45.

affected. Shippers even in those states that were blockaded could still engage in blockade running without the additional burden of trying to evade government policy.[5] Despite his cogent arguments, Calhoun could not break the administration's majority in Congress. And rather than risk a party split, or take up the lonely position of a political independent, he eventually, though reluctantly, supported the restrictive measures.

With the fall of Napoleon, the administration finally came round to Calhoun's position. On the last day of March, 1814, it proposed a bill repealing all restrictions on trade. Calhoun supported this change in policy with a report from his committee on foreign relations and a speech he delivered on April 6, 1814. The bill passed both houses and became law on April 14.[6]

In the debates over these trade measures, Calhoun, who usually maintained self-control under the most flagrant provocation, lost his temper with Grosvenor after the New York congressman bitingly accused him of inconsistency for party purposes. Heated words between the two congressmen led to a challenge—the only time in Calhoun's career that he was brought to the brink of a duel. Matters, however, were resolved satisfactorily. That Calhoun should have let his emotions govern his public behavior was a manifestation of the personal, political, and public pressure he was under at the time.

When Calhoun left home for Washington, D.C., to attend the second session of the Thirteenth Congress, Floride was again seven months pregnant. Her condition was a source of grave concern to Calhoun, particularly since her mother would not be with her. In the isolated plantation Bath, Floride would have to depend on her cousin-in-law Dr. Thomas Casey should any complications arise from her second confinement.

Worried about his family, Calhoun was equally concerned with the fate of the nation. In addition to the usual strain of public office in wartime was the sensitivity that went with his leadership role in the dismal affairs of state that he himself had done so much to precipitate. The war was going badly; all the hasty conclusions he had made about national honor, patriotism, the spirit of the militia, the innate strength of the country, and its ability to win quickly and overwhelmingly this "second war of independence" had not materialized—indeed, seemed to the sensitive Calhoun to have been misconceived. Unlike the ebul-

5. *Ibid.*, 126, 134, 163, 181, 184; *Life of JCC*, 10, 11, 13; Ravenel, *Lowndes*, 126, 127.
6. *Calhoun Papers*, I, 240–48.

lient Henry Clay or even the diffident Lowndes and the careful, cautious Cheves, Calhoun at this stage in his career was inclined to make assessments of his own conduct. A realistic judgment of past events and a tendency to shape forecasts on experience led him to question whether the beliefs he had acted upon were in fact sound and whether deeper and more compelling adversities were about to befall the country. For Calhoun in these trying days, guilt was always near the surface.[7]

47

Aside from the economic hardship that the war was bringing to Calhoun, to other planters, and to commercial interests everywhere, the British blockade of the nation's coastline was inciting separatism in the Northeast. The modest victory of Winfield Scott at Chippewa and the naval success of Oliver Hazard Perry on Lake Erie had, it appeared to the government in Washington, earned only a brief reprieve before the full force of the British army fell upon the nation. With Britain's command of the coastal waters, the expected invasion or many invasions could well partition the nation, especially disaffected New England and New York and the loosely held western territories.

Calhoun, more than any other war hawk, had that speculative habit of mind that could calculate the logic of disaster and its consequence. The more critical he perceived the nation's affairs, the more he sought to justify himself. His speeches in the early days of the second session of the Thirteenth Congress reveal his inner anguish. On the dark, chilly afternoon of February 25, 1814, Calhoun rose to make a formal speech supporting a bill for a loan of $25 million to finance the war effort. For the past two weeks the debate on this bill had raged in the House, with the most formidable speakers on both sides engaged in a verbal controversy that extended to whether the war policy had been in the national interest. Calhoun had prepared himself well, again determined to explain and defend the reasons for going to war. As he saw them, the motives were impressment, neutral rights, commercial monopoly, and the broad but fundamental issue of liberty, which he claimed British policy had endangered. And he did not ignore what he stigmatized as factious opposition and its perils for a democracy.

Calhoun had followed the debate carefully; and he had studied various works that he felt would help illustrate his position, like Emeric De Vattel's *Law of the Nations, The Tenth Federalist,* volumes of Jean Charles Sismondi's as yet incomplete *History of the Italian Republics Dur-*

7. For instance, in a speech on the army bill delivered on January 14, 1813, Calhoun remarked: "Whether it is the destiny of our country to sink under that of our enemy or not. Mr. C. said he was not without his fears and his hopes" (*Calhoun Papers,* I, 160).

ing the Middle Ages in English translation, and several histories of the Roman Republic and Empire, probably including Edward Gibbon's *History of the Decline and Fall of the Roman Empire.*[8] Calhoun's two-hour speech was a model of clarity and organization in which he subjected the arguments of Pickering and Webster, among others of the Federalist opposition, to penetrating analysis and vigorous rebuttal. But Calhoun could not conceal the defensive note that permeated his address. "Our existence is at stake," he said at one point, "no less than that of England, or rather the danger to her is imaginary to us real and certain." He reverted to the theme of possible defeat while describing the United States as the champion of neutral rights in the world. "But if unfortunately," he said, "we should be left alone to maintain the contest; and, if, in consequence which may God forbid, necessity should compel us to yield for the present, yet our generous efforts will not have been in vain." He took notice of the crumbling morale that seemed pervasive. "Government, it is true," he declared, "can command the arm and hand, the bone and muscle of the nation; but these are powerless, nerveless without the concurring good wishes of the community."[9]

Calhoun managed to keep his emotions under control, apart from the abortive duel with Grosvenor. He found a useful anodyne for his feelings in intense labor. Almost every day during the remainder of the session, he was engaged in debate, submitting long reports he had written in committee, or making lengthy speeches on a wide range of topics that concerned the conduct of the war. He looked forward to the end of the session, when he could be home with his family, far removed from the monastic surroundings and the mounting tensions of Washington.[10] Still, his speeches in the main showed no faltering of purpose, even though a careful listener could detect the occasional lapse in which his uncertainties were marked. In late April, Congress adjourned. A weary, subdued Calhoun journeyed south, where he would recoup his energies in the comfort of home and family, which now included his three-month-old daughter, another Floride.

During the summer of 1814, Calhoun devoted himself to managing his plantation. This entailed spending the day on horseback personally directing his slaves in cultivating crops of corn, wheat, and cotton that had been sown before his arrival, mending fences, repairing tools and

8. See especially *Calhoun Papers,* I, 211, 214, 215, 216, 233, 234. The works cited are from internal evidence.

9. *Ibid.,* 279, 227, 235, X, 42, 43.

10. *Ibid.,* I, 205, 206.

outbuildings, feeding livestock, and making all other preparations necessary for the fall harvest. It was hard physical work, but a labor that Calhoun enjoyed. Apart from a lifelong habit of practical study (he had no use for novels or other light reading) and a growing passion for politics, Calhoun was devoted to farming as a pleasure and as a vocation. He was never happier than in watching his green fields come to maturity and in experimenting with the latest agricultural techniques. He was a considerate master with his slaves, but he insisted on discipline in their work, and when he thought it necessary he employed the lash. This type of punishment he seems to have used sparingly except on those occasions when fears of slave revolt swept his region.

While at Bath, Calhoun kept himself posted on national affairs. Like others of his countrymen, he felt humiliated at the disgraceful rout of the militia at Bladensburg and the burning of Washington. Unlike many, however, he did not regard the Washington raid as anything more than a raid. With a clear view of British resources and strategy, he could see no military gain for the enemy in capturing and destroying a city of no military importance. The prompt retreat of the British and their inability to seize Baltimore, which did have military significance, confirmed Calhoun in his analysis. He was far more concerned with the projected British invasion of the Hudson River Valley, which, if it succeeded, could result in the capture of Albany and New York City. Such a disaster would inevitably separate the entire Northeast from the rest of the nation, and would probably detach it for good. Calhoun was much relieved at the naval victory of Thomas Macdonough on Lake Champlain that effectively cut communications for the invading British and Canadian army. Another victory closer to home, that of Andrew Jackson over the powerful Creeks, the action at Horseshoe Bend on the Tallapoosa River in what is now eastern Alabama, assured the security of the southwest frontier for the time being.

British terms at Ghent, however, where commissioners from both sides were seeking to make a peace treaty, were initially so harsh as to prolong the war. The terms included a British protectorate over an Indian state that encompassed most of the Northwest Territory, the cession of the entire northern half of Maine to Canada, and surrender of New Orleans. Only a total defeat of the United States, it would seem, could end the conflict.

While Calhoun pondered these draconian terms and worried about their apparant acceptance by some arch-Federalists in New England, he became seriously ill with what was termed bilious fever but was probably a recurrence of the dysentery that he had suffered when a student at Yale. The Thirteenth Congress had already been in its third session for a month when a gaunter than usual Calhoun took his seat in late October, 1814. Members of both houses of Congress were occupying temporary quarters in the post office, the only government building the British had not destroyed. The rooms available were far too small and cramped to accommodate the membership, but Calhoun made no complaint. Nor was he demoralized, as many were, by the smoke-blackened ruins of the public buildings. Rather, he used the dismal appearance of Washington, D.C., to emphasize the absolute necessity for prompt and vigorous action.[11]

President Madison in his address to the session had insisted that Congress provide more funds for the war, and urged conscription to bring the regular army to its authorized strength. On October 24, 1814, Daniel Webster attacked both proposals. In what was now familiar language, he arraigned the administration's conduct of the war and accused it of stalling on peace negotiations because of its land hunger for Canada. Calhoun countered the next day with a speech that denounced Webster's charges as absurd. Canada was the proper sphere for offensive operations in any sound strategy, nothing more. The American effort on the seaboard must be a defensive one. Obviously referring to the destruction of Washington, he said, "The enemy can make no permanent conquest of any importance there; but he hopes, by alarming and harassing the country, and putting us under enormous expense in defending it, to break the spirit of the nation, and bring it to his terms."[12]

For the remainder of the session, Calhoun, though chairman of the foreign affairs committee, concerned himself almost exclusively with manpower and financial problems. Active on the floor, in the anterooms, and in visits to colleagues' messes, he was largely responsible for securing congressional acceptance for drafting, if necessary from the militia, to complete one corps of volunteers whom he hoped would be tempted to enlist by a generous land bounty. There was a certain desperation about his activities during the fall and early winter of 1814, which is best expressed by his remarks supporting a direct tax to be levied on the states. "You have for an enemy," he said, "a power the most implacable and formidable; who, now freed from any other contest, will the very next campaign direct the whole of his force against you. Besides his deeprooted enmity against this country, which will

11. Constance M. Green, *Washington: Village and Capital, 1800–1878* (Princeton, N.J., 1962), 63, 64.

12. *Calhoun Papers,* I, 255, 256.

urge him to exertion, he is aware of the necessity, on his part, to bring the contest to a speedy termination."[13]

Calhoun had been studying the problem of national finance for some time and had decided that another central bank was necessary, along with additional loans and taxation, both direct and indirect. Gallatin's successor as secretary of the treasury, Alexander J. Dallas, a Philadelphia lawyer, had presented a new revenue bill along with a letter recommending a national bank with a capital of $ 50 million. The proposed institution, patterned on the first Bank of the United States, would finance the government debt and any future loans that might be necessary. Dallas would have the government subscribe 40 percent of its capital stock in 6 percent bonds while private capital would purchase 60 percent of its stock with $ 6 million in specie, $ 12 million in government war bonds, and $ 6 million in treasury notes. Although the president would appoint five of the fifteen directors on an annual basis, the federal government would not control the bank, which was, however, required to lend the government up to $ 60 million at 6 percent interest.

Calhoun was familiar with Dallas' plan, which John W. Eppes, Randolph's successor, reported on behalf of the ways and means committee. The House responded favorably, and a bank bill to that end was introduced on November 7. As he had on all previous issues that he regarded important, Calhoun made a major speech on the bank. While favoring its charter, he proposed a bank completely free of government support or control, except that it would be required to subscribe to treasury notes that had been issued to finance the war. It would not be compelled to make loans to the government, and the treasury notes it purchased could be sold at its pleasure. But the bank bill, which had excited strong opposition in both houses of Congress, was lost in the euphoria of Jackson's victory at New Orleans and the news of the treaty of Ghent, which brought peace at last.

In the few weeks that remained of the Thirteenth Congress, the House committee on military affairs reported a bill that fixed the peacetime army at 10,000 men. An amendment was at once offered, reducing the army to 6,000 men. Calhoun was prepared for this move and gained the floor in an effort to defeat the amendment. He pointed out that the army must be strong enough to protect the western frontiers and that it must be large enough to "keep alive military service and serve as a seminary for that purpose." He seems not to have been

13. *Ibid.*, I, 254.

prepared to debate the precise size of the peacetime army, but he voted against the reduction amendment, which carried. The House, however, reconsidered the original bill and finally accepted the 10,000-man limit.[14]

Quite clearly, Calhoun felt that the War of 1812 had taught a useful lesson—that the nation should never again be so ill-prepared to defend itself. The two speeches he made on the peace treaty and the military establishment in late February, before the Thirteenth Congress adjourned, revealed his sense of relief that the war had ended. Calhoun seemed to be saying that even if the peace treaty was inconclusive, the nation, considering its condition, had been fortunate not to have fared worse, despite Jackson's victory at New Orleans. War, he had discovered, was something more than heady ambition and frothy rhetoric.[15]

Calhoun returned to his home in late March, 1815, and remained there until November. On his return trip to Washington, D.C., he journeyed overland to within fifty-three miles of the capital and completed his trip by steamboat, which he found an enjoyable experience. He had, however, been reluctant to leave. Floride was again pregnant. A family tragedy that occurred during his stay at home made him all the more sensitive to the perils of her impending confinement. He had only been at Bath about six weeks when his little daughter, Floride, was suddenly taken ill with a violent fever; she died within twenty-four hours. The parents were grief stricken. "Thus early was stached [snatched] from us in the bloom of life, our dear child . . . so healthy so cheerful, so stought [sic] . . . she had just begun to talk and walk," he wrote his mother-in-law, "and progressed so fast in both as to surprise everyone."[16] He was also concerned about his son, Andrew, who he learned as soon as he arrived in Washington, was ill with fever. This time he would not chance Floride's giving birth in isolated Bath. She must go to Charleston, where she would have the care of his friend and Yale classmate Dr. James MacBride.

As he had done the year before when worried about his family in distant South Carolina, Calhoun plunged into the work of Congress with renewed zest. Many of the faces that had been missing from the Thirteenth Congress were once again seen in the House. Henry Clay had resumed the Speakership; gadfly John Randolph was once more in his seat, his hunting dogs at his feet and his "toast water" near at hand. Calhoun's friend Lowndes was chairman of the ways and means com-

14. *Ibid.*, 278.
15. *Ibid.*, 277–82.
16. *Ibid.*, 283.

mittee, while Calhoun retained his chairmanship of foreign relations. The prestige he had gained from his speech on the bank bill prompted Speaker Clay to appoint Calhoun chairman of a select committee to consider the state of the currency. In his message to the new Congress, President Madison had recommended that steps be taken to put the nation's disordered financial affairs on a sound basis. Since a central bank was considered essential for this objective, Calhoun and his committee, using Alexander Hamilton's bank of 1791 as a rough model, brought in an elaborate bill of twenty sections on January 8, 1816.

Aside from technical aspects, the new bank would function as a privately held and managed institution rather than as one subject to close government control. It would, of course, be chartered by Congress and must pay a bonus set at $ 1.5 million for the privilege. The bank had the power to establish branches in the various states. Its notes would be payable at par for all government taxes, direct or indirect, including excises and imports. Apart from five of its twenty directors and its president, who were government appointees, the management was independent, responsible only to its shareowners. The bank would act as the sole depository for government funds—a most valuable asset and one that Calhoun counted on for establishing a uniform currency standard because the bank's notes were backed by the nation's monetary reserves.

After some minor alterations were made in the bill, both houses of Congress approved the measure. It became law on April 10, 1816—a record of only six weeks from introduction. Sensing the expansive mood of Congress in the debates over the bank, during which the objections of Webster for the Federalists and Randolph for the extreme Jeffersonians were brushed aside, Calhoun worked with Lowndes to bring in a revenue bill that would continue the wartime direct tax. There was considerable opposition. Randolph warned that Calhoun and the Madison administration were tending toward consolidation and away from the federative character of the government. Calhoun was not concerned with Randolph's strictures. He perceived the establishment of the bank and the tax as a necessary and practical application of government power that promoted the interests of his class, his state, and the major interests involved. Indeed, when pressed on this point, he stated that liberty and sound morals were served by a sound currency and a nation free of debt. Disordered, depreciated currency, an empty treasury, and general economic depression were the breeding grounds of those dread opposites tyranny and anarchy.[17]

17. *Ibid.*, 331–39.

But Calhoun was more concerned with national defense than with any one subject of public policy in the Fourteenth Congress. Even proposing and defending the bank and tax measures were a part of his anxiety about the military posture of the nation. He argued for an expansion of officers' training schools from the one at West Point to three others located in the South and West. He pushed vigorously for the military education at government expense of poor but ambitious and intelligent young men. "Rich men," he said, "being already at the top of the ladder, have no further motive to climb. It is that class of the community who find it necessary to strive for elevation, that furnishes you with officers."[18]

Calhoun equated defense with national self-sufficiency. In his arguments favoring a protective tariff for the fledgling cotton and woolen textile industries, he did not, as he explained later, draw "the proper distinction between duties for revenue and duties for protection." The tariff act he supported contained the principle of minimum valuation, which was decidedly protective to the woolen and cotton industries in the Northeast. In a public letter published during the fall of 1832, Calhoun observed, "The provision was then new, and not well understood. My attention was not particularly directed to it."[19] But even if he had understood the principle and the distinction between protection and revenue at the time, the chances are he would have supported the act.

American manufactures were in danger of being driven out of the domestic market by a flood of cheaper, better British goods, and Calhoun's argument was strictly along lines of security to be enhanced through national self-sufficiency. Implying that Britain was still the principal antagonist, he pointed out that in the event of another war, that country would cut off imports of essential manufactured goods like textiles and cause great economic distress. He wanted revenue to meet the war debt and to promote security and prosperity for all interests. "When our manufactures are grown to a certain perfection," he said, "as they soon will under the fostering care of government . . . the farmer will find a ready market for his surplus produce; and what is almost of equal consequence, a certain and cheap supply of all his wants. His prosperity will diffuse itself to every class in the community."[20]

Congress adjourned on April 30, 1816, having accomplished much

18. *Ibid.*, 287.
19. *Life of JCC*, 17; *Calhoun Papers*, XI, 592.
20. *Calhoun Papers*, I, 350.

towards providing a cohesive framework for the future development of a peacetime economy. But among the many important measures that were passed, a compensation bill that raised the salaries of congressmen and that Calhoun had supported was the target of intense criticism throughout the nation. Calhoun to his dismay found that his constituents were more caustic about the alleged salary grab than voters in other areas. His safe seat appeared to be in jeopardy when his cousin Colonel Joseph Calhoun announced himself a candidate for Congress and community leaders denounced Calhoun unsparingly.

Other congressmen confronted by the same hostility had openly disavowed their vote for increased compensation and thrown themselves on the mercy of the community. Calhoun was advised to do likewise but adamantly refused. For the important work that he and his colleagues had done to strengthen the nation's economic and social institutions, he declared that they deserved just compensation. Calhoun organized two mass meetings in his district, where he not only explained what the Fourteenth Congress had done but argued forcefully that if just compensation were not paid to the people's representatives, public service would not attract the best men. Underpaid congressmen would be tempted to follow the path to corruption.

Calhoun was at his best in facing his audience of planters and professionals. His pose earnest, seemingly disinterested, and transparently honest and courageous, the tall, thin figure with flashing eyes and matter-of-fact delivery reminded his audience of what they chose to believe were the attributes of the founding fathers. He seemed to be republican virtue incarnate, and he won his reelection handily. During the short session of the Fourteenth Congress that began on December 2, 1816, Calhoun steadfastly defended his course. Other congressmen were not so valiant. The compensation law remained for the present Congress, but was repealed for the Fifteenth Congress.[21]

Calhoun returned to the short and final session of the Fourteenth Congress in December, 1816, refreshed and eager to push on with what he regarded as the capstone of his program for national security—internal improvements. Although optimistic about passage of a public works bill, he continued to develop his defense theme. A self-sufficient nation would still be vulnerable to attack if its communications remained in the primitive state that presently existed in the nation, he reminded the House. A barrel of flour normally costing two to three dollars when delivered to Detroit during the war cost sixty dol-

21. *Ibid.*, 361, 362; *Life of JCC*, 23.

lars, he said, while a cannonball transported to Lake Erie or Lake Ontario from Albany cost fifty cents a pound after transport charges were paid. "We occupy a surface prodigiously great," said Calhoun, "in proportion to our numbers. The common strength is brought to bear with great difficulty on the point that may be menaced by an enemy. . . . Good roads and canals judiciously laid out, are the proper remedy."[22] As a first installment towards paying for these public works projects, which would be nationwide in scope, Calhoun proposed using the bonus that was to be paid for the bank charter.

Although his position on all of these measures was certainly nationalistic, Calhoun's first and overriding concern was defense. He was reacting to the near collapse of the nation during the war and was resolved that such a condition should never again arise. In this case, what was beneficial to the security of the nation as a whole was also most useful to his state and region. If any part of the United States desperately needed improved transportation, it was the seaboard slave states, the most underdeveloped region in the East. But uppermost in Calhoun's mind was a nation in which all sections and interests reinforced one another. This was the lesson of the War of 1812, and Calhoun, more than any other member of a Congress that included Henry Clay and William Lowndes, was responsible for driving this program through over the spirited and able opposition of Webster, Randolph, and Pickering. There was one difficulty, however, that was completely unexpected—a difficulty that would in the end wreck Calhoun's vision. It was a tragic irony for him that a southern president, a slaveholder, and the principal father of the Constitution, James Madison, at the very end of his term vetoed the bonus bill.

Calhoun had gone to the Seven Buildings, the president's temporary residence, to congratulate him on the success of his administration. The two chatted briefly. As Calhoun prepared to leave, Madison in a carefully phrased comment said that he was about to veto the bonus bill, and explained his constitutional objections to it. Calhoun was surprised and deeply chagrined. If anyone in the nation understood the absolute necessity of good internal communications during wartime, it should have been Madison. His administration had been responsible for the conduct of the war. A British raiding party had chased him from the capital, a disgraceful departure that Calhoun thought would have been avoided if the military establishment had been able to move regular troops and supplies fast enough to threatened areas.

22. *Life of JCC*, 21; *Calhoun Papers*, I, 399.

Calhoun, however, had to bow to the president's constitutional objections, which he admitted he and his colleagues had not considered thoroughly. Madison's knowledge and prestige on constitutional matters were not to be challenged.[23] Calhoun made the best of his disappointment, but he must have wondered whether the states, the localities, and private capital outside of the Northeast could ever raise the funds necessary for the kind of development he believed was essential. Public works of this nature would maintain the various sections of the Union in economic balance. And that economic balance would provide the security and stability he sought above all.

23. *Life of JCC*, 21.

V

Erecting Defenses

A new president was elected in 1816. James Monroe, like the two previous presidents, was a Virginian, a planter, a slaveholder, and a Republican. Rather a remote person, he was not as popular as his predecessor, and his nomination by the congressional caucus of his party had not been achieved without opposition. William H. Crawford, a citizen of Georgia but a native son of Virginia, also a Republican, a slaveholder, and a planter, opposed the nomination. Crawford had been in conspicuous public service for the past ten years as a member of the United States Senate, minister to France, secretary of war, and secretary of the treasury during the last year of Madison's administration. An instinctive politician and an able, highly ambitious public servant, Crawford had made the most of his brief tenure in Madison's cabinet and his congressional connections to challenge Monroe in the caucus. He almost succeeded, garnering fifty-four votes to Monroe's sixty-five.

During the years he was chairman of the House foreign relations committee, Calhoun had worked closely with Monroe, and he took an active part in promoting his canvass. It is possible that Calhoun's efforts on behalf of Monroe in Congress helped defeat Crawford's nomination. What is certain is that Crawford's relations with Calhoun were correct but scarcely cordial after his defeat. Henry Clay had also watched Calhoun's activities with his accustomed care and marked him as a future rival.[1] Calhoun seems not to have concerned himself with either the big Georgian's ambitions at this point or Clay's distinctly cool demeanor.

Monroe's priorities in selecting his cabinet were sectional balance, ability, political importance, and personal preference, in that order. For the all-important post of secretary of state, whose occupant was considered to be heir apparent to the presidency, he chose John Quincy Adams. Adams would represent the North, and as an ex-Federalist, he

---

1. *Calhoun Papers*, I, 316, 317; *Clay Papers*, V, 658; Charles Wiltse, *John C. Calhoun, Nationalist: 1782–1828* (Indianapolis, 1944), 114, 115.

would dramatize the nonpartisan character Monroe wanted for his administration. There was no doubt in the president-elect's mind that Adams had both experience and ability. He had been a United States senator, minister to the Netherlands, Prussia, Russia, and Great Britain, and most recently peace commissioner at Ghent. Nor was there any question about his ability. Adams was a classics scholar and was fluent in French and German; indeed, he was quite the most cultivated man in Washington, D.C., and perhaps in the Union. He was besides supremely industrious. Unfortunately, he had a pedantic turn of mind, a biting temper, and a tendency to patronize those whom he considered intellectually inferior. Short, stout, balding, and testy, Adams, however, had been for years a loyal supporter of Monroe, and he always deferred to the president.[2]

Monroe persuaded his erstwhile competitor Crawford, representing the South, to continue in the Treasury Department because of his obvious ability and his standing with Congress. To obtain a representative of the West, he offered the War Department to Henry Clay, who refused but urgently recommended the governor of his state and a political ally, Isaac Shelby. Richard M. Johnson, one of Clay's colleagues in the House, backed him. Monroe was persuaded and offered the post to Shelby, who refused to leave his comfortable berth in Kentucky for what he knew would be a politically difficult post. The War Department had had five secretaries in the space of four years and among the knowledgeable was considered to be in a shambles.

Since the West had declined the offer of an appointment, Monroe felt released from any obligation to that region. The two South Carolinians Lowndes and Calhoun had always been uppermost in his mind for the position. He thought highly of both men and decided to offer the post to Lowndes because, as he later explained, "the appointment had been offered by my predecessor . . . and for that reason . . . I thought it proper to renew the overture." Lowndes also declined. Before Monroe made the offer to Calhoun, he consulted with Crawford, who made no objection but did not express any particular enthusiasm. The other members of the cabinet were holdovers from the Madison administration—Benjamin Crowninshield in the Navy Department and Richard Rush, attorney general, both of whom would soon be replaced. Smith Thompson of New York would become navy secretary, and William Wirt of Maryland, a large-limbed, genial lawyer, part-time

2. Samuel Flagg Bemis, *John Quincy Adams and the Foundations of American Foreign Policy* (New York, 1949), 260, 261.

novelist, and father of a bevy of beautiful girls, would become attorney general.[3]

Calhoun was at Bath when Monroe's offer arrived on October 10, 1817. Considering that all the other cabinet posts had been filled by this time, Calhoun knew that he had not been first choice for the War Department. Whether he had learned that he was the fourth person to be offered the position is unknown. If he had known, it probably would not have made any difference. Calhoun was blocked from any advancement in Congress. Henry Clay was Speaker of the House and had shown no disposition to step down from that post. The South Carolina legislature had just elected his old enemy William Smith to the United States Senate to fill the unexpired five-year term of John Taylor. South Carolina's other senator, John Gaillard, had such a reputation for honesty, courtesy, and ability that he would retain his seat as long as he desired. The War Department represented a fresh opportunity for this complex, ambitious person whose latent insecurity demanded the reassurance of public acclaim. The fact that the War Department was recognized to be in parlous condition actually attracted Calhoun because he saw more clearly than Shelby and even Lowndes, who advised him not to accept, that with the support of the president, which he would surely have, he would not just restore the department but reform and expand it.[4]

Calhoun's close connection with Monroe had shown him that the new president would be most responsive to defense in the interests of national security. And this objective was the most compelling reason why Calhoun decided to accept Monroe's offer. He was determined that the frightening experiences of 1812 would never happen again if he could prevent them. "For none felt more deeply than myself," he wrote one week after he took office, "that total want of preparation which preceded the last war, and which had nearly been succeeded by the most disastrous consequences." A reformed, reinvigorated War Department, including a highly trained professional army with able officers, was, of course, the means that would counter the ambitions of any foreign power to expand in North America at the expense of the United States. Other, lesser motives like a felt political need to gain visible administrative experience and an urgent desire to participate in

3. *Calhoun Papers,* X, 319, 320; Ammon, *James Monroe,* 357–63.
4. Ammon, *James Monroe,* 418; Thomas Hart Benton, *Thirty Years' View* (2 vols.; New York, 1854–56), I, 77, 78.

affairs of state, to assist in framing policy rather than defending it in Congress, were also factors in his acceptance.[5]

Once Calhoun had made up his mind, he moved rapidly to settle the affairs of his plantation and to make all the arrangements necessary for moving his family to Washington, D.C. He had decided that he would not brave the discomforts of the capital without Floride and the children. Soon after he accepted the War Department appointment, the Calhouns left Bath in their carriage, which their black coachman, Hector, managed with more skill than they had expected. The children coped well with the boredom of travel and were, as Calhoun wrote his mother-in-law, "far less troublesome" than they had anticipated. The family arrived in Washington in early December and were guests of the Lowndes while they looked for a suitable rental.[6]

Washington still bore the scars of the British raid, though they were rapidly being removed. The White House would not be ready for occupancy until September, 1817, but the four-story brick building next to it that housed both the War and Navy departments had been restored and renovated. Calhoun was able to move into his rather cramped office in the southeast corner of the first floor immediately after his arrival.[7]

Before he had been able to sort out the responsibilities of his new position and become acquainted with his staff of twenty-five clerks and messengers, Calhoun was confronted with a serious problem involving the powers of the secretary of war as they related to the authority of the general officers. At stake was whether civilian control of the army would prevail over the pride and sensitivity of the most popular military hero in the nation, Andrew Jackson. Could the secretary of war give a direct order to any officer in Jackson's command, or must he transmit the order through Jackson as the latter demanded? That such a situation had developed reflected the confused state of the War Department, which had, in effect, lost control of the army's command structure.

Calhoun was determined to reimpose civilian authority. Both he and

5. *Calhoun Papers*, II, 17. That Calhoun considered the appointment very carefully is in part borne out by the fact that it took him three weeks before he answered the president in the affirmative (*ibid.*, I, 418).

6. *Ibid.*, I, 420, II, 37.

7. Constance M. Green, *Washington: Village and Capital, 1800–1878* (Princeton, N.J., 1962), 67; Lurton D. Ingersoll, *A History of the War Department of the United States* (Washington, D.C., 1879), 110.

Monroe, however, were well aware of the difficulties in dealing with the politically potent, highly independent general. Firmness was essential, but so was tact. It would not do to issue any peremptory orders. Calhoun, who had never met Jackson, counted on the general's good sense in respecting civilian control and in his understanding that some flexibility had to be maintained if the department were to control the operations of forces scattered over thousands of square miles along which communications were slow and uncertain. He drafted a most diplomatic letter in which he seemed to agree with Jackson's contention and declared that it would be War Department policy to issue orders through the commanding generals whenever possible. Yet at the same time, he noted that there would have to be exceptions to this procedure when unforeseen contingencies arose. In these cases, said Calhoun, "The exception becomes the rule." Jackson was satisfied with this arrangement, which allowed him the control he desired but also asserted the War Department's authority to issue orders directly to subordinate officers.[8]

Calhoun may have been well advised on the politics of personality, but he was almost completely ignorant of military science. During his career in the House, he had been primarily concerned with foreign and economic affairs, though he had a good layman's grasp of strategy. He had read only one slim volume on military tactics before he took over the War Department. He knew some of the top army officers but had not made a study of their fitness for the positions they held. Fortunately, they were an outstanding group of professional soldiers, most of whom had performed well, if not brilliantly, in the War of 1812.

The military establishment was divided into a northern branch, commanded by Major General Jacob Brown, and a southern branch, commanded by Major General Andrew Jackson. Brown was forty-two years old; his health, never particularly sturdy, was now poor. He had been wounded in the war and had not completely recovered. Self-taught in military science, this son of a Pennsylvania Quaker was a bold, vigorous army commander, and he had good tactical and organizational sense. He also had his share of vanity and was somewhat of a complaining soul. His headquarters were at Brownville in northern New York, on the shores of Lake Ontario.

Brown's two deputies were Winfield Scott, stationed in New York City, and Alexander Macomb, at Detroit. Scott, a fine officer who had distinguished himself at the battles of Chippewa and Lundy's Lane, was

8. *Jackson Correspondence*, II, 343.

immensely self-assured, with the most extravagant pretensions. Formerly a lawyer, Scott possessed a litigious personality that seems to have been sharpened by his brief experience at the bar. His Virginia birth and background exaggerated his sense of honor and self-importance. He was a magnificent figure of a man, six feet five inches tall with a heavily muscled frame. He had a fondness for spectacular uniforms and display that emphasized his majestic appearance. Scott was an excellent leader and an earnest student of military science.

Macomb was a regular army officer in service for the past eighteen years. He was a dependable, rather plodding person who could be counted on to be a stubborn defender of any position assigned him, whether it be a fort under attack or a table of organization in which his duties were detailed. In an unfortunate attempt to praise Macomb's qualities, a sympathetic contemporary observer said of him: "Superficial judges, who think gravity (notwithstanding it is proverbially a cover-fool) synonymous with weight of character and solidity of judgment, draw unfavorable conclusions, as to his stability."[9] Yet this amiable, paunchy figure was a better politician in both army and government circles than Scott.

Jackson's headquarters were at Nashville, Tennessee. His two brigadiers—Edmund Gaines, who was stationed at New Orleans, and Eleazer Wheelock Ripley, whose headquarters were at Augusta, Georgia—had both distinguished themselves in the War of 1812. Like Scott, Gaines had a legal background and was almost as particular as his northern counterpart about his rank and perquisites. The brigadiers were frequently at odds with each other and the War Department over fancied preferences they perceived one or the other had been given. Ripley, a New Englander, had also a record of insubordination under Brown's command, though he seems to have kept his place under the more inflexible Jackson. All in all, the senior officers were a seasoned lot who would perform well if their duties were clearly outlined and a firm but tolerant hand were exercised over them.

The army stood at 8,221 officers and enlisted men—30 percent below authorized strength—when Calhoun became secretary of war. Morale was bad, pay was meager, discipline was harsh, and rations were poor; and the rank and file had to face a well-nigh universal stigma against the military that the war had not appreciably changed.[10] In addition, the organization of the army into two geo-

9. George H. Richards, *Memoir of Alexander Macomb* (New York, 1833), 127, 128.
10. *Military Affairs*, 669–80, vol. I of *American State Papers: Documents, Legislative and Executive, of the Congress of the United States* (38 vols.; Washington, D.C., 1832–61).

graphical divisions thousands of miles apart was a badly flawed arrangement. The military establishment consisted of three corps—engineers, artillery, and infantry. Ordnance, medical, and supply officers were scattered through the two divisions and reported to their commanders. Although a general staff organization existed on paper, most of the top positions had not been filled; headquarters were not centralized in Washington, D.C. Nor was there any chain of command except through the secretary. Uniforms, rations, and even powder and shot were contracted out as needed by individual supply officers and as a result were of variable quality and overly expensive. Calhoun found unpaid accounts on his desk that totaled more than $ 45 million, which, if translated into modern equivalents, would equal not less than a half-billion dollars.

In addition to its specific military duties, the War Department administered the government's Indian policy and was responsible for the settlement of pensions for revolutionary war veterans. Both areas were extremely sensitive to partisan and other criticism. Much of even the routine correspondence in connection with the department's duties fell to the secretary and his chief clerk, Major Christopher Vandeventer, a capable man who was formerly Jackson's deputy quartermaster general. Adding immeasurably to the perplexities of the office was a serious Indian war being waged against the Seminoles in southern Georgia. Hostilities had drifted dangerously into Spanish-held Florida.

Calhoun was fortunate in one respect. The energetic Crawford, during his brief tenure as secretary, had studied the problems of the military establishment and submitted a plan that detailed the organization of a general staff. He recommended a combined adjutant general and inspector general to supervise the army's personnel, a quartermaster general to oversee all military equipment, a commissary general to purchase and distribute rations, an apothecary general to be in charge of medicine and give general supervision to medical personnel, and a paymaster general. Subordinate officers in these staff positions would be distributed within the two divisions but would be responsible in carrying out policy to their respective heads of staff. Crawford had also made provision for three judge advocates, who would direct the army's legal system, but he recommended no staff changes in the artillery corps or corps of engineers. Despite this rough plan for a complete reorganization of the department, Calhoun realized that he had an immensely difficult task simply in putting his own office in order. After a week on the job, he was, as he said to Charles J. Ingersoll, "impressed with the magnitude of its duties." Very little had been done to "give exactness, economy and dispatch to its monied transactions."[11]

For the next two months, Calhoun was busier than he had ever been before in his life, where not a spare moment had been neglected for useful work. The Seminole war claimed urgent attention. Gaines had been ordered to Amelia Island just off the north Florida coast before Calhoun took office. The island, nominally Spanish territory, was a nest of adventurers and freebooters who had been inciting Indians and fugitive slaves to plunder outlying frontier settlements in Georgia. In new orders, Calhoun gave Gaines wide latitude. If he found it necessary after capturing the island, he could cross into Spanish territory in pursuit of the Seminoles and "attack them within its limits, should it be found necessary, unless they should shelter themselves under a Spanish post. In the latter event, you will immediately notify this department." But fresh information from the Georgia-Florida border indicated that a much larger force was needed. After consulting with the president and cabinet, Calhoun ordered Jackson to assume field command at Fort Scott in southwestern Georgia of a force of three thousand professionals and militia, along with two thousand Indians, and to go on the offensive.[12]

While analyzing the news from the Georgia frontier and acting accordingly, Calhoun was planning a reorganization of the army in response to a Senate resolution of January 20, 1818. He solicited advice from Brigadier General Joseph G. Swift, head of the engineering corps; Major John Abert, the army's topographical chief; Brigadier General David Parker, adjutant and inspector general of the northern command; and Major General Brown, who came to Washington, D.C., to consult on all aspects of the proposed reorganization. By February 4, when Brown arrived at the War Department, Calhoun had already drafted a plan that would create a general staff in Washington. Brown read the draft, which was copied and sent on to the Senate military committee on February 5. He may have made some suggestions, but he did not, as he later claimed, make any substantial corrections or additions. Calhoun's plan was, however, indebted to Crawford's report of a year earlier.[13] Brown and others were of assistance in drawing up the details of the reorganization bill that went to the Senate on February 18.

11. *Ibid.*, 627–35; *Calhoun Papers*, II, 16.
12. *Calhoun Papers*, II, 20, 39, 40; *Jackson Correspondence*, II, 340–42.
13. *Calhoun Papers*, II, 121, 131, 132, 147.

The bill centralized all of the staff responsibilities in Washington, D.C., and added to the existing arrangement a surgeon general, a judge advocate general, and a quartermaster general. In the future, supplies and rations would be purchased in bulk by the requisite officers in Washington, D.C., and, where possible, stored at depots and arsenals throughout the country. The staff officers attached to the various commands reported directly to their chiefs in the capital. There would be no more dependence on local suppliers who routinely charged the government monopoly prices for inferior rations, which were often not delivered at the time and place specified. Unfortunately, the plan did not go into effect soon enough to support the Seminole campaign. During the summer of 1818, Jackson's and Gaines's forces most of the time subsisted as best they could through direct purchases.[14]

By late April, 1818, the staff reorganization bill had passed both houses of Congress substantially as Calhoun had drafted it. There would be additional changes, such as an accounting system for the quartermaster general's department, but these simply filled out the framework already provided. Calhoun was also anxious to improve the procedures of his office. Economy and efficiency were uppermost in his mind, but he recognized the need for caution. Administration, unlike congressional service, was hedged about with a thicket of personal, political, and public responsibilities that had to be weighed carefully before any sudden or radical changes were made. The brash congressman of 1812 who helped drive an unprepared nation into war was now the careful though reform-minded executive of 1818. "It is dangerous to reform," he said, "before we know the precise state of the disease; and in a business so complicated as the affairs of an army, this cannot be done at once." What Calhoun had achieved in his first three months of office was a bureau system wherein the staff chiefs exercised direct authority and bore direct responsibility under the secretary for maintaining the military establishment.[15]

While reorganizing the staff, Calhoun was implementing a program for coast defenses that had been set in motion before he became secretary. These forts, which were of special interest to Monroe, also claimed Calhoun's strong support, for coastal defense and especially defense of

14. *Ibid.*, 341, 341n.
15. *Ibid.*, 258, 405, 406, 407, 408, 147. For an admirable discussion of Calhoun's reorganization of the army, see *Calhoun Papers*, II, LXI–LXIX. See also Lloyd M. Short, *The Development of the National Administrative Organization of the United States* (Baltimore, 1923), 125–29, and Chase Mooney, *William H. Crawford* (Lexington, Ky., 1974), 79–81.

the frontiers were important aspects of Calhoun's drive for national security. He feared above all Britain's power in Canada and along the thousands of miles of vaguely defined border from the district of Maine to the Pacific Northwest. The vulnerability of New Orleans and the border areas between Georgia and Florida were also sources of deep concern.

Calhoun was suspicious of British traders whether they operated in the Northwest or the Southwest. He was as certain as Andrew Jackson that they were the agents of British expansion at the expense of the United States under the guise of the fur trade. East and West Florida were loosely held by Spain. They constituted a power vacuum that Calhoun believed the British would fill if the United States did not acquire the territory. All members of the Monroe administration were anxious about the possibility of Florida in British hands, but none more so than Secretary of State John Quincy Adams, who had been negotiating with the Spanish minister, Luis de Onís, for the purchase of that territory before Calhoun came to Washington.

Under the direction of General Swift, preliminary work had been done on forts at the entrance to Chesapeake Bay, the harbors of Mobile and New Orleans, Lake Champlain, Fort Niagara on Lake Ontario, Pea Patch on the Delaware River, and New York Harbor. Congress, reacting to urgent requests of the Monroe administration, had provided adequate though scarcely generous appropriations to begin these projects. And Monroe, who had just returned from his tour through New England, was anxious to inspect the site in Chesapeake Bay and the unfinished canal through the Great Dismal Swamp to Elizabeth City in North Carolina. Calhoun was invited to join the party. He welcomed the opportunity to leave his desk for a brief respite, particularly since the tour's end would place him about three hundred miles, or a week's journey, from Bath, where urgent business affairs required his attention.[16]

Calhoun needed to raise funds to purchase furniture, hire servants, and secure other incidentals necessary to establish his own home in Washington, D.C. He had found the cost of living for a family in Washington higher than he had counted upon; particularly expensive was the official entertainment he was expected to provide as a cabinet officer. The Lowndes family was most hospitable, but he had to acquire permanent accommodations soon. The second session of the Fifteenth Congress would convene in mid-November, and with it would begin

16. *Calhoun Papers*, II, 4–7.

the round of official and private dinners, teas, and balls that marked the winter social season of Washington. Calhoun's salary of $ 4,500 a year would not cover his living and entertainment expenses. Since his last year's crop had been cut in half because of extreme drought conditions, he was short of cash. Calhoun had to sell some of his property, but he felt he could not depend on his brothers or brother-in-law to negotiate the sale. Moreover, he wanted to inspect this year's crop of cotton and corn so that he could estimate for himself his probable revenue. It was urgent that he visit home, however briefly, and the president's tour was most timely.[17]

Calhoun reached Bath the last week in June to find that his crops were again drought stricken. There was little he could do to increase his yield, but presumably he was able to raise enough cash for the winter season through the sale of land. He spent only nine days at home, returning to Washington, D.C., in mid-July.

Meanwhile, alarming news had come from Florida. In May, just before Calhoun and Monroe left for their southern tour, the administration had learned that Jackson had taken the Spanish fort of St. Marks in East Florida, which he claimed was necessary to the defense of his army. During his invasion Jackson had captured several Indians, whom he had hanged summarily. He had seized also a British trader, Alexander Arbuthnot, and a former British marine officer, Robert Ambrister, both of whom he was holding for trial, and he had burned several Indian villages. Adams, voicing the only criticism in the cabinet to Jackson's actions, objected strenuously to a war conducted in such a barbarous manner. Monroe and Calhoun believed that Jackson was acting within orders that enjoined him to "adopt the necessary measures to terminate the conflict."[18]

During Calhoun's southern trip, news had often appeared in the papers of Jackson's apparent summary execution of Arbuthnot and Ambrister, of his capture of Fort Barrancas at the entrance to Pensacola Bay, and of his taking of Pensacola itself, the main Spanish base in West Florida. Previous dispatches from Jackson had satisfied Calhoun that all objectives against the Seminoles had been achieved. Now it would appear that Jackson was attempting to seize Florida even if the action brought on a war with Spain. The execution of the two Britons might well involve the nation in a war with Great Britain, too. When Calhoun

17. *Ibid.*, 37, 38, 407.
18. *Jackson Correspondence*, II, 355–57, 358–60; *Adams Memoirs*, IV, 87.

reached Washington, D.C., and found what he perceived to be the confirmation of his fears in official dispatches from Florida, he was certain that Jackson was fomenting a war with Spain. Surely the seizure of Pensacola was entirely unauthorized. As he wrote his friend Charles Tait: "It belongs to Congress, and not the Executive to make war on Spain. However improper the conduct of Spain has been, and however desirable to us to possess the Floridas, I am decidedly of the opinion that the peace of the country ought to be preserved. Should other powers be involved, and the war general, the wisest man, cannot see the result, we must suffer. We want time. Let us grow."[19]

Calhoun's state of mind was decidedly different from what it had been five years earlier. In matters involving war and peace, he was uncertain how to proceed except to disavow Jackson's course and Jackson himself. Calhoun saw quite clearly that he could not tolerate Jackson's insubordination because it threatened civilian control of the military and the entire chain of command structure. An ever-present fear of military despotism loomed large, deeply ingrained as it was in the Whig political theory he had inherited. He was unaware that Jackson had been in touch with the president and had objected strenuously on grounds of military expediency to Calhoun's orders to Gaines that obligated the latter to consult with Washington before he pursued fugitive Indians into Spanish posts. In his letter to the president, Jackson had also proposed that in addition to the capture of Amelia Island, the whole of East Florida be taken and held "as an indemnity for the outrages of Spain upon the property of our citizens."[20] Monroe had never answered the letter. Much later, he said that he had been ill at the time and had not read it. Whether or not this was the case, Jackson had some grounds to consider Monroe's silence as consent.

If Calhoun was deeply concerned about the gravity of the situation in Florida, Monroe was more so. It was the president's policy to convene the entire cabinet on all important questions and make a consensus determination of administration policy. Adams drew a caustic conclusion from the frequent cabinet meetings. "There is slowness, want of decision," he wrote, "and a spirit of procrastination in the President."[21] On the events in Florida, Monroe certainly bore out Adams' contention. In the president's mind, there was the prospect of war if he did not condemn Jackson's action and make appropriate restitution.

19. *Adams Memoirs*, IV, 107; *Calhoun Papers*, II, 408.
20. *Jackson Correspondence*, II, 345, 346.
21. *Adams Memoirs*, IV, 37.

Yet the disciplining of a popular general carrying out a popular cause could have unfortunate political consequences.

It was a worried Monroe who convoked his cabinet on July 18 and held extended discussions over the next five days. At the first meeting, Adams was the only member who defended Jackson's conduct. The secretary of state had seen the captures as important bargaining chips in his negotiations with the Spanish minister, though his argument was that Jackson had acted in a defensive manner and that "there was no real, though an apparent violation of his [Calhoun's] instructions." Calhoun made the principal argument against Adams' position at this meeting and the next four meetings. The fat, balding Adams with his harsh voice and clipped accent was an agile opponent. His long defense of Jackson made him at once more wary in debate and more emotional. His face reddened with the effort, and his right hand shook with palsy as he tried desperately to swing his colleagues around to his viewpoint. But Calhoun pressed the constitutional issue that Jackson's seizure of Pensacola constituted an act of war against Spain. Only Congress had the power to declare war. And Adams at the end of the debate had to concede that there were difficulties in holding Pensacola without an act of Congress.[22]

Adams thought that Calhoun was personally "offended with the idea that Jackson has set at naught the instructions of the Department." He may have been so, because Calhoun was a proud and arrogant man, but he was also an insecure person who saw threats nearly everywhere—from Spain, from Britain, from military tyranny, even from what he construed to be law and order violated by a popular demagogue. As he debated with the seemingly recalcitrant Adams, he, too, let his emotions rise with the heat of argument. At length he made the error in that highly charged political atmosphere of suggesting that Jackson be censured. He recommended this knowing that Monroe had never answered Jackson's letter to him suggesting that all of East Florida be seized as hostage to the good behavior of Spain.[23] Just before the meeting, Monroe had shown Calhoun the letter in question.

After the final cabinet meeting, and moved no doubt by Adams' argument that public opinion would go against the administration if Jackson's conduct were punished, Monroe disregarded Calhoun's intemperate outburst. There would be no censure; but there would be no hostages, either. Pensacola and Forts Barrancas and St. Marks must be

22. *Ibid.*, 108, 111; Ammon, *James Monroe*, 421–23.
23. *Adams Memoirs*, IV, 108–15.

returned to Spain. Jackson had acted without authorization yet in good faith. Above all, both Jackson and the administration must be relieved of any responsibility for making war without congressional approval.

In his long, wordy letter to Jackson that reflected his own views and those of the cabinet, Monroe even suggested that he and Calhoun would, if the general consented, alter some of the warlike phrases in his reports from Florida for the public record. The president managed to avert a rupture with the temperamental Jackson and, by giving up the posts, any break with Spain; his position, however, was not straightforward.[24] Since the record of the court-martial proceedings of Arbuthnot and Ambrister had been unaccountably lost in the mails, a response to the British was delayed for some time. When copies were finally received, Whitehall was not disposed to reject the evidence on which the two men had been tried and executed.[25]

Dealing with Jackson and debating with Adams in cabinet session was but a part of Calhoun's daily ration of work. Implementation of Indian policy and two expeditions into the Northwest that were closely associated with that policy claimed much of his time. His most pressing problem apart from the Seminole war was the Cherokee nation, whose lands extended from western Georgia to the Mississippi River, embracing much of northern Alabama and southeastern Tennessee. Georgia and frontier settlers near Cherokee lands had been pressing for the extinction of Indian titles since the end of the revolutionary war. The Jefferson administration had worked out a policy that it hoped would satisfy the land hunger of the frontiersmen and the safety of the Indians. The federal government would negotiate with the various tribes for land cessions; it would promote emigration of the Indians far westward to lands that it would purchase and guarantee title on; and it would encourage the training of Indians in farming pursuits so that they would eventually either be assimilated or coexist with the dominant white population.

The War Department had been given responsibility for executing this policy. Calhoun did not press for any change in Indian affairs, but he did make the policy a significant part of his drive for national security. He also expanded its scope dramatically. Extinguishing Cherokee titles in Georgia and encouraging the southwestern Indians to

24. *Ibid.*, II, 400–404, 405; *Jackson Correspondence*, II, 105, 106; Ammon, *James Monroe*, 423, 424. See Bassett's analysis in *Jackson Correspondence*, II, 382–83n, and Robert Remini's in *Andrew Jackson and the Course of American Empire, 1767–1821* (New York, 1977), 368.

25. *Calhoun Papers*, III, 131.

adopt settled ways of farming their tribal lands would encourage white emigration to Georgia and would, he felt, stabilize that frontier.

The program would, of course, be popular in the West, and the establishment of peaceful Indian settlements in the Arkansas Territory would bring that remote area into closer touch with the rest of the nation. Indian emigration westward encouraged by the government would, Calhoun thought, lessen the incidence of costly and barbarous tribal wars. In furtherance of these objectives, he brought heavy pressure to bear on the Cherokees to emigrate, but he emphasized that the move was voluntary. "It is better for you and for us that all of the Cherokees should go to Arkansaw," he told a deputation of chiefs who had come to Washington, D.C. "If however any should choose to remain [in the East], I will treat them with justice." All emigrating Indians would be supplied with muskets, powder and shot, corn, and other necessary supplies.[26]

Calhoun also secured a large cession of Cherokee lands in Georgia, but not enough to satisfy the rapacious whites, genuine settlers and speculators alike.[27] Although a westerner himself with boyhood memories of Indian raids, Calhoun was not impressed by the demands of land-hungry frontier interests that the Indians be exterminated or forcibly removed. He recognized their value as sources of the important fur trade and their presence, if friendly and socialized, as a defense, especially in the Southwest but also along the Canadian border, where they would act as a buffer against a potentially unfriendly power. And curiously enough, he saw the Indians as eventual citizens, a distinction he refused to confer upon free Negroes. Calhoun managed to wring a $ 10,000 grant from a reluctant Congress to begin a pilot program of education for selected Indian youths of both sexes. He channeled these funds out through Catholic and Protestant missionaries, who achieved limited success before the grant ran out and was not renewed.

While still engaged in cabinet discussions over the Florida crisis, Calhoun received and read carefully a report from Thomas McKenney, superintendent of Indian trade, that commented harshly on the license system then prevailing in the Northwest. McKenney's self-interest was involved, so he may have exaggerated the evils, but there was no doubt that numerous private traders, many of them British, were plying the Indians with whiskey, a prime source of the unrest along the frontier.

26. *Ibid.*, II, 180, 181.
27. *Ibid.*, 436–38, III, 693.

Government regulation of the Indian trade had evolved in piece-meal fashion over the past quarter century. A system of factories had been established under the auspices of the War Department, and Congress had eventually created the position of superintendent of Indian trade. Among the duties of the superintendent was the management of the various factories and their coordination with the army posts.[28]

McKenney, a red-haired, sharp-featured, engaging person, and like Calhoun of Scotch-Irish descent, was a thirty-three-year-old store-keeper first in Washington, D.C., and then in neighboring George-town. He was a native of Maryland. Knowledgeable in the ways of government and politics as practiced in the Washington community, McKenney combined business experience with a certain skill in analyzing and reporting on information that impressed Calhoun.[29] McKenney, the various Indian agents and subagents—like the honest and reliable Return J. Meigs for the Cherokees and the dishonest, unreliable David Mitchell for the Creeks—and the territorial governors constituted Calhoun's personnel for implementing the government's Indian policy.[30]

Most of the personnel agreed that the factory system should be tightened up and that licenses to private traders ought to be either abolished or managed under much more stringent conditions. But there were powerful forces other than British agents and unscrupulous traders who were interested in shaping Indian policy to their own ends. John Jacob Astor, head of the American Fur Company, maintained two lobbying agents in Washington, D.C., and made frequent trips himself to influence members of Congress and Calhoun. The Missouri Fur Company maintained a close connection with Thomas Hart Benton, Missouri Territory's representative in the capital. Both companies, though fierce competitors, were determined to

28. Francis J. Prucha, *Sword of the Republic* (New York, 1969), 75–76, 99–100, 199–200.

29. Herman J. Viola, *Thomas L. McKenney: Architect of America's Early Indian Policy, 1816–1830* (Chicago, 1974), 1–22.

30. See, for instance, McKenney's report of July 17, 1818, and Mitchell's memorandum of October 20, 1818, on the Creeks, *Calhoun Papers*, II, 393–95, III, 236, 237. The War Department had twenty-seven agents and subagents. Besides McKenney, there were eleven factors and assistant factors and twelve clerks (*Indian Affairs*, 163, vol. II of *American State Papers*). Mitchell, a political power in Georgia, was a Crawford appointee. He soon allied himself with a half-breed Creek leader, William McIntosh, and proceeded to swindle the Creeks and the federal government. He also engaged in slave smuggling and other nefarious activities that came to light in 1821. Calhoun dismissed Mitchell on February 16, 1821. See Michael D. Green, *The Politics of Indian Removal* (Lincoln, Neb., 1982), 53–57.

remove the government's presence in the fur trade and eliminate private operators, too. With Benton's help, they had managed to secure a House resolution advising the abolition of the government factories.

Calhoun, who was asked for a report and recommendation, received conflicting advice. McKenney, able bureaucrat that he was, staunchly upheld the factories but suggested certain reforms in the system. Lewis Cass, the governor of Michigan Territory, argued vehemently for abolition.[31]

Calhoun decided to offer a compromise solution, but he went far beyond the issue of the fur trade and enunciated the government's policy on Indian affairs in general. He proposed that a new bureau be established in the War Department that would be responsible for all aspects of the government's involvement with the Indian trade. The superintendent of the bureau would, in addition to his other duties, be charged with the granting of licenses and the regulation of the trade. For the privilege of trading with the Indians, Calhoun set a large enough sum to discourage the small operator and reduce the number of traders to a manageable group. The traders would be subjected to heavy penalties if they did not conform to the strict regulations the new bureau would draw up. In place of the factory system, Calhoun recommended that Congress charter a stock company that would be a private corporation and would pay an annual bonus for the privilege of trading with the Indians, but would be subject to the same regulations as individual licensed traders.

Having disposed of the trading issues, Calhoun then articulated the administration's position in dealing with the Indian tribes. He wrote: "They neither are, in fact, nor ought to be, considered as independent nations. Our views of their interest, and not their own, ought to govern them. By a proper combination of force and persuasion of punishments and rewards, they ought to be brought within the pales of law and civilization. . . . Those who might not choose to submit, ought to be permitted and aided in forming new settlements at a distance from ours." Calhoun's recommendations coincided with the most advanced thinking of the time. His paternalistic remarks reflected the predominant belief that the Indian nations must be deprived of their sovereign status, a legal fiction in his eyes, and either socialized and absorbed into the white culture or removed far distant from contact with whites. Calhoun's principal argument was based on the impossibility of a traditional Indian society existing side by side with a settled farming society.

31. *Calhoun Papers*, III, 44–56, 123–27.

He candidly expressed his opinion that if this policy of separation on the one hand and integration on the other were not carried out, the Indians would become extinct. A case in point was the contemplated removal of the remnants of the Six Nations from western New York. "Experience proves," wrote Calhoun to the responsible subagents, "that when surrounded by whites, they always dwindle and become miserable."[32] Education, training, and individual land ownership under federal auspices were to be the means of assimilation.

Removal, too, would be conducted as humanely as possible under federal auspices to areas west of the Mississippi, which were well stocked with game and relatively free of indigenous hostile tribes. The government would guarantee Indian holdings in the new lands, and the army would keep out intruders. There, too, Calhoun hoped that through government-sponsored education and training programs, the immigrant Indians would eventually be prepared for assimilation with the dominant white culture. His ideas on removal contained the germs of the reservation policy adopted seventy-five years later, though Calhoun had no interest in preserving native Indian culture, which he felt was an impractical and wasteful use of land resources.

This report was the first of Calhoun's major communications to Congress as secretary of war. Like his speeches, it was well organized and expressed in plain English, yet it conveyed a sense of compelling nervous energy. The argument was clear and strong; the facts were interesting and not only buttressed the argument but clarified it. As a thoughtful piece addressed to a major problem of state, it received wide publicity, mostly favorable. The report made a positive impression on Congress. Henry Clay and especially William H. Crawford, both ambitious to succeed Monroe, cocked a wary eye on the energetic secretary of war.

Meanwhile, Calhoun was engaged in mounting two expeditions into the Northwest. His objective was the establishment of army posts to secure that frontier from the incursion of unfriendly Indians and, as he believed, hostile British traders. Calhoun had the enthusiastic support of Monroe for the venture, and a favorable reception from Congress and the press. In his planning, he drew up a new geographic line between the northern and southern divisions of the army, relieving the overburdened southern division from any involvement in the venture. He extended General Brown's jurisdiction westward and gave him the command responsibilities for the expeditions. At

32. *Ibid.*, 341–55, II, 294.

first Calhoun thought of establishing a military post at what is now the northeastern border of Montana, where the Yellowstone River empties into the Missouri to form Lake Sakakawea on the border of North Dakota and Montana. Such an imperial push westward would, he felt, constrict the activities of agents of the British Northwest Fur Company and defend American interests against the powerful Sioux tribe. Information from the frontier indicated that the tribe was being supplied and armed by the British for possible attack.[33]

But Calhoun soon determined that the far reaches of the Yellowstone River were simply too ambitious for the resources at his command. He settled upon the Mandan Villages (the present city of Bismarck, North Dakota) at a bend in the Missouri River three hundred miles east of the Yellowstone and the point on the river nearest to the British trading post on the Red River of the North. Calhoun's grand scheme envisaged another fortified post some four hundred miles to the southeast at the mouth of what was then called the St. Peters River, now the Minnesota. A post here would also serve the purpose of interdicting British trade coming south along the Red River of the North. "I am very desirous," he wrote Andrew Jackson, "by taking strong and judicious posts to break British control over the Northern Indians."[34]

At this time, Calhoun was organizing not just the strategic Yellowstone expedition but also an exploration of the territory north and west drained by the Mississippi River. A group of scientists would accompany that expedition and investigate the plants and animals of the region, collect data on the Indian tribes there, and make geographical and meteorological surveys. Calhoun selected for this assignment one of the army's senior topographical engineers, Major Stephen H. Long.[35] For the command of the larger, more important, essentially military expedition to the Mandan Villages, Calhoun, on Jackson's advice, named Brigadier General Henry Atkinson. Sensitive to the political and public reaction to both expeditions, he awarded the transportation and supply contracts to James Johnson, the brother of Richard M. Johnson, who was an old associate of Calhoun in the House, a political power in the West, and chairman of the House military affairs committee.

It was early decided that both expeditions would utilize specially

33. *Military Affairs,* 69, vol. II of *American State Papers; Calhoun Papers,* III, 214–16, 431–32.
34. *Calhoun Papers,* III, 61.
35. *Ibid.,* 395, 396.

designed light-draft steamboats along with the traditional river keel-boats.[36] As Calhoun commented later, "The employment of one or two steamboats if there is a reasonable prospect of their success . . . would give much more interest and eclat to the expedition and would proba- **77** bly impress the Indians and the British."[37]

Unfortunately, Johnson, to whom the War Department entrusted the design and construction of the steamboats, had sufficient knowl-edge neither of engine technology nor of the varying depths, the shift-ing sandbars, and the snags on the rivers the boats would travel. Knowledgeable army officers and experienced riverboat men thought steamboats would fail unless smaller than eighty tons burden, but the four vessels constructed by the Johnsons for the expedition were each from 150 to 200 tons burden. The experienced officer Colonel Cham-bers, in describing the *Expedition,* one of Johnson's boats, said that she drew seven feet of water when loaded. A four-foot draft was deemed the maximum for river passage. The *Expedition's* engines he pro-nounced "feeble," noting that it had taken her five days with frequent strandings to make twenty-five miles against the current. No accom-modations existed for the troops except a platform on the upper deck. Crews were inexperienced, and the boats were not equipped with an-chors for kedging. Eventually, the Yellowstone expedition reached Council Bluffs in western Iowa, where Atkinson encamped for the winter. Keelboats had carried most of the soldiers and provisions, though three of the four steamboats did make the thousand-mile river journey. Major Long's steamboat, the *Western Engineer,* a small vessel that drew only nineteen inches of water, had arrived at Council Bluffs three months before the Yellowstone flotilla.[38]

Despite Long's success, public criticism was beginning to surface in those newspapers that gave voice to the complaints of disappointed contractors. And in the Congress, the fur trading lobby that distrusted Calhoun's Indian policy stepped up its pressure. Its artful campaign caught the ears of ambitious politicians who would grasp at any issue to advance their own fortunes.

36. Only ten years had passed since Robert Fulton's steamboat made her maiden trip on the Hudson River. Steamboats were still a novelty in the East and almost completely unknown in the Far West.

37. *Calhoun Papers,* III, 633, 634, IV, 646.

38. *Ibid.,* III, 498, IV, 68, 69; Prucha, *Sword of the Republic,* 145.

VI

Panic, Politics, and Personality

A misplaced faith in steamboats was not the only factor that hampered the Northwest expeditions, frustrated Calhoun, and tarnished his reputation. The inept performance of James Johnson and his numerous tribe of brothers and in-laws was a particular target for the critics. Yet to some extent the Johnsons were not entirely at fault. No sooner had preparations for the expeditions gotten underway than the panic that preceded the depression of 1819 fell with crushing force on all business activities in the West.[1]

The Johnsons, who were overextended like most western entrepreneurs, immediately felt the constriction of credit. Several of their agents went bankrupt and defaulted on their contracts. These failures forced the Johnsons to demand further advances f. ⁓ the government so that they could arrange alternate sources of supply. At the same time, they had to defend themselves from creditors who threatened to confiscate stores already in the process of delivery at St. Louis, the base for the expedition.[2] Continuing financial pressure caused vexing delays that the army officers on the spot, notably General Jesup of the quartermaster corps, did not fully understand but that were obvious to Calhoun and Monroe, both of whom saw the broader picture. By the summer of 1819, so much had been paid in advances to the Johnsons that the administration could not afford to let them become bankrupt.

From Bath, Calhoun wrote the army's commissary general, George Gibson, that though he was "opposed to free advances . . . there are instances, in which, if the general rule is rigidly adhered to, the publick may suffer an essential injury." He favored allowing additional payments to the Johnsons if they could be safely made. President Monroe, who was traveling in Kentucky at the time, ordered another and final advance of $ 107,000 on the personal plea of Richard M. Johnson, backed by a strong letter of support from Andrew Jackson, Governor Shelby of Kentucky, and other western notables. Monroe did insist,

1. *Calhoun Papers*, IV, 255, III, 702, 708.
2. *Ibid.*, III, 702–704, 708, 709, IV, 74, 75, 38.

however, that the four steamboats the Johnsons built for the Yellow-stone expedition be transferred to government ownership as security.[3]

An attack on the War Department's management of the expeditions had already begun in the St. Louis *Enquirer* when Monroe allowed further advances to the Johnsons, who had by now received some $200,000. Thomas Hart Benton, just beginning his political career and with ties to both the Bank of Missouri, a Johnson creditor, and the Missouri Fur Company, an opponent of Calhoun's Indian trading plan, was the newspaper critic. He spoke, however, for more powerful interests than just those in Missouri.

Clay and Crawford were determined to neutralize what they perceived as Calhoun's popularity and at the same time to score his vulnerability not just in the apparent mismanagement of the western expeditions but in the War Department's handling of revolutionary war pensions and especially in the expensive fortification program. Hard times following on the panic of 1819 gave the two a forum for their criticisms and demands for retenchment. Since most of the funds appropriated for the executive branch went to the War Department— $7,180,000 for 1819—Calhoun was the obvious target. Throughout the winter of 1819–1820, Congress demanded reports on all War Department projects and responsibilities. These were in the form of resolutions that were obviously framed to embarrass Calhoun. In the main, he was able to answer them without giving his congressional critics any significant opening. Despite the problems of the Johnsons, both the Long and the Atkinson expeditions had accomplished worthwhile objectives at no significant additional costs beyond that for the maintenance of troops on the northwestern frontier.[4]

Expenditures for the military had almost doubled since 1811, during a period when army strength had remained relatively the same. As Jessup explained, the increase had to be attributed to the expansion of the nation's frontier, which made transportation charges the major items in the army's budget.[5] The rather elaborate fortifications program, now well under way, also swelled military appropriations, as did the enlarged pension list and increased subsidies to the various Indian tribes. None of these programs could have been considered extravagant by any thoughtful contemporary considering the size of the nation, its undeveloped state, its pattern of growth, and the responsibilities of the military for the defense of thousands of miles of frontier

3. *Ibid.*, IV, 98, 134–37.
4. *Adams Memoirs*, IV, 509–11.
5. *Calhoun Papers*, III, 219, 220.

wilderness. But Congress was not in a thoughtful mood. Before the depression set in or the problems with the Yellowstone expedition surfaced, the House had asked what reductions, if any, could be made in the military establishment. Calhoun chose this occasion to lay before Congress a full record of his accomplishments as secretary.

In a report of over five thousand words, to which he added four statistical documents, Calhoun demonstrated most forcibly the added responsibilities of the army during the past fifteen years. He explained again in greater detail the efficiencies that had resulted from the staff reorganization. In commenting on the staff, he remarked how much more difficult its task was in the United States than that of its counterparts in Europe. "It has here to encounter," he said, "great and peculiar impediments, from the extent of the country, the badness, and frequently the want of roads." He wrote of rations, of compensation, and of the liquor problem among the troops, and even spoke to the old Whig fears that a standing army imperiled liberty. Such a view, he wrote, "is conceived more of timidity than wisdom . . . what well founded apprehension can there be from an establishment distributed on so extended a frontier, with many thousand of miles intervening between the extreme points occupied?"[6]

Calhoun's report elicited admiration from the *Niles' Register,* the Washington *National Intelligencer,* and other papers outside of the capital. It certainly did not detract from Calhoun's popularity in Congress, and it further alerted major presidential contenders to a potentially serious rival. They reacted accordingly. Clay and Crawford prepared to challenge Calhoun's assumptions on army strength and the need for the coastal forts; John Quincy Adams began thinking about getting him out of the country by way of a foreign mission. Crawford was the principal source of the political pressure in Congress, though he covered his tracks carefully. As a leading member of the Monroe administration, he could not remain in the cabinet while challenging one of its major policies and openly criticizing a colleague who enjoyed the president's confidence. Calhoun was aware of Crawford's moves, but comity among cabinet members and the president dictated that he act with prudence and civility. He did, however, begin building his own political defenses.

Calhoun's first significant move in this direction was to suppress his feelings about Jackson and seek to enlist that popular public figure in supporting the War Department. Calhoun distrusted Jackson, but he also recognized that the general would prove a vigorous champion of

6. *Ibid.,* 374–80.

the military establishment. Jackson had come under severe attack from Clay, who condemned his course in Florida, especially his execution of Arbuthnot and Ambrister. Crawford's allies in Congress were also outspoken opponents of the general.

Given their common political enemies, it was quite natural that Jackson and Calhoun would make common cause in defending the military policies of the administration. Although neither man really trusted the other, Jackson made a public display of his cordiality towards Calhoun. And Calhoun did whatever he could among his supporters in Congress to blunt the attacks of Clay and of Crawford's friends. After Jackson's role was vindicated in Congress, the general vigorously supported the War Department's defense program.[7]

Of lesser immediate importance to Calhoun's policies and future career were his political communications with his college friend Micah Sterling about developments in New York between the Bucktails, who were followers of Martin Van Buren, and those who looked to De Witt Clinton. Another friend and alumnus of Tapping Reeve's law school, Virgil Maxcy, kept Calhoun posted on affairs in Maryland. In Congress, Eldred Simkins, a personal friend from home and another alumnus of the law school, worked with Lowndes to protect the War Department from its enemies, as did Samuel Ingham, who represented a Philadelphia constituency in Congress. A rather starchy individual, Ingham was, nevertheless, an influential member of the so-called Family party that controlled the Republican organization in Pennsylvania. Although he had resigned from Congress for business reasons in 1818 and would not return to the House until 1822, Ingham maintained his political ties. These individuals represented the core of Calhoun's political support; but he had already begun to build upon his cordial relations with army officers in key situations—men like Winfield Scott and Jacob Brown in New York, a crucial state.[8] His need for broader support became increasingly necessary, not just because hard times affected his public programs, nor because a political coalition seemed to be forming against him in Congress, but because a cleavage, part ideological and part geographical with factional and economic overtones, suddenly opened wide in the spring of 1819. This political crisis over the organization of the Missouri Territory threatened to force Calhoun into a controversial position on slavery.

7. Ammon, *James Monroe*, 422; *Jackson Correspondence*, II, 408–11, 415; Jonathan Roberts, "Memoirs of a Senator from Pennsylvania, Jonathan Roberts," *Pennsylvania Magazine of History and Biography*, LXII, No. 3 (July, 1938), 400–403.

8. *Jackson Correspondence*, II, 223, 224, V, 500.

Just before the financial panic erupted in 1819, James Tallmadge, Jr., a congressman from upstate New York, tossed an incendiary amendment into the debate over the bill that would organize Missouri as a slave territory preparatory to its admission into the Union as a state. His amendment prohibited slavery in the proposed state constitution. The admission of Missouri as a slave state would have tilted in favor of the slave states the regional balance that had existed for the past seven years. Tallmadge's amendment passed the House on a purely sectional vote. It was defeated in the Senate, but not before another New York congressman, John W. Taylor, and one of the New York senators, the venerable Rufus King, subjected slavery to a withering attack that upset southerners in Congress and their more articulate constituents, while it called forth Jefferson's famous admonition on the stability of a Union. The tenor of the Missouri debates unquestionably reflected the economic tensions of the times, which sharpened the sectional aspects of the debate, but underlying political currents figured as important motives, too. Calhoun viewed with particular interest the part the three New Yorkers played in Congress as they pushed for the containment of slavery in the West.

Tallmadge and Taylor were both political followers of De Witt Clinton, who was locked in a fierce struggle with Martin Van Buren for control of the Republican party in New York. Rufus King, the last Federalist candidate for president in 1816, was the leading figure in a small but distinguished group that was bent on destroying Clinton's influence in the state. Dubbed "high-minded" Federalists by Van Buren because they had supported the war effort, the members of the King faction were cooperating with his anti-Clinton group, the Bucktails.[9] As Calhoun diagnosed the situation quite accurately, New York's participation in the Missouri debates was in part an extension of the power struggle between Van Buren and Clinton. Both politicians were bidding for western support in their own state and in the new states of Ohio, Indiana, and Illinois.[10] Calhoun could not ignore, however, the

9. Everett S. Brown, *Missouri Compromises and Presidential Politics* (St. Louis, 1926), 58, 59.

10. There is no substantial evidence that Van Buren was using the Missouri issue to create a southern-dominated party that would protect slavery, as Richard Brown contends in his article "The Missouri Crisis, Slavery and the Politics of Jacksonianism," *South Atlantic Quarterly,* LXV, No. 1 (Winter, 1966), 58–72. This article is a prime example of reading history backwards. Van Buren's creation of the North-South party alliance was some seven years in the future. It is straining a point to argue that Van Buren, given his expertise in maneuver and the everchanging political scene, would have engaged in such long-term political planning.

moral questions that King so eloquently raised. That there was a question of sectional balance was certainly obvious, yet the vehemence of the attack on the institution of slavery and its fierce defense from southern members could not simply be brushed aside as either the result of political jousting in a key state or a product of the tensions of hard times.[11]

John Quincy Adams worked out a dark mosaic of interconnecting political, social, and economic problems that he found most distressing: "The bank, the national currency, the stagnation of commerce, the depression of manufactures, the restless turbulence and insubordination of the State Legislatures, the Missouri slave question . . . the rankling passions and ambitious projects of individuals mingling with everything."[12] But the president was much more optimistic, and his projections about the immediate future were more accurate than Adams' were. Separation of Maine from Massachusetts and its request for admission to the Union as a free state preserved the sectional balance, permitting Missouri to retain its slave constitution. One of the Illinois senators, Jesse B. Thomas, had offered a compromise amendment that would prohibit slavery north of latitude 36°30' in the Louisiana Territory except in Missouri, an arrangement that satisfied enough members from the free states to gain passage in Congress. Still, Taylor's speeches on the floor of the House and those of King in the Senate posed a series of constitutional, moral, and social arguments that the Monroe administration could not overlook.

The president requested members of his cabinet to give him their opinions on two points that had been raised in the Missouri debates before he took action on the Maine and Missouri bills. Did the federal Constitution empower Congress to prohibit slavery in a territory? Did the eighth section of the Missouri bill, prohibiting slavery forever in the territories north of the compromise line, apply only to the territorial condition? It was also necessary to determine whether that section of the bill also applied to states that might enter the Union at a later date. When the cabinet met to consider these questions at 1:00 P.M. on March 3, 1820, all agreed that Congress had the power to prescribe conditions, including abolition of slavery, in the governance of the territories. Adams alone argued that the power extended to the people as well as the land embraced in the territories. Other cabinet members, including Calhoun, were not yet prepared to make that distinction, though

11. *Adams Memoirs*, IV, 398.
12. *Ibid.*, 498.

their quibble was more a matter of expediency than of logic. On the second question, Adams followed King's argument that the Declaration of Independence created a moral climate that forbade government, whether state or national, to establish slavery where it had never existed.

Crawford challenged Adams' assumptions, arguing that the Missouri bill was following a precedent set by the Ordinance of 1787. As a general principle, that ordinance could not be binding on a state legislature. Monroe leaned towards Adams' position that Congress' powers over the territories extended to their inhabitants as well as to their lands. He doubted whether the restriction could apply to a sovereign state, however. Calhoun had remained silent during the debate, but when Monroe asked for written opinions, he proposed a compromise whereby those in the cabinet (all but Adams) could answer the second question in the affirmative, assigning their reasons why the restriction applied only to the territorial status, while Adams could also answer in the affirmative but without adding his reasons. Monroe and Adams agreed to this procedure.

The Missouri debates and the arguments Adams advanced in the cabinet had deeply disturbed Calhoun. He had, of course, political ambitions, and he feared that if Adams' free soil stance became a part of the record, it could force him to make a public avowal of his position, which he felt would be prejudicial to his career. He was well aware of antislavery attitudes that were developing in the northern states, and he did not want at this point to flaunt a proslavery opinion, such as Crawford seemed quite willing to do. Calhoun quite agreed with Adams that the Georgian's decided opinion on this point was part of his "canvass for the presidency."[13]

After the meeting, Adams and Calhoun carried on the discussion as they walked up Capitol Hill. Calhoun praised Adams' natural rights principles as "just and noble," but he added that "whenever they were mentioned in the Southern country, they were always understood as applying only to white men." There was an ingrained prejudice against whites being employed in domestic service, but not in some aspects of farming, manufacturing, and mechanical labor. Calhoun said that "he had often held the plough; so had his father." Manual labor in general, however—hoeing, hand harvesting, and the like—was considered degrading, "the proper work of slaves."[14]

13. *Ibid.*, V, 5–12.
14. *Ibid.*, 5.

According to Adams, Calhoun then made the standard argument for slavery as a mechanism for social control. "It was the best guarantee for equality among the whites," he observed. "It produced an unvarying level among them. It not only did not excite, but did not even admit of inequalities, by which one man could domineer over another." Adams responded with a vigorous indictment of slavery, whose supporters he declared were "mistaking labor for slavery, and dominion for freedom."[15] Yet it seems unlikely that Adams lectured Calhoun with the passionate antislavery convictions he confided to his diary.

Adams did imply, however, that Calhoun, along with other slaveowners, admitted slavery to be evil in the abstract sense. And the statements on both sides seem candid and pungent enough to have aroused a sense of moral rectitude and certainty on one side and moral guilt and uncertainty on the other. In the end, Adams went along with his cabinet colleagues and supported the compromise because, as he said, he believed "it to be all that could be expected under the present constitution."[16]

Calhoun was relieved that the Missouri difficulties had been resolved without endangering the Union.[17] But in the fall of 1820, he became concerned about another seemingly insurmountable problem connected with slavery that appeared when Missouri applied for statehood. Its constitution contained a slavery clause, and also a clause prohibiting free blacks from entering its territory. Debate immediately became tempestuous in Congress. Representatives of free states charged that the Missouri constitution violated the equal privileges and immunities clause of the federal Constitution, while slave-state representatives claimed that the exclusion of free blacks was a local issue which Missouri, when it became a sovereign state, had sole power to determine.[18] Calhoun was at a loss as to how this new crisis could be resolved; the only apparent solution was for Congress to declare the anti-immigration clause null and void as repugnant to Article IV of the Constitution.[19] He was relieved when Henry Clay returned to Congress in January, 1821, and effected a compromise whereby the Missouri legislature was required to agree that it accept the equal privileges and immunities clause of the Constitution. Through other

15. *Ibid.*, 10.
16. *Ibid.*, 12.
17. *Jackson Correspondence*, III, 24.
18. For contemporary commentary on this debate, see William Plumer Jr.'s correspondence in Brown, *Missouri Compromises*, 18–34.
19. *Adams Memoirs*, V, 199.

means, Missouri later managed to keep free blacks from immigrating into the state.

The rhetoric of the Missouri debates had enhanced Calhoun's passionate concern for stability. Whatever he may have said to Adams about slavery, he perceived the danger it posed to the Union. If the free states were determined at some future date to emancipate the slaves or, as he said, to enter into "a conspiracy either against our property, or just weight in the Union . . . [it] might and probably would lead . . . directly to disunion with all of its horrows [*sic*]."[20]

Calhoun was worried about a future in which he saw slavery as a divisive, destabilizing factor. His latent fears were also exaggerated by the savage and continuous attack on his administration of the War Department that had begun during the Sixteenth Congress and suddenly became sharply focused on an unfortunate transaction of his chief clerk, Major Christopher Vandeventer. In the summer of 1818, Vandeventer's brother-in-law, Elijah Mix, a sharp-eyed merchant and roving speculator, had learned that the War Department was about to purchase large quantities of a special type of granite to be used for the underwater foundations of the fortification to be built on Chesapeake Bay at Old Point Comfort.

Government policy did not require advertised bids for contracts, and normally, as had been the case with the Johnsons during the Yellowstone expedition, successful contractors could receive advances while the work progressed. This was an ideal setup for a shrewd businessman who had War Department connections but little available cash. The department did require bondsmen who would guarantee performance, but otherwise exercised little control over the actual contract once it had been approved. Mix made a low bid for the stone based on prices for material and labor as they stood at the time. General Swift, the chief engineer, himself a part-time speculator in New York real estate, awarded the contract to Mix as the lowest bidder. Mix then had to raise enough cash to satisfy bondsmen. He approached Vandeventer with a proposition to sell him on favorable terms a one-quarter interest in his contract.[21]

Before concluding any arrangement, Vandeventer sought Calhoun's opinion. The busy secretary made a serious blunder when he advised his chief clerk that there was nothing illegal in his participation, though it could expose him to criticism. Since Calhoun was not explicit in ordering him to keep clear, Vandeventer without his knowledge purchased the quarter interest and later another quarter interest

20. *Calhoun Papers*, V, 413.
21. *House Reports*, 19th Cong., 2nd Sess., No. 79 *passim*.

to rescue Mix from bankruptcy. Not long after these transactions, the panic and depression ensued, with a consequent drop in the cost of materials and labor. The contract accordingly rose in value. Mix bought back Vandeventer's shares in January, 1820, and their father-in-law purchased the other quarter interest. Vandeventer profited considerably from these deals.[22]

At this point, the president received an anonymous letter detailing Vandeventer's involvement. Calhoun suspected that Crawford was behind the letter—a suspicion that seemed confirmed when the *Gazette*, a Washington, D.C., paper, revealed some of the contract details in an editorial denouncing the fortifications program as wasteful and of dubious value.[23] A coalition that had formed in the House demanded and obtained an investigation that spread before the public all the contracts made by the War Department since Calhoun had become secretary.

As expected, the Johnson advances were again denounced, Vandeventer's impropriety scouted, and Swift's real estate deals criticized. But the committee could find nothing illegal, fraudulent, or even extravagant in the conduct of the department or the military. It was clear that Calhoun had only peripheral knowledge of the details of contract administration. His position with respect to the Mix contract had been quite proper, even if his judgment of Vandeventer's character could be faulted.

The Monroe administration may have avoided public censure, but its image as the custodian of public virtue was surely not improved. Yet Calhoun kept Vandeventer in his post of responsibility and did not even give him an official reprimand. He seems to have regarded the Mix affair as a further example of how unprincipled politicians were using the depression as a pretext to score points against the administration. The panic and depression atmosphere of unease in the country, to which Calhoun himself was not immune, was being exploited, he felt, for the benefit of would-be presidential contenders. He characterized the movement as a manipulation of the national mood. "It was," he said, "a vague but widespread discontent, caused by the disordered circumstance of individuals, but resulting in a general impression that there was something radically wrong in the administration of the government."[24]

22. *Ibid.*
23. Washington *Gazette*, February 4, 1820.
24. *House Reports*, 19th Cong., 2nd Sess., No. 79 *passim; Annals of Congress*, 16th Cong., 1st Sess., 1594; *Adams Memoirs*, V, 128.

Whatever the underlying causes, the House, after listening to harshly critical attacks condemning what were termed extravagance and waste in Calhoun's administration of the War Department, again passed a resolution calling for plans to reduce the army by about one-third of its allowed strength. Although the resolution was ostensibly an economy measure, the antiadministration leaders in Congress had not overlooked the fact that in reducing the military establishment, Calhoun would be forced to demote or dismiss politically potent officers in order to meet congressional guidelines.

Calhoun may not have had the highly developed political sense of Clay or Crawford, but he was quick to recognize this trap that had been set for him and, in circumventing it, to develop a means of preserving potential military strength while still conforming to congressional demands for economy. He would retain insofar as possible the officer corps, including the military academy at West Point, as a cadre that would be capable in times of national emergency of expanding the regular army rapidly and efficiently. But Calhoun needed more precise information than he had available and advice on whether his rough ideas for reduction were practical. Above all, he needed counsel on the best way to balance the public necessity, as he saw it, with the politically delicate assignments of the command structures in the reduced army. Two other problem areas, he anticipated from the current mood of Congress, needed attention if the administration was to be prepared for further cuts—the coast fortifications program and the unresolved policy on Indian affairs.

For all these reasons as well as to strengthen his political position, Calhoun decided in the summer of 1820 to make a tour of inspection through the Middle Atlantic states and the Northeast. Accompanied by Major Isaac Roberdeau, who acted as his aide, and Peter Hagner, a treasury official, Calhoun left Washington, D.C., on August 15. He visited Philadelphia, New York City, Albany, Sackets Harbor on Lake Ontario, and Boston. To satisfy his own curiosity and his nagging sense of insecurity about British power on the northern frontier, he made the lengthy trip from Sackets Harbor to Montreal, two hundred miles along the St. Lawrence Valley. On this detour General Brown accompanied him. From Montreal, the Calhoun party turned south down Lake Champlain to Plattsburg and Albany.

While passing through Albany, Calhoun did not meet either Van Buren or Clinton. Perhaps he decided to keep completely clear of the rivalry that was raging furiously at the time between Van Buren's Bucktails and the Clintonians. He went directly from Albany to Boston, where he visited factories, the navy yard, and the forts in the city and its vicinity, and spent an entire day in Daniel Webster's company. The two men talked politics and must have exchanged guarded words about the presidential succession and the motives of Clay, Clinton, and Crawford. Calhoun returned to Washington, D.C., by way of New Haven and New York City for a round of official entertainment and reviews in the company of William Wirt, his cabinet colleague who was in the city on personal business. Calhoun was back at his desk in Washington by October 1.[25]

Calhoun's journey, though fatiguing, did afford relief from the daily routine of office business. The change, he felt, had also benefited his health. "I think it better than what it has been for several years," he told Richard Johnson. Apart from receiving information and guidance from the army officers with whom he consulted, he satisfied himself that the Missouri crisis was not as serious as he had supposed but was largely the result of a few ambitious politicians in New York and the middle states.[26] Calhoun's conversations with leading men in the northern states also confirmed his impression that economy in government would continue to be the major theme for a political offensive against the Monroe administration as soon as Congress reassembled.

That the Crawford, Clinton, and Clay factions in Congress would concentrate on him Calhoun had little doubt, but he felt that he had prepared himself well to meet them successfully. He had failed, however, in one important if not crucial respect. Henry Clay had resigned his seat and returned to Kentucky. The Speakership was thus thrown open; and Calhoun was presented with an opportunity to have an ally in this powerful position, but he had been unable to have his candidate, William Lowndes, elected. John W. Taylor, a Clintonian, had finally prevailed over Lowndes in a lengthy and bitter contest. As outspoken on economy in government as he was in restricting slavery in the territories, and one of the congressmen in the antiadministration coalition, Taylor appointed a majority of Crawford and Clinton partisans to the committees that would consider the administration of the War Department and its appropriations.[27]

Calhoun was under no illusions in believing that the Bucktails and

25. Isaac Roberdeau, "Journal of Col. Roberdeau's Journey with John C. Calhoun, Secretary of War in 1820" (MS at Historical Society of Pennsylvania); *Calhoun Papers*, V, 408.

26. *Calhoun Papers*, V, 375, 412–14.

27. *Ibid.*, 425, 389; Edward K. Spann, "John W. Taylor, the Reluctant Partisan" (Ph.D. dissertation, New York University, 1957), 262.

the Clintonians in New York were both reaching out for Crawford's support in discrediting the Monroe administration. Under the loose rubric of Radical, whichever political group won in New York was bound to coalesce in Congress and seek to make political capital over the alleged extravagances of the War Department. Clinton was enjoying a brief ascendancy in New York, and Taylor's election confirmed Calhoun's opinion.[28]

If Calhoun's administration had been considered objectively, the Radicals would have been hard put to justify their attack even under the widest definition of strict economy. Under the new organization of the War Department, Calhoun had made such substantial savings that even with the additional costs for fortifications, expeditions, Indian affairs, and pensions, the military establishment in 1821, according to his estimates, would cost 40 percent less than it had in 1817 when he took office.[29] But accomplishment and objectivity were not factors in the arguments of the Radicals; nor were concerns about the defense of the nation and its Indian policy of particular moment as they aimed their barbs at their most tempting target, whom Clinton and Crawford judged to be their most dangerous rival. The fact that Monroe had just been reelected president with only one dissenting electoral vote did not deter the Radicals from their efforts to embarrass his administration through Calhoun.

While hoping that Congress would not insist on reducing the army by one-third in accordance with the House resolution and urging his friends to resist any cuts, Calhoun nevertheless prepared for the worst. He asked General Brown for a plan to reduce the army in accordance with the resolution. Brown complied with a detailed recommendation that made reductions in the enlisted ranks, leaving the officer and noncommissioned officer corps intact.

Brown's argument was simple and direct. Most of the commissioned and noncommissioned officers were experienced veterans of the war. "By retaining them," Brown wrote, "with a reduced number of rank and file as a basis for enlargement, the establishment might be extended with great facility and promptitude upon any sudden emergency."[30] Calhoun readily accepted Brown's point, which merely restated a principle he had advanced in speeches and debates when he was a member of the House. This plan also spared him the antagonism

28. *Calhoun Papers*, V, 425.
29. *Ibid.*
30. *Ibid.*, 378.

that would surely arise from those officers who might otherwise have to be dropped from the rolls.

Calhoun's report of more than 5,000 words and 7 statistical tables was a finely crafted state document in which he managed to preserve the army leadership yet reduce the size of the army to 6,316 noncommissioned officers and enlisted men, almost precisely the reduction asked by the House. At the same time, Calhoun made it abundantly clear that the welfare of the United States would be better served if no cuts were made, and he pointed out how his reorganization had reduced costs significantly. As a policy document, the report was a *tour de force* that established Calhoun as one of the ablest administrators who had ever managed a government department. As a political document, it must also receive high marks. Calhoun had complied, however reluctantly, with the wishes of a group in the House that he knew had partisan motives; yet he had evaded the trap set for him in tampering with the officer corps, most of whose members had important political connections.

Unfortunately, as had happened with his previous reports, the plan's very success as a public document made Calhoun's detractors redouble their efforts to whip the military establishment with the scourge of economy. Two days before the adjournment of the Sixteenth Congress on March 2, 1821, both houses passed a bill that the president felt he had to approve. It cut the army by 40 percent, not sparing the officer corps, and threw the onus of removal back upon Calhoun. Congress also slashed appropriations requested for the fortifications program.[31]

Calhoun was faced with the unenviable task of reducing in rank all officers if he was not to destroy the army's organization. What was particularly painful to him and politically embarrassing was the enforced lowering of the number of senior officers. Besides reduction in rank, Calhoun would authorize lateral transfers of these men wherever possible. Enforced retirement was the last resort. Retention of the military academy at West Point without any cuts in its complement of cadets he considered absolutely indispensable.[32] To achieve these cuts in the numbers of senior officers, Calhoun brought Brown, Gaines, and Scott to Washington, D.C., for consultation. Most difficult of all was the removal of one of the major generals.

In strict seniority, Jacob Brown's federal commission antedated Jack-

31. *Annals of Congress*, 16th Cong., 2nd Sess., 1789–1830.
32. *Calhoun Papers*, V, 669.

son's. But Jackson was popular and politically necessary if the attacks on the army were to be countered. One possible way out of the dilemma was to make Jackson governor of the new territory of Florida, whose acquisition had been anticipated for some months. Monroe had broached the governorship to Jackson almost two years before, and he had persisted in urging Jackson to consider the position when the transfer from Spanish to American sovereignty was made, only to meet with refusals. After the House passed the bill reducing the army in late January, 1821, Monroe again offered the governorship to Jackson, pointing out that if his decision were affirmative, his answer must be received before Congress adjourned. Jackson delayed his reply until he learned that the Spanish government had agreed to the treaty, and then reluctantly accepted the post. Monroe and Calhoun were much relieved that this turn of events had provided adequate consolation for Jackson and that they did not have to brave a possible political storm whichever man they chose to head the army.[33]

The four brigadier generals were cut down to two with the usual recriminations from those who were reduced in rank. Lesser ranks throughout the army also felt the effects of the bill. Calhoun's desk was piled with complaints from officers who had been affected adversely and their spokesmen in Congress and out. Both Adams and Calhoun and to a lesser extent Jackson had been under almost constant attack through two sessions of Congress. Crawford, the chief instigator, was, as Adams observed caustically, "a worm preying upon the vitals of the administration within its own body."[34]

Calhoun's reaction to the criticism he was receiving was one of anger mixed with despair as he wondered if there really was some substance to the campaign against him. Not quite sure about his policies now that depression gripped the land, and faced with not just harsh criticism from Congress but the formidable and in most respects much more searching arguments in cabinet council from his colleague Crawford, Calhoun at times gave way to uncertainty, though in more reflective moments he decided a partisan plot was responsible for his troubles. Of course, in his correspondence with political friends and army officers, he maintained an air of supreme confidence that his past actions were beyond reproach. In unguarded moments and in the heat of argument with Crawford, his composure was not that certain. After all, the appropriation for Indian affairs had been cut in half, and along

33. *Jackson Correspondence,* III, 38, 41; *Calhoun Papers,* V, 663; *Adams Memoirs,* V, 321, 322.

34. *Adams Memoirs,* V, 315.

with the reduction of the army, the fortification program had been slashed heavily. Could these actions reflect the popular mood? Were they broader and deeper than the designs of aspiring men? Had he been too impulsive in pushing the administration farther and faster than public opinion would justify? Or were the actions of the Congress simply a response to the depression?[35]

Answers to these questions were important in Calhoun's troubled state of mind, for his ambition to be president had never flagged, however uncertain he might be on occasion about his policies. His friends at home, in Congress, and in the army were encouraging. While keeping silent, even denying that he had any interest except to keep Crawford at bay, Calhoun made a move in late March that was aimed at preparing the way to the presidency.

In a conversation with Adams, who was angling for Calhoun's support of his own candidacy, he urged that William Lowndes be given the mission to England when Albert Gallatin vacated the post. Adams, who was almost always sensitive to a political gesture, failed at the time to notice that Calhoun was trying to move a potential rival from his home state out of the country. Calhoun's motive became clear, however, when, late in 1821, the South Carolina legislature unanimously presented Lowndes's name for the presidency. Before news of this event reached Washington, D.C., Calhoun had announced to a group of congressional friends that he was a candidate. He had in a way been forced into this position, which was certainly premature, by Adams' campaign that had quite suddenly associated Calhoun with the New Englander as a vice-presidential candidate.

Calhoun had already decided that Adams had little or no chance of election, and was unwilling to be marked for second place on what he perceived to be a losing ticket. After impetuously making public his own candidacy, he was confronted with the action of the South Carolina legislative caucus. Embarrassed and shaken, Calhoun immediately sought out his friend Lowndes, now a rival. Lowndes listened to Calhoun's explanations and agreed to write his friends in South Carolina, but he would not absolutely take himself out of the contest, which chagrined the impatient, aggressive, yet curiously uncertain Calhoun.[36]

Some weeks before, Calhoun had made a serious mistake that was already wreaking havoc with his position in the House. On November

35. *Ibid.*, 333, 334, 514, 515.
36. Ravenel, *Lowndes*, 221–29; *Calhoun Papers*, VI, 595, 596.

5, 1821, the short, balding Martin Van Buren had reached Washington, D.C., and secured temporary quarters at Strothers' boardinghouse, where Fourteenth Street intersected with Pennsylvania Avenue. Van Buren, who had been elected a United States senator from New York, was about to take his seat in the Seventeenth Congress. Although their acquaintance was slight, Calhoun was well briefed on Van Buren's career and his present standing in New York politics. At the moment, he and his band of Bucktails were the masters of the Republican party in New York, having bested De Witt Clinton in the state elections. Clinton's eclipse had weakened, at least for the time being, one of the factions in the House that had been tormenting Calhoun.

Calhoun saw in Van Buren an ally in removing John W. Taylor from the Speakership and in strengthening his own position with Congress. He lost no time in visiting Van Buren at his quarters. The two men got along well and their political ideals seemed compatible, though Calhoun was unable to discover Van Buren's views on the presidential contenders. As for Van Buren, he had quickly and accurately appraised the strength of the various factions in Congress.

What the New Yorker had concluded was that Crawford's not only was the strongest faction but also represented the power bloc that coincided with his own views about future political arrangements. In his long-range plans for himself and his state, Van Buren felt that he must accomplish three things. He had to achieve mastery over the New York congressional delegation. He had to defeat Taylor's bid for reelection to the Speakership. Finally, he had to strengthen the alliance between Virginia and New York that had been the source of Jeffersonian-Republican political power, but that had slowly weakened during the Madison and Monroe administrations. Thus he had already decided to support the Crawford faction, though he was delighted to accept Calhoun as an ally in his campaign against Taylor. In this kind of game, Calhoun could not possibly compete with a master player who had trained himself in the often mysterious ways of New York politics.

Van Buren proposed to Calhoun that they back for the Speakership Caesar Rodney, an undistinguished member of the House from Delaware. Calhoun agreed. But Rodney, as Van Buren had probably calculated, could not command undivided support from western border states or from Virginia and Maryland. Next, with Calhoun's concurrence, Van Buren proposed Louis McLane, the other Delaware representative. When he proved to be weaker than Rodney, Samuel Smith from Maryland was put forward. He also made a poor showing. Van Buren now suggested that they try Philip P. Barbour of Virginia, who was secretly in Crawford's interest and who may have been Van Buren's candidate all along. Calhoun, who should have sensed the Virginia connection with Crawford, unaccountably agreed. After five ballots, Barbour finally eked out a two-vote majority over Taylor and was elected Speaker.[37] The new Speaker promptly appointed antiadministration members to head all the important committees that dealt with the military. The House committee structure for the Seventeenth Congress would, it appeared, be more hostile than its predecessor.

Calhoun was concerned about public acceptance of his defense policy and the imbroglio touched off by his premature candidacy. But he was heartened to have George McDuffie, a close friend from the Edgefield district of South Carolina, replace Eldred Simkins in the House. Even this measure of support was threatened, however, when McDuffie, a quick-tempered advocate, was disabled for some months, and nearly killed, in two duels with a Crawford supporter, Colonel William Cumming.

Calhoun was shocked that political differences could be carried so far that they endangered life itself. Moreover, the young McDuffie was more than just a congressional ally; he was devoted to Calhoun and had been for some years almost a member of the family. Left an orphan at an early age, this blue-eyed, black-haired lawyer was an exceptionally able person. He had been befriended by Calhoun's elder brother James, for whom he worked as a clerk. Since Moses Waddel's school was nearby, James Calhoun saw to it that McDuffie attended his classes. He made such rapid progress that after three years of intense education, he was accepted as a junior at the recently established South Carolina College. After college, McDuffie studied law. Admitted to the bar, he opened an office in the village of Pendleton, where Calhoun's mother-in-law owned a plantation known as Clergy Hall.

A diligent lawyer with a fine business sense, McDuffie soon built up a lucrative practice and a large following among the planters and community leaders of the Pendleton and Edgefield districts. When the Sixteenth Congress adjourned, Simkins decided to retire from the House. At Simkins' request and with the earnest backing of the Calhoun clan, McDuffie ran for Congress and was elected without opposition.[38] Of average height, he had the sharp features and the nervous temperament of his Celtic forebears. Although many found him grim

37. J. C. Fitzpatrick (ed.), *The Autobiography of Martin Van Buren* (Washington, D.C., 1920); *Calhoun Papers*, IV, 316, 317, 546, 597; Van Buren to Joseph Yates, November 6, 1821, VBLC; John W. Taylor to Richard Taylor, December 12, 1821, in John W. Taylor Papers, New-York Historical Society.

38. *Calhoun Papers*, V, 96.

and forbidding, McDuffie was sociable enough when he relaxed. But in the public forum and especially in debate, he was harsh, abrasive, and unrelenting.

The duels temporarily removed McDuffie from the political scene. An overwrought Calhoun believed wrongly that Crawford had deliberately engineered McDuffie's near murder, just when his services were most needed to resist the renewed attack on the War Department. And Calhoun could not escape the unpleasant fact that he bore some responsibility for the duels. When he thought McDuffie would die, he "over whelmed us all with grief," remarked Calhoun. "It falls on us as a deep national calamity," he added. "I now experience the consolation resulting from the efforts, which I made at an adjustment." The affair, besides affecting Calhoun personally, dramatized the scope of the contest between him and Crawford, which now extended to the Deep South as well as to Pennsylvania, Ohio, New York, and even New England.[39]

There were other circumstances surrounding Calhoun's presidential candidacy that were upsetting. His cordial association with Adams changed to a correct but scarcely warm relationship. Van Buren in the Senate and Barbour in the House were working against him; Adams, Crawford, and Smith Thompson, the recently appointed navy secretary in the cabinet, were either completely hostile or coldly impersonal. Calhoun felt that he was surrounded by enemies. Only the president and the genial attorney general, William Wirt, remained friends as before; but Wirt had no political following, and Monroe, despite his power and prestige, kept himself aloof from the political fray. The president did, however, threaten to veto another army reduction bill that was before Congress. Fortunately, there were enough men of good sense in the Congress to resist the pressure applied by Calhoun's antagonists. Monroe, however, approved a bill that abolished the factory system, a chain of Indian trading posts under the direct authority of the War Department.[40]

Since 1795, the War Department had conducted trade with the Indians on as equitable a basis as possible considering the lack of proper auditing and accounting procedures. The Indian trade was now thrown open to private enterprise, specifically, Astor's American Fur Company and the Missouri Fur Company, whose congressional repre-

39. *Ibid.*, VII, 165; *Adams Memoirs*, VI, 65, 66, 76; Edwin L. Green, *George McDuffie* (Columbia, S.C., 1936), 8–14, 9, 23–27, 32, 33–36.

40. *Adams Memoirs*, VI, 515; Prucha, *Sword of the Republic*, 205, 206; Viola, *Thomas L. McKenney*, 70.

sentative, Thomas Hart Benton, was no friend of Calhoun. The War Department would still monitor the agents who had to post high bonds, but the trade would henceforth be conducted on a profit basis with little or no consideration of the welfare of the tribes. This legislation deprived Calhoun's close associate Thomas McKenney of his job as superintendent of the Indian trade just when Calhoun's campaign was achieving some momentum, especially in Pennsylvania through Ingham.[41]

Calhoun's apparent gains in Pennsylvania stimulated the Crawford partisans to greater efforts. The chorus of criticism that Crawford was orchestrating in Congress now worked its way into influential papers like the Washington *Gazette,* Thomas Ritchie's oracular Richmond *Enquirer,* and Van Buren's New York papers—the Albany *Argus,* the New York *Courier,* and the *National Advocate.* Besides its carping refrain of economy and lax administration, the *Enquirer* bitterly arraigned Calhoun's alleged constitutional theory of loose construction and accused him, among other crimes, of seeking to foist a military despotism on the nation. None of these papers or those that followed their line made mention of Crawford, but there was little doubt that his organization was responsible for the opinions expressed.

The abolition of McKenney's post as superintendent of Indian trade coincided with the rising tempo of the press war. It made sense, therefore, that the embattled Calhoun should turn to McKenney, one of his closest working associates, for support and that the two men should consider the publication of a paper to defend themselves against what both regarded as gross fabrications for partisan ends. McKenney had no formal journalistic experience, but Calhoun knew him to be a writer of clear prose and, in his many reports on Indian affairs, a forceful advocate. With Calhoun's own funds and with some financial assistance from his friends, the first issue of the Washington *Republican and Congressional Examiner,* a four-page, semiweekly paper, appeared on August 7, 1822. No sooner had a few issues of the new journal been published than the Washington *Gazette* and other anti-Calhoun papers threw off all pretense and came out boldly for Crawford. Van Buren, too, removed all doubt as to where his preferences lay. His papers now openly supported the Georgian.[42]

41. The Family party and its newspaper, the Franklin *Gazette,* were supporting Calhoun.

42. John Niven, *Martin Van Buren: The Romantic Age of American Politics* (New York, 1983), 126, 129–33; Robert V. Remini, *Martin Van Buren and the Making of the Democratic Party* (New York, 1959), 50; *Clay Papers,* III, 300, 313, 314.

McKenney had begun his newspaper project with a studied effort to offer reasonable arguments in defense of Calhoun and his policies, but he was soon drawn into the same vitriolic pamphleteering of his journalistic foes. Notable were a series of articles signed "A.B.," which accused Crawford of speculating with treasury funds in several western banks. These articles were the work of Ninian Edwards, an expansive and reckless politician who had gained a reputation of sorts as a Kentucky judge and later as territorial governor of Illinois, where his principal achievement seems to have been land speculation at the expense of two Indian tribes, the Sacs and the Foxes.

Edwards had personal grievances against Crawford. He was only too eager to embarrass the secretary of the treasury with whatever means possible. Whether Calhoun had a hand in opening the columns of the *Republican* to Edwards or McKenney alone was responsible is not known. In any event, under the pseudonym of A.B., Edwards impeached Crawford's integrity as a public officer, claiming that he had positive evidence of malfeasance. The result was an instant and successful demand from the Crawford forces for a congressional investigation. Although unable completely to clear Crawford, the inquiry did demonstrate that A.B.'s claims had no basis in fact. The newspapers, even the *National Intelligencer,* partial to Crawford, made much of the affair. Crawford's partisans were zealous in seeking out the identity of A.B., presumably to indict him for libel.

Late in 1823 Monroe appointed Edwards minister to Mexico, and he was en route to his post when Congress learned that he was the author of the A.B. articles. Edwards was brought back to Washington, D.C., where a select House committee made an intensive investigation of his conduct. Nothing came of this inquiry except a repetition of the charges against Crawford and the exposure of Edwards as a perjurer. The whole affair did dim Crawford's image as an exemplary public servant, but Calhoun's obvious connection with Edwards was not the sort of link a disinterested candidate for the presidency would cherish.

Yet the period during which the A.B. affair was claiming national attention coincided with the peak of the Calhoun boom. The Family party in Pennsylvania, and former Federalists in New York, New England, Maryland, and South Carolina who applauded Calhoun's reputed nationalism, were vocal in their support. Westerners like the powerful Johnson family in Kentucky approved of his military policy and pushed his candidacy. Although there were exceptions, high military officers on active duty, whose status he had upheld, utilized their patronage to sustain him.[43] Calhoun himself wrote encouraging letters to his friends and supporters, while McKenney kept up the attack on Crawford in the self-contained Washington community.

Two developments occurring in rapid succession improved Cal- **99** houn's position while practically removing Crawford from the contest. The burly treasury secretary, while on a visit to Virginia, became ill and, through a gross example of medical malpractice even for that time, was bled and poisoned to such an extent that he nearly died and was left a physical wreck. While Crawford was experiencing a slow, uneven convalescence, his skillful manager Van Buren made a serious error. He rejected as so much empty rhetoric the appearance of a popular movement protesting the selection of presidential candidates by congressional caucus. Calhoun may have often been out of touch with political reality, but in this case he judged the situation correctly and joined Adams, Clay, and Clinton in charging that the caucus was undemocratic. They urged that their followers plan state nominations either through popular meetings or through the legislatures.[44]

Calhoun's supporters in New York City launched what they called the People's party, based squarely on the popular nomination of presidential candidates. With Calhoun's blessing and financial support from his friends in New York, they launched a paper, the *Patriot,* to propagate their anticaucus views. Meanwhile, Lowndes, who may have offered a serious challenge in the South, died at sea. His untimely death was a timely occurrence for Calhoun. The South Carolina legislature now came out almost unanimously for his candidacy despite bitter opposition from one of its senators, Calhoun's old enemy William Smith.[45]

All these circumstances gave Calhoun a sense of optimism not warranted by events that had already begun to occur with a measured regularity. Adams, whose supporters had been quietly marshalling his strength in New York and New England, had also acquired a Washington, D.C., paper, the *National Journal.* It quickly mounted an editorial offensive against Calhoun, calling into question his maturity and his judgment in practical affairs. And Calhoun's loosely knit band of supporters could not match in political effectiveness the tight Craw-

43. *Adams Memoirs,* VI, 241, 242; Niven, *Martin Van Buren,* 130.

44. Niven, *Martin Van Buren,* 139; *Calhoun Papers,* VIII, 70.

45. *Calhoun Papers,* VIII, 70; Morgan Dix (comp.), *Memoirs of John Adams Dix* (2 vols.; New York, 1883), I, 66–68; Charles Wiltse, *John C. Calhoun, Nationalist: 1782–1828* (Indianapolis, 1944), 253.

ford organization that Van Buren had put together. And in the summer of 1822, the Tennessee legislature startled all of the contenders when it unanimously presented Jackson for the presidency. The Old Hero himself was now on display in Washington, having been elected to the Senate.[46]

As the year 1823 opened, all was not well for Calhoun in Pennsylvania, which he had counted on as the primary source of his strength in the North. A split in Pennsylvania's Republican party began when Connecticut-born Henry Baldwin of Pittsburgh, a former Federalist, sought better representation for the West in the legislature. His political program brought him into a direct confrontation with the Family party, based in Philadelphia and its environs.[47] The president, possibly at Calhoun's urging, had unwittingly encouraged division by his neutral appointment policy. Just as the Jackson candidacy began attracting popular attention, Ingham and his political henchman, George M. Dallas, were faced with a serious challenge to their control of the Family party. Baldwin had quickly seized upon Jackson's popularity to advance his own and his region's interests.

Baldwin's following, soon to be known as the Amalgamators, made such rapid headway that the Family party began to reassess its support of Calhoun. Dallas, acting as Calhoun's manager, shied away from bringing his name before a party conclave when delegates from western Pennsylvania indicated that they would present Jackson. In relaying this news to Virgil Maxcy, Calhoun predicted that "the election is with Pen[nsylvani]a and New York. If they unite they choose their man; if they divide their respective candidates must become the rival candidates."[48]

At that time the *Patriot* and the People's party were contributing significantly to the anti-Crawford, anticaucus sentiment in New York. But they were helping Adams and to a lesser extent Clinton, rather than Calhoun. Party opinion in New York, whether controlled by Van Buren or divided among the other four candidates, tended to oppose another southern president. A poll of the New York legislature taken just before the caucus nomination of Crawford disclosed eighty-eight votes for Crawford, thirty-six for Adams, and a mere eleven for Calhoun, while Clay had six and Jackson four. No one voted for Clinton.

46. Robert V. Remini, *Andrew Jackson and the Course of American Freedom, 1822–1832* (New York, 1981), 59.

47. John M. Belohvlek, *George Mifflin Dallas: Jacksonian Politician* (University Park, Pa., 1977), 19, 20.

48. *Calhoun Papers*, VII, 515.

Calhoun's hopes for New York were dashed. If he could carry Pennsylvania, however, he still had a chance, he believed. His close friend John McLean, a political power in Ohio who had replaced Return J. Meigs as postmaster general, thought that Calhoun had an excellent chance to defeat Clay in Ohio and win the state.[49] But Jackson's candidacy changed the situation, even though Calhoun persisted in discounting its impact.

When Dallas capitulated to the Jackson fervor, and the Family party in caucus instructed its delegates to vote for the general at the Republican convention in Harrisburg, Calhoun's candidacy received a mortal blow. Had he been more attuned to the tensions that existed between east and west in Pennsylvania, he would not have been so startled by the sudden change in his fortunes. The Harrisburg convention gave an overwhelming endorsement to Jackson. As a consolation, Dallas managed to secure solid backing of Calhoun for the vice-presidency.

Van Buren and the Crawford cause sustained an equally shattering rebuff. The New York senator had refused to accept the popular verdict on caucus nominations and had gone ahead with his plans. On a wintry evening in February, 1824, two weeks before the Harrisburg meeting that foreclosed Calhoun's chances, Van Buren was forcibly reminded that he had been wrong in his assessment of both the popular and the congressional mood. He secured a caucus nomination of Crawford but by scarcely a third of the congressional membership.[50]

49. Benjamin F. Butler to Van Buren, March 27, 1824, VBLC; *Calhoun Papers*, VIII, 112, 132, 135, 226.
50. *Calhoun Papers*, VIII, 554, 555.

VII

Vice-President

Legislatures of other states followed Pennsylvania in nominating Calhoun for vice-president. Adams thought that Calhoun engineered these later nominations, but this seems unlikely. As Calhoun remarked to his friend Maxcy: "Jackson's friends indicate a disposition to add my name to his ticket in Pen[nsylvani]a as VP. We have determined in relation to it to leave events to take their own course, that is to leave the determination to his friends."[1]

Although the zest that the try for the presidency had engendered was now gone, Calhoun had more than enough work and responsibilities to consume his driving energy and satisfy his inquiring mind. With the termination of his and, as he thought, Crawford's presidential hopes, there was now no need to continue publication of the Washington *Republican,* which had been a drain on his funds and those of his friends. Again he was able to provide a living, though rather a meager one, for McKenney. He had just created the Bureau of Indian Affairs within the War Department. On March 10, 1824, he appointed McKenney chief of the new bureau at a salary of $ 1,600 a year.[2]

For the seven years he had lived in Washington, D.C., Calhoun's home life had served as a respite from the tension of cabinet meetings, political councils, and ever-present administrative problems. His health had been uncertain. Since a serious illness, probably cholera or typhoid, which he suffered in the fall of 1819, he had seemed unusually susceptible to colds and fevers. Washington, D.C., after all, was not a particularly healthful place; it was raw and wet during the winter months and hot and humid during the summer, with open drains, unpaved, unsanitary streets, and no safe water supply. Floride was also ill much of the time, primarily from the complications of repeated pregnancies. During Calhoun's term as secretary of war, she had given birth to six children, two of whom died in infancy, and had suffered one miscarriage. Many of the confinements had been difficult for the now-plump little woman, and often postnatal complications had followed.

1. *Calhoun Papers,* VIII, 554.
2. *Ibid.,* 78, 574, 575.

In May, 1823, she gave birth to John C. Calhoun, Jr., and though she had not fully recovered, by July she was again pregnant. The Calhouns' fourth daughter (two had died as infants), Martha Cornelia, was born in April, 1824.[3]

Despite her frequent pregnancies, the vivacious Floride led the social set among the cabinet wives entertaining at balls, receptions, and those all-female teas that kept boredom at bay for the congressional and cabinet ladies. Whenever her condition permitted, Floride acted as hostess for the dinners, receptions, and balls Calhoun gave to entertain members of Congress, his colleagues in the cabinet, high-ranking military officers, foreign diplomats, and the constant stream of important constituents from home and elsewhere. Dinners were heavy, elaborate affairs with three to four wines, oysters prepared in various forms, game birds, hams, tongues, roasts, and always a variety of fruits and cakes.

The Calhoun household was well staffed with servants, but most of the official dinners were catered affairs.[4] Besides acting as hostess for her husband, Floride did her share of informal electioneering either among the wives of influential politicians or directly with their husbands. She was effective enough in this arena to attract the spiteful attention of John Quincy Adams.

By far the most popular of the Washington ladies, Floride was almost overwhelmed with attention when her infant daughter Elizabeth became critically ill with pneumonia. The president called every day. Mrs. Adams and Mrs. Margaret Bayard Smith, a leader of Washington society and its prime retailer of gossip, were among the many women who sat up each night with the dying child. Mrs. Smith, who had lived in the capital since 1800, said, "I never in my life witnessed such attentions."[5]

The Calhouns had rented a large house near the Capitol (Mrs. Smith described a ball she attended there at which five rooms were thrown open for dancing), but in 1823, they moved into the more spacious and private accommodations of Calhoun's mother-in-law in Georgetown. A year previously, Mrs. Colhoun had purchased for ten thousand dollars a red-brick mansion on the heights overlooking Georgetown. The home, known as Oakly, was surrounded by twenty acres of land, most of it in virgin forest of lofty pines and magnificent

3. *Ibid.*, VII, 132, 135, VIII, 78.

4. See Margaret Bayard Smith, *The First Forty Years of Washington Society*, ed. Gaillard Hunt (New York, 1906), 361.

5. *Ibid.*, 149.

hardwoods. Mrs. Colhoun, who had lived with the family for the past three years, was in her middle fifties.[6] She was still an attractive, though an increasingly difficult, frequently ill-tempered person given to sudden whims. Without consulting anyone, she purchased Oakly, which Calhoun described as a "splendid establishment." He thought she had gotten a bargain, but as he explained to his brother-in-law, "she had no need of it. I fear she will in the long run find it dear." But Mrs. Colhoun had for once been more prudent than Calhoun usually gave her credit for being. The purchase came at a time when Floride was expecting another child and a cholera epidemic was endangering the family. Oakly provided large and presumably more healthful accommodations for the growing family. It was spacious enough for Mrs. Colhoun to have her own living arrangements whenever she wished, and it was particularly well suited for entertaining. The grounds provided Calhoun with a countrylike setting for relaxation; and the site, perched on a hilltop, was dry and relatively free from the summer insects that swarmed about the malarial swamps of the city and the filth and offal of Washington's streets and winding backyard lanes.[7]

Mrs. Colhoun's decisions were not always so fortunate. Calhoun and her older son John Ewing Colhoun, both of whom managed her properties and accounts, were frequently concerned about her expensive habits and her impetuous investments. As she grew older, Mrs. Colhoun became deeply involved in highly emotional religious activities, which must have been disturbing to the freethinking Calhoun. She was especially addicted to evening revival meetings, which she would attend whatever the weather conditions to "beat up recruits." And she did not confine her exhortations to strangers; she constantly urged Calhoun and her daughter to assist in her missionary activities.[8] Neither was attracted to the revivals that swept through Washington, D.C., in the twenties, and neither was responsive to the emotional fundamentalism that inspired Mrs. Colhoun. Floride clung to her Episcopalian faith, and Calhoun, rejecting the Calvinism of his forebears, drifted into Unitarianism like that other formidable intellect, John Quincy Adams.

Providing official entertainment, meeting living costs, and maintaining an extensive establishment in Georgetown were costly undertakings that required more funds than Calhoun's salary, now raised to six thousand dollars a year. Throughout his cabinet tenure, Calhoun had

6. During this time, she spent summers in South Carolina (*Calhoun Papers,* V, 95, 96).
7. *Ibid.,* VII, 298, VIII, 290–91, 213.
8. *Ibid.,* V, 133, 134, 408, 454, VIII, 171; Smith, *Washington Society,* 153, 159, 160.

to depend on the additional income he received from the family plantations near Abbeville and Pendleton, which were looked after by his brothers. His income varied with the world cotton market and the fluctuating rates of exchange in Augusta or Charleston, where he had his crops sold, and in London. Freight and wharfage costs averaging 1.1 cent a pound cut into profits that averaged about ten cents a pound net during the comparatively good year of 1823, when cotton rose to over sixteen cents a pound in Augusta.[9]

Calhoun dealt with a number of different factors, but his most trusted agent was John C. Bonneau, Floride's cousin, a Charleston cotton broker and merchant. Despite his heavy burden of duties, Calhoun kept careful track of world cotton prices and import and export figures for cotton in London, New York, Boston, and several southern ports. Although cotton prices had sunk to a new low in 1822, Calhoun noted that consumption was "enormous" and that competition from Indian cotton had almost disappeared.[10] But whatever price cotton fetched, Calhoun realized all too well that his income was reduced substantially because he was an absentee owner. His brothers and his brother-in-law, burdened with their own responsibilities, could not give his plantations the detailed supervision they required for peak production of quality cotton. Overseers, even the best of them, were no substitute for owner management.

From time to time during his tenure as a cabinet officer, Calhoun had to sell off lands in South Carolina to make ends meet. Thus far he had not been forced into long-term debt for his livelihood, though he and others in his circumstances often gave notes at sight for from ninety days to six months on anticipated earnings from harvested crops. And Calhoun's salary as vice-president, an office he knew he would win by late 1824, would be one thousand dollars less than his salary as secretary of war.

Calhoun's last months as secretary of war were less turbulent than the last several years had been. The depression had lifted to a considerable extent. As a noncontender in the presidential campaign, he was no longer the object of partisan fury. Nor was his administration of the War Department the prime target for congressional economizers.

Shortly after the first session of the Eighteenth Congress adjourned on May 24, 1824, Calhoun combined business with pleasure and left Washington, D.C., for a surveying trip in western Pennsylvania to de-

9. *Calhoun Papers,* VIII, 164, 223.
10. *Ibid.,* 218, 198.

termine the feasibility of a canal route from the Chesapeake Bay to the Ohio River at Pittsburgh. The Erie Canal project, now nearing completion, had prompted a surge of canal-building activity that modified to some extent congressional demands for economy and constitutional objections to federally funded internal improvements. Neither the Congress nor the Monroe administration was ready to underwrite any scheme to develop a national system of canals and turnpikes that Calhoun had favored, but the government did support appropriations for the army corps of engineers to assist state and private agencies in laying out prospective routes.

The Chesapeake and Ohio venture was one that stirred Calhoun's imagination. When the little expedition of army and civilian engineers left the capital on August 18, 1824, Calhoun was an enthusiastic member of the party. The men traveled on horseback and foot through the trackless wilderness and the mountainous country of the Allegheny range. Since his youth, Calhoun had enjoyed outdoor life. He reveled in the exercise and the companionship he found in the group. He was also, as always, a keen observer of the country they traveled through— its wildlife, its rivers and streams, the occasional frontier hamlet they came upon.

In his report to Monroe, Calhoun stressed repeatedly the unifying aspects of canals and turnpikes in a nation of such diverse interests and great distances. He felt that the proposed Chesapeake and Ohio canal would be the principal agent in binding together the three great sections of the country. The region that bordered the Great Lakes would be "firmly united," he said, "to that on the Western waters, and both with the Atlantick States, and the whole intimately connected with the centre." This report was another of Calhoun's luminous state papers. It reflected his unease about the sectional patterns he had observed in the Missouri debates, and it offered a plan to overcome them with a nationwide network of improved transportation and communication.[11]

The scope and difficulty of the undertaking caused Calhoun to cast aside any constitutional scruples he may have had. He conceded that the projected canal was "too great to be executed by a company, or by the State through which it will pass, and even were it less stupendous the necessity of the concurrence of three states, each of which has a powerful opposing interest, would I fear, long postpone the period of execution." Only the federal government had the resources and the single interest to build the canal.[12]

11. *Ibid.*, IX, 309, 343, 344, 421–29.
12. *Ibid.*, 514–15.

106

On his return from western Pennsylvania, Calhoun was caught up in the nationwide celebration of General Lafayette's visit to the United States forty-three years after the British surrender of Yorktown. As secretary of war and the senior cabinet member in Washington, D.C., at the time of Lafayette's arrival in New York, Calhoun made most of the arrangements for celebrations at the capital and the tour through Virginia. When the fat, ruddy-faced French aristocrat, bearing little resemblance to the vibrant, lithe young officer of a half century before, appeared in Washington, Calhoun acted as host until the president arrived from his Virginia home. Thereafter it was a constant round of dinners, military reviews, and triumphal processions while Lafayette, accompanied by Calhoun, made his way through Virginia to Yorktown, where over six thousand people turned out to honor him.

Calhoun must have regretted the expenditure of time and the occasional inconveniences of the tributes, which lasted more than two months in the Washington, D.C., and Virginia area alone. But he must also have been impressed at the outpouring of popular sentiment for one of the last of the revolutionary war heroes. Certainly he found an encouraging unity in the spontaneous national feeling, reports of which he had read in the papers as Lafayette journeyed south from New England.[13] He was still too realistic, however, to imagine that the tour evoking memories of the revolutionary war struggle would, in his own words, "conquer space." And he had already come to the conclusion that the manufacturing interests of the North were manipulating public policy through the tariff that had just passed Congress to levy tribute on the entire nation and especially the plantation South for its own class and sectional interests. Calhoun noted that the census of 1820 had shown a decided increase in the population of those states favoring the increase in the tariff of 1816 with a corresponding increase in their representation in the House of Representatives. Those states that inclined toward free trade had increased their representation by only six members, while those favoring a protective tariff by twenty-eight. The Senate, too, had gained twelve seats from regions that generally supported higher rates.

Calhoun had not been particularly concerned about tariff increases, provided they gave what he considered a reciprocal advantage to agriculture, particularly the cotton plantation agriculture of the South. But the tariff of 1824 seemed so blatantly particularistic, so lacking in the mutuality of interest that he felt was indispensable to the proper func-

13. See Fred Somkin, *Unquiet Eagle: Memory and Desire in the Idea of American Freedom, 1815–1860* (Ithaca, N.Y., 1967), 131–74.

tioning of the Union, that he encouraged McDuffie in the House and Robert Y. Hayne, newly elected senator from South Carolina, to work against the proposed legislation. The fact that Henry Clay, a political enemy, had unfolded his American system of national planning in support of the tariff bill was another factor, albeit a personal one at this time, in Calhoun's indirect opposition.[14]

Another aspect of the tariff debate that affected Calhoun's thinking, though to a minor extent, was the significant drop in world cotton prices. A doubling of rates on cotton cloth imports that the manufacturing interests demanded would place a real hardship on the planters of his region, as well as consumers everywhere. But numbers counted. Unlike the attitude during the Missouri debates, there was no willingness to compromise on the part of the tariff forces. Was this the opening round of a power grab by Henry Clay? Calhoun had not long to wait for his suspicions to be confirmed. From his neutral position as vice-president elect (the Crawford contingent were still bitter opponents), he watched the political jockeying for the presidency that went on after the second session of the Eighteenth Congress assembled on December 6, 1824. None of the contenders had a clear majority in the electoral college. Jackson led with ninety-nine electoral votes, followed by Adams with eighty-four. The Constitution provides that if no candidate has a majority, the House must choose the president from among the three candidates with the greatest number of electoral votes, each state casting one vote. Clay, with thirty-seven electoral votes, was thrown out of the competition; Crawford, with forty-one, remained as the third candidate.

Although excluded from the contest in the House, Clay, always the political gamester, was determined to play all his cards for future preferment. He controlled the electoral votes of Kentucky, Ohio, and Missouri, and he could count on some votes in several other state delegations. Clay bargained with all the contenders but eventually decided to cast his lot with Adams. He made this unwise move in the face of instructions from the legislature of his own state, Kentucky, to vote for Jackson, who, in addition, was the most popular candidate in the House delegations Clay controlled. Calhoun was aware of all the deals and projected deals that virtually converted the House chamber into an auction room. Perhaps from disgust at the entire procedure, but more likely because it would be futile for him to espouse any candidate at this point, Calhoun maintained his neutral stance. His own state had

14. *Life of JCC*, 18, 19; *Annals of Congress*, 18th Cong., 1st Sess., 686, 687, 2207, 2208, 2361.

gone for Jackson, yet he was uneasy about the general. He was not free of an inherited Whig bias that opposed military leaders in high political office. Calhoun had, besides, a high regard for Adams' intellectual attainments and his experience in public office, though he was wary of the apparent influence of Clay, whom he disliked and distrusted.

But when Adams with 31 percent of the popular vote was elected primarily through Clay's efforts, and the new president chose Clay to be his secretary of state, Calhoun was shocked at what appeared to be the political theft of the executive branch of the government. Would the social and economic organization of the nation follow the same lines that had been exposed in the recent tariff debates? Would Clay's American system be the policy of the new administration? And if this policy should prevail in both the executive and legislative branches, what was to become of the slave-plantation system in the South? Six days after the inauguration of Adams, Calhoun wrote General Swift that "the voice and the power of the people has [sic] been set at naught; and the result has been a President elected not by them, but a few ambitious men with a view to their own interest." He was particularly upset at Clay's appointment, declaring that it was "the most dangerous stab which the liberty of the country has ever received." Calhoun was quite certain, however, that in the next election the popular will would triumph. "Principles cannot be violated in this country with impunity," he said.[15]

When he wrote these words, Calhoun was already abandoning his neutral position. Although he refused to be drawn into any immediate move to form an antiadministration party in Congress, he was making overtures to the Jackson partisans. And he meant to use his office of vice-president, as far as its severely limited powers permitted, to enhance what he regarded as the popular mandate.[16]

Meanwhile, for the first time in almost eight years, Calhoun was going to spend seven months in his home state. He had much to do in restoring his plantations to more profitable enterprises after years of absentee management. His entire 1824 cotton crop had been destroyed in a warehouse fire, so it was absolutely essential for his and his family's welfare that good crops be harvested, whatever the price of cotton. This required Calhoun's close attention to the lands and to all stages of the crop cycle, not just in cotton, but in corn, wheat, and other produce for home consumption and for marketing.[17]

15. *Calhoun Papers,* X, 10.
16. *Ibid.,* 7, 8.
17. George P. Fisher, *Life of Benjamin Silliman, M.D. LL.D.* (2 vols.; New York, 1866), I, 325.

Calhoun's properties, Bath and the Clergy Hall plantation in the Pendleton district, which his mother-in-law owned, were both in the extreme southwestern part of South Carolina near the Georgia line. The topsoil in these picturesque foothills was thin, but the red clay beneath had excellent properties for retaining fertilizer. Deep plowing, manuring, and ditching for drainage yielded results that were good, though not as spectacular as those of the productive lands to the east in the Edgefield and Greenville districts. River-bottom lands in the vicinity that were reclaimed through levies matched any yields of cotton or cereal grains raised in the state.

The Tugaloo River and the Seneca, which flowed through Pendleton, were branches of the Savannah River and afforded cheap transportation for bulk products like cotton to Augusta, though both streams were shallow and needed improvement, and some portages were required. The climate of the Pendleton area was the most moderate in the state. Winters were mild, rarely dipping below twenty degrees Fahrenheit, and summers generally escaped the humid, tropical heat that afflicted areas to the east. Calhoun decided to make Clergy Hall, rather than Bath, his South Carolina residence. The nearby village, with its district courthouse, two churches, an academy, a printing office, a weekly newspaper, and an agricultural society, provided some rudiments of culture.[18]

Clergy Hall itself was a plain farmhouse quite similar to Calhoun's birthplace, but it served quite well for what Calhoun thought would be a temporary lodging until he could find a site on which to build. In the spring of 1825, however, Clergy Hall was barely large enough to accommodate the family, let alone any visitors who might make their way to Pendleton. And the roads south from Washington had not improved since Calhoun had moved his family to the capital six years before. Here was an area where Jefferson's notions of states' rights and a wise and frugal government had not worked for either man or beast. But Calhoun in his first public announcement to his friends and neighbors at a dinner in his honor at Pendleton couched his comments on the state of the nation in far loftier terms than any disquisition on the wretched condition of the southern roads. After praising the American system of government, he referred only obliquely to the recent events in Washington. "Education, Election and the Press," he concluded in a rhetorical flourish, were "the hope of Freemen and the dread of Tyrants."[19]

18. Robert Mills, *Statistics of South Carolina* (Charleston, 1826), Pt. 2, pp. 671–84.
19. *Calhoun Papers*, X, 130–31, 16, 17.

Later, during a summer of strenuous physical activity on the plantations and much thought on his own future and the future of the nation, Calhoun began seriously to lay the groundwork for another try at the presidency. Jackson would undoubtedly be in the field, but this did not deter Calhoun from keeping his name and especially his record before the public. His soundings among the local leaders and opinion makers confirmed for him that political operations in the South had been directed against Crawford and that both Jackson and Adams had gained in popularity because both were staunch supporters of the Monroe administration.

Now that the election was over, the means employed to select Adams and the Clay appointment were already compelling issues. "As it is," he wrote Ingham, "there is no disposition for a systematick opposition to the measures of the administration, whether right or wrong . . . but I do not doubt of an entire union of the South against the principles on which Mr. Adams had been elected, and on which he has organized his adm[inistratio]n."[20] He was satisfied that Adams had failed to secure the Crawford contingent, but that faction continued to oppose both himself and Jackson.

His enemy Governor Troup, Crawford's political lieutenant in Georgia, remained a formidable obstacle. Calhoun's Indian policy of gradual resettlement west of the Mississippi and the assimilation of the Georgia Indians with white society was not popular in Georgia or anywhere else along the southwestern frontier. The Crawford organization, which controlled Georgia politics, was the exponent of immediate extinction of all Indian titles whether the Indians were "civilized" or not. "From this source," Calhoun observed, "springs the Georgia movement; and hence the blending of the Slave with the Indian question in order, if possible to consolidate the whole South." He regretted deeply this state of affairs, blaming it on Adams' failure to follow the policies of the Monroe administration.[21]

At Abbeville on May 27, 1825, in a major address Calhoun reviewed his career in government. He stoutly defended his course in advocating the recent war, which he again repeated had "justly been called the second war of independence." Alluding darkly to those in high places "who preferred submission with all its humiliation," he studded his remarks with electioneering phrases like "the virtue and intelligence of the American people." He did not neglect in closing to state that the

20. *Ibid.,* 28.

21. *Ibid.,* 38; *Indian Affairs,* 259, 260, 473, 502, vol. II of *American State Papers: Documents, Legislative and Executive, of the Congress of the United States* (38 vols.; Washington, D.C., 1832–61); *Adams Memoirs,* VI, 255, 256, 271, 272; *Calhoun Papers,* X, 40.

voice of the people must always prevail. "I cared much less," he said, "who should be elected than how he should be; nor do I confine this principle to others without extending it to myself." After all, he had been elected vice-president by popular and electoral votes, not by private auction in the House of Representatives.[22]

Calhoun had his eye on New York when he made these statements. The New York legislature had just enacted a law providing for a referendum on the popular election of presidential electors by district. "Let the people have the powers directly," he wrote Monroe's son-in-law, Samuel Gouverneur. "Let the votes be by districts; and if there be no choice, let the two highest candidates be sent back to the people and all will be well." Beyond the New York situation, Calhoun, like other aspiring politicians, was backing a constitutional amendment that would abolish the electoral college and provide for the direct election of the president and vice-president by popular vote.[23]

After making final arrangements for both the Pendleton and the Bath plantations that included the interviewing and hiring of new overseers, Calhoun left for Washington, D.C., early in October. His slow journey north was delayed further by public dinners and other entertainments in his honor. At these gatherings, Calhoun invariably repeated his new campaign theme, the "virtue and intelligence of the people." Before he left for Washington, he learned that Van Buren had joined the Jackson movement. As he surely recognized, Van Buren's move cancelled out for the time being his chances of securing New York, where he still maintained an active organization of able politicians and editors. Calhoun had hoped that Clinton would break his temporary alliance with Van Buren and divide the opposition to his candidacy in the Empire State. The reverse had happened. Clinton and his following were decisively defeated in the fall elections. Van Buren emerged the leader of the party in New York. With this power base and his connection to Crawford, he might well carry Calhoun's South into Jackson's ranks under the banner of Jeffersonian states' rights.[24]

Calhoun must now have realized that his hope of rallying a united South behind his candidacy was a forlorn one at best. Yet he was re-

22. *Calhoun Papers*, 21–24.
23. *Ibid.*, 26, 27.
24. Fitzpatrick (ed.), *Autobiography of Martin Van Buren*, 198, 199; *Calhoun Papers*, X, 38, 39, 56, 57; Silas Wright to Azariah C. Flagg, November 18, 26, 28, 1826, Richard Hoffman to Flagg, November 28, 1826, FNYPL; Albany *Argus*, November 26, 1826.

solved to take a stand against the Adams administration even if he had to defer again to Jackson in 1828. There was 1832 to consider, and he was still a young man.

Calhoun's reaction to the president's message was ambiguous, however. He could not help but be impressed by the scope of Adams' national vision and his bold program of internal improvements, which in many respects resembled his own thinking. He was troubled by the long-term aspects of the president's program, however—its placid assumption that the federal government would not only underwrite internal improvements as a fixed policy but also by implication promote industrial development. Were not the administration's proposals simply Clay's American system in another guise, a rebirth of Federalism? Calhoun also had to respond to the political implications. Van Buren and all of the Crawford contingent had immediately charged Adams with "amalgamation," a restatement of Federalism and a rebuke to the revered Republican principles of "Ninety-eight." Presumably Jackson's friends agreed with this tactic.

Calhoun expressed his dilemma in a letter to General Swift five days after Congress assembled. "The friends of state rights," he said, "object to it as utterly ultra, and those, who in the main, advocate a liberal system of measures, think that the Message has recommended so many debateable subjects at once, as to endanger a reaction even to those measures heretofore adopted."[25]

Adams followed up his message with another bold proposal, that the United States send a mission to a conference of the recently independent South and Central American republics that would meet in Panama and devise means for a common defense against Spanish efforts to reimpose imperial rule. The Panama project was aimed in part to gain popularity for the administration as an official expression of support for the cause of liberty in the western hemisphere. But the manner in which Clay and Adams presented the mission proposal made it vulnerable to partisan attack. Van Buren quickly sensed its political weakness and moved to exploit it. The slight, immaculately dressed senator from New York called upon Calhoun at Oakly and after the usual amenities proposed that they combine forces against the mission. Calhoun had now to make up his mind. He hesitated no longer. He avowed himself opposed to the measure, but he was not quite ready to align himself completely with the opposition. Meanwhile, he would take full advantage of whatever limited powers he had as vice-presi-

25. *Calhoun Papers*, X, 56.

dent to counter the administration and especially to neutralize Clay.[26]

Calhoun's predecessor, the alcoholic Daniel D. Tompkins, had for the past four years rarely appeared to preside over the Senate. Thus in 1824, the Senate adopted a rule that delegated the appointment of committees to its presiding officer, who in the absence of the vice-president would be its own elected president *pro tem*. Rather than excuse himself and defer to the president *pro tem*, Calhoun appointed the committees, taking care that antiadministration senators controlled the most important ones, such as finance, foreign affairs, military affairs, the judiciary, and naval affairs.

As Henry Clay assessed the situation, there were fifteen to sixteen senators who would oppose the administration on every point of policy. Another eight to ten were politically or personally hostile to Adams and Clay, but were restrained by public opinion at home and were more cautious in their opposition. Together these groups formed a majority against the administration. It was a majority difficult to maintain, however, especially when antiadministration leadership had to contend with Clay's subtle intervention backed up by the patronage at his disposal. Thus, Calhoun's packing of the strategic committees was an important move. With such articulate antiadministration senators as the able but eccentric Littleton Tazewell of Virginia, the popular, persuasive Nathaniel Macon of North Carolina, Jackson's close friend Hugh Lawson White of Tennessee, and the politically astute Martin Van Buren of New York, Calhoun had brought to bear a phalanx of knowledgeable opponents to Clay's maneuvering.[27]

An equally important asset for the antiadministration men, though more for his colorful, vituperative language that made for spicy gossip than for sustained, substantive attacks, was the presence for the first time in the Senate of John Randolph. This incongruous figure with his boyish head that appeared to be joined directly to his shoulders, his tiny torso attached to long, storklike legs, and long, spindly arms had grown even more bizarre in his behavior over the years. In his high-pitched voice loaded with venom, he began lacerating Clay and Adams from the very beginning of the session to the vast amusement of the galleries and the antiadministration senators. Randolph's digressions may have been exasperating, and his rantings undignified and fre-

26. J. C. Fitzpatrick (ed.), *The Autobiography of Martin Van Buren* (Washington, D.C., 1820), 200; *Calhoun Papers*, X, 72; *Webster Papers*, II, 98.

27. *Clay Papers*, V, 117, 118; Worthington Chauncey Ford (ed.), "Letters to John B. Davis," *Massachusetts Historical Society Proceedings*, XLIX (February, 1916), 192.

quently irrelevant, but his capacity for bringing administrative measures into ridicule was particularly galling to Adams and Clay.[28]

The Panama mission, as Calhoun expected, became a prime target for those senators who were bent on embarrassing the administration. And it was a handy lever for them to swing over uncommitted colleagues from the slave states who were concerned about the recognition of black republics like Haiti and newly independent Central American states where mulattoes and blacks held important government positions.

A legacy of distrust over the race and slavery issues raised in the Missouri debates still lingered in the minds of southern congressmen. Calhoun was especially sensitive and defensive about any remarks touching on the social implications of race. Just the idea of recognizing Haiti, which some northern papers had floated, called forth a nervous comment from him. "It is a delicate subject," he wrote Adams' secretary of the navy, Samuel Southard, "and would in the present tone of feelings to the south lead to great mischief. It is not so much recognition simply, as what must follow it. We must send and receive ministers, and what would be our social relations to a Black minister in Washington? Must he be received or excluded from our dinners, our dances and our parties, and must his daughters and sons participate in the society of our daughters and sons?" He closed his letter with a solemn warning. "Small as these considerations appear to be they involve the peace and perhaps the union of the nation."[29]

The Panama mission raised again these potentially explosive political issues, which Randolph and other administration critics seized upon. From his lofty seat overlooking the Senate chamber, Calhoun made no effort to restrict Randolph's harangues. The scarecrow figure in blue and buff with hip-length boots heaped obloquy on Clay and Adams, pausing only now and then to quaff drinks of porter and other alcoholic refreshments. Occasionally he would excoriate the racial composition of the Latin American republics, but his ire was directed at administration supporters, whom he referred to as earwigs, dunces, pimps, knaves, scoundrels, and liars. In one of his rambling remarks studded with choice invective, Randolph drew upon Henry Fielding's *Tom Jones* to label Adams as "Blifil" and Clay as "Black George," who directed a coalition, "unheard of till then, of the puritan with the black

28. William Cabell Bruce, *John Randolph of Roanoke* (2 vols.; New York, 1922), II, 199, 200–203.

29. *Calhoun Papers*, X, 39.

leg."[30] This last remark precipitated a challenge from Clay and a se-riocomic duel in which happily neither of the participants was injured.

116

Calhoun could not have been pleased at Randolph's references to slavery; nor was he amused, as Van Buren and other antiadministra-tion senators were, at Randolph's abusive drolleries, for he had little sense of humor and much sense of decorum. But he had studied carefully and widely the role of a presiding officer whose powers were circumscribed as the vice-president's were. Besides Jefferson's *Manual of Parliamentary Practice,* he had perused several volumes of John Hat-sell's *Precedents of Proceedings in the House of Commons* and William Coxe's *Memoirs of Sir Robert Walpole* with particular reference to the restricted role of Parliament's Speaker, which in many respects resembled the functions of the vice-president. He had also thoroughly acquainted himself with the Senate rules. Rules six and seven, which related specif-ically to the powers of the vice-president over debate, were somewhat ambiguous as to whether the chair could call a senator to order. There was no question that the chair had ultimate authority to decide the point when the decorum of the Senate had been breached, but the rules were silent on whether the chair or a senator would make the call. Calhoun decided that the "right to call to order on questions touching the latitude or freedom of debate, belongs exclusively to the members of this body, and not to the Chair."[31] He made public his interpretation of the rules in a brief speech to the Senate and in response to the pointed criticism he had been receiving from the administration press for his failure to curb the intemperate remarks of Randolph.

Two weeks later there appeared a long article in the *National Journal,* the administration's Washington paper, signed "Patrick Henry," that was severely critical of Calhoun's interpretation of the Senate rules, and was wide ranging in its argument. The major thrust of this able piece was that Calhoun had been elected by the people and that he was responsible not to the Senate but to the public at large. Its language seemed so similar to that of the president's messages and other public papers that Calhoun assumed Adams himself was the author. He pre-pared himself accordingly, and on May 20, 1826, three weeks after the "Patrick Henry" article appeared, Calhoun, signing himself "Onslow" after the celebrated parliamentary speaker Arthur Onslow, replied in the columns of the *Daily National Intelligencer* and the new Jacksonian paper, Duff Green's *United States Telegraph.*

30. Charles R. King (ed.), *The Life and Correspondence of Rufus King* (6 vols; New York, 1900), VI, 666, 667; *Register of Debates, 1825–26,* 19th Cong., 1st Sess., II, Pt. I, 401.
31. *Calhoun Papers,* X, 89.

Calhoun's reply gave notice that a well-prepared and logical mind was at work. His rebuttal was in line with what he had previously declared in his recent speech to the Senate. He maintained that "Patrick Henry"'s attack and other editorial recriminations were directed at him personally and only used Randolph as a pretext. Whatever his protests that he was a neutral in the contest between Van Buren's Crawford following, the Jacksonians, and the Virginia ultra-Republicans, his strict interpretation of his powers was surely of assistance to all who opposed the administration.

In all, there were five "Patrick Henry" articles and six from the pen of "Onslow." Whether "Patrick Henry" was the president or not, the views he expressed were in line with Adams' inaugural address and his first annual message. Calhoun's position was close to the thought of the Virginia school of states' rights and strict interpretation. Both essayists quickly moved away from the narrow point of the vice-president's parliamentary functions and on to the broader theme of the essence of government. To Calhoun, the issue had become one of liberty versus power, and with keen dialectical skill he turned the political tables on "Patrick Henry."

In arguing against any inherent powers for the vice-presidential office, Calhoun questioned the assumption of inherent powers in the presidency. He scorned the executive's use of patronage to extend his control over legislation and proclaimed it an unconstitutional subversion of liberty. Randolph, Calhoun wrote, was "highly talented, eloquent, severe, and eccentric; always wandering from the question, but often uttering wisdom worthy of [Francis] Bacon and wit that would not discredit [Richard Brinsley] Sheridan, every Speaker had freely indulged him . . . and none more freely than the present Secretary of State."[32]

The exchange was a spirited one. Calhoun's argument could not conceal the fears he felt about the future. He was deeply concerned about his own exposed position in the political storm he saw approaching, the problem of liberty as opposed to power, the menace he saw to the slave institutions of his native region from the economic and social pressures of the free states, and those states' growing preponderance of wealth and population over the plantation South.[33]

In the midst of his rebuttals to "Patrick Henry," Calhoun finally decided that he could no longer maintain his neutral position politi-

32. *Ibid.*, 154.
33. The "Patrick Henry" and "Onslow" exchanges are all reprinted in the *Calhoun Papers*, X.

cally. He wrote Andrew Jackson on June 4, 1826, formally offering his services to assist in the campaign against Adams. This had been a difficult decision for him, because he did not entirely trust Jackson's devotion to liberty, remembering all too well his conduct in the Floridas. But Calhoun distrusted Clay and Adams more, and then there was always the possibility of the succession. Jackson had already declared that one term in the presidency was enough. He responded favorably to the offer and assured Calhoun that he should consider himself to be Jackson's running mate in 1828.[34]

Calhoun had made no bones about his contempt for Clay, whom he pictured as the master spirit of an administration that he was beginning to feel was subtly opposed to slavery. Clay was a prominent advocate of colonization, and he knew firsthand of Adams' antislavery views. Were not these attitudes part and parcel of special-interest legislation like the tariff, Clay's American system, and Adams' proposals for a continuous federal public works program of internal improvements, which would undermine state power and eventually submerge under wealth and the weight of numbers the society and the value system of his own cherished region? Calhoun expressed these fears privately in his correspondence with close friends and political supporters.[35]

Calhoun's alleged neutrality had not fooled Clay, whose political antennae were especially sensitive. The first session of the Nineteenth Congress was scarcely a month old when he observed that Calhoun was an important part of a congressional coalition that Van Buren was putting together, though the terms had not as yet been settled. A few weeks later, one of the terms became evident to him when Tazewell, Hugh Lawson White, and Robert Y. Hayne all touched on slavery in their speeches against the Panama mission. Hayne, who reflected Calhoun's views, was the most outspoken on the slavery issue within the context of the recognition of Haiti and the attitudes on this issue of other Latin American states.[36]

Calhoun was certain that Adams and Clay were plotting to bring the slavery issue before Congress, to reopen, as he stated in a letter to Tazewell, "the Missouri Question" for political gains in Pennsylvania. Charles Miner, a Federalist congressman from western Pennsylvania and a close friend of Adams and Clay, had presented a resolution that would abolish slavery in the District of Columbia and would look toward the eventual abolition of slavery throughout the nation. The

34. *Ibid.*, 110, 111.
35. *Ibid.*, 27–30, 72–73.
36. *Clay Papers*, VII, 126, 221–22; *Register of Debates*, 19th Cong., 1st Sess., 165–66.

resolution excited apprehensions already raised by the Panama debates.[37]

Calhoun was not entirely comfortable with his new political arrangement, as he explained in a long letter to former president Monroe. "Never in any country, in my opinion, was there in so short a period, so complete an anarchy of political relations. Every prominent public man feels that he has been thrown into a new attitude, and has to re-examine his new position, and reapply principles to the situation into which he was so unexpectedly and suddenly thrown."[38]

During that winter, early in the session, Calhoun had been a guest along with Martin Van Buren at Ravenswood, the plantation of William Henry Fitzhugh in nearby Fairfax County. The clever New Yorker had sought to draw Calhoun out on whether he would support Jackson in 1828 and whether he would consider an alliance with the Crawford men. Van Buren was well aware of Crawford's antipathy towards Calhoun. Calhoun himself knew that Thomas Ritchie, the editor of the Richmond *Enquirer,* and others of the politically powerful Richmond junto were suspicious of Jackson. No commitments were made on either side, but both men established areas of mutual interest and understanding for future discussions.[39] By early summer, they had apparently agreed that Calhoun would use his influence in the Carolinas, with those adherents in Virginia, and in the Northwest to rally behind Jackson, while Van Buren would bring in the Crawford contingent, who would be expected to support Calhoun for another term as vice-president.

But then the "little magician" made a move that aroused suspicions always near the surface. Some months before, Calhoun had been in-strumental in establishing a Jacksonian daily newspaper in Washington, D.C. Its editor, the tall, thin Missouri journalist, speculator, and indefatigable promoter Duff Green, was the brother-in-law of Ninian Edwards, Calhoun's friend of A.B. notoriety. The *Telegraph* under the capable but scheming Green began subtly to build up Calhoun's stature while belaboring the administration and praising Jackson. Van Buren had noticed the bias and, understanding Green's personality and background, resolved to bring another (impartial on his terms) editor to town. He was also bent on preserving the old alliance between New York and Virginia that for so many years had proved an unbeatable political combination. Thomas Ritchie seemed an ideal choice for both

37. *Register of Debates,* 19th Cong., 1st Sess., 128.
38. *Ibid.,* 132–34.
39. Fitzpatrick (ed.), *Autobiography of Martin Van Buren,* 514.

objectives. But it would not do to alienate Calhoun and disrupt their current tenuous relationship by any overt act if indeed, as Van Buren suspected, Green was his secret partisan. Nor was it politic for Van Buren to suggest that another paper be established in Washington, D.C., that would divide the patronage of the Jacksonians.

Van Buren made the suggestion indirectly through a recent convert to his cause, Churchill C. Cambreleng, a member of Congress from Suffolk County, New York. Van Buren had Cambreleng write him a letter advocating another antiadministration paper in Washington. Then he sent the letter on to Calhoun, who tactfully rejected Cambreleng's suggestion, remarking that another paper was certain to arouse jealousy and undermine the common front of opposition to the administration. Van Buren, however, persisted in his efforts to replace Green's *Telegraph*. He contacted Ritchie through Tazewell, but the Virginia editor refused to leave his assured position for the uncertainties of Washington. Moreover, he and his fellow members of the junto distrusted both Calhoun and Van Buren. For the next three years, the *Telegraph* flourished as the sole spokesman for the Jacksonians in the capital.[40]

Politically, Calhoun had sustained considerable injury during the long session of the Nineteenth Congress despite the support of Green and his own able rebuttal in the public debate over the powers of the vice-president. Primarily through the activities of Henry Clay, Calhoun's popularity in Pennsylvania was sharply reduced. The long arm of the vengeful William H. Crawford had reached into his home state to defeat his old friend Eldred Simkins, who had been seeking election to the South Carolina senate. In a more impressive display of power, Crawford partisans managed to elect Calhoun's inveterate enemy William Smith to the United States Senate to replace John Gaillard, who had died suddenly on February 26, 1826.[41]

Still, it had been an interesting even if disappointing session. When it became apparent to the administration that Calhoun's neutrality had ceased and that he and his supporters were moving toward Jackson, the group led by Adams and Clay reacted vigorously in the *National Journal* and other kindred papers, and through the patronage it controlled and the members of Congress whom it could count on for support. Clay directed the offensive; and Adams, despite his noble

40. *Ibid.*, 514, 515; *Calhoun Papers*, X, 156, 157, 252, 253.
41. *Calhoun Papers*, X, 157, 158, 165.

utterances in his diary, did nothing to deflect the attack. Indeed, he may well have written the "Patrick Henry" articles.

Of the major antiadministration men in Washington, D.C., Calhoun's following was certainly least in numbers, but he was on display, and had been elected by a majority of the popular vote, which could not be said for the president. Yet he found himself in a position where he must defer to Jackson and accept a partnership with Van Buren, whom he had come to dislike personally because of what he had observed of the New Yorker's devious political style and whom he perceived to be a future rival.[42] And Calhoun did not have any firm commitment from Jackson that he would be backed for the presidency in 1832. The Panama mission that had aroused his fears and those of his supporters in Congress about slavery and race had finally passed the Senate by a close vote—a distinct rebuke to Calhoun, Van Buren, and the Jacksonians even though the American delegation never attended the Congress.

Quite clearly, a political struggle was underway that would polarize the Republican party. Calhoun recognized the signs of discontent and was rethinking his position on public policy to bring it more in tune with the states' rights sentiment on the rise in the South. His own state was continuing to experience economic difficulties. Public opinion there was blaming the centralizing policies of the Adams administration, particularly the tariff, for the high prices manufactured goods commanded while cotton and wheat prices in the world market fell to new lows.

But the ambitious vice-president had to emerge from his absorption in the political scene and devote his energy and concern to family matters. Just before Congress adjourned in May, 1826, his son Patrick broke his arm just below the elbow. Then three-year-old John C. Calhoun, Jr., came down with a heavy cold that rapidly grew worse and developed alarming symptoms. Calhoun had planned to journey south and remain at Pendleton until November. The serious illness of his second son forced him to remain in Washington through what he knew would be a hot, humid, and unhealthful summer.[43]

42. See Calhoun's comments on the New York radicals in his letter to Joseph Swift, June 6, 1820, in *Calhoun Papers*, X, 112.

43. *Ibid.*, 90, 91, 105, 106.

VIII

Reluctant Jacksonian

Congress adjourned on May 22, 1826, but Floride Calhoun, caring for a household of sick children and nursing the six-week-old infant James Edward, was in no condition mentally or physically to endure the discomforts and the hardships of carriage travel over the muddy, stump-studded roads that meandered through the wilderness to South Carolina. She would wait until fall after the roads dried, when, she hoped, she and her family had recovered health and strength. And her husband, though there were urgent reasons for his presence in Pendleton and at Bath to oversee his and his mother-in-law's properties, agreed with his wife that they should all remain in Washington, D.C.

Then a situation developed beyond the Calhouns' control, changing their plans. Their three-year-old, John C., Jr., whom they thought was recovering from what was probably influenza, became gravely ill with pneumonia and other complications. For weeks, as the humid summer of Washington pressed down on Oakly, rendering the dark, shuttered chambers almost unbearable even to adults accustomed to the damp heat, the child lay in a fevered torpor, each breath a labored rasp. The physicians gave little hope to the distraught family, and they could not seem to alleviate John Jr.'s painful symptoms.

Finally, the parents could not bear to remain longer with the torment of the sickroom. All the other children had recovered, and a change seemed necessary to the family's well-being. The Calhouns decided to chance the uncertain roads and return home. It seemed a desperate measure to travel with such a sick child, and at first John, Jr., became worse. By the time the family reached Salisbury, North Carolina, 250 miles from Washington, his condition was critical. The parents again tried medicine in a last desperate move, and the child responded. He grew slightly better each day until they reached Pendleton, when the choking cough that had persisted throughout his illness suddenly stopped. From then on, the drier, cooler climate of the uplands seemed to work a miraculous change not only on the health of the convalescing child but on the drooping spirits of the entire family.[1]

1. *Calhoun Papers*, X, 239.

The improvement in health of John, Jr., and the rest of the family on their arrival in Pendleton led the Calhouns to decide that they would avoid exposing their family for any lengthy period to what they now regarded as the disease-laden atmosphere of Washington, D.C. Their decision coincided with Mrs. Colhoun's inclination to sell Oakly. Pending the sale, Calhoun arranged to rent the property to Major Vandeventer, who was still chief clerk of the War Department.[2]

A factor contributing to the establishment of a permanent home at Clergy Hall near Pendleton was the improvement in services that were becoming available in the area, particularly schools for the children. Soon after the family's arrival, Calhoun arranged for Andrew, his oldest child, to become a pupil of H. W. McClintock, a well-educated young man who had opened an academy in the village. Anna Maria, now nine years old, was sent to a highly recommended female school in Edgefield. She boarded with Calhoun's old friend and schoolmate, Eldred Simkins, and his family.[3]

Calhoun worked with a Mr. Brough, his young, industrious, but inexperienced overseer on the Pendleton plantation and on his other properties near Willington. Calhoun was expecting a good cotton harvest but little or no profit because of the drastic drop in prices for that commodity on the world market. His other crops were also bountiful, and while corn, wheat, and other staples had not experienced such rapid declines, they too were being affected by a world market glut in all agricultural products and a worldwide depression that still lingered on after seven years.[4]

For the first time in over a year, Calhoun found some time to relax and put away the cares of Washington, though for him, relaxation meant drafting three more "Onslow" letters, giving a speech at Pendleton, and writing at least a half dozen letters a day to friends and supporters after eight to ten hours on horseback directing the affairs of the plantation. He was happy to note that Pendleton was becoming a summer resort for wealthy low country families who fled the humid, malarial plains for the cooler, drier air of the foothills.

Calhoun was not an especially sociable person. He was far too serious for the rounds of balls and parties that most of these absentee planters and their families so much enjoyed. He had had enough of such entertainment in official Washington. But he did like interesting company, and as a politician as well as a local celebrity, he found that he

2. *Ibid.*, 49, 50.
3. *Ibid.*, 239.
4. *Ibid.*, 45, 303.

could not ignore his rich neighbors. Calhoun was also hospitable in the tradition of all southerners of his class and station. Even though Clergy Hall was rather cramped for entertaining, the Calhouns found beds for the many visitors. Their table, while not serving the lavish meals of Washington, was always provided with vegetables of the season, plentiful meats fresh and cured, fish, and game. Claret accompanied the meals, and madeira closed them. On festive occasions there was champagne. Calhoun purchased most of his wine through General Swift in New York, though he also received shipments from Charleston.[5] Later he planted grapevines and experimented with the production of native wines.

And so the summer of 1826 passed agreeably for Calhoun. He continued to be a target for the administration press, especially in the northern states—a campaign that worried some of his supporters, who urged him to make a tour through Pennsylvania, New York, and New England. Calhoun would not comply. With rather lofty condescension, he said that "time and circumstances" would clarify his position on public affairs.

As the new session of Congress approached, Calhoun was loath to leave his family and friends and again endure the discomforts of a bachelor's mess in Washington. Yet there was one compensation; he looked forward to a more tranquil session than that of the previous year. He felt that the administration onslaught upon him would be lessened now that the question of his powers as presiding officer of the Senate had been thoroughly vetted. John Randolph, a prime cause of all the difficulties, had been defeated for reelection. The Panama question was a thing of the past. There would be fewer distractions and more time for reflection, for reexamining his new political relationships and planning his future.

With evident relief, Calhoun told his brother-in-law that he had "ceased to be the object of the malignant attack of those in power."[6] But even as he wrote these words, the Phoenix *Gazette,* an administration paper published in Alexandria, Virginia, raked up the old Mix affair in a most invidious way, accusing Calhoun of sharing in the profits of the contract. Along with the indictment, the *Gazette* furnished a purported copy of a letter from Mix to an army officer that seemed to prove the allegation. Mix promptly declared the letter a forgery, and the matter would soon have been forgotten. But Calhoun immediately demanded

5. *Ibid.,* 46, 56, 66, 112–13.
6. *Ibid.,* V, 240.

an investigation in the House and dramatized this action further by temporarily vacating his post as presiding officer of the Senate until there was a resolution of the charges.[7]

Calhoun knew he was free of complicity in the Mix contract affair; he also knew that he might not get a fair hearing from a committee that was sure to be packed by administration partisans. Had he been a better politician, he might have ignored the *Gazette*'s smear tactics. Calhoun, however, felt that he must have public vindication, and his sense of honor and propriety, always acute in such situations, overcame his sense of caution. Van Buren would have ignored the ill-founded charge. But the sensitive, impulsive Calhoun never calculated that an investigation, whatever the outcome, would keep the subject before the public for weeks, even months, and would become a rich harvest for partisan editors bent on distortion and useful innuendo.[8]

John W. Taylor, who was again Speaker of the House, followed Clay's direction in appointing a seven-member committee, five of whose members were either political or personal enemies of Calhoun. Calhoun nevertheless made an effort to gain an impartial investigation. He had his protégé McDuffie attend the hearings. McDuffie, however, was unable to make much of an impression and was unable even to have the committee hear witnesses for Calhoun.[9]

For almost six weeks, the hearings dragged on, making newspaper copy both for and against the vice-president. The committee's report eventually cleared Calhoun of any wrongdoing but in such a confusing way that the public could believe whatever it chose. And there were plenty of administration papers in key states that helped the public to decide that he must somehow have been involved in a betrayal of the public trust. The Jacksonian papers defended the vice-president, but so cleverly contradicting was the report Clay engineered that they found it difficult to present Calhoun in the martyr's guise of innocent victim.[10]

Behind the scenes, many of the Radicals, spurred on by their vindictive leader William H. Crawford, retired now to his Georgia plantation

7. *Ibid.*, 243, 244.

8. *Ibid.*, 274, 275.

9. *Ibid.*, 250, 252, 256, 257.

10. Gerald M. Capers, *John C. Calhoun, Opportunist: A Re-appraisal* (Gainesville, Fla., 1960), 113. Capers states that the investigation did not satisfactorily clear Calhoun's name. Also see *House Reports*, 19th Cong., 2nd Sess. No. 79, pp. 152–55; *Register of Debates*, 19th Cong., 2nd Sess., 575–76; Worthington C. Ford (ed.), "Letters to John B. Davis," *Massachusetts Historical Society Proceedings*, XLIX, 195; *Jackson Correspondence*, III, 332; *Calhoun Papers*, X, 248, 250–52, 254–55.

though still a political force, sought to have Calhoun read out of the Jacksonian alignment. Van Buren was tempted to follow Crawford's lead for both personal and ideological reasons, but eventually he held back. He still had need of Calhoun in the grand alliance he was formulating. Moreover, the vice-president was too visible, too clearly respected in the post he occupied, and too politically powerful in certain areas, including Van Buren's own state of New York, to be summarily pushed aside for what were obviously trumped-up, blatantly partisan charges.

While the Mix investigation ground on, Van Buren was reelected overwhelmingly to a second term in the Senate. His triumph over Clinton impressed all of official Washington, and especially Calhoun. The two men resumed their discussions on how to meld their personal followings into a firm political alliance that would elect Jackson president and reelect Calhoun vice-president. As Van Buren saw it, Calhoun's national reputation and his well-known views on public policy would strengthen the ticket. They would help counter the image (that was being projected in the North) of Jackson as a military despot and a demagogue who had no platform to offer. The Georgia and North Carolina legislatures had already declared for Jackson; South Carolina could be counted on with certainty. But Van Buren would have to convince the Crawford following in all the southern states that Calhoun should be on the ticket. Thomas Ritchie was a key factor in achieving this objective, as well as in strengthening Jackson's image. Ritchie was an important member of the junto and the most influential editor in Virginia, perhaps in the entire South.

From the discussions between Calhoun and Van Buren two important decisions emerged—the formation of a national nominating convention and the establishment of a party alignment based on party loyalties that transcended sectional divisions. Van Buren embodied these conclusions in a letter to Ritchie that Calhoun read and approved. In proposing a party alliance based on Jeffersonian principles between the "planters of the South and the plain Republicans of the North," Van Buren called for the organization of parties on issues even if this meant the resurrection of the defunct Federalist party. "We must always have distinctions," he wrote, "and the old ones are the best of which the nation and the case admit."[11]

11. Martin Van Buren to Ritchie (copy), January 13, 1827, VBLC; J. C. Fitzpatrick (ed.), *The Autobiography of Martin Van Buren* (Washington, D.C., 1920), 513, 514.

Calhoun, who continued to be concerned about renewal of antislavery agitation, was especially intrigued by Van Buren's ideas about a political settlement that he thought would protect the slaveholding states from attack. He also thought well of Van Buren's assertion of states' rights as a counter to what he regarded as sectional agitation for special interest groups like northern manufacturers who sought protective tariffs. Calhoun had come to believe that this class would utilize public policy to enrich itself at the expense of farmers throughout the nation, but particularly those in the South, who were dependent on the cotton crop and the international market. As he wrote Bartlett Yancey, one of his supporters in North Carolina, "I do not doubt, that the more daring sperits [sic], that guide the councils of the coalition, count the slave question, as among the ways and means of uniting what is [sic] called the free States."[12]

To many contemporary observers, Calhoun seemed to be moving away from his nationalist position, but he did not see his political stance that way. He had always been, he maintained, a states' rights Jeffersonian, an unwavering member of the Republican party. He had always striven for the liberty of individuals and had fought against national power as expressed in the executive branch. His support of internal improvements and the tariff of 1816 had been to provide for the common defense and to utilize the resources of all to strengthen the states as individual entities. Now that both policies were being used to promote what he regarded as northern sectionalism and the enhancement of executive power, he was merely trying to restore the balance that had begun to erode in the aftermath of the War of 1812.

Meanwhile, manufacturing interests had managed to gain House approval for a steep increase in the tariff on imported woolens. Leading Jacksonian senators, who were not ready to commit their candidate on the tariff, absented themselves when the final vote was taken. Van Buren, for instance, was visiting the congressional graveyard that day to pay his respects, it was reported, to the illustrious dead. Fearing that administration senators would contrive a tie and require Calhoun to disclose his position, the Jacksonians also urged him to be absent. But he refused, and when a tie did occur, his vote tabled the bill. On the whole, Calhoun was satisfied with the political arrangement on the tariff and hopeful that he would succeed Jackson. He perceived De Witt Clinton to be his only serious opponent and was counting on Van

12. *Calhoun Papers*, X, 253.

127

Buren to keep that worthy in check. As soon as Congress adjourned, Calhoun left for home.[13]

At about the same time, though taking a different route, Van Buren and Cambreleng, who had become his congressional lieutenant, also journeyed south. Accompanying them as far as Charleston were two of Calhoun's close associates, both members of Congress, James Hamilton, Jr., and Colonel William Drayton. Van Buren and Cambreleng visited Crawford at his plantation in Georgia and sought to persuade the former Radical chieftain to support a Jackson-Calhoun ticket. Crawford grudgingly agreed to the Jackson candidacy, but no arguments could bring him to support Calhoun.

By prior arrangement, George McDuffie arrived in Richmond at the same time as Van Buren and Cambreleng on their return journey from Georgia and North Carolina. McDuffie's spirited presentation, combined with Van Buren's plausible explanations and Cambreleng's nimble wit, convinced a hitherto skeptical Ritchie and other members of the junto that a Jackson-Calhoun ticket would sweep the Adams administration out of office.[14]

Calhoun had reached Pendleton before the Richmond meeting. Despite his happiness at being with his family and delight at the prospect of bumper crops in cotton and cereal grains, he was more deeply concerned than ever before about the continuing economic depression that seemed to have the cotton planters, himself included, in a vise grip. Cotton that had sold as high as twenty-nine cents a pound at Charleston and Augusta two years earlier had fallen to an average of twelve cents a pound the past year and gave every indication of falling another four to five cents a pound when the bountiful 1827 crop was harvested.[15]

At the same time, prices for those manufactured and imported items that were deemed essential to the livelihood of the planters either

13. There is some controversy regarding Van Buren's role in the tariff vote. He says in his autobiography that he was absent visiting the graveyard, but apparently he was present for an earlier vote on another bill. I have chosen to take him at his word and believe that he left the chamber just before the vote on the woolens bill. See Fitzpatrick (ed.), *Autobiography of Martin Van Buren*, 169.

14. *Ibid.*, 368; Joseph H. Harrison, Jr., "Oligarchs and Democrats: The Richmond Junto," *Virginia Magazine of History and Biography*, LXXVIII, No. 2 (April, 1970), 188–91; Joseph H. Harrison, Jr., "Martin Van Buren and His Southern Supporters," *Journal of Southern History*, XXII, No. 4 (November, 1956), 438–41.

15. *Calhoun Papers*, X, 113, 130, 257, 268; George R. Taylor, "Wholesale Commodity Prices at Charleston, South Carolina, 1796–1861," *Journal of Economic and Business History*, IV, Pt. 2, pp. 848–68.

remained stable or increased in price. The planters blamed the most visible target, the recent tariff, for their economic woes. And two able spokesmen appeared to voice their protests—Thomas Cooper, the tiny, atrabilious political economist, and Robert Turnbull, a Charleston planter whose legal background had sharpened a naturally adversarial mind. Turnbull's arguments were actually a reply to Hezekiah Niles, editor of the influential Washington, D.C., weekly that bore his name and a protective-tariff zealot. He had written and given wide currency to the report of a convention of woolen manufacturers, journalists, and politicians that had met in Harrisburg, Pennsylvania, on July 30 while the Calhouns were en route to Pendleton with their sick child.

Turnbull blamed the tariff squarely for the continuing economic depression in the South. He claimed that it raised prices for manufactured goods and restricted the domestic market, which in turn reduced European consumption of raw cotton. He considered the tariff special interest legislation that plundered one section in favor of another and, recalling the Virginia and Kentucky resolutions of 1798, suggested a similar remedy of state action to redress the planters' grievances. Turnbull's analysis reflected the thinking of Cooper and even of McDuffie, who had spoken out in a similar vein. The Charleston planter's solution was of course couched in unalloyed Jeffersonian idiom.[16]

Calhoun had studied world market trends for years and was more conversant with cotton production figures in his own state as well as other staple-producing states than Turnbull or Cooper. He knew that much of the problem came from the planters themselves, who had tried to compensate for falling cotton prices by increasing production, thus compounding the decline. But he also felt the tariff was a factor in the hard times that had overtaken the South and, politically, an issue that was fast becoming an urgent one. One aspect of Turnbull's anti-tariff philippic made a good deal of sense to him—his strictures on the partial legislation that he saw as a result of the administration's efforts to use its power and its patronage for the enrichment of one section over another. Henry Clay and John Quincy Adams were not nationalists in Calhoun's eyes; they were sectionalists using the strident trumpet tones of nationalism as a pretext for invidious special interest legislation that tended to undermine individual liberty. He had already

---

16. Dumas Malone, *The Public Life of Thomas Cooper, 1783–1839* (New Haven, 1926), 294, 301, 323; Robert J. Turnbull, *The Crisis; or, Essays on the Usurpations of the Federal Government* (Charleston, 1827), *passim;* Thomas Cooper, *Two Essays: 1. On the Foundation of Civil Government: On the Constitution of the United States* (Columbia, S.C., 1826), 26 *et passim.*

made public his position on the tariff by his vote on the woolens bill.[17]

When Calhoun returned to Washington, D.C., for the short session of the Twentieth Congress, he knew that the tariff issue would be so deeply involved with the presidential campaign that it might not be politic for him or the Jacksonians to take such an open antitariff position. But what was politic and what was the best stance for his state and region brooked no equivocation. The best policy for the South was also the best policy for the nation, as he saw it, not the narrow, special interest legislation of Clay and Adams and the American system—an arbalest of power squarely aimed at breaching equality of opportunity.

Foes of the administration had triumphed in the fall elections. Calhoun would not at least be faced with a repetition of the Mix investigation. Van Buren had engineered the election of Andrew Stevenson as Speaker of the House over John W. Taylor. Stevenson was a member of Ritchie's junto, thoroughly committed to the Jackson-Calhoun ticket and a moderate on the tariff issue.[18] Randolph, who had been elected to the House, was appointed chairman of the powerful ways and means committee. He was too ill to accept, so Stevenson selected McDuffie in his place. Majority membership on all other House committees went to opponents of the administration. The same result occurred in the Senate, where antiadministration members were elected to chair all important committees. Daniel Webster was the only formidable spokesman for the administration and the tariff supporters in the Senate. He was beginning his first term in the upper house, to which he had been elected from Massachusetts, having changed his residence and his constituency from the free-trading merchants of Portsmouth, New Hampshire, to the bankers and their industrialist clients of Boston and its vicinity.

But Calhoun could not count on the various factions, still seeking to coalesce into an effective party, to follow a consistent line on public issues. The session was not two months old when De Witt Clinton, whom he regarded as his principal rival in the emerging party organization, died suddenly of a heart attack. Van Buren moved swiftly to merge Clinton's following into his own political group. He now took Clinton's place as the northern contender for the presidential succession. The fragile ties that were binding him and Calhoun together in the Jackson campaign were strained.[19]

Calhoun's suspicions about Van Buren were certainly not alleviated

17. See, for instance, *Calhoun Papers*, X, 421.
18. Niven, *Martin Van Buren*, 196.
19. *Calhoun Papers*, V, 308, 309, 337, 338.

by the more or less continuous efforts of the Crawford Radicals to remove him from the ticket or embroil him in a controversy with Jackson. A letter of Monroe to Calhoun alluding to the possible disciplining of Jackson for his conduct in the Seminole war had been stolen from Calhoun's files. It had speedily made its way in mutilated form to Jackson, who demanded an explanation. In this case, Calhoun's honor deferred to political necessity. He neither denied nor admitted that he had disapproved of Jackson's course in the Indian war, but he cleverly ascribed their respective roles to honesty and patriotism.

Jackson and his political advisors in what came to be known as the Nashville committee felt that they could not afford a break with Calhoun. Although Jackson was acutely sensitive about his activities in the war, he agreed to shelve the issue for the time being. He, too, had long harbored resentment toward Calhoun for his independent policies when secretary of war and was suspicious about his ambitions. And Duff Green's *United States Telegraph*, the only Jacksonian paper in Washington, injured Calhoun's standing with the general and his fervent supporters by its frequent editorials extolling the virtues of the vice-president while blandly assuming that he would succeed Jackson in the presidency.[20] Calhoun believed Van Buren was trying to remove him as Jackson's running mate when in fact the New Yorker was doing his best to keep the ticket intact against the forays of Crawford, who still maintained a substantial following. Van Buren's efforts bore fruit when party conventions or legislative caucuses in state after state endorsed Calhoun as the vice-presidential nominee.

The campaign itself was becoming increasingly vitriolic, though Jackson, not Calhoun, was now the principal target. In the administration press, he was pictured as a bloody-minded tyrant who executed militiamen without trial, a sensualist who lived in sin with a woman to whom he had never been married, an ignorant, irreligious desperado who could scarcely write his own name. Jacksonian papers and especially the *Telegraph* responded in kind, accusing Adams of, among other things, acting as a pimp for Tzar Alexander when he was minister to Russia. But it was not the journalistic barrage and the poisonous rhetoric, nor even the covert activities of Crawford, that threatened serious divisions among the Jacksonians. It was, as Calhoun knew it would be, the tariff issue, on which the Adams administration was united but on which the Jackson forces were in disarray.

Calhoun participated in discussions with Van Buren and Speaker

20. *Ibid.*, X, 342, 345, 354, 355–56, 357–59, 361–64, 378–79.

Stevenson on the proposed tariff bill. None of them wanted the tariff question to play a part in the presidential campaign, but they saw no way to circumvent it since their opponents were determined to make it the prime political issue. Moreover, Washington boardinghouses and hotels were crammed with individuals of a new type—special interest lobbyists who were representing all manner of businesses that would benefit from increased tariff rates. Spokesmen for the woolen industry were the most prevalent and the most persistent in attempting to influence congressmen.

Van Buren came from a state that had a plethora of conflicting interests. His constituents included woolen manufacturers, farmers who raised sheep exclusively, and farmers whose main reliance was on other commodities but who also raised sheep on the side. Almost all, except those in the most remote farming communities, who depended in part on the putting-out system, wove woolen cloth at home. In addition, New York had a prosperous, articulate mercantile community and a substantial shipbuilding industry, both of which were vehement supporters of free trade. It had been, and still was, a cardinal rule for Van Buren to protect his position at home. Thus his approach to the tariff question would have to be based on a series of compromises that would arouse the least criticism in New York and if possible elsewhere. Yet his underlying philosophy leaned towards agriculture and free trade—towards reducing duties that raised prices on consumer goods and tended to restrict the domestic and foreign market for agricultural products, whether they be cotton, wheat, raw wool, or flax.

Speaker Stevenson, according to plan, appointed a high tariff man and an administration supporter, Rollin C. Mallary of Vermont, to head the House committee on manufactures that would report a tariff bill. The majority of the committee members, however, were Jacksonians, the ablest of whom was Silas Wright, a Van Buren lieutenant now serving his first term in Congress. Wright persuaded the committee to hold hearings that continued throughout December, 1827, and January, 1828.

At night after the committee had adjourned, Wright, with Van Buren at his side, worked out the tariff schedules state by state, calculating the lowest or the highest rates depending on the product that could be assigned without serious political repercussions. Woolen rates were increased as high as Van Buren and Wright deemed would be acceptable to the consuming states in the West and the South, but were far lower than those demanded by the manufacturers in New England and their home state of New York. Raw wool duties were raised sharply, a boon to sheepherders everywhere and an additional cause for complaint from the manufacturers. Other increased duties on molasses, cordage, pig iron, and fabricated iron bore much more heavily than before on the shipbuilding and rum distilling industries of New England, while offering incentives to Pennsylvania iron-masters, Kentucky hemp growers, and grain whiskey distillers.

Whether Van Buren and Wright deliberately devised this poison pill strategy to defeat a tariff bill they knew would face a close vote with New England and New York voting against it, or whether they sold it to southern members of the House as the best compromise they could get, is unknown. What is known is that Calhoun approved the bill as reported and that McDuffie, his spokesman in the House, said, "We saw this system of protection was about to assume gigantic proportions, and to devour the substance of the country and we determined to put such ingredients in the chalice as would poison the monster . . . a policy, which, though I did not altogether approve, adopted in deference to the opinions of those with whom I acted."[21]

Van Buren had met with Calhoun and presented him with two alternatives. The first was for southern members to join with New Englanders and defeat the bill as reported. But, argued Van Buren, this would result in ultimate passage of a protective tariff because westerners would join with eastern interests to gain a modified bill. The second alternative was for southerners to resist all amendments that would raise rates and take a chance that the New England members would join the southerners and defeat the bill during its passage in either house. Van Buren stressed the fact that this arrangement risked a union of moderate and high tariff members, which would pass the bill, but it also held out the prospect of defeating the bill entirely. Calhoun accepted his reasoning and urged southern members to adopt the poison pill strategy. Thus the tariff passed the House with southern votes. On January 31, 1828, the House version was greeted by a storm of criticism, most of it leveled at the woolens schedules. Manufacturers claimed that these were so low that they would ruin the industry, while cotton-producing states found them too high, indeed confiscatory.[22]

When the bill reached the Senate, however, the union of the tariff men became apparent. Henry Clay had passed the word to administra-

---

21. *Congressional Globe*, 28th Cong., 1st Sess., 747.

22. *Calhoun Papers*, XIII, 469–72; Fitzpatrick (ed.), *Autobiography of Martin Van Buren*, 409, 410; *Calhoun Works*, III, 48–51; *Congressional Globe*, 20th Cong., 1st Sess., 921; Thomas Hart Benton, *Thirty Years' View* (2 vols.; New York, 1854–56), I, 95–102.

tion supporters that the duties on woolens and other articles of northern manufactures were as high as they could expect. Van Buren voted with the majority in defeating amendments from cotton and other special interest groups that would have lowered rates on key items. To Calhoun's chagrin, Van Buren voted for the crucial amendment that raised the schedule on woolens, and his vote was enough to pass the measure. President Adams approved the bill that would be stigmatized as "the tariff of abominations."[23]

Calhoun charged treachery, but in fact he misunderstood Van Buren's position, which was to enact a tariff that would carry New York and Pennsylvania for Jackson and not alienate the moderate tariff states of Kentucky and the Northwest. Van Buren firmly believed that if the compromise he and Wright had worked out was defeated, a much higher tariff would have been enacted, which would cost Jackson dearly in Virginia, the cotton states, and possibly even in New York.[24]

But Van Buren underestimated the hostility increased rates on such necessities as woolen cloth would generate in the depression-stricken South. And he did not consider the fears this legislation aroused among southerners like Calhoun who saw it as an encroachment of the central government on individual liberties. To them, the tariff reached straight through state borders and acted upon individuals, thus denying them a measure of freedom. It seemed also to be a compulsory tax on agricultural interests everywhere in the nation to support a form of enterprise from which they gained no reciprocal benefit. Indeed, those southern planters who listened to Thomas Cooper or Robert Turnbull were convinced they were subsidizing an interest and a section that were positively inimical to their prosperity.[25]

23. *Calhoun Works,* 5, 50–51.

24. Niven, *Martin Van Buren,* 196–99; Robert V. Remini, "Martin Van Buren and the Tariff of Abominations," *American Historical Review,* LXIII, No. 4 (October, 1958–July, 1959), 914–16; *Calhoun Papers,* XIII, 457–60.

25. See an interesting interpretation of what is deemed a unique patriarchal, family-oriented culture in the South Carolina of the 1830s in James Brewer Stewart, "'A Great Talking and Eating Machine': Patriarchy, Mobilization and the Dynamic of Nullification in South Carolina," *Civil War History,* XXVII, No. 3 (September, 1981) 197–230. Because of its disproportionately heavy concentration of slaves and overwhelming reliance on the world cotton market, which had been in a state of deep depression since 1825, South Carolina doubtless presented an extreme case of social and economic paranoia. Thus the tariff exhibited a clear-cut issue to the leaders of a society that felt itself not only endangered but entrapped. Patterns of male dominance and familial connections, and other anthropological considerations in varying degrees, can be applied to all of American society in this period.

Members of the South Carolina delegation met in Senator Hayne's boardinghouse to discuss the tariff and what their future actions should be. Calhoun did not attend, though he kept himself informed of the discussions, which went on for several days. Most of the congressmen agreed with McDuffie that if the tariff policy were continued, it would lead to a breakup of the Union. But it was finally decided that they would make every effort to dampen public meetings and other emotional attacks on the tariff when they reached home. All were determined to use whatever influence they possessed to keep the presidential contest out of the tariff debate.[26]

Calhoun unquestionably acted as a moderating force. He felt strongly that the Adams administration must be defeated before there would be any hope of reducing tariff rates. The administration had come into power, he was convinced, through corrupt means and had sought throughout its term of office to enhance its power at the expense of the legislative branch and the states. With its ally, the Marshall-dominated Supreme Court, it had enacted much of its ideology into the supreme law of the land. However he felt about Van Buren, Calhoun regarded the tariff issue as essentially of a piece with the Adams-Clay program of centralizing power at the expense of liberty.

Congress adjourned on May 26, 1828. Calhoun left Washington, D.C., a few days later for Pendleton. On his route through Virginia, North Carolina, and his home state, he found overwhelming support for the Jacksonian ticket. As he had suspected, there was an upsurge in antitariff sentiment among the large cotton planters and even among the yeoman farmers. It was especially acute and vociferous in South Carolina.[27] Despite the efforts of Calhoun and his associates of the congressional delegation, community anger grew in intensity during the summer. Turnbull and Cooper, both of whom disliked Calhoun intensely, kept agitation at a fever pitch. At times antitariff orators at public meetings, overflowing with furious rhetoric, demanded extralegal action and insisted that if grievances were not redressed, secession might well be the only alternative.

To alarmed friends in the North and in neighboring states, Calhoun wrote lengthy letters downplaying the excitement. He opposed calling a special session of the legislature and counseled constitutional remedies. But as the summer wore on and efforts at molding dominant public opinion along more moderate contours seemed to be having

---

26. *Niles' Register*, XXXV, 183–85, 199–203.
27. Stewart, "A Great Talking and Eating Machine," 208, 209.

little or no effect, Calhoun began to reassess the situation. What had been an oppressive sectional tax that bore heavily on an already burdened southern economy now became a concentrated effort on the part of the Adams administration to change the slave-plantation system into an industrial economy. "From the settlement of this section of the country to this day, our labour and capital have been wholly turned to agriculture," he wrote John McLean. "To this pursuit we owe our slave population. Without it we should have had as few blacks as Pennsylvania or New York. It is a fearful experiment to compel us rich in land and Negroes, but destitute of money capital, skilled in the culture of corn, cotton, rice and tobacco, but utterly without experience or skills in merchanick [*sic*] labour to turn manufacture[r]s."[28]

Although he specifically singled out Clay's American system for this state of affairs, Calhoun was more concerned about long-range trends that he now discerned emerging in the North and Northwest. He was, in addition, uncomfortable with the new party system that was developing. After the tariff votes of Van Buren and Jackson's close associate John H. Eaton, a Tennessee senator, he became concerned about the course of a new administration. As so often in the past when he felt surrounded by political enemies and assailed by doubts about the future, Calhoun began seeking a way out of his own and his state's dilemmas in what he hoped would provide a realistic solution to an impending political and constitutional crisis.

Calhoun had brought with him from Washington, D.C., Jeffersonian political pamphlets challenging the Alien and Sedition acts. He had been studying Wheaton's Supreme Court *Reports,* Hobbes's *Leviathan,* Cooper's and Turnbull's articles on the southern economy, Elliot's *Debates,* and Yates's Minutes. He was also reading carefully the first two issues of the *Southern Review,* a new magazine of political and economic opinion that he had helped establish. On a more practical level, he received a series of warnings laced with sound political advice from Duff Green. The Washington editor was particularly critical of McDuffie, who had cast off his moderate stance and was making speeches charging a hostile alliance between the North and the West and hinting darkly at secession. "Your leading men," wrote Green, "should not look to the little squad who collect at your public dinners and cry 'no tariff.' You must look to the nation and *act* for the people as they *are.*"[29]

28. *Calhoun Papers,* X, 406.
29. *Ibid.,* 412, 422.

Thus, when William C. Preston, on behalf of the South Carolina legislature, asked him to prepare a report on the tariff, Calhoun was not only happy to comply but had already roughed out his arguments. He still needed a copy of Jefferson's Kentucky resolutions and a statement of imports and exports for the past five years. He asked Preston to send him these documents from Columbia. Calhoun was prepared to decry the wrongs he believed were being inflicted on the cotton-growing states, but as he remarked to Preston, "all moves aiming at *reform and revolution as ours is, must, to be successful be characterized* by great respect for the opinion of others." And though he had now become quite wary of Jackson's policy on the tariff, he would not indulge in any language that might be construed as criticism of the new administration whose election he anticipated.[30]

Once he had received the data he requested from Preston, Calhoun wrote two documents, "Exposition" and "Protest," rapidly in his billowing scrawl. Although visitors interrupted, forcing halts in his work, he had a draft of 35,000 words completed in about two weeks. Once he had the argument clear in his mind, his pen raced across page after page of foolscap. In plain but vigorous language buttressed by an impressive display of data, he set forth the grievances of the planter class in his state. He also gave vent to his own frustrations—his deep-felt feelings of insecurity for his own future and the future of a social order and of a nation that he felt were in deadly peril.[31]

30. *Ibid.*, 431.
31. *Ibid.*, 431, 434.

137

John C. Calhoun, late 1840s

National Archives

Charleston, South Carolina, late 1840s
South Caroliniana Library, University of South Carolina

Floride Calhoun, tidewater heiress, early 1820s
South Caroliniana Library, University of South Carolina

Andrew Pickens Calhoun, Calhoun's eldest son
South Caroliniana Library, University of South Carolina

Anna Maria Clemson, Calhoun's gifted daughter

South Caroliniana Library, University of South Carolina

Thomas Green Clemson, Calhoun's son-in-law, as a young man

South Caroliniana Library, University of South Carolina

*Francis Wilkinson Pickens, Calhoun's cousin and sometime political
advisor*

South Caroliniana Library, University of South Carolina

Joel Roberts Poinsett, Unionist, brilliant horticulturist, and political enemy of Calhoun

South Caroliniana Library, University of South Carolina

Robert Barnwell Rhett, restive anti-Unionist.

South Caroliniana Library, University of South Carolina

Franklin Harper Elmore, Calhoun's advisor, Charleston banker and politician

South Caroliniana Library, University of South Carolina

Dixon Lewis, heavy of body but not of mind, Calhoun's advisor and antebellum senator from Alabama

South Caroliniana Library, University of South Carolina

George McDuffie, Calhoun's tempestuous friend and supporter

National Archives

Henry Clay, whom Calhoun considered to be all style and no substance

The godlike Daniel Webster, early 1840s

Cartoon of the presidential campaign, 1844

Print Collection, Miriam and Ira D. Wallach Division of Art, Prints and Photographs, The New York Public Library, Astor, Lenox and Tilden Foundations

Fort Hill, Calhoun's modestly pretentious home in Clemson, South Carolina

South Caroliniana Library, University of South Carolina

John Quincy Adams, Calhoun's sometime friend, longtime foe

National Archives

Martin Van Buren in the 1840s, Calhoun's political nemesis

James K. Polk, as he appeared during the early years of his presidency

National Archives

IX

"Exposition" and "Protest"

While Calhoun was pondering the impact of the tariff and speculating about a grim future for the South during the hot summer of 1828, he was suddenly struck down with fever, arthritic pains, and wracking cramps. His whole family as well as the slaves became ill with similar symptoms. They had dengue fever, a mosquito-carried African bacteria brought by slave ships to the West Indies and transmitted from there to the plantations of Florida, Georgia, and South Carolina. More alarming, two cases of yellow fever also appeared in the Pendleton area, but fortunately the disease did not become epidemic. The dengue fever lasted for about a week, causing acute discomfort before rapidly subsiding. It left Calhoun, his family, and his slaves weak, but within a short time all completely recovered.[1]

Until now, the Calhouns had found Pendleton free from serious disease, but Calhoun himself was susceptible to colds and was frequently ill for short periods. Floride and her mother, who spent much of each year with the family, enjoyed remarkably good health. Although she had had nine pregnancies and at least two miscarriages, Floride was much stronger physically than her tall, raw-boned husband.

At Pendleton, nevertheless, Calhoun led a vigorous outdoor life with plenty of exercise as he rode for miles every day inspecting and directing his plantations. For the past three years, he had derived his sole relaxation from politics and the confining atmosphere of Washington, D.C., in the improvement of his house and lands at Pendleton. One of his first projects was the enlargement and remodeling of Clergy Hall, which he renamed Fort Hill. After he was unsuccessful in purchasing lands nearby where he planned to build a new home, he had finally decided on converting the simple, boxlike parsonage into a home that suited his own and Floride's taste and was large enough to accommodate his family of six children with rooms for guests and his mother-in-law. Compared to Oakly, Fort Hill was a much smaller,

1. *Calhoun Papers*, X, 411.

more modest dwelling. No hay wagon could be driven through its central hall as had been said of Oakly. When all the family was present along with guests, its eight bedrooms had to serve double, perhaps triple, occupancy. Not as pretentious as the summer mansions of Calhoun's Charleston neighbors, Fort Hill was a comfortable, rambling home with broad porches on two sides and Doric pillars in the Greek revival style, which the wealthier classes north as well as south had adopted in their architecture as a visible badge of their success and prominence.

Calhoun personally supervised most of the conversion work, utilizing his own skilled slaves and borrowing additional craftsmen from his brother-in-law, John E. Colhoun, whose plantation, Keowee, was within a day's ride.[2] Calhoun had a one-room study built for himself with a short, stone-flagged path that led to the main house. Here he placed maps of the state and the Union on the walls so that he could reflect on "the immense distances and diversity" of the nation. Here he also kept his books, volumes of the *Register of Debates* and other government documents, philosophical works, histories, biographies, treatises on scientific subjects, and works of political economy, but no popular literature, for which he had little use. The study, like the man, was spartan, a place of work, not of pleasure or relaxation.

Yet Calhoun did have an aesthetic side to his nature, which expressed itself in the attention he paid to the grounds about the house. In April, 1827, he wrote his mother-in-law, who was then in Charleston, to send him a few orange trees, which he thought might survive if carefully cultivated on the south side of the house. He also wanted two or three pomegranate shrubs. That fall he planted Kentucky bluegrass as a lawn that sloped down the hill for several acres to the entrance of the property. He and Floride had a fondness for the exotic in shrubs and flowers. They also appreciated the appearance and the shade of the huge virgin oaks, pines, and other native trees on the grounds. Calhoun's overriding sense of privacy and of security was most evident in the long road through a dense forest that one traveled before reaching the house. A visitor remarked that the mansion was "so concealed that you hardly noticed it until you are within a very short distance of the white pillars of the north and east front of his house."[3]

Although abstemious in both food and drink, Calhoun relished a glass of good claret with his meals and some madeira during the evening. There was also champagne for special occasions. Apart from the

2. *Ibid.*, 296.

3. Harriet Hefner Cook, *John C. Calhoun* (Columbia, S.C., 1965), 80.

wines and such staple items as salt, spices, tea, and coffee, basic foods for the family and slaves were raised on the plantation. Their meals tended to be the plain, wholesome fare of a well-to-do farmer: ham, beef, poultry, mutton, cornbread and wheat bread, and fresh vegetables in season, supplemented by preserved fruits, potatoes, and root crops. Calhoun was especially fond of melons that he planted himself in the kitchen garden.

Of course, slaves performed all of the household chores and took care of the children, though the Calhouns did employ a teacher-governess. Some eighty slaves worked the plantation, which consisted of about nine hundred acres, 10 percent of which was devoted to the cotton cash crop. Another ninety acres were planted in corn and wheat, with smaller allotments for barley and rye. There were peach, pear, apple, and apricot orchards. Fig trees and various nut trees provided fruit and variegated foliage on the southern exposure of the mansion. The remainder of the acreage was meadow for the grazing of farm animals, except for the two 3-acre plots each slave family cultivated for its own use or sale to Calhoun. Slave families were housed in attached individual stone houses that were usually divided into three or four rooms. From his study, Calhoun could see the quarters perched on a lower hill about six hundred feet from the mansion.

During his occupation of Fort Hill, Calhoun employed no drivers but was fortunate in having several overseers—especially, in later years, Mr. Fredericks—who seem to have been able managers and humane persons. Calhoun himself was eminently fair and understanding with his helpless slaves. Unlike many of his neighboring planters, he encouraged religion and religious marriage among the blacks, many of whom he had known all of his life. Indeed, one black woman, one hundred years old, who was born in Africa, had been with the family since the 1750s. Yet Calhoun and his overseers resorted to punishment when they deemed it necessary. In January, 1827, Calhoun learned from Floride that there were blacks on the plantation who had been "in some instances disorderly." She was concerned about the situation. Calhoun wrote from Washington, D.C., to his brother-in-law John E. Colhoun to "see that all is right, and if not the most decided measures be adopted to bring them to a sense of duty."[4]

Cotton prices in the world market during the late twenties and early thirties were so low that they scarcely paid the cost of raising the staple, baling it, and shipping it to market. But Calhoun and his overseers

4. *Ibid.*, 84; *Calhoun Papers*, XV, 393, 395–96, 403, 411, 416, 417, 420–21, X, 254.

were such good planter-managers that they managed to wring out small profits almost every year. Despite his long absences from Fort Hill, Calhoun kept a careful watch on his plantation, and though never free of debt to his factors in Augusta and Charleston, he and his family maintained for the times and the region a high standard of living. He was also able to indulge his passion for experimental agriculture and the latest in farm equipment, which he usually purchased in the North and had shipped to Pendleton. Active in the Pendleton Agricultural Society, Calhoun subscribed to several agriculture journals. He and Mahlon Dickerson, a senator from New Jersey and an avid horticulturist, exchanged information on the grafting of fruit trees. Joel Poinsett, a congressman from northeastern South Carolina and a political opponent, shared with Calhoun his expertise on subtropical plants, flowers, and trees.

During his vice-presidential years, Calhoun was able to spend much more time at home engaging in his beloved agricultural pursuits and enjoying his family. He was an indulgent father who took great pride in his four sons and two daughters. Seventeen-year-old Andrew was tall and lean like his father, but a far more relaxed person than Calhoun had been at his age. He also had a touch of humor in his makeup, which his serious-minded father never seemed to understand. With Calhoun's encouragement Andrew decided on a military career, but when his father secured an appointment for him at West Point, he changed his mind. Then he expressed an interest in attending Yale and with his father's assistance was accepted for the class of 1831. Calhoun wrote his former teachers at Yale asking that they give Andrew a private examination to determine whether he should enter the sophomore or the junior class. He was particularly concerned about Andrew's possible roommates. "I would deem an idle and immoral room mate a great misfortune," he wrote. "He leaves me with habits of industry and correct moral deportment and I would consider it *the* greatest misfortune if he should return without them."[5]

Andrew's sister Anna Maria was eleven years old in 1828. In appearance she resembled her mother—dark hair, dark eyes, small in stature. Her personality, however, was more like her father's. Even as a child, she was a serious person who gave every indication of a deep interest in current economic and political events. Calhoun responded to his studious, petite daughter. Of all his children, she remained his favorite and in later years became his confidante. Patrick, who was

5. *Calhoun Papers,* XI, 82.

seven, three-year-old Martha Cornelia, and the babies John C., Jr., and James Edward, completed the family, for the time being. Theirs was a busy household, with relatives and friends appearing at all hours. Although Calhoun, even at home, was either supervising his work force or closeted in his study, he tried his best to make up for his long absences in Washington. Still, the major responsibility for educating and training the children fell to Floride, who also had her share of responsibilities in the management of the plantation. Her duties included caring for sick slaves, supervising the black midwives, and always catering to her mother, who spent much of her time with the Calhouns and was becoming increasingly eccentric as she grew older.

Distractions apart, Calhoun managed to set aside several hours each day for study and writing early in the morning before his customary tour of inspection. But in the fall of 1828, he had to break his routine in order to complete the task the South Carolina legislature had asked him to perform, the formulation of a statement of grievances on the tariff that would appear as a legislative report. At the same time, he had to make preparations for his journey to Washington, D.C., and the second session of the Twentieth Congress. The Jackson-Calhoun ticket had triumphed in November. Jackson would take office on March 4, 1829, and Calhoun planned to take Floride and their youngest child, James Edward, with him for the inauguration. The rest of the children would remain in South Carolina under the care of various relatives. Calhoun had to have frequent conferences with his overseer, and he drew up detailed instructions on all aspects of plantation management for his employee's guidance. Despite these demands on his time, Calhoun gave the report he was preparing for the legislature priority. By late November, it was finished and being copied for transmission to Columbia.[6]

Calhoun began his report, or more properly his essay, with a familiar statement—that the tariff of 1828 was unconstitutional because it subsidized one branch of industry, manufacturing, at the expense of commerce and agriculture. He did not deny that Congress under the tax and commerce clauses of the Constitution had the power to regulate trade among the states and with foreign powers or the power to tax for the general welfare. But, Calhoun maintained, a tariff must be for revenue only; it should not tax one section for the benefit of another. It must not be levied on all the people for the exclusive enrichment of a part of the people. He granted the fact that a revenue tariff might

6. *Ibid.*, X, 431–32, 433–34.

incidentally provide protection, but its sole purpose must be the support of the national government; and it was the duty of its framers carefully and scrupulously to arrange tariff schedules to that end. Undoubtedly, Calhoun had read Thomas Cooper's free trade treatises, especially his pamphlet on the tariff of 1824, but the vice-president's economic and constitutional positions were more flexible than those of the learned president of South Carolina College. **159**

With his ground staked out, Calhoun then addressed himself to the current tariff. Were its burdens fairly distributed? What were its effects on the domestic economy and foreign trade? What was the nature of the American economy? From these specific considerations, he developed a broad analysis of power, liberty, and responsibility in which he attacked what he declared was the tyranny of majority rule. His argument developed speedily from special pleading and a restatement of the free trade position to an inquiry into the basic problem of man and society and of the nature of sovereignty. Noting the class aspects of the tariff legislation, Calhoun envisaged a gloomy future in which the worst aspects of a monied European aristocracy would be imposed on the United States and individual liberty would be extinguished in a corporate state, or what he called a "great joint stock company." He then indulged in a kind of ruthless determinism: "After we (the South) are exhausted, the contest will be between the Capitalists and Operatives, for into these two classes it ultimately must divide society. The issue of the struggle here must be the same as in Europe. Under operation of the system wages will sink much more rapidly than the prices of the necessaries of life, till the operatives will be reduced to the lowest point, where the portion of the products of their labour left to them, will be barely necessary to preserve existence."[7]

Calhoun saw this development as inevitable, stemming from the nature of man, independent of circumstances. "Irresponsible power is inconsistent with liberty," he wrote in a pre-Actonian phrase, "and must corrupt those who exercise it." What then was the remedy? Calhoun fell back on a political solution that he insisted was the original intent of the framers of the Constitution. Drawing on Madison's *Federalist* 51 (which he incorrectly attributed to Hamilton), his report of 1800 on the Alien and Sedition Acts to the Virginia legislature, Jefferson's Kentucky resolution of 1798, and a new work that had just been translated into English, Barthold Niebuhr's *History of Rome*, Calhoun focused his attention on the problem of sovereignty.[8]

7. *Ibid.,* 445–79, 480.
8. *Ibid.,* 486, 488, 494.

Originally, the states had been completely sovereign but had delegated certain enumerated powers to the national government. These were all specified and hence circumscribed while those retained to the states and the people were not. If the sovereign power were divided, what entity was to be the judge of where the boundaries lay? Not the national government, because it would have a direct interest in defining its own powers. Not the state legislatures, because they did not directly represent the people on any given issue on which sovereignties might conflict. The proper judges were conventions elected by the people on a particular issue. Calhoun dismissed the amendment provision in the Constitution as unworkable. His solution was a veto or interposition on the part of a convention in one state or several states. "Under the operation of this supreme controlling power to whose interposition no one can object, all controversy between the States and General Government would be thus adjusted and the Constitution would gradually acquire by its constant interposition in important cases, all the perfection of which the work of man is susceptible."[9]

Calhoun, in his resort to state sovereignty, went beyond both Madison and Jefferson in their reaction to the Alien and Sedition Acts. They had sought simply to assert the rights of states, not to claim original sovereignty for them. Yet once Calhoun advanced this theory, he hastened to couch it in a historical context.[10] He drew a clear distinction between the substance and the exercise of power. The states held the substance of original sovereignty; the central government within prescribed limits exercised the collective will of the people as expressed through the states. Calhoun accepted judicial review as the appropriate source for interpreting the constitutional limits of the central government but emphatically not as an arbitrator between reserved and enumerated powers.[11] To those who might argue that interposition, state veto, or, as it came to be called, nullification, would place the minority over the majority, Calhoun countered with the assertion that he sought balance, not supremacy—an additional counterpoise that was now warranted by economic change not foreseen by the framers.[12] The states would act in a Niebuhrian sense as the Roman tribunate in protecting established institutions with their vetoes and ensuring minority interests against the incursions of an oligarchy that he saw in the making.

9. *Ibid.*, 523.
10. *Ibid.*, 504.
11. *Ibid.*, 524. Gerald M. Capers does not make this distinction (*John C. Calhoun, Opportunist: A Re-appraisal* [Gainesville, Fla., 1960], 131).
12. *Calhoun Papers*, X, 526.

Only towards the end of the document did Calhoun depart from the high plane he had taken in developing an eloquent and original defense of minority rights against class legislation. He could not forebear from charging that Clay's American system was a cover for special interest groups who were usurping sovereignty, "as men invariably do, who impose burdens on others for their own benefit." It mattered not that representatives of the interests the manufacturers had put together in a protective tariff combine had been elected by a majority in their communities and were not the result of edicts from hereditary rulers; to Calhoun the evil remained the same. Nor could he abstain from adverting to "the great political revolution which will displace from power on the 4th of March next, those who have acquired authority by setting the will of the people at defiance" and which would restore the "pure principles of our government."[13] Although he counseled delay in taking any impetuous action to nullify the tariff, Calhoun remained adamant about the dangers to the Republic from uninhibited majority rule and class legislation. Notwithstanding his brilliant theoretical display, his bold generalizations on power and sovereignty, Calhoun still conveyed the threat of direct action.

Yet Calhoun was deeply concerned that the situation in Columbia might get out of hand and that the hotheads, like his close friend McDuffie, might stampede the state legislature into rash action against the general government. All through that hot and humid summer, emotions among the vociferous planter population had been worked up to a near-frenzy of excitement. The whole tenor of the argument Calhoun built up in the "Exposition" was aimed to present the case in a cool, considered manner that would dampen any drastic moves yet would set in motion the machinery for repeal of the tariff act. It would also warn other sections of the Union against any future legislation that an increasingly self-conscious South might consider punitive, especially on the subject of slavery.

The document was cast in a defensive mode, reflecting Calhoun's sense of personal isolation and alienation from what the Union of his youth and young manhood had become. Repeatedly he underscored the growing weakness of his state and his region in terms of population, of wealth, of the inflexibility of its capital, bound up as it was in land and slaves at the mercy, as he saw it, of outside sources, northern and European bankers and markets, that were surely reducing his state and region to a colonial status. Judging Calhoun's thought from this viewpoint, which in some respects foreshadows the agrarian populism

13. *Ibid.,* 531.

of a later day, and in other respects an extension of the original intent of the founding fathers, one sees that his understanding of a national union based on reciprocal interests had never changed. Despite the censure of Thomas Cooper, who had accused him of being a Federalist, Calhoun had gone beyond the Madisonian position on a division of powers and, in emphasizing the contractual nature of the government, claimed original sovereignty for the states.[14]

To some extent, like Jefferson before him, Calhoun was emphasizing a balance of interests and hence of power. This balance rested on what he took to be a common understanding under which a republican government operated for the benefit of not just individual liberty but equality of opportunity for the free white population wherever they resided. It was his understanding that the framers of the Constitution meant to protect and encourage local institutions as the best entities for promoting freedom and adapting to a changing environment while at the same time providing both security and stability for society.

Calhoun's argument went farther than that of Jefferson and of John Taylor in reshaping the ideas of republicanism. In his formulation, the republican stance was not merely a static defense of the old order but a means of instilling a new vigor in the South's attitudes whereby the slave-plantation system would strengthen itself through subordinate economic activities like commerce, manufacturing, and transportation, which were to be developed locally at local expense and controlled through local auspices. These interests would of course interact with the plantation economy but would never become dominant in the culture.

Calhoun saw in the Clay-Adams "coalition" an engine that, in its drive for change, was seeking to subvert the Union of the fathers for the particular interests of a certain class in a certain region. Clay's American system was the means through which the instrumentalities of government would extract maximum capital for the growth of industry from the agricultural economy, particularly the one-cotton-crop producers. In what might well be termed an early expression of Manchester economics, Calhoun advanced a theory of interests that focused on the centrality of markets. The livelihood of southern cotton producers and their commercial auxiliaries was determined by prices set in the world market. Other agricultural interests like hemp, wool, and foodstuffs and manufactured items like textiles were produced

---

14. See Cooper's pamphlet *Consolidation: An Account of Parties in the United States from the Convention of 1787 to the Present* (Columbia, S.C., 1824) *passim*.

primarily for domestic consumption. Hence plantation commodities, according to Calhoun's thinking, that were sold in the world market were being unfairly taxed through protective tariffs for the benefit of interests outside of the South.[15] As a careful scholarship has argued, Calhoun sought to institutionalize compromise in such a way that it would protect ever-changing minority interests.

Thus Calhoun would prevent any significant displacement of resources as much for the future of the Union as for the security and prosperity of his admittedly weaker section. He intended to achieve this end through what he perceived to be constitutional and lawful means. He was so concerned about the fate of his report that he postponed his trip to Washington, D.C., for almost a month while the state legislature debated his propositions.

Already the party apparatus in South Carolina showed signs of polarization. Two of Calhoun's closest friends and associates, James Hamilton, Jr., and McDuffie, had joined with Chancellor William Harper and a new face in South Carolina politics, the red-haired, impetuous editor of the Charleston *Mercury,* Robert Barnwell Rhett, to demand radical measures even if they led to secession from the Union. On the other side, counseling patience and relying on lawful means of protest, were the misshapen, scholarly lawyer from Charleston, Hugh Legaré, and the rich rice planter and congressman Colonel William Drayton. Calhoun had cast his lot with the moderates and had drawn on his political power and prestige in the legislature to hold the extremists in check. He did not leave for Washington until he was assured that the legislature would have his "Exposition" printed and that the "Protest" resolutions did not threaten a resort to force if the Congress balked at immediate action.[16] The legislature had five thousand copies of the two documents printed and distributed but took no further

15. John Taylor, *Construction Construed and Construction Vindicated* (Richmond, Va., 1830), 49–50; Robert Shalhope, "Thomas Jefferson's Republicanism and Antebellum Southern Thought," *Journal of Southern History,* XLII, No. 4 (November, 1976), 544–55. See Calhoun's opinions voiced years later on this point in *Calhoun Works,* I, 48, 49, 87–89; T. P. Govan, "American Below the Potomac," in Charles Sellers (ed.), *The Southerner as American* (Chapel Hill, 1960), 21; Pauline Maier, "The Road Not Taken: Nullification, John C. Calhoun, and the Revolutionary Tradition in South Carolina," *South Carolina Historical Magazine,* LXXXII, No. 1 (January, 1981), 16.

16. See Calhoun's letter to William C. Preston and that of January 6, 1829, in which he states emphatically that he is seeking reform, not revolution (*Calhoun Papers,* X, 545, 546). William H. Denney, in "South Carolina's Conception and the Union in 1832," *South Carolina Historical Magazine,* LXXVIII, No. 3 (July, 1977), 171, argues persuasively that Calhoun took a conservative stance on nullification, as opposed to the extremists.

action. Calhoun's authorship was concealed, though word soon leaked out that he had drafted the reports.

Calhoun realized that his public indictment of northern and western entrepreneurs was not politic for a man in his position of national importance and that it might indeed injure his standing with the Nashville committee, which was anxious to avoid controversial issues. But three overriding considerations had determined his course. First, he was determined to maintain his political position in South Carolina in the face of inveterate political foes like Senator Smith, Dr. Cooper, and other Crawford followers in the state. The tariff issue had become far too significant among the electorate for him to sidestep, if he had had any desire to avoid taking a position. Second, he saw opportunity in the tariff controversy to consolidate enough nationwide opinion so that the new administration would be required to make repeal or effective compromise a matter of policy from the outset. Finally, he intended his "Exposition" to be a direct challenge to Martin Van Buren—an argument that would appeal to all southerners, but especially the Crawford contingent and the shaken alliance of "planters and plain Republicans" that he had once espoused.

Calhoun had been somewhat disconcerted when he learned that Van Buren would run for governor of New York. After Van Buren's election to that highly visible and politically important post, Calhoun must have wondered whether his rival would remain for a time out of national politics.[17] When Calhoun reached Washington, D.C., for the short term of the Twentieth Congress in late December, 1828, however, any hopes he may have harbored about Van Buren's future had been dashed. Van Buren was virtually certain to be named secretary of state. The New York governorship seemed now simply a tactic to provide the "little magician" with additional political stature in the new administration.

Observers in Washington, D.C., saw three distinct factions emerging among the Jacksonians—those who favored Van Buren, Calhoun's group, and some congressmen who were attracted to Postmaster General John McLean, primarily because of his patronage.[18] At this stage it appeared that Calhoun's friends, among whom were Littleton Tazewell, the senior senator from Virginia, and Samuel Ingham of Pennsylvania, were the most numerous. The Van Buren men, headed by Silas Wright and C. C. Cambreleng, were unable to thwart the election of

17. *Calhoun Papers*, X, 425, 426.
18. Edward Everett to Joseph Blunt, November 23, 1828, EMHS.

Duff Green as printer for both houses. Jubilant, overconfident Green at once began an editorial campaign in the *Telegraph,* which took for granted that Jackson would serve only one term and hinted that Calhoun was a logical candidate to succeed him. The casual Tennessee senator John H. Eaton, who had recently married the equally casual Peggy O'Neil Timberlake to the scandal of official Washington, represented the president-elect, but few knew his policies, except that he had supported the tariff of 1828 along with Van Buren.

Van Buren had early decided that he needed a personal emissary who enjoyed a relationship with Jackson. James A. Hamilton, the urbane son of Alexander Hamilton, fit the bill. As one of Van Buren's "high minded Federalists," he was now a Jacksonian in good standing. He had represented Van Buren at the celebration commemorating Jackson's victory at New Orleans. Rachel Jackson had been particularly taken with this handsome scion of a great New York family—a factor that counted much with the general. Hamilton had acted also as an intermediary between the Crawford group and the Nashville committee. He was trusted by Jackson's advisors and those Crawford followers who still bitterly opposed Calhoun.

When Jackson arrived in Washington on February 12, 1829, and set up temporary headquarters at Gadsby's Hotel, Hamilton was on hand to represent Van Buren. Calhoun was also an early visitor. He must have been somewhat chagrined to find Hamilton with the president-elect when he called late in the evening of February 13. As soon as Hamilton excused himself, Calhoun came directly to the point. Later, Jackson reported their conversation to Hamilton: "He wishes me to appoint Tazewell Secretary of State and urged it upon me with great earnestness, dwelling much on his great knowledge and wisdom and particularly the great influence this appointment would have upon Virginia."[19] Since Jackson had already made up his mind to offer the post to Van Buren, he listened carefully but made no comment. However, Calhoun's visit must have had some impact, because Jackson soon afterwards offered the post of minister to England to Tazewell without consulting his secretary of state designate. At about the same time, he offered the lucrative, politically powerful office of collector of the port of New York to Samuel Swartwout, an old crony of dubious speculative instincts. Swartwout was close to Calhoun, and his appointment was a distinct affront to Van Buren—indeed, a move that struck at the core of

19. James A. Hamilton, *Reminiscences of James A. Hamilton during Three Quarters of a Century* (New York, 1869), 63, 65–69, 75, 79–82.

the Albany Regency's base in New York City. If Van Buren failed to exclude a dangerous partisan in a subordinate, though politically powerful position, Calhoun failed to have two of his close associates included in secondary administrative posts. Eaton rebuffed his overtures in favor of his former War Department chief clerk, Christopher Vandeventer, for appointment to the same position he had held under Calhoun. And neither Jackson, to whom Calhoun made a direct appeal, nor Ingham, his friend and supporter in the Treasury Department, would appoint Virgil Maxcy to be treasurer of the United States. Jackson and Van Buren felt that they must placate Virginia and especially Ritchie's junto. The appointment, at Ritchie's behest, went to John Campbell.[20]

Calhoun had no direct influence on the makeup of Jackson's cabinet, which all thought would indicate who would be the guiding spirit of the new administration. Eaton, Jackson himself, and his two aides, the hulking William B. Lewis and his nephew and namesake Andrew Jackson Donelson, determined the composition of the cabinet. Through Hayne and Hamilton, Calhoun had sought the treasury post for Langdon Cheves, formerly head of the Bank of the United States and widely respected as a financier. Cheves, a close associate of Calhoun during his early years in Congress and the War Department, had recently returned to South Carolina, his native state, from a long sojourn in the North. He was considered to share Calhoun's views on the tariff, and it was thought he would use his position as secretary of the treasury to move the administration towards free trade. But Jackson turned down the Carolinians. They did manage to have Ingham, their second choice, installed in the Treasury Department. Van Buren, however, received the State Department, considered to be of the first rank.

McLean, a friend of Calhoun, while maintaining an independent course, stayed on as postmaster general, a temporary carry-over from the Adams administration. John Branch and John M. Berrien, both southerners and slaveholders, were appointed secretary of the navy and attorney general, respectively, primarily through the influence of Eaton and Jackson's aides. Eaton himself became secretary of war, and after a brief period of some confusion, McLean resigned to become an associate justice of the Supreme Court. William T. Barry, an amiable westerner and a friend of Jackson's who had just been defeated for the

20. *Ibid.*, 101; *Calhoun Papers*, XI, 143; J. C. Fitzpatrick (ed.), *The Autobiography of Martin Van Buren* (Washington, D.C., 1920), 262, 263; *Calhoun Papers*, XI, 26–28, 48, 63; Andrew Jackson to Van Buren, April 4, 1829, Van Buren to Campbell, April 17, 21, 1829, Van Buren to Ritchie, April 13, 19, 1829, VBLC.

governorship of Kentucky, took his place as postmaster general. With the exception of Van Buren, the cabinet was considered by Jacksonians and their opponents alike to be definitely lackluster—"the millenium of minnows," as one contemporary observer remarked. Yet Calhoun had "no reason to complain"; he wrote Major Vandeventer, "a majority, I believe to be friendly."[21]

Jackson and his aides had made an earnest though clumsy effort to show no preference for either Van Buren or Calhoun in the composition of the cabinet. Unfortunately for the future effectiveness of Jackson's councilors and the harmony of his administration, the Eaton appointment would be most disruptive. Not only was Eaton incompetent in an administrative sense, but he and his new bride, Peggy, had exaggerated pretensions, originating probably in her background, which had a whiff of scandal about it. It was said that the shapely daughter of a Washington, D.C., tavern keeper had had affairs and perhaps even an abortion, and that she had lived with Senator Eaton without benefit of matrimony. Much of this was speculation, but there had been enough gossip about fair Peggy around the tea tables of the Washington ladies to stamp her a woman of easy virtue. Calhoun was well aware of the rumors that circulated about Peggy and the president's heated defense of her. He also knew enough about Jackson's personality and his concepts of loyalty to realize that any social rebuff to the Eatons could create difficulties.[22]

When the Eatons paid their first social call on the vice-president, Calhoun was not at home, but Floride was. Although again pregnant and somewhat indisposed, she was civil to the Eatons, who, after a brief conversation, took their leave. The following day Floride mentioned their visit and said that she would not return the compliment. In the tight little protocol-bound world of the capital, this could only be interpreted as a calculated snub. Floride said that she knew nothing about Peggy, whether the rumors about her sex life were true or false, but she would certainly not take the lead in recognizing someone socially about whom there were so many questions. Calhoun foresaw problems in his relationship with the president but bowed to Floride's decision as essentially her prerogative.[23] Soon afterwards, the Cal-

21. James A. Hamilton to Van Buren, February 18, 19, 1829, in Hamilton, *Reminiscences*, 99; William Wirt to William Pope, March 22, 1829, in John P. Kennedy, *Memoirs of the Life of William Wirt* (2 vols.; Philadelphia, 1849), II, 228; *Calhoun Papers*, XI, 11.

22. Van Buren to Churchill C. Cambreleng, February 1, 1829, VBLC; Fitzpatrick (ed.), *Autobiography of Martin Van Buren*, 364.

23. Fitzpatrick (ed.), *Autobiography of Martin Van Buren*, 476, 477.

houns returned to South Carolina and escaped for the time being the social imbroglio that rapidly took on political overtones. Peggy and the White House, however, had noted Floride's snub.

Calhoun's suspected authorship of the South Carolina "Exposition" and his involvement with the nullification movement had already aroused Jackson's suspicions about his Unionism and his personal loyalty. Calhoun himself had recognized that his support for the antitariff position in South Carolina would open him up to criticism in other areas of the nation and might well jeopardize his succession to the presidency. He was not surprised when Marcus Morton, a Massachusetts Jacksonian, wrote that "there are two subjects permanent and unavoidable operating against you. These are the slavery subject and the tariff subject." But Calhoun felt that he had to make a stand, that he had to articulate what he had come to believe was an impending offensive on the social and economic institutions of his state and region.

The Calhouns had not been in Pendleton long when complaining letters began to arrive from his friends in Washington, D.C., which seemed to portend not just confusion in appointments but a concerted effort to isolate him politically. Shortly before he left for Washington, James Hamilton, Jr., governor of South Carolina, spent several days at Fort Hill en route from an extended visit north. Hamilton fancied himself a master player in the political game but was often embarrassing to Calhoun. He convinced Calhoun that the latter should make an effort to reestablish cordial relations with Van Buren. Hamilton agreed to act as spokesman and wrote a fulsome letter to "the little magician," which put that subtle operator on guard.[24]

Calhoun had learned that Jackson would be a candidate for a second term and that Van Buren now seemed to have superceded Eaton, Lewis, and Donelson as his most influential advisor. Despite his efforts through Hamilton to conciliate Van Buren, it was with no enthusiasm that Calhoun left Pendleton in mid-November of 1829.[25] Floride did not accompany him. In August she had borne her fifth son and last child, William Lowndes Calhoun. With Martha Cornelia five and James only three, and with the new infant to consider, the Calhouns judged it best for the family not to undertake the difficult trip. Calhoun's suspicions that the Peggy Eaton affair was being used to discredit him with the president were confirmed when he reached Washington. The cabi-

24. *Calhoun Papers*, XI, 30, 31, 48, 49, 43; James Hamilton, Jr., to Van Buren, November 16, 1829, VBLC.

25. *Calhoun Papers*, XI, 109, 117, 122, 123.

net was now divided into opposite camps, and Calhoun had no choice but to range himself with those who would not receive Peggy. But it was the president's first annual message to Congress that really put Calhoun on the defensive and created an instant uproar among many southern congressmen, especially those in the South Carolina delegation.

On the all-important issue of the tariff, southerners found Jackson's message deeply disappointing. It proposed no significant changes, and certainly no tampering with the protective principle. A federally funded internal improvements program, a policy that southern and western interests favored, was found to be unconstitutional unless clearly interstate and directly related to national security. The president anticipated a revenue surplus, which he recommended be distributed to the states on the basis of population—another means, as Calhoun saw it, to discriminate against a minority section. Finally, Jackson castigated the Bank of the United States, suggesting that it was not too soon to consider whether its charter should be renewed.

To Calhoun and most of his fellow South Carolinians, the message proved that the president was but a puppet in the hands of Van Buren. The administration's position on internal improvements was clearly a device to protect New York's Erie Canal while forcing the rest of the country, particularly South Carolina with its slender resources, to fend for itself. Tariff policy was of course dictated by northern manufacturers, and the bank recommendation was simply a move by northern bankers to monopolize credit and currency for their own section. How could the underdeveloped South and West be misled by an administration so wholly incompatible with their basic interests? As Calhoun, Hayne, and other southerners who had now endured amost ten years of agricultural depression cast about for a means to form a viable coalition that would check Van Buren's influence in the administration, Samuel Foote, a Connecticut senator, provided them with one.

Foote, formerly a Federalist and an Adams supporter, moved a resolution that would suspend the sale of government-owned lands in the West. When Thomas Hart Benton of Missouri, speaking for the land-hungry West, reacted heatedly to the Foote Resolution, Calhoun and Hayne saw their chance to isolate the Northeast on the land issue. They simply awaited a better opportunity. It came on January 18, 1830, when Benton again attacked the resolution.[26]

That burly, large-featured senator, in full, grandiloquent flights of

26. Thomas Hart Benton, *Thirty Years' View* (2 vols.; New York, 1854–56), I, 130–32.

rhetoric, accused the manufacturing states of trying to limit westward migration so that they might preserve their labor supply—an argument that had been leveled against the Federalists some thirty years earlier. Before he closed, Benton indicated that the West might well reverse its position on the tariff and no longer support what he declared was a subsidy to eastern interests. After several New England senators offered rebuttals and Calhoun's enemy, fellow Carolinian William Smith, spoke of state sovereignty and even brought up the threat of secession if the tariff were not modified, the handsome, spare senator Robert Y. Hayne, resplendent in gleaming white stock and London-tailored frock coat, rose to make his reply. This scion of one of South Carolina's most illustrious families, well-bred, rich, and highly intelligent, was a match for any speaker in Congress. In mastery of material and in extemporaneous argument few men of his day could compare with Hayne's wit and fluency on the public rostrum. Instead of excoriating the New Englanders, as Benton had done, Hayne proposed a practical solution to the problem, a federal land policy that would be most beneficial to the western states. Clearly bidding for western support on the tariff, Hayne was offering in return southern assistance on the public land issue. He did not allude to Smith's position, nor was there even a hint of secession in his remarks. Other southern senators supported Hayne.[27]

By now all Washington was aware that a great debate was in the making. The Northeast had to reply and recapture if possible the initiative that Hayne and Calhoun had seized. Daniel Webster was the only spokesman for the manufacturing states who had the ability to articulate their position and compete on even ground with the polished, adroit Hayne. On January 20, 1830, before a capacity audience composed primarily of Washington's ladies in the galleries and even on the floor of the Senate chamber, the stocky, deep-browed Webster began his reply to Hayne. His was an effective speech delivered in his rolling periods replete with dramatic pauses, but as Calhoun quickly recognized, he had shifted the argument from land policy directly to the constitutional aspects of the tariff issue.

Webster had studied the problem of sovereignty carefully and was familiar with the arguments set forth by Cooper, Turnbull, McDuffie, and other South Carolina extremists. He was thoroughly cognizant of Calhoun's own arguments on the subject in his "Exposition." And as

27. *Ibid.*, 186, 132–38; Theodore D. Jervey, *Robert Y. Hayne and His Times* (New York, 1909), 233–39.

Webster developed his points one by one, Calhoun understood what the great orator was attempting—to draw Hayne into a constitutional debate on nullification. Both Calhoun and Hayne welcomed the opportunity not just to defend their cause but to expose, as they saw it, New England's consistent attacks on liberty, its own near-treason in the War of 1812, its responsibility for the slave trade, and Webster's convoluted stand on tariff policy. Hayne made these points in a long address the following day.[28]

Webster began his second reply to Hayne on January 26. Again the small Senate chamber was filled to overflowing. Over a period of two days he spoke, occasionally glancing at one or two notes, his deep baritone voice alternating in cadence and pitch, his gestures carefully but dramatically used to emphasize a point or a turn of phrase. The first day he spent repudiating Hayne's charges, gradually shifting his emphasis to a constitutional position that stressed the supremacy of the national government within its prescribed limits. His argument followed closely Marshall's opinion in the McCulloch case. He brushed aside Calhoun's compact theory of state sovereignty and pointed out that the Constitution was the supreme law of the land acting through the states directly upon the people.

Webster did not ignore Calhoun but, pausing in his declarations and staring directly up at the vice-president, implied that Calhoun's position on internal improvements could be construed as inconsistent. Calhoun interrupted him. "Did he understand the Senator from Massachusetts to say that the person now occupying the chair of the Senate has changed his opinion on the subject of internal improvements?" Webster denied any imputation. When he reached the climax of his speech, he had his audience's sympathy completely as he intoned those ringing phrases on the permanence of the Union and asked his fellow countrymen to join him in celebrating the triumph of patriotism and nationalism over nullification and disorder. Even Calhoun, who viewed the scene with a dispassionate calm, was momentarily affected by the wave of emotion that engulfed the chamber.[29]

After the debate was over, Webster had certainly scored the most points, perhaps not in the Senate hall or in South Carolina, but in the country at large. When he had edited his remarks carefully, Gales and Seaton, the publishers of the *Intelligencer,* sent thousands of copies of the speech in pamphlet form throughout the land. Andrew Jackson

28. Benton, *Thirty Years' View,* 241–52.

29. *Webster Papers,* III, 18, 19; Maurice G. Baxter, *One and Inseparable: Daniel Webster and the Union* (Cambridge, Mass., 1984), 179–93; Benton, *Thirty Years' View,* I, 134–42.

read the speech in the White House. He had followed the entire debate with mounting interest. Although his sympathies were entirely with Webster, he, and Van Buren especially, realized that prompt action was needed or the South and the West might unite and force a drastic reduction in the tariff. Should this occur, Calhoun, not Van Buren, would assume leadership in what was being referred to as the Democratic-Republican party, or more increasingly, the Democratic party.

An opportunity arose for the administration to make public its opposition to nullification. Benton had taken the lead in arranging for an elaborate dinner at Brown's Indian Queen Hotel to celebrate Jefferson's birthday on April 13, 1830. Benton's purpose was to emphasize the existence of the new Democratic party, to identify it with Jeffersonian principles, and to head off any change in government policy on public lands. He brought together all the leaders of the recent Jacksonian coalition, including Hayne, who represented the slaveholding planters, and Cambreleng, a spokesman for the northern entrepreneurs.[30]

Calhoun, who still hoped for a change in administration posture and a party consensus on the tariff issue, accepted an invitation as one of the guests of honor. Jackson indicated that he would attend, as did Van Buren. Calhoun expected some announcement from the president, and he prepared himself accordingly. Hayne had been selected to make the address of the evening; the remainder of the program would be taken up with toasts.

Just before the dinner, Van Buren met with Jackson and Major Donelson at the White House. Assuming that Hayne's remarks would be vigorously against the tariff and that he would probably allude to nullification, the group decided that the president's response in the form of a toast would announce his policy on what they all felt was a divisive issue. The program indicated that Calhoun, who would be seated to the right of the chairman, the elderly John Roane of Virginia, would respond to Jackson's lead-off special toast. Van Buren would follow. The group thought that, for prime effectiveness, Jackson's toast should be short and as pungent as possible, but should express clearly Webster's position on the indivisible union. The few words were written out on a scrap of paper and no doubt sounded for effect. Recalled Van Buren, "Thus armed, we repaired to the dinner with feelings on the part of the old Chief akin to those which would have animated his

30. Benton, *Thirty Years' View,* I, 148–49.

breast if the scene of this preliminary skirmish in defense of the Union had been the field of battle instead of the festive board."[31]

At Brown's, Hayne was in his usual fine form. He denounced the tariff but avoided any blunt remarks in support of nullification. Nevertheless, when volunteer toasts began and took an antitariff turn, the Pennsylvania delegates walked out. Tension rose in the dining hall. Everyone could sense a contentious mood that seemed to sharpen the noise of conversation, the clatter of dishes, and the tramp of waiters. Calhoun became increasingly tense as the time for the special toasts began. Roane gestured for silence and in a few brief words introduced the president. Jackson rose, holding his glass before him, but instead of directing his gaze out over the audience, he turned and stared directly at Calhoun. "Our Union," he said, "It must be preserved." Then he held up his glass, indicating that all should stand. When everyone, including Calhoun, had risen to his feet, Jackson sipped his wine and sat down. Calhoun was next to offer a toast. With all eyes upon him, his hand shook slightly as he in turn addressed the president, but his voice was firm. "The Union," he said, "next to our liberty most dear." Calhoun should have ended it there. He felt, however, that he had to make his point unmistakably clear. In doing so, he muted the effectiveness of his reply and at the same time increased Jackson's suspicions of his intentions. "May we all remember," he continued, "that it can only be preserved by respecting the rights of the states and by distributing equally the benefits and the burdens of the Union."[32]

For the next several weeks, the Washington press debated the meaning of the dinner and the toasts.[33] The *Intelligencer* claimed that the affair, under the guise of a Jeffersonian celebration, had been designed to force free trade on the country, and it hailed Jackson's toast as a forthright rejection of such an ulterior motive. Quick to respond, the *Telegraph* insisted that Jackson was merely calling upon all parties to compose their differences, particularly those expressed through the extreme pretensions of the manufacturers.

While the debate ground on, in a gesture of political support for the administration Calhoun broke a tie in favor of Amos Kendall's appointment to the fourth auditor's position in the Treasury Department. Kendall was a Massachusetts-born, New Hampshire–educated Yankee who had moved to Frankfort, Kentucky, where he edited the *Argus of*

31. Fitzpatrick (ed.), *Autobiography of Martin Van Buren,* 414.
32. *Ibid.,* 257; Benton, *Thirty Years' View,* I, 148–49.
33. *Clay Papers,* VIII, 195.

Western America and, together with Francis Preston Blair, had been a major force in carrying Kentucky for Jackson. Calhoun was also instrumental in the confirmation of another newspaperman close to Van Buren, Mordecai Noah, the mercurial editor of the New York *Courier.* But he was unsuccessful in rallying his supporters behind Isaac Hill of the Concord *Patriot,* who had also been nominated for a treasury post.[34]

Despite these services, the president remained distant from Calhoun. The Peggy Eaton affair had seemingly split the cabinet, aligning Berrien and Branch with Ingham on the Calhoun side against the president, Van Buren, Eaton, and Barry. Although the cabinet appeared to be divided into roughly equal parts, Calhoun had been forced into the weaker position and he knew it. Yet he found himself unable to make any headway in improving his relationship with a president he basically disliked and distrusted. And he was aware that Van Buren and the men around Jackson were seeking to rake up the old charges that he had disapproved Jackson's forays in West Florida and had wanted the general court-martialed for insubordination.

James A. Hamilton, Van Buren's unofficial envoy, had corresponded with Calhoun about these allegations during the presidential campaign. Factors that had to be considered were the letter Monroe had written to Calhoun that was stolen from his file and the unwavering enmity of William H. Crawford, who might well break cabinet confidentiality if he could injure Calhoun. Calhoun believed that he had acted correctly in cabinet counsel. But given Jackson's acute sensitivity about his past actions in Florida, Calhoun must not have been completely surprised when he received a terse note from the White House enclosing a copy of a letter from Crawford to John Forsyth, a senator from Georgia, that gave his version of Calhoun's position. Jackson claimed that Crawford's account was at variance with letters of Calhoun in his possession and requested an explanation. Had Calhoun been a better politician or even a person less conscious of his own rectitude, he could have disarmed Jackson with a personal explanation of his and Crawford's differences in this matter. A defensive attitude governed Calhoun's actions, however. His indignant reply was as curt as the president's note had been and implied that Van Buren was the source "of secret and mysterious attempts, which have been in making by false insinuations for political purpose for years to injure my character."[35]

34. *Calhoun Papers,* XI, 143, 149, 191, 192, 201, 202; Thomas Ritchie to William C. Rives, April 15, 1830, in William Cabell Rives Papers, Library of Congress.
35. *Calhoun Papers,* XI, 162, 163.

Jackson replied in kind, and for the next eight months the two men conducted occasional written skirmishes that brought into the fray former president Monroe and his entire cabinet, Van Buren, James A. Hamilton, Forsyth, and various other politicians on both sides of the argument. Faced with the impending presidential campaign against Clay, Jackson, on the advice of Van Buren and others in the party, sought to compromise the difficulty. By now, Calhoun had so completely backed himself into a corner on matters of policy as well as politics that he spurned the offer. Rather, he sought vindication by presenting his views to the public in the form of thirty-five documents that he placed in the hands of Duff Green for publication in the *Telegraph* and later distribution as a fifty-two-page pamphlet.[36]

There were some last-minute efforts to forestall publication, and Calhoun did make the manuscript available to the president for any changes he might wish to make. But Eaton, to whom it was passed, never brought it before Jackson. With the appearance of the pamphlet, the break between the president and vice-president became final.

Although Calhoun did not directly accuse Van Buren of being an accomplice of Crawford in the conspiracy, he strongly implied Van Buren's involvement through the agency of James A. Hamilton. Green was more direct in accusing Van Buren in the editorial column of the *Telegraph*. Green was not only defending Calhoun but battling for his paper's survival against a new press, the *Globe*, that had now become the administration's mouthpiece. Kendall, whom Calhoun had originally supported, was the architect of the administration's change in its public information policies.

In December, 1830, just as Calhoun had decided to make public his side of the controversy with Jackson, Kendall had brought his former partner Francis Preston Blair from Kentucky to establish a paper, the *Globe*, that would vie with the *Telegraph* for government patronage and articulate much more closely the administration's political and economic position. Blair, a wraithlike figure with broad temples and a sharp chin, was a master of the cut-and-thrust journalism that was long on innuendo and heated rhetoric, and short on fact. His penetrating style, which soon became apparent, had the peculiar facility of goading his adversaries to a frenzy. In this kind of journalistic savagery, Green, for all his bravado, was an easy target. It would not be long before Calhoun's principal defense in the capital would be driven out as much

36. Lyon G. Tyler, *The Letters and Times of the Tylers* (2 vols.; Richmond, Va., 1884), I, 424.

from loss of patronage as from Green's own indiscretions in print.[37]

Van Buren publicly denied any complicity in the Jackson affair, which countered somewhat the bad image Calhoun's pamphlet had fixed upon him in the South. The effectiveness of Calhoun's pamphlet can be seen in the angry expostulation of Alfred Balch, Van Buren's close friend and supporter in Tennessee. Balch wrote James K. Polk a worried letter on January 6, 1831, which he concluded by saying that Calhoun's "ambition is as hot as the crater of a volcano."[38]

Van Buren, however, had earlier taken a step that helped isolate Calhoun and detach South Carolina from neighboring southern states. This was the Maysville veto, which he had drafted and persuaded Jackson to accept as a matter of public policy. The veto countermanded a bill that would have provided federal support for completing a road entirely within the state of Kentucky. In the administration's reasoning, which was couched in the purest Jeffersonian terms, the commerce clause of the Constitution did not give Congress the power to provide for road projects entirely within the boundaries of a given state unless there was an explicit need to provide for the common defense. The message was a ringing affirmation of states' rights that was most pleasing to the strict constructionists in Virginia, North Carolina, and Georgia. Not mentioned, of course, was that the wording of the veto was also incidentally a protective device for projects like New York's Erie Canal and canals already built or under construction in Pennsylvania, Maryland, and Virginia.

The Maysville veto also attacked Clay's American system at its most vulnerable point—the interests of powerful states and of expansive entrepreneurs. Politically, its Jeffersonian accents coincided with the aspirations of the less populous states. Although the underdeveloped South and West were in desperate need of public assistance for internal communications, the veto's rhetoric disguised the fact. Calhoun had long staked his political reputation on an imperial plan of internal improvements. He would never give up his vision, even though it ran counter to popular prejudice. The Maysville veto opened Calhoun to the charge of inconsistency on his concept of state sovereignty. It made his attacks on the American system seem to many, who did not comprehend the changes taking place in the social order, as merely a dis-

37. William Stickney (ed.), *Autobiography of Amos Kendall* (Washington, D.C., 1872), 370–72; Lynn Marshall, "The Early Career of Amos Kendall: The Making of a Jacksonian" (Ph.D. dissertation, University of California at Berkeley, 1962), 199.

38. *Polk Correspondence*, II, 375, 402, 403.

play to cover his insensate ambition. Even in his home state, Calhoun had to confess, the veto was well received.[39]

Van Buren had one more move to make that would eliminate the last vestige of Calhoun's influence with the president and at the same time would ease his own burden of being at the head of a cabinet that was so bitterly divided. In addition, he needed a respite from the political wrangling and the daily drudgery of his life in Washington. Van Buren managed to convince Eaton, who was likewise a target for political abuse, that both of them should resign and thus permit the president to reshape his cabinet into a more harmonious group of advisors. Eaton never understood that he and his wife Peggy were being purged, that Van Buren had concluded a reshuffled cabinet would function far better if it did not have to contend with their mischief-making activities. Van Buren's and Eaton's resignations were followed by Ingham's and, after considerable pressure from the president, those of Berrien and Branch. They were replaced with men who were closely identified with the Van Buren faction.[40]

Calhoun was at Fort Hill when these unprecedented changes were made. He had left Washington in early March after Congress adjourned and returned home by way of Richmond. There he met with Governor Floyd, the erratic governor of Virginia, and several other supporters of nullification who were also hoping to break the power of Ritchie and the junto in the state. If Calhoun had been deeply despondent at the turn of events in Washington, his spirits were raised by the encouragement of these Virginia supporters. And his optimism soared as he made his way through North Carolina and his home state.

In Columbia, where he stopped for a few days, he had several meetings with a young, brash editor, James Henry Hammond, whose paper the *Southern Times and the State Gazette* had been making an impression not just on the planters in the vicinity of the state capital but also on those in the tidewater region and even in the foothill counties. Calhoun had been a subscriber to Hammond's paper and heartily endorsed his editorial emphasis on political unity within the state. He was unusually candid with Hammond. After speaking of what he perceived to be a falling-off in Jackson's popularity, he expressed his belief that the Democratic party was about to be broken up into sectional alignments. As he warmed to his subject, Calhoun became increasingly confident of his ability to reorganize the party segments on constitutional and eco-

39. *Calhoun Papers, XI,* 259–62.
40. *Ibid.,* 267–69.

nomic issues that the Jackson administration had either ignored or pushed aside. A southern political leader like himself should be put forward for the presidency because there was a natural affinity of agricultural interest between the South and the West and even most of the North. Calhoun's comments and especially his volunteering of himself for the presidency did not move the politically astute Hammond. Nor was the youthful editor at all reserved in contradicting the great man. "I told him candidly," said Hammond, that "such a step would be imprudent at the moment."[41] Calhoun apparently took Hammond's remarks in good grace, because later they had tea and dinner together.

As the 1832 campaign for the presidency grew closer, Calhoun's capacity for self-delusion became more intense until it was brought to an abrupt halt. A rapid escalation of nullification sentiment threatened civil war in South Carolina, and at the same time the most serious slave revolt that ever occurred in the South flared up in Virginia. These two outbreaks quickly became interrelated but, instead of uniting the South with the West, produced counteracting forces that eventually isolated South Carolina and terminated for the time being Calhoun's unrealistic hopes for the presidency.

41. *Calhoun Papers*, XI, 298, 299; Drew Gilpin Faust, *James Henry Hammond and the Old South: A Design for Mastery* (Baton Rouge, 1982), 59, 60.

X

Nullification, 1831–1833

On the night of August 21, 1831, a self-taught black minister, Nat Turner, led a group of some seventy fellow slaves on a murderous expedition through Southampton County, Virginia, only fifteen to twenty miles north of the North Carolina border. Before armed local whites and a hastily gathered militia force apprehended them, the band had murdered fifty-five white men, women, and children. A tumult of horror swept through the slaveholding South. Nowhere were these fears more acute than in South Carolina, whose slave population even in the backcountry was over 50 percent of the inhabitants.

The news of the uprising reached a state whose ruling class was already seething with anger at the course of the Jackson administration on the hated "tariff of abominations." This emotional situation had become more intense as bitter arguments developed over the means to be employed for relief. The more impetuous nullifiers toyed with the thought of secession if the tariff were not modified. There was in addition a large body of highly respectable conservative opinion that counseled patience and political pressure on the federal government. Headed by Joel Poinsett, a rich rice planter, gifted horticulturist, and not so gifted diplomat, the Unionists, as they were beginning to call themselves, included such Charleston notables as Colonel William Drayton, Daniel Huger, and Hugh Legaré, who cherished a personal grudge against Calhoun. The Unionists were already in secret correspondence with President Jackson and his new secretary of war, Lewis Cass.

George McDuffie and Governor James Hamilton, Jr., of South Carolina were the leaders of the extremists, who commanded a slight majority of opinion among the planters and the yeoman farmers of the up-country. Those who followed Calhoun's reasoning that nullification, or state veto, as he preferred to call it, was a peaceful, theoretically sound process included one of Calhoun's cousins, the ambitious young Francis Pickens; Senator Hayne; and the newspaper editor James Henry Hammond.[1]

1. William W. Freehling, *Prelude to Civil War: The Nullification Controversy in South Carolina, 1816–1836* (New York, 1966), 166, 206.

The radicals gained the initiative in late May, 1831, when McDuffie, by arrangement with Governor Hamilton, electrified a Charleston audience with a three-hour speech in which he demanded nullification at all costs even if it meant revolution and disunion. This inflammatory address was printed and distributed throughout South Carolina and adjoining states. It evoked an immediate reaction from Duff Green and other friends of Calhoun in the South, who felt that unless he could somehow disassociate himself from McDuffie's passionate utterances of defiance, he was finished as an aspirant for the presidency. "I tell you in sober sadness," said Green, "that you have no other hope . . . the country cannot be made to believe in McDuffie[']s *doctrine* . . . I can hardly be mistaken in the fact that a widespread opinion prevails that there is at work in South Carolina a powerful passion of disloyalty to the government of the United States."[2]

Calhoun was as shocked as Green at McDuffie's address. The Charleston meeting "was wholly unexpected," he wrote Ingham. "I think it every way imprudent, and have so written Hamilton . . . I see clearly it brings matters to a crisis, and that I must meet it promptly and manfully." He believed that he had to take charge of the nullification movement and seek to guide it along peaceful, constructive channels while at the same time keeping up the pressure on the Jackson administration, or relinquish his position of political leadership in the state. The latter alternative was impossible for a man of Calhoun's convictions. He now realized that if he let events take their course, there could be armed hostilities between South Carolina and the central government as well as civil war within the state itself. He was well aware that in assuming leadership of the movement he would be openly identified as a nullifier, which in many parts of the Union meant traitor. As Green remarked: "His friends had been taught to believe that he was not a Nullifier. Little considering what the term implied they expected him to denounce the doctrin[e] because they expected such a measure would promote his popularity."[3]

Just when Calhoun felt that his political future looked more promising, he made this bitter decision and gave up all hope of succeeding Jackson in the presidency. To a considerable extent, he himself had been responsible for the upsurge of savage rhetoric in the state that seemed to be polarizing the political community. He had counseled the South Carolina firebrands in Congress to oppose the tariff of 1824 and

2. Edwin L. Green, *George McDuffie* (Columbia, S.C., 1936), 108–11; *Calhoun Papers*, XI, 399.

3. *Calhoun Papers*, XI, 399, 404, 459, 460.

had gone along with Van Buren's tactic in supporting the tariff of 1828. He may have been deceived, as he claimed, but he had nevertheless put his prestige and his influence behind the latter bill. Finally responding to the tariff and its reception in the South, he had overreacted and had formulated the nullification doctrine in the "Exposition" he wrote for the South Carolina legislature.

Calhoun had been driven by what he believed was the growing weakness of his state and his section in an industrializing society. Uncertain about a future in which the slave-plantation system seemed to be increasingly on the defensive, Calhoun, with his speculative mind and his latent insecurity, tended toward rationalizing a potential minority position as the only proper political logic that was blessed by Jeffersonian precedent and confirmed by historical fact. But hampering his vision of restoring the political and economic balance were two contradicting interests that he did not, and perhaps never would, recognize.

Calhoun was as interested as any other educated American in the benefits of industrial development, particularly improvements in transportation, for his state, his section, and his nation. On the other hand, he was determined to preserve the agricultural order with its accompanying system of values that was fast becoming obsolete and was essentially incompatible with the enterprise system and the free labor ethic of the North and of western Europe.[4] Practical and impractical by turn, Calhoun despite his powers of reasoning could never reconcile these two divergent themes. And complicating all was his ambition, his quest for the presidency, which to some degree shaped his course in the current controversy.

Throughout June, 1831, Calhoun waited for an appropriate time to make his position on the tariff controversy known. By mid-July, he began drafting a document that would again set forth his doctrine of state veto, which he insisted was a calm, reasonable, and practical solution to the crisis. While he studiously avoided the term *nullification,* Calhoun restated in stronger language points he had made in the "Exposition." Again basing his argument on Madison's report to the Virginia legislature and the Virginia and Kentucky resolutions, he predicted that unless the general government was confined "strictly to the sphere prescribed by the constitution, and preventing it from interfering with the peculiar and local interests of the country," the Union would be in grave jeopardy. He added the notion of concurrent majority to his essay, maintaining that the proper course of political parties

4. Stewart, "A Great Talking and Eating Machine," 205–206.

was to take the sense of all the diverse economic interests in the Union and give each its proportional weight in the governance of the country. Calhoun was aware that he was hazarding his northern and western support, but considering the situation in the state and his own convictions, he wrote Ingham: "I deemed it not only a duty, but indispensable. If I have erred, it is not because I have acted with preciptancy . . . I can scarcely dare hope, that my friends to the North will sustaine me in the positions I have taken. . . . But let me assure you, that there is not the slightest tincture of disunion in it. It is accompanied with an ardent attachment to the Union, but a still stronger one to liberty."[5]

Calhoun's paper, which came to be known as the "Fort Hill Address," appeared in the Pendleton *Messenger* on July 26. The "Address" was written for a general audience and was replete with concrete examples that were persuasive to anyone who professed to be a Jeffersonian-Republican. It was difficult for the Jackson press to refute its arguments, but the paper had one major weakness. However much Calhoun abjured the term *nullification,* the "Address" placed him squarely in the radical camp. Whatever justification Calhoun made for his action, he had unwittingly damaged his national reputation. As that shrewd diviner of political trends, John McLean, wrote Samuel Gouverneur after reading the address: "Our friend Calhoun is gone, I fear, forever. Four years past he has been infatuated with his southern doctrines. In him they originated. . . . He will not sustain himself anywhere, not even in his own state." Yet Calhoun had elevated the nullification cause beyond noisy and boastful rhetoric to a matter of constitutional and political right. If he had sacrificed his presidential ambitions, perhaps forever, he had at least supplied a ballast of reason to the frail bark of emotion. Webster's reaction to the "Fort Hill Address" was that it "was the ablest and most plausible, and therefore the most dangerous vindication of that particular form of Revolution which has yet appeared."[6] Unfortunately, the stars in their courses seemed to be striving against Calhoun.

Scarcely had the "Fort Hill Address" been published than word was received in South Carolina of the Nat Turner uprising. All classes of whites in the seaboard slave states succumbed to an instant panic that was not eased by Virginia governor John Floyd's response to an inquiry from Governor Hamilton, which was given wide circulation. Floyd claimed that there was extensive unrest among the slaves in his state.

5. *Ibid.,* 442–43.
6. Quoted in Gerald M. Capers, *John C. Calhoun, Opportunist: A Re-appraisal* (Gainesville, Fla., 1960), 148; *Webster Papers,* III, 195.

Yankee peddlers and traders had stimulated it, aided and abetted by abolitionists in New England. Religion had been the means, and though Floyd seemed to be unconscious of the fact, he condemned the alleged propagandists of spreading a doctrine that sounded much like the Declaration of Independence. They told the blacks, Floyd said:

> God was no respecter of persons; the black man was as good as the white; that all men were born free and equal; that they cannot serve two masters; that the white people rebelled against England to obtain freedom; so have the blacks a right to do. He went on to say that their own Virginia preachers and many of the white women had taught the blacks to read so that they could understand the bible. From their efforts large groups of slaves met for religious services where they listened to subversive sermons and received abolitionist tracts.

Without any substantial evidence, Floyd concluded that there was a widespread conspiracy among slave leaders to launch at some appropriate time a slave revolt throughout the South. Almost as an afterthought, he absolved the masses of slaves from any complicity, but there was no doubt about the incendiary theme of Floyd's letter.[7]

Such publicity, which was distorted out of all proportion when it permeated the emotional climate of South Carolina, swept aside Calhoun's reasoned arguments in the "Fort Hill Address." Fiery speeches led to hastily organized patrols and demands that abolitionists be harried out of the state. Personal rights and liberties guaranteed by the state and federal constitutions were set at naught. Religious services for slaves on many plantations were banned.

Even Calhoun, who was far more perceptive about such things than his neighbors, reacted much more severely than he ever had before to the insubordination of Alec, one of his house slaves. Shortly after Floyd's letter had been made public, Alec had irritated Floride, who had just had a miscarriage. When she threatened him with a "severe whipping," he ran away but was soon found near Abbeville fifty miles away. Calhoun sent instructions that he be jailed for a week and fed only bread and water, and that someone be employed to give him "30 lashes well laid on at the end of the time." By way of explanation Calhoun wrote, "I deem it necessary to our proper security to prevent the formation of the habit of running away, and I think it better to punish him before his return home than afterwards."[8] It is unknown

7. Charles Ambler, *The Life and Diary of John Floyd* (Richmond, Va., 1918), 89–91; Freehling, *Prelude to Civil War*, 64.
8. *Calhoun Papers*, XI, 463.

whether Calhoun responded to Floyd's letter and forbade religious services at his plantations; he probably did not. But the Nat Turner revolt, coinciding with an upsurge in abolitionist activity, made a decided impact. Calhoun had been increasingly concerned about antislavery agitation since the Missouri debates and had begun to associate the abolition movement with the class and sectional aspects of the tariff controversy.

Altogether, it had been an unfortunate summer for Calhoun. Despite his hazarding of his political future with the "Fort Hill Address," his risky effort had not calmed the radical nullifiers, nor had it fared well with the president, who saw treasonable intent. Floride had been ill and querulous. His son Andrew had been expelled from Yale for joining in a student fracas. And weeks of rain had caused the Seneca River to overflow its banks, flooding much of Calhoun's cotton and corn crops, which were largely destroyed. He would be deeper in debt for the coming year. The political and economic future seemed bleak indeed as he prepared to leave for Washington, D.C.[9]

Calhoun made a leisurely trip north by way of Raleigh, North Carolina, where he was feted at a public dinner, and Richmond, which he reached in early December. During the several days he spent in Virginia's capital, he discussed politics, theories of government, nullification, and the tariff with Governor Floyd and others who opposed Ritchie and the Virginia junto. A newcomer to the Calhoun circle, Richard Crallé, the youthful editor of the *Lynchburg Jeffersonian and Virginia Times,* met with the group and summarized Calhoun's conversation.

On the evening of December 4, Calhoun was particularly expansive. He attributed positive power to the general government and negative power to the states. This division, he maintained, led to an encroachment on state power. He denied that secession was applicable in any dispute between one or more states and the central government because the central government was the agent of the states. His most interesting point to his small audience involved the relationship between capital and labor. Calhoun said that capital had a tendency to destroy and absorb the property of society and produce a collision between itself and its workers. "The Federal Government by its distribution of revenue creates Capitalists, and operates upon the labour of the States," he remarked. Commenting on the current political scene, Calhoun rejected any joining of forces with Henry Clay. And he

9. *Ibid.,* 462.

would not support Jackson, whom he had earlier, in a letter to Hammond, chastised as "too ignorant, too suspicious and too weak to conduct our affairs successfully."[10]

Henry Clay, who had just been elected a senator from Kentucky, had revised his tariff ideas and was supporting internal improvements in his bid for the presidency. His position now seemed close to that of Calhoun. But the Carolinian distrusted Clay and would not respond to the feelers put out to him. He resolved to follow an independent course for the time being, probably because the Virginia legislative caucus, which met on December 17, voted overwhelmingly for Jackson but made no nomination for vice-president.[11]

185

The administration had proposed in general terms a modification of the tariff and softened its stand on the Bank of the United States. But the new secretary of the treasury, Louis McLane, cast doubt on the administration's intentions. His report disclosed that the South would experience little relief from the proposed legislation. Duties would be repealed or slashed on articles that were not being manufactured in the country; they would be retained on items of consumption basic to the plantation South, like woolens and iron. Calhoun conceded that such a tariff would lower general rates, but argued that in specific terms it would bear more heavily on the South.

Before any debate on the administration's program began, however, the recent nomination of Martin Van Buren as minister to Great Britain became of prime political importance. For weeks the appointment had been a major topic of gossip in the capital and in New York. Van Buren's many enemies were divided on whether his rejection by the Senate would help or hinder his political career. Everyone knew that the result of the congressional vote would have a significant impact on a second Virginia legislative caucus scheduled for February 29 to select a vice-presidential candidate. And this in turn might well affect the outcome of the first Democratic convention, scheduled to meet in Baltimore from May 21 to May 23, 1832. Henry Clay summed up the opposition stance in a letter to Peter B. Porter. "I think there is a more prevalent opinion among our friends as to the expediency of his rejection than existed when you left us," he said. "Of its justice none of them doubted."[12]

Calhoun understood that a rejection of Van Buren "would strengthen, rather than weaken him," but he had already decided to veto the appoint-

10. *Ibid.*, 523, 383.
11. *Clay Papers*, VIII, 437.
12. *Ibid.*, 445.

ment should he need to break a tie with his vote. That this action would be construed as a purely partisan move seems not to have concerned him. Yet the atmosphere in the Senate chamber when the Van Buren nomination came up for a vote was thick with political rhetoric. No evidence was presented that he was, as alleged, a corrupting influence in government. Clay's charges that Van Buren had toadied to British interests when he was secretary of state were without foundation.[13] Other attacks on Van Buren in executive session were even more farfetched.

The heated debate finally came up for a vote to table the nomination. At this point Daniel Webster rose and left the chamber. A tie had been contrived, whether Calhoun was a party to it or not. He promptly cast his vote to table. When the nomination was finally voted on, Calhoun again broke the tie rejecting Van Buren. Calhoun knew that the rejection virtually assured Van Buren of the vice-presidential nomination on the Jackson ticket, but he felt he had no alternative to voting as he did. With that quality of self-deception which sometimes clouded his judgment, he merged his personal feelings of dislike, distrust, and thwarted ambition with a sincere belief that Van Buren was unfit for any high office. He also shared with some of his colleagues the notion that Van Buren was so unpopular in the South and the West that he would drag the ticket down, thus leaving open the possibility of the election going into the House. Should this unlikely situation come to pass, Calhoun might have a chance for the vice-presidency if he could unite his section.

If Calhoun's judgment had been closer to the mark, he would have seen that Clay would be the principal beneficiary if the election went to the House. Calhoun's view of Clay was about the same as his attitude towards Van Buren. In assessing his vote, Calhoun commented on the damage he felt the pairing of Jackson with Van Buren had done to the Union. "Either," he wrote Ingham, "would have been comparatively harmless, without the other; but united they formed a combination which will long be remembered for its disasterous [*sic*] consequences."[14]

Calhoun did, however, briefly consider joining his fortunes with Clay. Governor Floyd of Virginia and Francis Brooke, Clay's representative in the Old Dominion, persuaded the men to come to an arrangement. In the end, Calhoun realized that he could not in good conscience accept Clay's stand on the tariff and other aspects of the American system. Clay also drew back when he learned that such a partnership would at best bring only local advantage for him in the seaboard slave states.[15]

13. *Calhoun Papers*, XI, 544, 388, 389.
14. *Ibid.*, 547, 548.
15. *Clay Papers*, VIII, 335, 484, 485.

The Van Buren rejection highlighted a session wherein the tariff debate and the bank issue were the dominant features. Calhoun took little interest in the rechartering of the Bank of the United States, which Clay was determined to make the platform for his presidential bid. Jackson was just as determined to defeat the bank and eventually destroy it as the government's depository. The South Carolina delegation split on the bank, with McDuffie, who was chairman of the House ways and means committee, its warm advocate. Calhoun continued to focus his energies on tariff reform, which, as he had remarked earlier to Ingham, seemed as far distant as ever in reducing the schedules on those basic articles deemed essential to southern planters.

Efforts were made to compromise the tariff issue, and for a time it appeared that the most blatant protective features would be scaled back. In the end, the manufacturing interests were able to maintain rates on key items though some reforms were made. The bill that Jackson signed did not meet any of South Carolina's objections—as perhaps no bill could have done at this point without a test of strength. The nullifiers in South Carolina had so conditioned themselves with their rhetoric, their preparations, and their statewide organization that only significant reform would have materially eased the situation. Political orators in South Carolina and other slave states in the aftermath of the Nat Turner revolt and the increased publicity of the abolitionists had associated the North and the tariff with emancipation.[16]

Representatives of the manufacturing interests in Congress had become just as adamant on the tariff, though they denied any attempt on their part to interfere with slavery. And they vehemently repudiated abolitionism. The administration likewise excoriated abolitionism in the columns of the *Globe* and saw the tariff as a legitimate and constitutional power of the general government. Nullification was both a threat to the Union and a step towards anarchy. Jackson, through his mouthpiece, Blair, put Calhoun and the nullifiers in South Carolina on notice that they would feel the full weight of the federal government if they tried to obstruct the law.

Despite the plain language used by the administration, Calhoun thought that it would act in the same manner as it had in a recent conflict between Georgia and the Supreme Court over the Cherokee Indians. Georgia had defied a judgment of the Supreme Court and numerous treaties between the United States and the Cherokee nation. In all these circumstances, it had nullified acts of the national government. Its position was similar to the one South Carolina contemplated,

16. Freehling, *Prelude to Civil War*, 250–52.

but Jackson had done nothing to discipline Georgia. Calhoun had counted on strengthening his case politically by exposing the administration's inconsistency, but he found himself again a loser. Public opinion, except in certain areas of New England, supported Georgia's callous treatment of the Indians. Still, Calhoun hoped to have the last word on the Georgia case. He planned to have first the state courts and then the federal judiciary decide nullification in a procedure that closely resembled the Cherokee action against Georgia. If the administration used force to compel obedience, it would be ignoring the courts as well as violating the sovereignty of a state.[17] But events moved too fast for any appropriate court test. Nothing came of Calhoun's plan.

By now, Calhoun had conceded that Jackson and Van Buren would be elected in November. His prospects for political advancement blasted, he spent the summer of 1832 seeking to explain and popularize the nullification cause with the Unionists in his own state and with what he hoped was a potentially sympathetic audience in other states. He eagerly responded to Governor Hamilton's request that he elaborate on his "Fort Hill Address." In the lengthy public letter he prepared, Calhoun admitted that a "great majority" of the people were confusing nullification with secession. He claimed that nullification, or interposition as he preferred to call it, differed from secession in nature and in objective. Again asserting original sovereignty for the states, he cast relations between the federal government and the states in the form of a contractual relationship. Secession was withdrawal, separation, a dissolution of the partnership. Nullification, on the other hand, assumed the relation of the principal with its agent, the states being the principals, the federal government their agent, and the Constitution the contract between the two, whereby all powers not specifically enumerated were reserved to the states.

Like Jefferson before him, Calhoun placed a strict construction on implied powers. If the contract was breached, then the act or acts breaching it, in this case the tariff, were null and void. The objective of nullification was to keep the agent within its prescribed limits, but not through secession, which would destroy delegated or trust powers. Calhoun warned, however, that secession could follow nullification if repeated or plenary abuses were not corrected. "Many," wrote Calhoun, "acknowledge the right of a state to secede, but deny its right to nullify and yet it seems impossible to admit the one, without admitting

17. *Calhoun Papers,* XII, 11, XI, 665.

the other." Hamilton had the letter published in mid-September during a colorful, highly emotional, and dangerously divisive election campaign in the state.[18]

Calhoun's explanation and argument changed few minds outside of the state. The *Globe* and the White House branded the letter another treasonable utterance. Whether Calhoun was concerned about the paradox that was developing before his very eyes in South Carolina, as the Unionist minority battled for its existence against a nullification majority, is not known. If he did realize the logical inconsistency in his arguments for minority rights, he must have also been concerned by the warlike aspect of affairs, particularly in Charleston. Yet he too was being swept along by the emotional currents of the hour. When Governor Hamilton visited Pendleton in mid-September, he and Calhoun agreed that a special session of the legislature be called right after the state election to consider another election for a nullification convention.

The nullifiers won a popular majority of 65 percent of the votes cast, but the Unionists almost carried the city of Charleston and ran well in several other districts. Most disturbing were the seemingly irreconcilable attitudes of both sides. No sooner had the election results become known than the Unionists made a formal complaint, which they addressed to the Tennessee legislature, bitterly condemning the theory and the tactics of the nullifiers. They singled out Calhoun as the ringleader and the originator of what they called dangerous and treasonable doctrines. The Nashville *Banner* published their indictment, which was reprinted widely. It was featured in the *Globe* with editorial comment that savaged Calhoun.[19]

The special session of the South Carolina legislature met on October 22. After listening to a message from Governor Hamilton that reviewed the recent tariff history and the failure of protest to achieve a reform, it passed a bill calling for a nullification convention over the spirited opposition of the Unionist minority. There followed another campaign, which, however, was so closely organized that the delegates chosen reflected the same small elite group of planters, newspaper editors, and lawyers that controlled most of the wealth in the state and comprised its largest slave owners. Although relatives and close friends of Calhoun constituted a large number of the delegates to the convention, he was unable to restrain the more radical spirits. Nor was there

18. *Ibid.*, 613–49; Freehling, *Prelude to Civil War*, 238–44. See also Maier, "The Road Not Taken," 16.

19. *Calhoun Papers*, XI, 667, 668.

any effort on either side to add moderate delegates to the ranks of the Unionists, who made up with ability and eloquence for their small numbers. The only temporizing document the convention passed was an address that Calhoun had written restating the peaceful, constitutional argument for nullification. This expression of intent was submerged in the ordinance of nullification itself, which came out flatly for secession if force were used to collect duties in the state. No judicial procedures were permitted. Setting all of Calhoun's careful reasoning at naught, the ordinance required a test oath of loyalty to the state of all civic and military officers, who would be empowered to enforce the ordinance.[20]

The South Carolina legislature that had just been elected, meeting in regular session, passed the necessary enabling legislation, including the test oath, over the bitter opposition of the Unionists. Everything up to this point had proceeded smoothly in accordance with the views of the radical majority. One concession to moderation was in setting the date two months hence for the ordinance to go into effect. But the extreme nullifiers had not reckoned with the determination and the ability of Joel Poinsett, who had unofficially taken charge of the Unionists. Poinsett, who had been for some time in communication with Jackson and Lewis Cass, the secretary of war, persuaded his associates to call a Unionist convention. It met in Charleston on December 10 and, resisting all efforts at intimidation, issued a resounding declaration of opposition to the ordinance.

On the same day in Washington, President Jackson struck at the nullifiers. Nullification, he said, was tantamount to treason. The national government within its constitutional limits was sovereign, and tariff legislation came clearly within these boundaries. No state could break its compact and leave the Union; nor could it defy a federal law. Jackson stated that he would employ whatever force was necessary to exact obedience from South Carolina.

Edward Livingston, the new secretary of state, had written a document that in effect restated the nationalist position of Webster and John Marshall. A member of one of the great New York families, Livingston had lived in Louisiana for many years and had represented that state in the Senate. He was, moreover, the foremost American scholar of juris-

20. Frederic Bancroft, *Calhoun and the South Carolina Nullification Movement* (Baltimore, 1928), 127–42. But even among the extremists there were heated differences of opinion. See John Barnwell (ed.), "Hamlet to Hotspur: Letters of Robert Woodward Barnwell to Robert Barnwell Rhett," *South Carolina Historical Magazine*, LXXVII, No. 4 (October, 1976), 241, 245.

prudence and author of the Louisiana legal code. The document he drafted for the president's signature was not merely a firm warning to South Carolina but a cogent constitutional argument that upheld the powers of the national government as the supreme law of the land. So vigorous were the document's phrases and so compelling the theory of government they expressed that the proclamation dismayed such moderate advocates of states' rights as Martin Van Buren, while it spurred a dying John Randolph to a spasm of adversarial rhetoric.[21]

To some, Jackson's frank avowal of nationalist statements seemed the essence of the Federalist party position; to others, it embodied executive tyranny and consolidation of central power. The document threatened to split the uneasy party coalition between the free and the slave states that Van Buren had put together. In South Carolina, the proclamation further divided public opinion. Governor Hayne issued a counterproclamation bitterly denouncing Jackson's course. And he speeded up military preparations, though it was clear to him and to the leading nullifiers that they were poorly prepared for any armed conflict. Express mail from Joel Poinsett to Jackson and Secretary of War Cass took on an even more urgent tone as the Unionist leader pleaded for arms.[22] Jackson had already ordered reinforcements to Fort Moultrie and Castle Pinckney in Charleston Harbor. He ordered General Scott to organize their defenses and to cooperate with the Unionists if armed resistance to federal authority developed over collection of duties. Two armed revenue cutters were patrolling off Charleston to assist federal forces. A clash seemed imminent, yet leaders on both sides were working to avoid hostilities.

Calhoun had contributed much towards the excitement. Long ago, during the debates over the Missouri Compromise, he had begun to concern himself with the slavery question and, as he saw it, the growing weakness of the South in the Union. He had early connected these two issues with what he chose to regard as the class and sectional aspects of tariff agitation. Calhoun's mind was at once acute and adversarial, realistic and unrealistic. He visualized a conspiracy of northern and western entrepreneurs under the guise of Clay's American system, who were utilizing an increasing majority in Congress to exact from the South most of the capital required for the economic development of their region through their control of public policy.

21. Roscoe Pound, *The Formative Era of American Law* (Boston, 1938), 5, 6, 166, 167; Van Buren to Jackson, December 27, 1832, VBLC; Hugh A. Garland, *The Life of John Randolph of Roanoke* (New York, 1850), 359–61.
22. *Jackson Correspondence*, IV, 48, 482, 483, 485–88, 490–94, 497, 498, 501–503.

Calhoun was certain that unless this economic juggernaut was curbed, once the industrial states had been developed and the South reduced to a colonial status, the institution of slavery and the entire elitist culture of the plantation system would be in grave jeopardy. Abolition, then, he believed, was tied to public policy. Just as Calhoun early in his career had charged that British impressment and Indian policies were simply a pretext to imperialist domination of the United States, so now he believed that abolitionist agitation, Van Buren-style party politics, the American system, and what he branded as consolidationist trends in the executive branch of the national government were but symptoms of a covert design to impose a different social order on the South. He saw the outlines of a program that would reduce the region to generations of poverty and expose it to the barbarities of slave war. Calhoun had not stopped to consider that these paranoid notions had contributed mightily to the present situation—that his gift of logical discourse and his exaggeration of the very real social and economic problems facing the South had prepared the ground for conflict and provided a rationale for it.

Calhoun did, as he had in the war hawk congresses, feel some sense of responsibility for his rhetoric and exerted himself to curb rash moves, but he had not by any means changed his views despite the immediate crisis, the gravity of which he had not foreseen. He grasped at evidences that a peaceful solution was at hand for the short term. The president himself had called for a further modification of the tariff in his annual message to Congress. The *Globe* was urging tariff reform in its editorials, and both the Virginia and Alabama legislatures passed resolutions in favor of conciliation. It was manifest to Calhoun and other leading figures in South Carolina that nullification did not command much support in the slave states. And it was looked at as akin to treason in the free states.[23]

Calhoun had just been elected a United States senator to replace Robert Y. Hayne, who, in a political reshuffling among the small, elite group of South Carolina planter-politicians, would now succeed Hamilton as governor. There is no doubt that these moves were part of a well-thought-out plan whereby Hayne would restrain the hotheads in the state legislature and Calhoun would defend his brainchild, nullification, in Washington against administration stalwarts and the likes of Daniel Webster, the new apostle of northern nationalism.

Even though Congress had been in session since December 6, Cal-

---

23. Washington *Globe*, December 4, 7, 1832; *Adams Memoirs*, VII, 503, 515.

houn delayed his departure until December 22. Floride had been taken ill suddenly, and for several weeks her condition was considered grave. As soon as she recovered, he left Fort Hill for Columbia, where he conferred with Hayne, Hamilton, and other members of the state government. From there he sent his letter resigning the vice-presidency on December 28, 1832.[24]

On his way to Washington, D.C., Calhoun unquestionably heard the rumor that if hostilities developed in South Carolina, Jackson meant to seize him and others of the South Carolina delegation for trial on treason charges. Knowing Jackson's penchant for precipitate action, Calhoun may have believed that he would be in danger when he reached the capital. But he certainly was not deterred in his convictions, though word of administration threats against his person may have made him more pliable to compromise—on his own terms, however.

Administration forces had already introduced a tariff bill, sponsored by one of Van Buren's "high-minded" Federalists, Gulian Verplanck, that conceded almost everything the South Carolina nullifiers were demanding. Yet Clay and Calhoun, for different reasons, were opposed to the bill. Clay considered that such a sudden and drastic abandonment of protection would impose crushing burdens on the manufacturers. He also yearned for the prestige that would redound to him if he were able to resolve the crisis.[25] Calhoun opposed the Verplanck bill in part because it was a Van Buren measure and in part because he was willing to back some relief to the manufacturers, provided protection was removed as a governing principle in a new tariff bill.

Not long after Calhoun was sworn in as a senator, intermediaries brought him and Clay together. Soon they were in agreement on the rough outline of a tariff bill that would afford diminishing schedules over a ten-year period until the rates on specific items were reduced to a level of 20 percent *ad valorem,* about the same rate as the tariff of 1816. Thereafter, a tariff for revenue only would go into operation. Calhoun understood that the tariff distinctly renounced the principle of protection. For a time, Calhoun and his supporters balked at an eleventh-hour amendment Clay had been forced to tack on his tariff bill. John M. Clayton, serving his first term as a senator from Delaware, but clearly a spokesman for the manufacturing interests, demanded

24. *Calhoun Papers,* XI, 685.
25. *Clay Papers,* VIII, 615–24; Merrill D. Peterson, *Olive Branch and Sword—The Compromise of 1833* (Baton Rouge, 1982), 2, 3, 32, 51–53.

that "home evaluation" rather than "foreign evaluation" govern the final schedule in 1842. Such a distinction would raise tariff rates to include hidden costs of imported goods, transportation charges, insurance, and the like. Without Clayton's support, the compromise measure would be lost. At first Calhoun would have none of Clayton's amendment, but after lengthy discussions in which it was pointed out that conditions over a decade hence would surely be different from what they were now and that there would be ample time to make changes, he agreed reluctantly to accept the proposal. Calhoun had cornered himself. If he refused to accept the compromise bill, he would have to face Jackson again and with less prospect of success than at the outset of the controversy.[26]

Still, the chances were that even with the combined forces in Congress of Clay and Calhoun, their compromise measure would be lost to the administration bill, which was far more favorable to the South. But when Jackson asked Congress for authority to coerce South Carolina, Calhoun immediately saw that his and Clay's compromise measure would gain significant support from southern members who may have doubted the constitutionality of nullification, but recoiled from such an overt invasion of states' rights. He was quick to exploit in an impromptu speech what he stigmatized as executive tyranny. And when the Senate judiciary committee reported a bill that gave the president the authority he sought, southerners dubbed it the "force bill." To Calhoun it became the "Bloody Act." On January 22, a day after the bill was reported, Calhoun rose again in the Senate to denounce it and the president. His angular features drawn from tension and his deep-set eyes blazing, he lectured his colleagues in an even, unemotional voice on his compact theory of government. He closed with three resolutions that embodied these ideas.[27]

Calhoun's speech and resolutions, while they were offered in the hope of gaining adherents of and publicity for South Carolina's cause, were primarily an effort to delay a vote on the force bill until Calhoun could get what he thought would be an affirmative vote on the tariff. Even if his tactic failed, he wanted to delay enactment of the nullification ordinance until Congress adjourned on March 4. By then Virginia's efforts at mediating the crisis, he felt, would strengthen South

26. Peterson, *Olive Branch and Sword*, 49–55, 65, 67, 68; *Webster Papers*, III, 213; *Calhoun Papers*, XV, 367; *Register of Debates*, 22nd Cong., 2nd Sess., 690–717; *Calhoun Papers*, XII, 96–101; *United States Telegraph*, February 21, 1833; Thomas Hart Benton, *Thirty Years' View* (2 vols.; New York, 1854–56), I, 342–44.

27. *Calhoun Papers*, XII, 18–26.

Carolina's stand. "We must take time; and, with that view," he wrote William C. Preston, "it seems to me desirable, that the convention of the State should be called to meet after the 4th of March . . . we would then have a full view of all the ground, and take our measures accordingly."[28]

Webster quickly realized what Calhoun was attempting and succeeded in having the resolutions tabled. Before the force bill was even debated and before Calhoun's letter to Preston reached Columbia, a mass meeting of nullifiers had met in Charleston and voted to postpone the ordinance until March 4. Although certainly not binding, Governor Hayne chose to accept its mandate. Virginia's special commissioner, Benjamin Watkins Leigh, was then in Columbia urging that the state refrain from any belligerent action.

Still, Calhoun gave every outward indication of defiance. When the force bill came up for consideration in the Senate, whatever feeling he may have had about his role in pushing his state and the national government to this point of near conflict, he presented a bold face as he spoke for several hours over a two-day period. His speech ransacked historical precedent from the Old Testament book of Kings through the Persian Wars to the decline and fall of the Roman Republic to the contests of more modern times between the Federalists and the Jeffersonians. He talked freely about his past as a member of Congress during the War of 1812 and rehearsed his arguments against special interest groups who would destroy liberty through their control of public policy.

Throughout his remarks there was a defensive strain. And while Calhoun attacked the president as the embodiment of tyranny, his eloquent address was a lengthy exercise in self-justification. Anticipating that Webster, who was scheduled to reply, was expecting him to develop his constitutional arguments, he gave only brief attention to the theory and practice of nullification. It was an old debater's trick to disarm one's opponent before he began by robbing him of his line of attack. And Calhoun had need of every device he could command because he knew he could not match Webster in oratory. He therefore chose to present his argument in direct and simple terms: The force bill was tyranny that threatened the integrity of all the states and inevitably the liberty of all citizens.

Calhoun's tactics may have been sound, but Webster was also a skilled debater. Although he feared that his speech would never match

28. *Ibid.*, 37.

his reply to Hayne, he actually made an even more powerful argument than he had in his previous efforts. Webster went straight for Calhoun's resolutions. To a Senate chamber whose galleries were packed with spectators, the senator from Massachusetts presented in arresting terms the case for national power within its prescribed limits. In doing so, he restated his own and Chief Justice John Marshall's position on the relationship between the states and the central government. He held that the Constitution derived directly from the people, agreeing with Calhoun that the people alone were sovereign but denying that the states as corporate bodies were the sole representatives of the people. The distinction may have been a subtle one to many in the audience and even to some of his fellow senators. It was, however, the compelling point at issue, as Calhoun well knew. Webster's rhetoric and his style of presentation were more than a match for Calhoun's logic. Certainly the administration thought so, and Webster was satisfied that he had acquitted himself well. Former president Madison, the ultimate authority on the Constitution, agreed with him.[29]

Calhoun's speeches, his constant writing and research, and especially the strain of the session had left him feverish and unwell. In the midst of his address on the force bill, he had become so hoarse that he could not go on and was given leave to complete his remarks the following day. Yet he drew on his slender reserves of strength to answer Webster. Near the end of his remarks, Calhoun turned to Senator John Forsyth, an administration senator from Georgia, who had declared that South Carolina had repudiated the republican form of government that the Constitution guaranteed to all the states.

Calhoun, looking directly at the lean, elegant Forsyth, who sat near him, said that this was the first "ominous" reference that had been voiced in the debate. Could not Forsyth recognize that the power claimed for the federal government could be used as "a pretext to interfere with our political affairs and domestic institutions in a manner infinitely more dangerous than any other power which has ever been exercised on the part of the general government?" Calhoun was not content to let his warning rest without specific implications. He insisted on making his allusion to slavery unmistakably clear. "There exists," he said, "in every Southern state a domestic institution, which would require a far less bold construction to consider the government of every State, in that quarter, not to be republican, and of course, to

29. *Webster Papers,* III, 214, 215, 216, 222, 223. See also praise from Joel Poinsett and B. F. Perry, the embattled Unionist leaders in South Carolina, *ibid.,* 227, 235.

demand on the part of this government, the suppression of the institution . . . in fulfillment of the guarantee." The abolitionists, he was certain, would soon seize on the guarantee as a pretext for demanding an end to slavery. Unless Forsyth's position was opposed by "united and firm resistance," it would ultimately drive the "white population from the Southern Atlantic States."[30]

Finally, the root of the nullification crisis was exposed. What had begun as a reaction to a depression in the cotton states, a slump that had been particularly severe in South Carolina, had rapidly resolved itself into an all-encompassing fear on the part of a majority of the planter elite class that the growing industrialism of the North, expressing itself politically through the majority will, would eventually demand emancipation, heedless of the social consequences.[31] Most of Calhoun's southern colleagues did not share these fears. Forsyth, for example, dismissed Calhoun's contention with a brief rejoinder.

Despite his admonitions, Calhoun was satisfied that the compromise tariff that passed by comfortable margins in the House and Senate had secured the objectives he sought. The force bill, which was agreed to by Congress a few days later, was another matter. Only eight of his fellow senators joined Calhoun in opposing the measure. When it came to a vote, he led his small band out of the chamber in a dramatic display of opposition. The Senate then passed the bill on March 1, 1833, with only one opposing vote, that of John Tyler, newly elected senator from Virginia. Jackson signed the tariff and the force bill the next day.

An exhausted Calhoun was unsure how his fellow South Carolinians would react to the legislation. In the course of debate over both measures, he saw clearly that both congressional and public opinion were decidedly against nullification. While most of his colleagues, even those from the North, accepted his views on the old Whig principle of the right to revolution, very few thought that the tariff constituted a direct danger to liberty, as Calhoun contended, or represented a trend that spelled the doom of democratic government. Similarly, his argument that the Hamiltonian doctrine of implied powers, once accepted in this guise, would surely be employed to effect broader social and economic ends convinced few in or out of Congress. Nullification had gained most of the tariff concessions South Carolina demanded. If the state persisted in its separatist resolve, not only would it be isolated in the Union, but its nullifier majority would in all likelihood be crushed

30. *Calhoun Papers,* XII, 136, 140.
31. *Ibid.,* 136.

between internal and external forces. In salty language, James W. Wyly, a Tennessee legislator, expressed a general opinion of South Carolina nullifiers. "The Old Chief," he wrote Polk, "could rally force enough if necessary, upon two weeks notice from other states to stand on the Saluda Mountain and piss enough . . . to float the whole nullifying crew into the Atlantic ocean."[32]

It behooved Calhoun to go to South Carolina as soon as possible, where his presence could help restrain those whom he knew were radical secessionists in the state. He left Washington on March 3 by fast stage from Alexandria. Winter still gripped northern Virginia. The stage made slow headway over the icy roads, for alternate frosts and thaws had frozen in place deep ruts that were negotiated with extreme difficulty. Calhoun counted on his lieutenants, Governor Hayne and Francis Pickens in particular, and Benjamin Watkins Leigh, the Virginia commissioner, to check the radicals until he reached Columbia, but he could not be certain of their success. Impatient with the halting progress of the stage, and heedless of personal discomfort and his poor physical condition, he switched to an open mail wagon that paused only for brief changes of drivers and horses. Bundled up among the mailbags, Calhoun pushed on day and night, arriving in Columbia late on March 11, the very day that the nullification convention met. He was relieved to find that it had convened only briefly to elect Governor Hayne its president and to appoint a committee on the Virginia proposals.

Calhoun refused to speak at the session of the convention the next day, but his presence and certainly his influence were felt in the committee report that recommended repealing the nullification ordinance. Although, the report conceded, the compromise tariff did not remove all grievances, it did ensure an eventual return to a "revenue standard." At the same time, the convention nullified the force bill in a face-saving gesture that was now of no effect but preserved the principle so dear to Calhoun and to most of the nullifiers.

There were still some rancorous arguments and a court proceeding over the test oath that placed allegiance to South Carolina over allegiance to the United States. This question was eventually resolved by yet another compromise in wording. The crisis was over. Or was it? Calhoun, as he had so often in his public career, had put himself in an untenable position. He, instead of his critics, had used the tariff controversy as a pretext for a defense of slavery, wherein no present but only a

32. *Polk Correspondence*, II, 16.

potential threat existed.[33] He had extended his own defensive posture to that of an entire state and would now, through an inexorable turn of events, feel compelled to instill his fears for the future throughout the slaveholding South. By these destabilizing means, he hoped to unify the region and extort through threats with real power behind them an impregnable defense of minority rights as he saw them. On March 25, 1833, he wrote his former assistant in the War Department, Christopher Vandeventer, that he had "no doubts the [tariff] system has got its death wound blow. Nullification," he exulted, "has dealt the fatal blow. We have applied the same remedy to the bloody act [Force Act]. It will never be enforced in this State . . . there shall be at least one free State."[34]

33. See, for instance, *ibid.*, II, 288, 293, and letters of B. F. Perry and Joel Poinsett to Webster, *Webster Papers*, III, 251, 252.

34. *Calhoun Papers*, XII, 145.

XI

An Unlikely Cause

The atmosphere in the Senate chamber was tense on Monday morning, February 6, 1837. It was petition day, and most senators were in their seats, awaiting the bitter argument that was sure to erupt over abolitionist petitions. They knew that the House chamber was still in an uproar as angry southern members sought to censure former president John Quincy Adams for his attempts to circumvent the "gag rule" that denied even the presentation of an abolitionist petition.

After Vice-President Van Buren called the Senate to order, he recognized John Tipton of Indiana. Much to the surprise of his colleagues, Tipton, a supporter of the administration, a personal friend of Jackson, and as rabid an antiabolitionist as any of the southern senators, began in his halting, ungrammatical style to present two petitions that asked Congress to abolish slavery in the District of Columbia. He was clearly embarrassed by his role, and when he completed his reading, he apologized to the Senate. Tipton said that the petitions did not represent his own feelings on the subject nor those of a majority of his constituents. It was only from a sense of duty that he had presented them.[1]

Tipton's dilemma typified a public debate that ranged throughout the nation in the press, in casual conversation at hotels and boardinghouses, on the river and sound steamboats, the trains, and the coaches, and in the halls of Congress. For six years, the abolitionists had been mounting an ever-increasing attack on slavery through the medium of petitions. At first there had been few, primarily from Quaker groups, and they had been tabled without much comment. But gradually these documents aroused criticism from sensitive slaveholders, especially after 1833, when the British Parliament abolished slavery in the West Indies. The American Colonization Society had been for years an opponent of slavery but had concentrated its efforts on the removal of blacks to Africa and eschewed emancipation.

---

1. See a description of Tipton in S. P. Chase, diary, March 4, 1830, S. P. Chase Papers, Library of Congress; *Congressional Globe*, 24th Cong., 2nd Sess., 157.

That there was an undercurrent of opposition to slavery in the North had been amply evidenced in the Missouri debates and in the prohibition against slavery in the constitutions of all northern states, including the newly admitted states of the Northwest. Calhoun himself admitted on the floor of the Senate that "the great mass of Northern people believed that this southern institution was radically wrong." Although the opposition was tacit and though slavery was amply protected as a local institution through the division of powers and specific clauses in the Constitution, the abolitionists were beginning to tap the reservoir of quiescent antislavery sentiment in the North and even in the slave states. Calhoun testified to antislavery sentiment that existed in the South when he said that "there were many, very many, in the slaveholding States, who, at the commencement of the controversy, believed that slavery, as it existed among us, was an evil to be tolerated, because we would not escape from it, but not be defended."[2]

The campaign device of sending abolition petitions to Congress was meant to arouse and organize public opinion. Frequently, petition language was deliberately loaded with pejorative words and phrases that excoriated slavery and especially slave masters. Outraged southern congressmen, many of whom were themselves uneasy about the moral implications of the institution, responded with demands that the agitation be controlled.[3] Congress, they claimed, should not provide a forum for what they held were subversive views couched in insulting language. Abolition of slavery and of the slave trade in the District of Columbia was a particularly sensitive point, for the abolitionists had a good argument—that Congress had plenary powers of government over the District of Columbia as it had over the territories and therefore controlled its domestic institutions, including slavery. The substance of such petitions, it could be said, was well within constitutional limitations.

No man in public office was more sensitive to the developing slavery issue than John C. Calhoun. At the time of the Missouri debates, he had watched with alarm the growth in population and wealth of the free states as compared with that of his own region. Policy measures like the

2. *Calhoun Papers*, XIV, 12, 549.
3. B. F. Perry wrote Webster in May, 1833: "Whatever of wrong and sin there may be in slavery we are compelled by force of circumstance to sanction and tolerate it. It is an evil which was entailed upon us by our ancestors, and which we can not remedy, without the ruin of ourselves and the injury of those whom we would think of benefitting. So interwoven is it with our interest, our manners, our climate and our very being, that no change can ever possibly be effected without a civil commotion from which the heart of a patriot must turn with horror" (*Webster Papers*, III, 251).

tariffs of 1824 and 1828, outside of their political contexts, were evidence of northern aggression to a mind that had always had a defensive cast, whether the threatening element was Great Britain, the class interests of northern manufacturers, or the executive tyranny of Andrew Jackson. Calhoun simply would not believe that party and policy measures could be independent of each other—that either might be pursuing legitimate aims of self-interest. He lived in a world where pretext ruled. All moves in the political or economic arena that did not directly support his preconceptions were, he believed, hostile to him personally and were a cover for some punitive factor aimed at his political career, his state, his section, and its basic institutions. Such a suspicious, insecure person, gifted as he was, with an unusually active mind, a fine sense of logic, a debater's skill of a high order, and a passion for self-justification, could and usually did find a conspiracy in the actions of others that would alter the social and political norms he valued. In argument Calhoun frequently placed himself in situations from which extrication was difficult and in which he compounded the problem by magnifying its potential rather than dwelling upon its actual import. His role during the nullification crisis amply bears out his tendency to indulge in self-fulfilling prophecies. That he had seen in the tariff of 1828 a pretext for an assault on slavery had forced him into an unprofitable clash with the president and public opinion. His own extrication and that of his followers in South Carolina from a contest they could not win had raised the level of a public issue to unwarranted heights and fostered a latent strain of particularist suspicion that was threatening to the Union.

It was quite in keeping that Calhoun would seize upon the abolitionist movement as a broad conspiracy to undermine southern institutions when it commanded but little support in the North. Unwittingly, he played into the hands of the abolitionist leaders, who wanted the maximum of publicity for their cause, and at the same time he stirred up that hitherto uncommitted majority in the free states who considered slavery to be a moral evil but, as law-abiding citizens, would never have disturbed it where it existed legally. William L. Marcy, governor of New York, voiced the sentiments of many conservative men when he said of the southern position as Calhoun articulated it: "I can fight your battles so long as you make the constitution your fortress. But if you go to the Bible or make it a question of ethics, you must not expect me or any respectable member of the free states to be with you."[4]

4. Gideon Welles Diary, March 3, 1849 (MS in Gideon Welles Papers, Huntington Library, San Marino, California).

Calhoun's extreme views on abolitionist literature were so well known that no one was surprised when he rose to make a point on Tipton's petitions. In his customary matter-of-fact voice, he asked that after these petitions were presented, the Senate vote not to receive such petitions in the future. When the Senate agreed to open debate on the subject, Calhoun made a short speech which he closed with the comment that abolitionists would imbue in the rising generation "a spirit of fanaticism and the North and South would become two people[s], with feelings diametrically opposite."[5]

No sooner had Calhoun completed his remarks than one of the senators from Virginia, William C. Rives, rose to his feet. In precise language, he sought to break the tension. Rives had "no objection that Senators should present their petitions, but he protested against the gratuitous exhibition of misery which had no existence." At this juncture, he made a comment that startled his fellow southern senators and brought Calhoun again into the debate. "He was not in favor of slavery in the abstract," said this master of the great plantation of Castle Hill. "On that point he differed with the Gentleman from South Carolina."[6]

Calhoun denied that he had ever expressed any opinion of slavery in the abstract. What he had said was that slavery "was an inevitable law of society, that one portion of the community depended on the labor of another . . . when two races of men, of different color, and a thousand other particulars were placed in immediate juxtaposition. Here the existence of slavery was good to both." Calhoun then turned and, fixing his dark eyes on the Virginia senator, asked him directly whether he did not consider slavery good. Undaunted, Rives said "no." Slavery was "a misfortune and an evil in all circumstances."

Nettled by Rives's cool response, Calhoun made a brief rebuttal that was not as cogent as usual, his major point being that slavery in the South was an experiment still in progress, but that so far, both races "appeared to thrive under the practical operation of this institution . . . the South had nothing in the case to lament or to lay to their conscience."[7] Rives's contention that slavery was morally evil was utterly wrong, Calhoun declared, and the source of all the abolitionist propaganda that was straining the bonds of union.

Since early 1834, Calhoun had suspected that a coordinated attempt would be made to have Congress emancipate slaves in the District of

5. *Calhoun Papers*, XIII, 389.
6. *Ibid.*
7. *Ibid.*, 390; *Register of Debates*, 24th Cong., 2nd Sess., 710–19.

Columbia.[8] But it was not until two years later that such a campaign began in earnest, as hundreds of petitions accumulated on the desks of congressmen. John Quincy Adams in the House focused national attention on the petitions when he insisted on reading some that he had received. The ones he selected were usually severe indictments of slavery that infuriated his southern colleagues.

In the Senate, Calhoun inveighed against these petitions in his usual vein, adding the argument that the Fifth Amendment to the Constitution, which declared that no person be deprived of property without due process of law, constituted "an insuperable barrier." He asked, "Are not slaves property? And if so how can Congress any more take away the property of a master in his slave in this District, than it could his life and liberty?" Again indulging himself in the potential rather than the actual case, he said, "To yield the right here, is to yield the right to Congress to abolish slavery in the States." Calhoun's constant efforts to apply a gag in the Senate similar to the one imposed on Adams in the House did not escape harsh criticism even from his southern colleagues. John P. King of Georgia argued with him over the receipt of petitions, while Thomas Hart Benton, Isaac Hill of New Hampshire, and John M. Niles of Connecticut, firm supporters of the administration, accused him of being as much an agitator as any abolitionist.[9] And Rives lashed out at Calhoun's patriarchal approach to slavery and southern society by accusing him of following the precepts of Sir Robert Filmer, the defender of divine right monarchy who had portrayed the king as the head of the nation-family. Calhoun misunderstood Rives. He thought the Virginia senator was calling him a defender of monarchy. He hotly denied that he was any follower of Filmer, whose work he "abhorred."

Eventually, Calhoun had his way. Petitions were received, and the question was called and routinely tabled. Tipton's petitions and the brief debate with Rives that occurred a year later ended the controversy over abolition petitions when the Senate reenacted its previous rule, automatically tabling them without debate.[10]

In the House, Van Buren's lieutenants had earlier devised a compromise formula which, while it did not accept Calhoun's argument that Congress had no power to interfere with slavery in the District of Columbia, declared that it was inexpedient to make any moves without

8. *Register of Debates*, 24th Cong., 2nd Sess., 710–19; *Calhoun Papers*, XII, 197.
9. *Calhoun Papers*, XIII, 25, 72–77.
10. *Ibid.*, 386–88, 391; *Register of Debates*, 24th Congress, 2nd Sess., 715–23, 341, 386–88.

the consent of the District's residents and the adjoining slave states of Virginia and Maryland. This formula, which conceded that Congress could abolish slavery in the District, was introduced by a South Carolinian, Henry L. Pinckney. Even though it effectively gagged Adams, Calhoun and many others among the state's political leaders were outraged that a southerner, a South Carolinian, and a member of one of the state's leading families should not have seen the implications of his actions. A campaign began almost at once in South Carolina to discredit Pinckney. His loyalty to the nullification cause was dismissed in the fury of the attack that the Calhoun organization mounted against him. Although Pinckney fought back and had supporters, the States' Rights party, presumably with Calhoun's approval, if not instigation, made a deal with his former adversary in Charleston to run Hugh Legaré against Pinckney in the ensuing congressional elections. Legaré triumphed; and with his victory, the Unionist group came firmly behind Calhoun's leadership in defense of slavery. There would be no further serious challenges to Calhoun's political rule in the state for the next eight years. Despite the so-called Pinckney apostasy, the Van Buren–inspired formula worked effectively. Petitions were automatically tabled in the House without discussion, as in the Senate.[11]

Another tactic the abolitionists employed at about the same time was deemed even more subversive by southern opinion leaders because it carried the antislavery message directly to all who could read in the slave states. This was the placing of abolitionist literature in the southern mails, so that, it was hoped, some portion of the literature would find its way into the homes of slaves and whites who might be converted. For the time being, the perceived dangers of widespread dispersion of abolitionist literature unified Unionists and nullifiers in South Carolina. Both factions approved of the course Calhoun staked out to meet what they regarded as an extreme threat to the existing social order.

Calhoun offered meager praise for the administration's recognition that these materials raised a problem in the South and for its order that postmasters remove them from the mails. In line with his position on the encroachment of delegated national power on the reserved powers of the states, he insisted that it was the right of the states to control any mails that might be dangerous to local institutions. With the same fine

11. *Calhoun Papers*, XIII, 434; *United States Telegraph*, February 10, 12, 1836; Pendleton *Messenger*, April 1, 8, 1836; James Hamilton, Jr., to James H. Hammond, February 10, 1836, Robert Y. Hayne to William C. Preston, February 18, 1836, JHLC; Charleston *Mercury*, August 19, 20, 22–25, September 22, 24, 27, October 1, 7, 8, 11–15, 1836.

disregard for civil rights that he had shown in the petition matter, he relied on a highly restrictive interpretation of the First Amendment, which he said expressly forbade the federal government from interfering with the freedom of press or expression. Thus any effort to open or stop the mails was strictly a matter for the states.[12]

A year and a half earlier, Calhoun had written Duff Green from Fort Hill that resistance to abolitionist tactics in the South "will be of the most determined character even to the extent of disunion." And on September 9, 1835, Calhoun joined a meeting at Farmer's Hall in Pendleton to review the flood of abolitionist literature in the mails and take action on it. He and Langdon Cheves were among the twenty-one community leaders appointed to prepare a report and resolutions that were presented to the meeting. The report was ready in an hour's time. After ranging briefly over the threat they saw in the circulation of abolitionist literature, the leaders maintained that southern whites had every right to protect themselves from the incitement of a slave uprising. "The liberty of the press," the report stated, "implies no privilege to disturb by seditious libels, the peace of the community—to throw firebrands amidst a peaceful and unoffending people."[13]

The resolutions followed closely Calhoun's line that abolitionist propaganda was unconstitutional because it struck at the compact on which "the union of these states rests." They reiterated the point Calhoun had made in the Senate—that any attempt of Congress to emancipate the slaves in the District of Columbia or to abolish the slave trade there was unconstitutional because it would take property without due process of law as prohibited by the Fifth Amendment. The last three resolutions recommended that the chairman of the meeting appoint a committee of vigilance to examine and remove any abolitionist materials from the mails.[14]

Calhoun had succeeded in demonstrating that the Constitution could be employed on both sides of the slavery argument. He did not hesitate to invoke the division of powers to establish censorship, which certainly violated the spirit if not the substance of the Bill of Rights; yet when he was confronted with the possibility of Congress abolishing slavery and the slave trade in the District of Columbia, he boldly as-

---

12. *Senate Documents,* 24th Cong., 1st Sess., No. 118; see also Calhoun's "Report from the Select Committee on the Circulation of Incendiary Publications," *Calhoun Papers,* XIII, 53–66.

13. *Calhoun Papers,* XII, 547.

14. *Ibid.,* 548–54. It is likely that Calhoun had already prepared a report and resolutions before the meeting was convened.

serted the Fifth Amendment. Few of his colleagues could match Calhoun's knowledge of the Constitution and its historic precedents, or his agility as a debater. His encounter with Rives must have been bothersome, but he recognized that only Daniel Webster was his peer on the basic constitutional argument.[15] He had also proven himself an adroit maneuverer in a Congress that was closely divided between what were now being called the Whig party and the Democratic party after the settlement of the nullification controversy.

For a time it appeared that Webster and his following would break out of the Whig ranks and join the Democrats. Webster had supported Jackson's firm stand against South Carolina and the nullifiers. The popularity of Jackson's handling of the crisis in his home region had impressed him. Not long after the settlement of the nullification controversy, Calhoun queried his former subordinate in the War Department, Christopher Vandeventer, about this political possibility. "I am curious to know how the Webster and Van Buren interests will act," he wrote. "Will they amalgamate? and if not what will be their relative strength and their respective course?" Overtures were made by both Webster's faction and the Democrats, but before they could ripen into any arrangement, Van Buren, who recognized the danger to himself, managed to quash any merger of the two.[16]

Calhoun's long-range political objectives were to consolidate his power in South Carolina and unify the slaveholding states behind his leadership in protecting their domestic institutions, enhancing their economic outlook, and maintaining their political integrity. He confidently expected an impending onslaught from the central government, with its entrenched executive branch growing steadily more powerful and menacing through its control of federal officeholders.

In his own state, there was still a minority of the elite ruling class that opposed Calhoun from both a personal and a political stance. Much of this opposition came from the remnants of the Crawford organization, which Van Buren cultivated. Adversaries such as the aristocratic Joel Poinsett, the talented and scholarly Hugh Legaré, the Charleston lawyer James Petigru, and Colonel William Drayton, the wealthy Unionist planter, either resented Calhoun's pretensions or suspected him of

15. Baxter, *One and Inseparable*, 213–17.
16. *Calhoun Papers*, XII, 145; Van Buren to Jackson, October 12, 1833, with endorsement, VBLC; *Jackson Correspondence*, IV, 420; J. C. Fitzpatrick (ed.), *The Autobiography of Martin Van Buren* (Washington, D.C., 1920), 673–79; Sydney Nathans, *Daniel Webster and Jacksonian Democracy* (Baltimore, 1973), 63–66, 69, 70; Norman D. Brown, *Daniel Webster and the Politics of Availability* (Athens, Ga., 1969), 32.

secessionist tendencies. In other slave states, the Jackson-Van Buren organization that stressed common interests between "the planters of the South and plain Republicans of the North" had formed powerful

combinations that were unresponsive or actively hostile to Calhoun's objectives. And the anti-Jacksonians, who were coalescing under the leadership of Henry Clay and advocating a broad national program under the American system, were inhospitable to Calhoun's free trade views and his constitutional theories.[17]

With all these factors working against him, Calhoun's political situation would seem to have been grim indeed. But he remained optimistic and even claimed that he had "never lost an hour's spleep [*sic*], nor a meal amidest [*sic*] the many trying scenes through which I have passed, from anxiety."[18] As he surveyed the membership of the Twenty-third Congress, he recognized that being a party pariah had its advantages. He could rely on some capable tacticians in both houses who remained true believers in the nullification cause. In the House, his cousin Francis Pickens and George McDuffie could be counted on for effective support. Dixon Lewis from Alabama, so fat he had to have a special chair, which became a tourist attraction, was a keen-witted and loyal advocate. His new colleague in the Senate, William C. Preston, was a faithful coadjutor, though Calhoun found him inclined to be independent on economic matters. Another ally was the vain, intemperate senator from Mississippi, George Poindexter, whose backing could sometimes be embarrassing.

Outside of Congress, Calhoun had some powerful adherents in the persons of Littleton Tazewell, now governor of Virginia, Duff Green, who was still lending editorial support and political advice, and free trade advocates in the New York and Massachusetts mercantile communities. His former colleague Samuel Ingham was still active in Pennsylvania politics. Calhoun's allies formed a small but active group, whose congressional members were more influential than their numbers warranted because they held a balance of power between the Whigs and Democrats. Considering the lonely position the nullifiers had occupied a year earlier, Calhoun was quite satisfied with their situation. "Our position is strong in both houses," he said, "particularly in the Senate. No measure can be taken but with our assent, where the administration and the opposition parties come into conflict."[19]

17. Van Buren to Ritchie (copy), January 13, 1827, VBLC; William J. Cooper, *The South and the Politics of Slavery, 1828–1856* (Baton Rouge, 1978), 53, 54.
18. *Calhoun Papers*, XII, 145.
19. *Ibid.*, 192.

When he was not defending slavery from abolitionist attacks, Calhoun ranged himself against the president and administration policies with bitingly severe indictments of presumed executive encroachment on liberty that infuriated Jackson and let loose a continuous counterblast in the *Globe* from the vitriolic pen of Francis Preston Blair. Calhoun's first effort in the Twenty-third Congress was to have the force bill, or "Bloody Act," as he invariably called it, repealed, even though it was due to expire within the current session of Congress. He was unable to secure any action on the bill until near the end of the session, but in a lengthy speech on the repeal of the Force Act he defended his and South Carolina's stand on the tariff and characterized Jackson's actions as "the bloody edicts of Nero and Caligula."[20]

Jackson's veto of the bill to renew the charter of the Bank of the United States over a majority in both houses of Congress, and his removal of the deposits after replacing William J. Duane, the refractory secretary of the treasury, with the more compliant Roger B. Taney, furnished Calhoun with further arguments of Jackson's personal rule. Addressing himself to Clay's resolutions censuring the president, Calhoun excoriated Jackson and Taney, reserving some choice criticism for Amos Kendall, whom he accused of "daily and hourly meddling in politics." The top figures of the administration Calhoun dubbed "artful, cunning and corrupt politicians, and not fearless warriors." He charged, "They have entered the treasury not sword in hand, as public plunderers, but with the false keys of sophistry, as pilferers, under the silence of midnight."[21] The main thrust of Calhoun's speech, however, was what he felt was the total irresponsibility and ignorance of the administration on matters of sound banking and finance. An extreme shortage of currency and the high cost of credit (largely a temporary phenomenon stemming from the retaliation of Nicholas Biddle, who had the Bank of the United States call in its loans from state banks) Calhoun utilized as an argument that a sound and stable currency was a responsibility of the government.

Calhoun took care not to associate himself with Clay and other supporters of the second Bank of the United States, though he admitted his authorship of the bill that had established it in 1816. With respect to the state, or "pet," banks that were receiving government deposits, Calhoun regarded them as no alternative to the Bank of the United States. A fair approach, he thought, would be "to divorce the

20. *Ibid.*, 45–93.
21. Richard Latner, "A New Look at Jacksonian Politics," *Journal of American History,* LXI (1975), 957, 958; *Calhoun Papers*, XII, 221.

government and the banking system"—in effect, the logic that would eventually determine Van Buren's independent, or subtreasury, system. "Whatever the government receives and treats as money, is money," he said, "and if it be money, then they have the right under the constitution to regulate it." Calhoun did agree with Clay, however, that philosophically the country was undergoing a revolution. He voiced his customary fear that Jackson was transforming the Congress into a legislative nullity, with the result of "uniting in the President the power of the sword and the purse." Calhoun observed, "The very existence of free government rests on the proper distribution and organization of power." Heedless of the consequences to him personally, he voted with the Whigs to censure the most popular president since Washington. And when Jackson sent in a bitter protest of the Senate's action, Calhoun was ready with an equally bitter reply, the substance of which was that the Senate regulated its own proceedings and that the president had no right to contest its actions. He then voted with the majority not to receive the protest.[22]

Calhoun had certainly strengthened his reputation as a sound economic thinker among many conservative business leaders, but his sober analyses did not impress the entrepreneurial interests, who resisted any restraints on credit and speculation in land or stocks. His opposition to Jackson, much of which was viewed as personal and vindictive, attracted few adherents outside of South Carolina. He achieved at least one of his objectives, however, in the fall elections of 1834. The nullifiers in South Carolina won an overwhelming victory after they compromised with the Unionists on the test oath question. "You have seen," Calhoun wrote Samuel Ingham, "that we have made peace in our state and that we are a united people. I trust and believe the restoration of harmony is complete."[23]

Calhoun was hopeful that he could extend his support in the Twenty-fourth Congress, which convened on December 7, 1835. There were many areas of public policy that a person with Calhoun's ability and industry could explore to embarrass the administration and enhance his own prestige. But it would be wrong at this stage, with so much ferment in social and economic institutions even in the Deep South, to attribute merely personal motives to Calhoun. As he was driven by what he regarded as grave threats to the fragile social order of his region from menacing forces—abolition being but one such force—his

22. *Register of Debates,* 23rd Congress, 1st Sess., 206–23, 1640–50; *Senate Journal,* 23rd Cong., 1st Sess., 252–53.
23. *Calhoun Papers,* XII, 378.

ambition and his positions on public issues like land policy, the treasury surplus, executive patronage, and foreign policy were interchangeable. His was a broad-spectrum opposition to what he perceived as a uniform manifestation of a transient majority seeking to subvert individual rights through political action. Ultimately, in Calhoun's mind, the will of a popular majority in the free states was being directed at the South and its slave society. Abolitionists were but symptoms, to utilize one of his favorite metaphors, of a deep-seated disease in the body politic.

High on Calhoun's agenda for the Twenty-fourth Congress was an investigation of executive patronage, or the spoils system, as it was commonly called. On January 5, 1835, he introduced a resolution that a committee of two members from each political party be appointed for this purpose because, as he tartly observed, "there are different political interests in the Senate." The next day, the Senate approved the resolution and appointed a select committee composed of Calhoun, chairman, and George M. Bibb from Kentucky, the States' Rights party members; Samuel L. Southard of New Jersey and Daniel Webster, of the Whigs; and Thomas Hart Benton and John P. King, of the Democrats. With Calhoun setting an example, the committee worked hard and in the main harmoniously, though Benton could not conceal his dislike for Calhoun and his strong feelings that the report would be a partisan document that reflected on the administration. Yet Benton could not ignore the fact that he himself had made a similar report on executive patronage nine years before when the Jacksonian coalition was mounting its offensive against the Adams administration.[24] Calhoun did not have much use for Benton, whom he frequently described in his private correspondence as a "humbug."

On February 9, the committee report, a seventy-six-page manuscript with four statistical appendices, was read in the Senate. Although a committee effort, it bore the stamp of Calhoun's close reasoning, and its scope (embracing not just the extent of executive patronage, but the surplus, public lands, and "pet" banks) suggested strongly that the chairman had influenced the committee to follow the broadest possible lines of inquiry. From a policy viewpoint, the problems facing the government were interconnected, and to Calhoun, if not to Benton, they all tended to enhance executive power.

Apart from its assertions of the encroachment of executive power

24. *Register of Debates*, 23rd Cong., 2nd Sess., 109; Thomas Hart Benton, *Thirty Years' View* (2 vols.; New York, 1854–56), I, 80–82.

over the years, the report demonstrated that the number of citizens who were dependent on the government for their support had far outpaced the growth of population. Government expenditures, almost all of which were concentrated in the executive branch, had doubled over an eight-year period (1825–1833). The report's principal disclosure was the amount of government funds held by deposit banks— some eleven million dollars—without proper restrictions as to its prudent use. The report scouted the connection between the deposit banks, the government surplus, and the land boom in progress. It was obvious that the committee members, excluding Benton, were concerned that without any restrictions, the deposit banks were using the surplus to fuel speculation in lands and in stock companies, which in turn increased the market in public lands and further added to the surplus.

After the report was read, Calhoun as chairman of the select committee introduced three bills. One would attempt to force a more stringent accounting from government employees who handled public funds. Another sought to set up controls over the use of public funds on deposit, and the third, in the form of a joint resolution, proposed a constitutional amendment for the distribution of the surplus. Benton immediately attacked the report, accusing Calhoun of improperly influencing the committee. Calhoun responded rather sharply, which brought the Missouri senator to his feet, angrily replying that Calhoun had deliberately lied. His allegation created an uproar in the chamber, and one of Calhoun's champions, George Poindexter, called for a point of order. During the parliamentary bickering, Calhoun sat immobile, seemingly far removed from the confusion around him. When the Senate finally voted that Benton was out of order, Calhoun rose. In a laconic voice he raked over Benton's pretensions and inconsistencies in such a merciless manner that the garrulous Missouri senator was for once effectively silenced.[25]

Calhoun's remarks on the patronage were not the last words about this subject of sensitivity to administration supporters. Silas Wright of New York, Van Buren's spokesman in the Senate and a highly intelligent man of simple dignity, bore the brunt of defending Jackson's patronage policy. Felix Grundy of Tennessee, heavy of body but not of mind, joined Wright with some telling blows on the distribution of powers between the executive and the legislative branches. Calhoun, who respected both men, was forced to shift his argument from a

25. *Calhoun Papers*, XII, 452–56.

constitutional to a political base. "When it comes to be understood that politics is a game," he said, ". . . all will be regarded as mere jugglers—the honest and the patriotic as well as the cunning and the profligate—and the people will become indifferent and passive to the grossest abuse of power."[26]

Despite all the work on the report and the lengthy, frequently acrimonious debate, the bills and the resolutions failed in the House. Speculative fever was too strong among leading spirits in the nation. The deposit banks, with their resident lobbyist in Washington, Reuben H. Whitney, were too influential in Congress. The president still regarded the report on executive patronage to be a partisan device concocted by Calhoun and the Whigs to embarrass him, rather than a signal of any serious difficulties in the economy or abuses in government. His views had great weight among the Democrats.

The last important issue to be raised in the Twenty-fourth Congress was Jackson's vigorous, even provocative policy towards France. The difficulties between the United States and France, beginning during the French Revolution and continuing through the wars of Napoleon, involved claims against France for millions of dollars worth of American ships that had been seized in violation of neutral rights. Successive administrations had been unsuccessful in obtaining a settlement until the shrewd diplomacy of Van Buren, Jackson's secretary of state, and his deputy, William C. Rives, American minister to France, managed to work out a satisfactory solution with the government of Louis Philippe, new king of the French. But the French Chamber of Deputies by a close vote rejected the agreement. This setback after so many months of patient negotiation enraged Jackson, who adopted a truculent stance against France that seemed to portend war.

Calhoun and Clay took the lead in attacking Jackson's policy and in signaling the ruling powers in France that there was a peaceful way out of current difficulties. Calhoun responded favorably to a plea from the aged former secretary of the treasury, Albert Gallatin, to use all of his efforts to preserve the peace. Gallatin was certain that war would be ruinous to American trade, but he was much more alarmed about its effects on "our internal concerns, on our institutions, on the Union."[27] That Jackson had reacted to France in such a belligerent manner was but another example to Calhoun of the general's tendency toward willful, despotic measures, going back to his rash actions in the first Seminole war.

26. *Ibid.*, 495.
27. *Ibid.*, 479, 480.

Calhoun saw other sinister forces behind the president—"a corps of office holders, contractors, jobbers and speculators, to whom war would [be] a harvest." And on March 3, 1835, as the clock in the Senate chamber marked the closing hours of the Twenty-fourth Congress, Calhoun again voiced his fears of a business-bureaucratic cabal that was inciting an impressionable president to drive the nation into war. Before the Senate was a House amendment to an appropriation bill that would raise an additional three million dollars for defense. The president was to have complete discretion as to how the money would be spent. As he had been so frequently during this stormy session of Congress, Calhoun was on his feet in opposition to an administration measure. "There was a war party," he said, "in this as well as every other country—a party deeply interested in the existence of war—a party who were engaged in the business of jobbing, and contracting, and of party making." After a short but spirited debate during which the Whig speakers accused Jackson of being a dictator, the Senate rejected the appropriation.[28]

Fortunately for the well-being of the country, Van Buren and Taney were counseling patience and moderation. And in France, the king strove mightily to secure a favorable vote in the Chamber of Deputies. The crisis passed. While Calhoun was conferring with supporters in Charleston on his way home, news was received that the Chamber of Deputies had acceded to the French government's request. An indemnity of five million dollars, which represented the minimum amount the United States demanded, was to be paid as soon as appropriate arrangements were made.[29]

Calhoun had left for home on March 7, 1835. He took a steamboat to Norfolk and from there traveled to Petersburg, where for the first time he rode south for some miles on a railroad. Within five days he was in Georgetown, a tidewater market center about sixty miles north of Charleston—the fastest trip he had ever made from Washington to his home state. After delivering a short speech in Charleston, he hastened to Fort Hill, where he found that late frost had reduced his cotton crops sharply. Over the past five years, Calhoun's plantations had experienced several good seasons, when crops were plentiful and cotton prices ranged between thirteen and twenty cents a pound, depending on quality.[30] Cotton prices held up well, even during the money panic of 1834, until the panic and depression of 1837 broke the market. Had it not been for the abolitionist excitement, the general prosperity of the

28. *Ibid.*, 500–501; *Register of Debates*, 23rd Cong., 2nd Sess., 731–36.
29. Washington Irving to Van Buren, February 24, 1836, VBLC.
30. *Calhoun Papers*, XII, 521–22, 357, 541.

plantation South would have eased sectional antagonism. As it was, planters like Calhoun became involved in those entrepreneurial activities that they had formerly spurned.

In 1832, Calhoun's eldest son, Andrew, who had left South Carolina College without taking a degree, while seeking some occupation had become interested in the gold-bearing region of northern Georgia at Dahlonega, some seventy miles west of Fort Hill. Enough gold had been discovered in the area's picturesque foothills and valleys three years earlier to precipitate a rush. After the first wave of prospectors, the easily obtainable surface deposits had been exhausted, and a lull in the frenzy had ensued. When Andrew became interested, it was necessary to have equipment and sufficient manpower to work the veins. He had, nevertheless, purchased for his father a share in what was known as the O'Barr mine. No sooner had he concluded the agreement than David C. Gibson, a local speculator, circulated rumors that the mine was a poor one, and Andrew, fearing a further loss, sold out to Gibson. Calhoun must have been distressed at the transaction because Andrew felt that he had lost his "reputation" in the deal.

Calhoun and his brother-in-law Colonel John E. Colhoun visited the goldfields during the summer of 1833. They managed to repurchase the mine from Gibson for six thousand dollars, the same amount Andrew had gotten for his share. From that time on, the mine competed with agricultural pursuits as Calhoun's principal source of interest apart from family and political affairs. Although much concerned with erosion on his plantation and by his own account a lover of nature, Calhoun seemed oblivious of the wanton destruction gold seekers like himself were wreaking in the beautiful valleys and hills of western Georgia. The British-born geologist George Featherstonhaugh, who visited Dahlonega with Calhoun, said: "To obtain a small quantity of gold for the wants of the present generation the most fertile bottoms are rendered barren for countless generations. . . . What was once a paradise will become a desert."[31] Calhoun worked his mine with slave labor and from time to time added to his holdings. An account of his mine published not long after his death described it as having very rich deposits of gold. The venture, however, was not a source of great profit.[32]

31. *Ibid.*, 158, 160, 174; George W. Featherstonhaugh, *A Canoe Voyage Up the Minnay Sotor* (2 vols.; London, 1847), II, 255.

32. Rev. George White, *Historical Collections of Georgia* (New York, 1854), 542, 543. After about nine months of operation, the mine paid Calhoun $612.98. On January 27, 1835, it paid him the sum of $110.62. There are other scattered references to small sums in *Calhoun Papers*, XII, 194, 227, 398, 533, 554, 555. Later, the mine yielded significantly more income, but it never met Calhoun's expectation of great wealth.

Another area of development that Calhoun had long cherished was improved transportation, whether it be the refurbishing and extending of the wretched roads of his native region or the construction of canals, steamboats, or the newest means of overland travel and conveyance, railroads. The accumulation of a federal surplus and the administration's proposal to distribute it to the states kindled anew Calhoun's thoughts on internal improvements. This time, in accordance with his current political and economic ideas, he saw an opportunity for the states themselves to underwrite the projects. Always keenly interested in technological change, Calhoun had been early attracted to railroads as a rapid, flexible, relatively cheap, all-weather means of transportation. He believed them to be particularly suitable to the southern seaboard states, which lacked navigable rivers flowing from the interior to the coast. He had looked with envy, mixed with admiration, at the wealth and the economic and political power the Erie Canal had brought to New York. Likewise, he had watched the progress of the Baltimore and Ohio railroad as it extended towards Harpers Ferry on its way to tap the trade of the rapidly expanding Northwest.

For some time Calhoun had been casting about for a means to promote railroads in South Carolina. The initiative for such an undertaking, however, came not from South Carolina but from Ohio. A group of Cincinnati businessmen met in the summer of 1835 for the express purpose of exploring the possibility of connecting by rail their city with Charleston. They wrote letters of inquiry to Calhoun and to James Edward Colhoun. Calhoun's response was prompt and enthusiastic. He had hoped that Stephen Long's survey of the Southwest would provide the impetus for launching a railroad project that would do for Charleston what the Erie Canal was doing for New York City. But Long's report was not comprehensive enough, and as Calhoun admitted, the abolitionist excitement "rendered it impossible, at this time, to attract public attention in this quarter."[33]

Well-versed in the difficulties of reconciling diverse interests, Calhoun anticipated problems arising from competing locales in the four states (South Carolina, Georgia, Tennessee, and Kentucky) the route would traverse before reaching the Ohio River at Cincinnati. He himself had a route in mind that would cross the Blue Ridge Mountains through a gap that was about forty miles west of Fort Hill. He wasted no time in enlisting his close political friends and relatives in a promotion campaign. His former colleague Robert Y. Hayne, who was then mayor

33. *Calhoun Papers*, XII, 557–62.

of Charleston, set up a citizens' committee.[34] With funds supplied by the city council, the committee hired three engineers to study the route the Cincinnati group had purposed and to make recommendations. By the summer of 1836, the Louisville, Cincinnati, and Charleston Railroad Company had been chartered.

Its board consisted of directors from the four states through which the railroad would pass. South Carolina had subscribed most of the capital stock of four million dollars, which included one million dollars from the state and a "guarantee of two million dollars more to the company for its purchase of properties within South Carolina necessary for the route." The route chosen, however, was not the one Calhoun thought the most practical.[35]

Two months after a convention of the states involved met at Knoxville on July 4, 1836, and settled on the route, Calhoun and two associates left Fort Hill to make a personal inspection of his preferred route. The region they visited was one of wild beauty, in which the headwaters of three rivers, the Saluda, the Keowee, and the Tugaloo descended in scenic falls and rapids. Calhoun must have been reminded of his excursion through western Pennsylvania when he was an ambitious young secretary of war with a brilliant career ahead of him. Now, with his early hopes blasted and his health uncertain, and acutely defensive about the future of his state and section with its slavery system and plantation way of life, he could not view the Union with his former confidence. Yet he enjoyed his trip, and his report of the expedition that had reinforced his original idea on the route presented a detailed and persuasive argument. It was published in the Pendleton *Messenger.* But the local arguments that Calhoun had anticipated prevailed. Hayne, a lifelong friend, broke with him over the issue. Then came the panic of 1837, which effectively squelched the project. It foundered in a sea of opposing views, and the state eventually lost three million dollars, and monied investors an equal sum.[36]

Calhoun's personal interest in mining and his wholehearted support for railroad development were in keeping with his long-range views on the economic development of his community, state, and region. Although he was never directly involved in the efforts of his brother-in-law and of William Gregg in neighboring Edgefield to build cotton mills, there is no evidence that he disapproved of these ventures, and there is every indication that he supported manufacturing in the South

34. *Ibid.,* 566–68, 573, 574–76.
35. S. M. Derrick, *Centennial History of South Carolina Railroad* (Columbia, S. C., 1930), 129, 130, 159, 160.
36. *Calhoun Papers,* XIII, 286–93, XV, 359, 360.

as he had supported manufacturing in the North in 1816. Unquestionably, he read the article Gregg wrote for the Charleston *Courier* in favor of establishing a cotton textile industry in South Carolina, and he must have known of and possibly visited Gregg's mill town at Graniteville, though at the time, the Mexican-American war was absorbing most of his failing energies.

Slave-plantation agriculture was uppermost in Calhoun's mind, of course, but industry and improved transportation and communication were surely important, if not essential, auxiliaries to a more profitable and stronger southern economy. Throughout Calhoun's letters, speeches, and reports of the thirties and forties, there are abundant references to economic development in the South—particularly improved roads and canals and an expanded railroad net. Whether Calhoun visualized a slave labor force manning the factories of a new South is never explicitly stated. But as far back as 1819, when he discussed the Missouri problem with John Quincy Adams, he found no difficulty in slaves working together with whites in the fields and presumably in any workplace. And later, in his replies to the free soil argument, he would reiterate his contention that whites and blacks, free or enslaved, could and did labor together in all areas save in domestic service and in certain menial field tasks. He did not share the fears of his associate James H. Hammond, who wrote that once slaves became artisans, they were halfway down the road to freedom.[37] Nor did he make any comment on the vast pool of landless poor whites that some southerners who wrote on the subject of industrialization thought would provide a cheap labor force for southern factories. If any paradox existed in Calhoun's defensive rhetoric against abolition and the pace and the scope of northern industrial development at what he regarded as the public expense, he certainly was not aware of it. And in the final analysis, it cannot be said that this sentinel of the South was opposed to entrepreneurial capitalism.

Calhoun's unfortunate involvement with the Louisville, Charleston, and Cincinnati railroad was soon put behind him, for the aftermath of the panic of 1837 and its political fallout claimed his complete attention. He had seen his hated rival Martin Van Buren elected to the presidency and, through a unique set of circumstances, found himself risking his political base in the South to support the new president's policies.

37. Laurence Shore, *Southern Capitalists: The Ideological Leadership of an Elite, 1832–1885* (Chapel Hill, 1986), 32–35. Hammond made this remark shortly after Calhoun's death.

XII

A Cautious Return

The years of stress in Calhoun's public career between the easing of the nullification crisis and the Whig victory in 1840 were relatively happy and rewarding in his private life. Tragedies, like the death of two infant grandchildren, had occurred. These were expected, though nonetheless painful, for the state of medicine was still primitive. The death of Calhoun's mother-in-law after a long illness, on April 21, 1836, was rather a relief to the family. For years she had been a difficult woman, willful yet dependent, and increasingly eccentric.

Mrs. Colhoun's large estate was divided among her three children— John Ewing, James Edward, and Floride. Her bequest eased temporarily Calhoun's financial problems. Fort Hill, which he had rented from his mother-in-law and which had been kept in John Ewing Colhoun's name, was finally his. But he still maintained himself and his family from year to year by loans from his factor in Charleston, Floride's cousin John C. Bonneau, and from other sources. Until old Mrs. Colhoun's death, Calhoun maintained cordial relations with his brothers-in-law, though he disapproved of John Ewing's extravagant ways. John Ewing, who apparently had hoped for Fort Hill, became estranged from Calhoun when his mother died. He was beginning to run short of funds, and he seems to have thought that as the oldest child, he had prior rights to his mother's properties.[1]

James Edward had all those thrifty, orderly, and industrious habits that his older brother lacked and that Calhoun admired. He had been a naval officer for a number of years, but finally tiring of the discipline, the politics, and the arduous life of the Old Navy, had resigned and purchased Calhoun's plantation at Bath, to which he added adjoining lands. He renamed his estate Millwood and quickly proved to be a successful planter. James Edward remained a bachelor until he was forty-one years old, and his famous brother-in-law's family he claimed as his own. He was especially fond of Calhoun's two daughters, Anna

---

1. *Calhoun Papers,* XIII, 278, 296, 297, XII, 236; Charles Wiltse, *John C. Calhoun, Nullifier: 1829–1839* (Indianapolis, 1949), 311.

Maria and her younger sister, Martha Cornelia, who had been crippled since birth. So close were the Calhouns to James Edward that they named their fourth son for him. Calhoun depended on the younger of his brothers-in-law to look after his plantation when he was in Washington, and he relied on James Edward's counsel in family matters.[2]

Although the Calhouns' marriage was a secure one, there were times of stress and tension. Floride was an excitable, temperamental person; she was also stubborn and, as she grew older, began to exhibit some of the eccentric qualities of her mother. She had been pregnant most of her married life. The birth of her tenth child, William Lowndes, in 1829 (three children died in infancy), when she was thirty-seven years old, finally terminated her reproductive career. The pregnancies, together with numerous miscarriages, had made her a semi-invalid for years. Floride's illnesses did not improve her disposition or her relationship with her husband.

Calhoun was extremely reticent about his married life. His correspondence with his children invariably portrayed Floride as a capable manager of the household and an inveterate gardener, always busy with various projects. In a letter to his daughter Anna Maria, he said, "I wish you had half the industry of your mother." But Floride had no interest in politics or philosophical speculations, subjects that fascinated Calhoun. And she could be carpingly querulous with her husband and her children over fancied grievances. After one such argument with Andrew, which he reported to his father, Calhoun relaxed his guard and commented on Floride's weaknesses. "As to the suspecious & unfounded blame of your mother, you must not only bear them, but forget them. With the many good qualities of her Mother, she inherits her suspecious & fault-finding temper, which has been the cause of much vexation in the family. I have born with her with patience, because it was my duty to do so, & you must do the same, for the same reason. It has been the only cross of my life."[3]

Andrew Pickens, Calhoun's oldest son, was a likable young man with a sense of humor that his father lacked. He had been somewhat of a trial to Calhoun because of his failure to complete his college education and his inability to settle on an occupation. But Calhoun supported Andrew in his various ventures, which included the gold mine in Georgia and a plantation in Marengo County, Alabama, that had to be carved out of virgin wilderness. Andrew had married Eugenia Chap-

2. *Calhoun Papers*, XI, 568, XII, 236.

3. *Ibid.*, XII, 239; Calhoun to Andrew P. Calhoun, April 12, 1847, John C. Calhoun Papers, Duke University.

pell, the winsome daughter of John Joel Chappell, a prosperous lawyer in Columbia and formerly a colleague of Calhoun during the war hawk Congress. After a little over a year of marriage, Eugenia died, leaving Andrew a distraught widower of twenty-three and the father of a little girl, Calhoun's first grandchild. Andrew doted on the infant, whom he described as having "regular features, black eyes, long black hair, dimple cheek"; she "never cries but always greets you with an outright laugh or loveliest smile that you have ever looked upon." Andrew was unconsciously prophetic when he remarked, "She is too interested, too precocious a child I fear to live," for his baby daughter died less than a year after her mother on January 1, 1835. Calhoun made every effort to direct Andrew's attention away from his grief. He persuaded his son to become a planter, borrowed funds for this purpose, and purchased slaves from his brother-in-law to provide Andrew with a work force.[4]

Despite his worries about Andrew and the tensions of the so-called panic session of Congress, Calhoun found relief and as much relaxation as his nervous temperament permitted in his family life. During much of 1835 and 1836, he maintained a household in Washington that consisted of Floride, Anna Maria, and five-year-old William Lowndes. While in Washington, Anna Maria was a frequent visitor at the Duff Greens' comfortable home near Capitol Hill. She became a close friend of Green's daughter, Margaret. When the Calhouns returned to Fort Hill in the early spring of 1835, Margaret accompanied them. Andrew enjoyed her company during the summer and fall, a feeling that was reciprocated and no doubt encouraged by Andrew's anxious parents. In May, 1835, Andrew and Margaret were married in Washington, D.C.[5]

Although Calhoun must have been relieved that Andrew was settling down, he was concerned about his little daughter Martha Cornelia, or Cornelia as the family called her—a quiet, rather withdrawn child whose deformed spine made it difficult and painful for her to move about, much less to play with other children of her age. When she was fourteen, Calhoun finally decided that she should be brought north to be examined by some of the eminent physicians in Baltimore and Philadelphia. After persuading Floride that this course of action was in Cornelia's best interest (no mean feat), he consulted Dr. Nathan Smith, a specialist in what was beginning to be termed orthopedics.[6]

4. *Calhoun Papers*, XII, 239, 370, 371.
5. Ernest M. Lander, Jr., *The Calhoun Family and Thomas Green Clemson: The Decline of a Southern Patriarchy* (Columbia, S.C., 1983), 8.
6. *Calhoun Papers*, XIV, 118, 157.

In March, 1838, Anna Maria, together with Eldred Simkins' son and daughter-in-law, Arthur and Emma, brought Cornelia to Washington, D.C. She stayed with the Greens while a number of physicians, including Dr. Smith, examined her. The general verdict was hopeful; and the doctors even managed to convince a skeptical Calhoun that a "good deal could be done," but he doubted whether Cornelia's spine would ever be completely straightened. The treatments did prove beneficial, however. With the help of braces, Cornelia was able to be much more active than she had been. She also suffered from a congenital hearing loss and always remained frail and dependent. Cornelia died in 1857 just after reaching her thirty-third birthday.[7]

Calhoun's second son, Patrick, was also of concern to his father. Like Andrew, Patrick had received an uncertain primary and secondary education at the local Pendleton Academy, first under H. W. McClintock and then under Frederick Furber, a Harvard graduate and formerly a teacher at George Bancroft's famous Round Hill Academy. Furber was succeeded by Thomas Wayland, whom a contemporary described "as a sensible looking Englishman."[8] Although a native-born American, Wayland had been educated in England. He came from an intellectual background, being the son of Francis Wayland, president of Brown University, a Baptist clergyman, and a moral philosopher of some standing. The younger Wayland was not an effective teacher, however. The Calhoun boys received what their father described as an "imperfect" education.[9]

Patrick overcame his educational shortcomings and was admitted to West Point. For a time, he gladdened his father's heart by studying hard and abiding by the strict discipline of the academy. But he early showed signs of extravagance and a fondness for liquor and gambling. On a brief leave in New York City, he borrowed $230 from one of his mother's cousins, James E. Boisseau, a wealthy merchant, to settle his debts. Somehow Calhoun learned of Patrick's escapades, but he did not censure his son. On the contrary, he managed to procure a holiday furlough for Patrick, which Anna Maria, who was in Washington with

7. Lander, *Calhoun Family*, 6, 87, 161, 162.

8. *Calhoun Papers*, XII, 176, 177. Some years later, when Patrick was at West Point, Calhoun wrote, "When I reflect how imperfectly prepared you were . . . I ought to be satisfied" (*ibid.*, XV, 559).

9. George William Featherstonhaugh, *A Canoe Voyage Up the Minnay Sotor* (2 vols.; London, 1847), II, 268. For the Pendleton Academy, see advertisement, November 6, 1833, in *Calhoun Papers*, XII, 176. See also "Prospectus for Pendleton Highschool," December 7, 1838, in *Calhoun Papers*, XIV, 479.

her father at the time, explained was a reward for his high marks in his studies and his deportment. "Father thought you would prefer it, to our visiting you," she wrote, "as it would enable you to see sister [Cornelia] who could not travel now for fear of setting her back, and as it would free you from the discipline of the Point, for a short time."[10]

Anna Maria, now twenty-one, was her father's closest confidante. She, of all his children, shared his interest in politics, and though a gay, outgoing young lady who, like her mother, enjoyed company and played the piano well, she inherited from both parents a large capacity for work. When she was still an adolescent, she held classes in reading and writing for her younger brothers.[11]

Calhoun saw to it that Anna Maria had the best education for women that South Carolina provided. After attending a girls' school at Edgefield, where she lived with the Francis Pickens family, she was sent to a boarding school in Columbia. Her education was furthered by her voracious reading, which included not just Sir Walter Scott's novels and romantic poetry, the usual fare of young women of her station, but those volumes her father enjoyed—essays on political philosophy, histories, and biographies. She followed Calhoun's course in Congress through the *Register of Debates* and the *Congressional Globe* and discussed with him the political topics of the day. Calhoun always took time out of his busy schedule to answer his daughter's letters promptly.[12] Lonely and uncomfortable in the various bachelor messes where he boarded in Washington, Calhoun relished Anna Maria's chatty, descriptive letters. Andrew and Floride were also good correspondents, but their letters usually dealt with business affairs of the plantations. "Were it not for you," wrote Calhoun to Anna Maria in the spring of 1834, "I would not have heard a word about the Hum[m]ing birds, their familiarity, the vines, their blooms, the freshness of the spring, the green yard, the children's gardens, and finally Patrick's mechanical genius and his batteaux."

Whenever Anna Maria spent the winter and spring with her father in Washington, she always managed to brighten Calhoun's drab social life. During the third session of Congress, in the winter and spring of 1838, the austere figure of Calhoun and his dark-eyed, dark-haired daughter could be seen in a box at the new National Theatre. On a warm evening in April they saw James Henry Hackett, the New York–born actor already famed for his character roles, play the lead in two

10. *Calhoun Papers,* XIV, 275, 318.
11. *Ibid.,* 318, XII, 275.
12. See, for example, *ibid.,* XII, 238, 240, XIII, 536, 537.

farces, *The Kentuckian in New York* and *Monsieur Townson.* The plays were "utterly ridiculous," said Anna Maria, but she thought Hackett's acting "superb." She also observed, "I never saw father laugh so much or seem to enjoy himself more." In what must have been a gala diversion for Calhoun, the two went to the horse races the next day and a ball that evening at the French embassy in honor of Louis Philippe's birthday.[13]

Anna Maria also found time to spend with a new acquaintance, the six-foot six-inch mining engineer Thomas Green Clemson, whom she found to be a handsome man of fine education, varied interests, and considerable wealth. They met probably at the home of Missouri senator Lewis Fields Linn, a practicing physician and a close friend of Calhoun's. Clemson had come to Washington, D.C., to confer with Linn on the Mine La Motte, a rich lead deposit that both men were interested in exploiting. Anna Maria and Clemson soon became devoted to each other, and before the congressional session was over in July, 1838, they planned to marry.[14]

Calhoun liked Clemson and approved of the marriage; but he must have been deeply saddened to learn that he would lose the constant companionship he had come to share with his daughter. Anna Maria was no less upset at the thought of leaving the person she idolized. For several years, she had acted as her father's secretary, answering some of his letters, copying his manuscripts, and helping him with his research for speeches, public letters, and the position papers frequently requested of him. It had been exciting to her and most satisfying to be so much appreciated for her services. In fact, Anna Maria had expressed on several occasions to her close friends her determination never to marry but to devote her life to her father's career and well-being. "I thought there were duties enough in life for me to perform," she wrote Maria Simkins, "I felt I was useful to my father and was not wholly without objects in life, while I contributed to his pleasure in the slightest degree. . . . You who know my idolatry for my father, can sympathize with my feelings."[15]

Calhoun may have been more disturbed at the impending marriage of his daughter had he not been so deeply involved in attempting to carry the administration's subtreasury bill and at the same time cope with a challenge to his political leadership in South Carolina. During the past year, he had finally decided to give up his independent stand

13. *Ibid.,* XII, 319, XIV, 278, 279.
14. Lander, *Calhoun Family,* 233.
15. *Calhoun Papers,* XIV, 397.

and move toward a more positive cooperation with the Democrats. He realized that he risked the certain enmity of the Whigs in Congress and, more seriously, a division among his supporters at home and in other states. For the past six years, Calhoun had taken the lead in attacking Jackson, Van Buren, and others in the Democratic coalition. He had held up Jackson as an irresponsible egotist bent on enhancing the powers of the chief executive at the expense of the Congress, and those of the national government at the expense of the states. He had represented Jackson as a demagogue who set individual liberty at naught.

Calhoun had characterized Van Buren as a willing catspaw in this process, a machine politician who would subvert the federal system of government for the spoils of office. Calhoun had derived certain political advantages from his posture, which had been of importance in unifying the factions in South Carolina behind his leadership. His stand had also consolidated scattered opinion, mainly in the South but also in northern states like New York, Massachusetts, and New Hampshire, where the Democratic front was weakening over patronage and local issues and where many who rejected the Whig persuasion were also opposed to Jackson-Van Buren policies on the tariff, Indian affairs, banking, and foreign policy. These groups found in Calhoun a national leader whom they could support.[16] They shared the scorn he poured out on Van Buren, who they knew was Jackson's personal nominee for the succession.

In the course of a lengthy speech on the treasury surplus on February 17, 1837, Calhoun fixed his deep-set eyes on Van Buren, who was lounging in the vice-president's chair above the floor of the Senate. The Carolinian said that "he would not deny that Jackson had many high qualities: he had courage and firmness, was bold warlike, audacious; though not true to his word or faithful to his pledges." Alluding to a remark that the Whig senator from North Carolina, Willie Mangum, had made, Calhoun then described Van Buren as not of the "race of the lion or the tiger; he belonged to a lower order—the fox; and it would be in vain to expect that he would command the respect or acquire the confidence of those who had so little admiration for the qualities by which he was distinguished."[17] Calhoun always referred to the Baltimore convention that had nominated Van Buren for the presidency in May, 1835, as a "mock convention" made up of officeholders

16. See Calhoun's remarks on the administration's Indian policy, *ibid.*, XII, 189–91, on "pet banks," 139–41, and on the surplus, 112.

17. *Ibid.*, XIII, 85–86.

whom the Democratic machine controlled. The growing surplus, he charged repeatedly, was being converted into a gigantic slush fund for party purposes.

So constant and so vigorous was Calhoun's public campaign to discredit the Jackson-Van Buren organization that the Whigs considered him to be one of them despite his independent pose. But he had serious doubts about their program and particularly so about their leadership. Clay's American system he had long opposed as the epitome of consolidation. As for the Kentuckian himself, Calhoun completely distrusted his motives.

Clay was a partisan gamester, Calhoun felt, who would embrace any cause he considered to have momentary popularity. In the Senate before all of his colleagues, Clay had charged Calhoun with being impractical—being too metaphysical, too abstract in his reasoning. Calhoun had retorted in a scornful tone that it was precisely these higher qualities of mind that Clay lacked. "To this it may be traced that he prefers the specious to the solid, and the plausible to the true. . . . It is a fault of his mind to seize on a few, prominent and striking advantages, and to pursue them eagerly, without looking to consequences."[18] The Union, he believed, would never be safe in Clay's hands.

Webster, however, Calhoun had to respect for his depth of intelligence and his sure grasp of fundamental issues facing the nation. But Webster was the creature of northern hegemony, the spokesman of narrow class interest—of the bankers and the manufacturers of the Northeast who were, in Calhoun's opinion, draining the lifeblood of the South. Moreover, Webster personified those forces that were reducing the South to a colonial status and were determined to remake it into their own image whereby its social structure based on slavery would be reorganized into that of a free society. As Calhoun wrote Ingham in June, 1836: "We have long been marching on the direct road to despotism. . . . The effect was to give the dominant interest of the Union the supreme and unlimited control. From this the American system draws its origin."[19]

With these notions of a grim future for his region bedeviling his mind, Calhoun in the last analysis preferred to put up with "humbugs" like Benton and foxes like Van Buren. But during 1835 and 1836, he kept these thoughts to himself as he played the role of the independent in Congress and extracted the concessions he sought for his own advancement as well as protection for what he always referred to as the

18. *Ibid.*, XIV, 187.
19. *Ibid.*, XIII, 246–47.

"weak and exposed" portion of the Union. For the presidency he favored Hugh Lawson White of Tennessee over the other Whig contenders—Clay, Webster, and William Henry Harrison of Ohio. Still, he made no attempt to push White's candidacy.[20]

Calhoun's political position began to change in April, 1837, when panic swept the land and swiftly settled into a deep depression. With his usual penetrating analysis of economic trends, Calhoun had long foreseen an impending disaster. By the fall of 1836, he was certain that a crash was imminent. Since the economy had weathered the "panic session" of 1834, a boom psychology had gripped the nation. Cotton prices rose dramatically year after year in northern and European marts, and textile and shipping industries experienced unprecedented growth; but it was speculation in land, public and private, and in railroad equities that epitomized the gambling spirit. Fed by government deposits, by paper profits, and by an unfettered expansion of paper currency through hundreds of new banks, chartered under easy state banking laws, the boom gained alarming momentum in 1836, prompting the Jackson administration to issue the Specie Circular, which for the first time in the history of the young nation required gold or silver to be paid for public lands. This move brought a sudden check to overspeculation in land—a check that was only temporary, however. When Van Buren was inaugurated on March 4, 1837, the signs of economic disorder were becoming quite apparent as European investors began cautiously liquidating their American investments. The Bank of England twice raised its discount rates to dampen what it perceived to be an overheated economy in England and in France.

Calhoun believed the principal cause of the panic and depression was the derangement of the currency and the disappearance of a sound credit system after the removal of the deposits from the Bank of the United States. As early as January, 1833, he correctly diagnosed the basic problem that would bring on the panic more than three years later. "The currency of the country is the credit of the country—credit in every shape, public and private," he told the Senate in one of his more powerful speeches, "credit not only in the shape of paper, but that of faith and confidence between man and man. . . . To inflict a wound any where, particularly on the public faith, is to embarrass all the channels of currency and exchange; and it is to this, and not to the withdrawing the few millions of dollars from circulation that I attribute the present monied embarrassment."[21]

20. *Ibid.*, 301.
21. *Ibid.*, XII, 216.

For the next few years, Calhoun watched the spiral of speculation and the disordered, unregulated state of currency and credit. Using a mixed metaphor, frequently he warned of an "explosion" in what he called the "deseased" state of the economy. Just a few weeks before Van Buren's inauguration, he said that the collapse was inevitable and impending. On March 9, 1837, Richard Crallé, then editing a paper in support of Calhoun, the Baltimore *Merchant*, published an interview between Calhoun and an anonymous person who asked his views on the current situation. He replied: "Live, sir, economically, pay the debts you owe, if any, and contract no new ones. . . . A revulsion, sudden and desolating, must come, and that at no distant day."[22]

Calhoun was not surprised, therefore, when word was received at Fort Hill that commission houses in New York, Boston, and Baltimore and the great cotton exchange in New Orleans had all closed their doors. Nor was he astonished at the prompt suspension of specie payments of all the nation's banks that followed the commercial failures. The panic he had so long foretold had come. With a sense of grim satisfaction, Calhoun wondered what the new administration would do. Would it become demoralized and sink into a marsh of ineptitude and indecision? He thought that very possible and even flirted with the idea of a parliamentary government. "In England, or even in France they [the administrators] would be instantly expelled; but here we must bear with them, I suppose, til '41, or even longer, if suff[ici]ent patronage be left in their hands to purchase the mercenary," he commented.[23]

Van Buren called a special session of Congress to meet on September 4, and from time to time during the summer, he solicited advice from various sources. Although he knew that Calhoun had deep insights on banking and economic affairs, the president never communicated with him, even indirectly, which he could have easily done through senators like Dr. Linn of Missouri. Remote from the Washington scene and isolated politically, Calhoun had no idea what program Van Buren would propose at the special session; he thought that any remedy put forth would be "utterly hopeless under the control of those in power."[24]

As the summer advanced, a move got underway to take advantage of the depression and call a convention under Whig auspices that would organize opposition to the Van Buren administration. Presumably, it would present a plan to solve the current economic difficulties.

22. *Ibid.*, XIII, 112, 114, 140, 175, 176, 251, 259, 426, 493–95.
23. *Ibid.*, 509, 12, 512.
24. *Ibid.*, 507.

Calhoun refused to have anything to do with the proposed convention until its objectives were more specifically defined. Obviously he thought this was a Clay- or Webster-inspired move to position a candidate for the presidency in 1841. The economic plan, if any was developed, would, Calhoun felt, simply be the American system he had so frequently denounced as "consolidationist," though perhaps refurbished in new rhetoric.[25]

Calhoun reached Washington, D.C., a day or so before the special session was called to order on September 4. After listening to Asbury Dickens, the clerk of the Senate, read Van Buren's lengthy address and studying the much longer document of the secretary of the treasury, Levi Woodbury, detailing the problems besetting the government, Calhoun reported to James Edward Colhoun that "things are doing well here." Van Buren's program to meet the financial situation consisted of four distinct recommendations: an increase in the money supply by issuing up to ten million dollars in treasury notes; postponement of distribution, which would have obligated the government to pay nine million dollars to the states from the currently frozen surplus in the deposit banks; a federal bankruptcy law; and the centerpiece of the program, the complete separation of the government from the banks— an independent, or as it became more popularly known, subtreasury, system.[26]

Calhoun was instantly attracted to the subtreasury plan, which in many ways resembled an idea he had broached to the Senate in a speech he had made more than three years before. "Van Beyren [*sic*]," he exulted, "has been forced by his situation and the terror of Jackson to play directly into our own hands. . . . We have now a fair opportunity to break the last of our commercial shackles; I mean the control which the North through the use of government credit acting through the banks, has exercised over our industry and commerce."[27] Despite his feelings for Van Buren, Calhoun was determined to support the administration, though he knew that he risked a division among his political supporters.

Already there were indications that the deposit banking interest within the Democratic party was breaking away from the president on the subtreasury issue and was forming an organized opposition. A new

25. *Ibid.,* 516, 528.
26. Van Buren, memorandum, May, 1837, VBLC; Appendix, *Register of Debates,* 25th Cong., 1st Sess., 1–50; James D. Richardson (ed.), *A Compilation of the Messages and State Papers of the Presidents, 1789–1897* (20 vols.; Washington, D.C., 1900), III, 324–46.
27. *Calhoun Papers,* XI, 219, 327, XIII, 535.

paper, the *Madisonian,* had just been established in Washington, D.C., to present the group's views. Senators William C. Rives of Virginia and Nathaniel Tallmadge of Van Buren's state of New York were heading the opposition group, which was calling itself the Conservative party. While this move spelled political trouble for the president, it also posed immediate problems for Calhoun if he supported the administration's program. One of Calhoun's colleagues in the Senate, William C. Preston, was outspoken in his condemnation of the subtreasury. At least half of the South Carolina congressional delegation, headed by the popular stump speaker Waddy Thompson, Jr., had joined Preston. In addition, the Whigs and some Democrats were urging the rechartering of the Bank of the United States as the only sure means of restoring both the public and the private credit to its former state.

Calhoun rejected all these opposing stands, admitting that his position was one "of great delicacy and will require consummate prudence with decision and boldness." His support of the administration must be on his own terms. Van Buren's subtreasury bill was an artful compromise measure that was aimed at gaining the support of hard-money men like Thomas Hart Benton and state-bank men like Tallmadge and Rives. Silas Wright, Van Buren's floor leader in the Senate, had piloted the bill through the Democratic caucus. Its key political feature was its silence on whether the government would accept the notes of specie paying banks for the purchase of public lands, excise taxes, and import duties—a modest concession to the Conservatives.

When the treasury note bill came up for debate, Calhoun asked for postponement until he had prepared an amendment. Administration senators objected but could not head off Calhoun's motion. On September 18, the treasury note bill again became the order of the day. Calhoun made a lengthy speech, during which he gave the administration his terms for support. He then offered his amendment, which seriously threatened the fate of the subtreasury. The amendment would have the proposed subtreasury accept three-fourths of the government's revenue in specie in 1838, one-half in 1839, one-quarter in 1840, and specie only from 1841 on. If the administration rejected Calhoun's amendment, it would lose the support of the hard-money men and Jackson. If it accepted the amendment, it would alienate the state-bank men, who held a balance of power in the House. The administration accepted the amendment, hoping that offering a bribe of the government printing to the *Madisonian* and applying judicious pressure on the Conservatives by Speaker James K. Polk and the chairman of ways and means, Churchill C. Cambreleng, would line up enough of them to pass the bill. Neither of these efforts succeeded; not one of the Conservative members would accept Calhoun's hard-money amendment. The subtreasury failed by thirteen votes.[28] Calhoun supported all the other administration measures, which were carried on close votes in both houses.

During the debate on these bills, Calhoun was embarrassed by the heated opposition of his colleague Preston, who fought him at every point and accused him of waging a secret war against the banks. Calhoun was not concerned about the charges of inconsistency from the Whig orators, but such open opposition from within his own state and region was undermining his painfully gained position of leadership and his hopes for unity among the slaveholding states. When he returned to Fort Hill after the special session, Calhoun found that the division within his state was deeper than he had thought. Governor Pierce Butler and former governors Hamilton and Hayne, on whom Calhoun had counted for support, were in favor of state banks. They insisted that further economic development in South Carolina, and especially railroads, had to have the support of the federal government through local lending agencies.[29]

Even George McDuffie sided with the state-bank men. It was essential that Calhoun explain his complete change in political direction to those who were steeped in opposition tactics and rhetoric towards the regular Democratic organization—those who thought Jackson an overbearing tyrant and Van Buren a supple little intriguer. Calhoun had prepared his defenses in Washington, D.C., by finally coaxing Crallé to edit a new paper, the Washington *Reformer*, which immediately took up the cudgel in his behalf. And John A. Stuart, who had succeeded Rhett as editor of the *Mercury* in Charleston, began a spirited defense of the subtreasury. But Calhoun realized that only he could properly inform his own constituency. Thus he utilized a reply to a public dinner proffered in his honor by a group of supporters in nearby Edgefield District to set forth his reasons for the change.[30]

Calhoun's letter, which was widely published, was an ingenious mixture of self-justification and demonstrated proof that his policies had forced the Democrats to return to the principles that he had originally espoused. His position had always been consistent, Calhoun maintained; his independence and that of his followers since 1832 had never faltered. Cooperation with the Whigs (he underscored the word

---

28. *Ibid.*, 544–73; *Congressional Globe*, 25th Cong., 1st Sess., 35–37.
29. *Calhoun Papers*, XIII, 588, 612, 621, 628.
30. *Ibid.*, 629, 631–34.

cooperation) had been solely a matter of expediency to combat the executive tyranny of Jackson and the corruption of Van Buren. Calhoun averred that he had never accepted the Whig program of central banking, protective tariffs, and federally directed and controlled internal improvements. The subtreasury plan was the first dividend in the rollback of the consolidation tendencies he claimed had infiltrated the Democratic party. The banking interest, whether expressed through a Whig bank of the United States or through Jacksonian deposit banks, still represented the money power that when joined with the central government would overcome the states and speedily destroy individual liberties.

Calhoun claimed that nullification had triumphed. The Democrats, he said, had conceded that banks and currency and credit control were beyond the powers of the federal government. The Van Buren administration and the Democratic party had changed direction, not Calhoun and his dedicated band. Oversimplification, even sophistry, burdened his argument, but the Edgefield letter was an amazingly adroit political document. One month later, Calhoun received convincing proof that his course on the subtreasury and his explanation had satisfied the voters of his state. He visited Columbia on his way to Washington, D.C., and was gratified that a series of resolutions supporting him and the subtreasury plan were carried in the legislature by more than a ten-to-one majority.[31]

The two months since the adjournment of the special session had been trying ones for Calhoun. Besides his political problems, he had to harvest his cotton and corn without the services of his overseer, William P. McDow, the best he had employed to that date. McDow had died of fever while Calhoun was in Washington. Calhoun had also found his entire family sick with the same illness, though they soon recovered. He himself came down with a heavy cold and a severe eye inflammation that made it difficult for him to read and write and was bothersome in the fields, where he spent most of the daylight hours.[32]

The support Calhoun received from the South Carolina legislature buoyed him up. He made the tiring, uncomfortable overland trip to Washington, D.C., without any detriment to his health. Although the Edgefield letter had announced his return to the Democratic party, he maintained his distance from Van Buren. As for the Whigs, Calhoun characterized them as "bitter as gall. . . . Their hired scrib[b]lers and

31. *Ibid.*, 636–40, XIV, 7, 22.
32. *Ibid.*, XIII, 630, 642, XIV, 7.

press are daily misrepresenting in the grossest manner everything I say or do."[33]

However Van Buren may have felt at Calhoun's continued enmity and his role in sidetracking the compromise subtreasury plan in the special session of Congress, he was grateful for the Carolinian's support. Calhoun was articulating a new populist theme that made sense to Democrats hard pressed by the depression. In Senate debate and in public letters, Calhoun saw a union of money power with political power as one of the central causes of the panic and depression. But going beyond the economic consequences, he declared that this combination, if permitted to flourish, would be "far more fatal to free and popular institutions, than that of church and state. . . . Let the union be renewed," he declared, "it matters not whether with a league of State banks or a national bank, let the money and political power be once more wedded, and there will be an end to State rights." In the course of the debates over the subtreasury, Calhoun became the most effective speaker for the administration and the principal target of Whigs and Conservatives alike. He acquitted himself well in arguments that frequently descended to personalities on both sides.[34]

Despite Calhoun's efforts, the subtreasury bill that presumably would cut the ties between the money power and politics could not overcome the combined Whig and Conservative resistance in the House during the third session of the Twenty-fifth Congress. Nor was the administration able to muster sufficient support for its principal reform measure until 1840, the last full year of the Van Buren administration, despite Calhoun's support. Calhoun persisted, however, in having his specie clause inserted in the bill.[35] There had been a brief flurry of recovery in 1839, when the banks resumed specie payment and the government recovered its deposits. This interlude proved only a temporary halt in the downward spiral of industrial production and commodity prices. Throughout the entire period, the Whig party gained in strength and organization. By 1840, most of the Conservatives who had threatened a third-party movement had joined the Whigs. Van Buren was faced with a serious organized opposition that was extending itself west and south from New York and Virginia.

Meanwhile, Calhoun had to descend to the actual hustings, which he had not done for years, to combat dissidents in his home state. He was able to deal with Preston, who lacked a combative style and whose

33. *Ibid.,* XIV, 9, 105.
34. *Ibid.,* 163–248; Baxter, *One and Inseparable,* 261–67.
35. *Polk Correspondence,* IV, 405, 474, 475.

political strength was localized in the professional and commercial elite in Charleston. Hayne was dead, and Hamilton and McDuffie had retired from public life and ceased to concern themselves publicly with the subtreasury or even the abolition issue. But Waddy Thompson, Jr., from neighboring Greenville was another matter. Calhoun found himself in an impromptu debate with the redoubtable Thompson at a barbecue in late August, 1838. The two men exchanged heated remarks—one of the rare occasions when Calhoun lost his composure. Thompson was not to be purged, though he, as well as Preston and another longtime foe of Calhoun, Hugh Legaré, joined the Whig party.[36]

Calhoun's summer campaign in South Carolina was, on the whole, successful. He had managed to unite both former nullifiers and Unionists behind the election of J. P. Richardson to the governorship. He had given a renewed impetus to the activities of a troop of young, restless men who were in the main more adept politically than he. Robert Barnwell Rhett, former editor of the *Mercury*, James H. Hammond, now becoming a highly successful planter, and Franklin Elmore, president of the Bank of South Carolina, provided ideas and, more importantly, funds for a Calhoun presidential campaign organization.

His transition from the lonely posture of nullification through an independent, Whig-leaning stance to a position in the Democratic party had been achieved with less difficulty than Calhoun had anticipated. Outside of South Carolina, Calhoun's long-term objective of unifying the South behind him in a defense of slavery and of states' rights had made some progress in Alabama, where Dixon Lewis was pushing his cause with considerable success. In Virginia, Littleton Tazewell, the gifted newspaper editor Thomas W. Gilmer, and the young lawyer Robert M. T. Hunter constituted an active nucleus of support.

Calhoun's return to the Democratic party helped his cause significantly in the Old Dominion. The Richmond junto and its influential leader Thomas Ritchie, while wary of Calhoun, were willing to join their erstwhile political foe to form a united front against the Whigs. The elections of 1838 had created a situation in the House of Representatives whereby the Democrats who supported Calhoun, if they could manipulate the congressional caucus, would hold the balance of power.

Two key administration leaders in the House, James K. Polk and

36. *Calhoun Papers*, XIV, 391–94; *Niles' Register*, LIV, 406; *Calhoun Papers*, XIV, 409, 410, 411–18; *Niles' Register*, LV, 74; Wallace, *South Carolina*, 475.

Churchill C. Cambreleng, were not members of the new Twenty-sixth Congress. With the two men's experienced hands no longer on the mechanisms of control, Calhoun's lieutenants saw a chance to elect a member of their faction as Speaker. Franklin Elmore devised a strategy that apparently was not communicated to Calhoun. First, Calhoun's contingent would agree to the caucus candidate but hold back enough votes so that the election would be deadlocked, with neither the Whig nor the Democratic candidate gaining a majority on the first round. They would then slip in their own candidate; if he was unsuccessful, they would fall back on two other choices. Their candidates were Dixon Lewis, Francis Pickens, and Robert M. T. Hunter. Elmore thought Hunter had the best chance because he was nominally a Whig and popular with many fellow party members, though he had supported the subtreasury bill.

235

The election proceeded exactly as Elmore had planned. Pickens had been delayed in South Carolina, and since he was not present, his candidacy was dropped, much to his chagrin. John Winston Jones, a colorless but dependable Virginian and the administration's candidate, won in the caucus by one vote over Lewis. The Whigs proposed John Bell of Tennessee, a veteran anti-Jackson man, shrewd, capable, and tough minded. After three ballots with no majority, while Lewis gained steadily, the Calhoun faction tried to stampede the House in his favor. But a solid phalanx of Whigs and a number of administration Democrats kept Lewis from a majority. After ten ballots, which showed Hunter's support increasing slowly, the Whig leadership threw its weight behind him. With Calhoun's contingent, joined by a number of administration Democrats, voting for Hunter, he was elected Speaker. Van Buren saw through the maneuver as a bid by Calhoun for the succession, but he was not displeased with the result. Hunter would support the subtreasury bill, a factor that was uppermost in the president's mind. There were now enough Democrats in the House backing Calhoun or the administration to pass the bill. The Senate was secure.[37]

With one of his supporters, albeit a Whig, the Speaker of the House, and his effective rhetoric gaining support for the subtreasury program, Calhoun felt that it was time to resume personal relations with the president. As he explained to his daughter Anna Maria: "There could be little doubt as to the time. It must be done, if at all, before the election is over. If delayed till after he was reelected, it would have lost

37. John Boyd Edmunds, "Francis W. Pickens: A Political Biography" (Ph.D. dissertation, University of South Carolina, 1967), 47–49; *Calhoun Papers*, XV, 20; *Congressional Globe*, 26th Cong., 1st Sess., 88–89.

all dignity on my part and exposed me to very improper imputations." On the train from Richmond to Washington, D.C., Calhoun met William H. Roane, a newly elected senator from Virginia. Roane urged him to visit the president, thereby signalizing to the public that he and Van Buren had composed their differences. Roane added that the junto was anxious for a formal accord with Van Buren. Calhoun was favorable but not to be rushed. He would await the president's annual message to Congress, and if he deemed it satisfactory, he would, as he said to Roane, make "my personal, conform with my political relations."[38]

Van Buren's third message, one of his strongest state papers, impressed Calhoun; yet he waited until he could be certain that Clay and Webster would support William Henry Harrison, who had been nominated for president at Harrisburg on December 8. If they did not back Harrison and the Whigs failed to unite on one candidate, Calhoun thought he might have a chance against Van Buren on the abolition and tariff issues. By December 20, Calhoun realized that neither Clay nor Webster would split the Whig party. He delayed no longer.[39]

On New Year's Day, 1840, he attended the president's public reception. Shortly thereafter, Roane arranged a meeting between the two men. At the appointed hour, Calhoun and Roane were ushered into Van Buren's office. The president rose and extended his hand to the gaunt figure that towered over him. Calhoun accepted the gesture but made it clear that restoring their personal relations was simply a matter of expediency. Van Buren was sensitive to the Carolinian's discomfort. He knew that Calhoun envied his position and despised him as the presumed architect of all his political misfortunes. And Calhoun did not attempt to hide his feelings from Van Buren. He said that he had not changed his opinion of Van Buren's past actions, but that whatever political transgressions may have occurred, they were not of "sufficient magnitude to influence my course." If Harrison should prevail in the coming election, Calhoun stated, "a national Bank and tariff certainly will follow." His visit was intended "to remove the awkwardness of defending the political measures and course of one, with whom I was not on speaking terms and the weakening effects resulting from such a state." Van Buren expressed his gratitude for the step Calhoun was taking. The two men shook hands again, and the brief interview was over.[40]

38. *Calhoun Papers*, XV, 97, 68, 69.
39. *Ibid.*, 22.
40. Martin Van Buren to Jackson, February 2, 1840, VBLC; *Calhoun Papers*, XV, 68, 69.

By now, the presidential campaign had begun in earnest. A severe economic downturn during the spring of 1840 hurt Van Buren's cause. The Whigs, for once well organized, made hard times the underlying strategy of their campaign. In northern and northwestern states, Whig newspapers and stump speakers blamed the continuing depression on the subtreasury plan, which had finally become law, and the compromise tariff. In southern states their emphasis was entirely on the subtreasury, which they claimed was responsible for the low prices cotton commanded in the world market. The Whigs embellished these issues with theatricals to impress the uninformed voters—log cabins, coonskin caps, and for the drinkers, hard cider and other spirits. Not neglecting the temperance vote, they also provided nonalcoholic beverages. All of these gestures disgusted Calhoun, who was equally repelled when the Democrats countered with similar crowd-pleasing tactics.

At first Calhoun thought that the Democrats would win easily, but by the end of April, 1840, he decided the election would be close. His feelings about Van Buren remained ambivalent. He was supporting the president and using his influence in South Carolina and throughout the Union to defeat Harrison. He agreed with Hammond, however, that "it is a bitter pill." Van Buren still bore the stigmata of the force bill and Jackson's proclamations against nullification. Nevertheless, he was the better choice of two evils. "His professions are fair," Hammond wrote, "and for nearly four years his conduct has been nearly unexceptionable but more far more than this, he is in every way more nearly allied to us in principle than his opponent." Although South Carolina's vote was never in doubt, Preston, Thompson, and William C. Dawson, a Whig congressman from Georgia, stumped the state against Calhoun. Despite their denials, Calhoun insisted that they had come out boldly "on the side of the bank, tariff, abolition, antimasonry and consolidation party."[41] He was also upset by Duff Green's defection to the Whigs. For a time this political cleavage caused some bad feelings in the family.

South Carolina cast its electoral vote for Van Buren, who was, however, defeated by about 150,000 popular votes. Harrison's victory in the electoral college was much more decisive, with 234 votes to 60 for Van Buren. In assessing the results, Calhoun perceived the Whigs as far too heterogeneous in outlook to coalesce behind any program. He was quite certain that the party would degenerate into quarreling factions before Harrison's term was over. Van Buren's defeat, he con-

41. *Calhoun Papers*, XV, 191, 187, 188.

cluded, was just retribution for "all the old sins of Jackson's times. Although I deplore the mode, in which they have been put down, and the immediate grounds on which it was done," he commented, "I am not prepared to say, but what it will, in the end contribute to a more thorough reform. . . . Individually I have nothing to regret."[42]

Calhoun would never have admitted it, even to himself, but Van Buren's repudiation opened up an opportunity for him. His loyal supporters were quick to grasp this implication. What Calhoun and his followers did not realize at the time was that while their ends—the security and prosperity of the slave-plantation system—were the same, their means to achieve these ends were diverging. Southern politicians, some of whom followed Calhoun's star, were committed to cooperation with their northern counterparts on the slavery issue and on other issues that benefited the South. Some, if not all, had personal motives at stake in the perpetuation of national parties. Lucrative and prestigious federal offices were of prime concern. And while national power protected slavery as a local institution, alliance with northern politicians for mutual benefit seemed the best way for these men to further their careers at home and in Washington, D.C., and to achieve the perpetuation of the slave republic. Calhoun also at times had been responsive to the utility of political cohesion, his return to the Democratic party in 1837 being the most recent example.

Even though Calhoun understood that cooperation with the northern wing of the Democratic party was essential if he were ever to realize his burning ambition for the presidency, he looked far beyond the immediate concerns of his political friends and foes and saw that the free and the slave sections of the country were basically incompatible. Compromise might last for a generation, but unless the North made substantial and lasting concessions there would be no ultimate security for the social and economic institutions of the South. One of the driving motives in Calhoun's unrelenting quest for the presidency was that he could utilize the office's powers and influence to fashion what he hoped would be an ironclad arrangement that would protect the South and that no future political process could sidestep or weaken.

42. *Ibid.*, 376.

XIII

Hope Springs Eternal

Calhoun made his way to the Senate chamber on December 15, 1840, through rain and slush resulting from a recent thaw after a heavy snowfall. For once he did not have a cold or the hoarseness that had afflicted him for years during the winter weather in Washington, D.C. He felt more fit than he had for some time.

As Calhoun took his seat, Henry Clay was just completing his remarks on the subtreasury law. He closed by moving a resolution that would repeal it "forthwith." Calhoun was looking for a pretext to set forth his ideas on the state of the nation, the Whig party, a program for the future—in short, a platform for his candidacy in 1844, when he assumed Clay would be his opponent. He rose to his feet, his smoldering eye on Clay.

Disclaiming that he had ever played or intended to play "the game of in and out politics," Calhoun said that he would support those measures of the new administration that he approved. Those he would not support, like Clay's resolution before the Senate, he would oppose as a matter of principle, not of party loyalty. Then Calhoun set forth what he called Jeffersonian principles of states' rights. He affirmed his belief in the value of the subtreasury, and he rejected Hamilton's idea that a national debt, funded or unfunded, was a national blessing. The use of extensive patronage for partisan purposes was corrupting and thus indefensible. He objected to the recharter of the national bank, any distribution scheme that further depleted the treasury, and any tampering with the compromise tariff. His silence on abolition indicated to his supporters in the Democratic party that he approved of the Van Buren administration's policies on this highly controversial issue.[1]

That he meant to demonstrate publicly his loyalty to the party Calhoun made evident when he ventured out on the cold, blustery afternoon of January 1, 1841, to attend Van Buren's last public reception. He would not have done so, he remarked to his daughter Anna Maria, had Van Buren won the last election. But to absent himself would have

1. Washington *Globe*, December 16, 1840.

been noted, he thought, and misconstrued. Many, he said, attended for the same reason. Calhoun was now paying attention to the small political details that he had spurned in the past.[2] And he watched with a jaundiced eye the flock of would-be Whig officeholders who were already crowding into the lobbies of Congress to seek out influential party figures. For future reference, he noted the more persistent and the manner with which his Whig colleagues received them. He also paid a courtesy call on President-elect Harrison, who greeted him effusively, as if they had been friends for years when in reality they had only a passing acquaintance.

A day or so later, when he was busy at his desk in the Senate, Calhoun felt a tap on his shoulder. He turned around to find Harrison, who had come into the chambers through the lobby behind the vice-president's desk. Calhoun immediately recognized the awkwardness of the situation, especially as Harrison began to speak about the policies he intended to pursue as president in a voice audible throughout the small chamber. Calhoun politely interrupted long enough to suggest that they resume their conversation in the lobby. Harrison agreed and followed the Carolinian out of the chamber. There, to Calhoun's relief, a crowd of congressmen, expectant officeholders, and visitors surrounded the president-elect, and Calhoun was able to excuse himself. "It is almost distressing to see him," he wrote Anna Maria. "He is now in his 69th year, with the full share of infirmity belonging to that age, and very little of even the physical strength necessary to encounter the heavy responsibility belonging to his station; yet, as unconscious as a child of his difficulties and those of his country."[3]

It was apparent that the supple Clay was controlling Harrison. His audacious colleague, Calhoun decided, was directing the Whig program through a weak president. But Clay would have to face the united opposition that Calhoun was determined to lead in the Senate. During the last week of the Van Buren administration, both Calhoun and Clay staked out more precisely their respective positions. John J. Crittenden, Clay's alter ego from Kentucky, resubmitted the bankruptcy bill. The following week he tacked an amendment to Benton's preemption bill that would distribute the income from the sale of federal lands to the states. Clay himself moved a resolution that would revise the tariff upward so as to provide additional revenue for the depleted treasury. Finally, several Whig senators opened up debate on the reestablishment of a national bank.

2. *Calhoun Papers*, XV, 409, 410.
3. *Ibid.*, 504.

Of these Whig propositions, the preemption-distribution scheme was the most politically sensitive and, as Calhoun saw it, the linchpin of the entire Whig program. Benton's bill had been before Congress many times in the past and enjoyed substantial western support. It provided settlers who had not paid for their land preemptive rights of purchase when it came to settlement of their debts. In combining distribution with preemption, the politically agile Clay was bidding for votes from the West and from all those states hard pressed for funds as a result of the continuing depression. But Clay's major underlying purpose was to deprive the treasury of much-needed income and thus create the necessity of raising the tariff.

All the leading Democrats in Congress recognized Clay's tactics. Calhoun, as usual more perceptive than his colleagues, took the lead in focusing on the preemption-distribution scheme, yet at the same time, he took care to advance his own theories of state versus federal power without alienating the land-hungry constituency in the West. His argument was a familiar one, a federal cession of the lands to the states under strict terms that would provide the federal government with 65 percent of the income from sales. He wanted a lean but solvent federal government that would have a minimum of executive patronage and no incentive to raise tariff schedules on the pretext of revenue needs.[4]

Neither preemption nor distribution survived in the lame duck session of the Twenty-sixth Congress; and Calhoun had the satisfaction of advancing his own conservative views while helping mightily to derail the Whig legislative program before it fairly got underway. Later in the session, he clothed his party loyalty with a high-minded appeal to the sanctity of contracts. On a Whig motion to dismiss Blair and Rives as printers for the Senate, Calhoun ignored his oft-expressed hostility to Jackson's waspish editors and praised them as public-spirited citizens whose faithful performance should ensure the continuity of their printing contract. His stand, of course, earned him the gratitude of party leaders and even elicited favorable comments from Jackson.[5]

Calhoun also showed political sense by restraining any premature moves regarding his candidacy. Well before the 1840 election, he had publicly disavowed an article in the Charleston *Mercury* hinting broadly that he was a candidate to succeed Van Buren. After the Whig victory, his advisors were certain that restraint regarding the next presidential campaign was the best policy until the political situation clarified. There had been hopes that Van Buren would not again seek public

4. *Ibid.*, 423, 443, 447, 449.
5. *Ibid.*, 524–30.

office after his defeat; these were quickly dispelled when Benton had the Missouri legislature nominate the New Yorker as the Democratic candidate in 1844. Van Buren moved quickly to squelch this move without offending his supporters or absolutely refusing a nomination. His public letter to Governor Reynolds of Missouri was a small masterpiece of political ingenuity that seemed to head off any more premature actions. But his statement put Calhoun and his advisors on guard.[6]

Calhoun remained in Washington, D.C., for Harrison's inauguration, and listening to the president's lengthy, vapid address confirmed him in his opinion that Harrison would be but a plastic figure that Clay and Webster would mold to their advantage. Calhoun joined other senators who, like himself, had just been elected to a new term of office for the simple ceremony of swearing-in conducted by Vice-President Tyler. The Senate then considered Harrison's cabinet appointments in executive session. Calhoun voted with his colleagues to approve the entire slate, headed by Daniel Webster as secretary of state. The Carolinian was anxious to leave for home and was actually passing through Charleston when the Senate adjourned on March 15, 1840.

Plantation and family matters were uppermost in Calhoun's mind. When he had left Fort Hill for Washington, D.C., the previous December, the fields, outbuildings, and equipment were all in poor condition. His overseer, Green Stevens, had mismanaged the estate during Calhoun's frequent absences visiting his Georgia gold mine or electioneering. Stevens either left Calhoun's employ or was discharged. Calhoun then made an arrangement, partially on a crop sharing basis, with Mr. Fredericks, who would act as overseer under the direction of Calhoun's son-in-law, Clemson.[7] Although Clemson tended to be fussy about details, he and Fredericks got along well and soon were making progress restoring the plantation to its former state.

Either Calhoun had not stipulated an adequate food allowance for his slaves, which seems unlikely, or the new management team was working them harder than he had anticipated, because there were constant complaints about insufficient rations. In less than a month, the Fort Hill work force had slaughtered the hogs and prepared a six months' supply of preserved pork, and had repaired the gristmill, cotton gin, dam embankment, and sluiceways of the millpond. The

240

6. *Ibid.*, 40, 41, 413, 414; Van Buren to Thomas Reynolds, March 6, 1841, VBLC, also published in the Washington *Globe,* March 20, 1841; William L. Marcy to Prosper Wetmore, March 12, 1841, in William L. Marcy Papers, Library of Congress.

7. *Calhoun Papers,* XV, 381.

slaves had begun filling the icehouse with a season's supply of ice they had cut. They had ginned and baled the cotton, plowed and manured the fields. Fredericks was proving to be not only a highly competent manager but also a versatile mechanic. In addition, he supplied some draft animals that were desperately needed. Calhoun was much relieved that the plantation was now in such capable hands after Stevens' neglect. "I know, that you will find every thing out of order," he wrote Clemson, "and I would be uneasy were it not that you were present with a superintending eye. As it is I have no anxiety about my business at home."[8]

But Calhoun was worried about Anna Maria, who was undergoing a difficult pregnancy and was confined to her bed. He was also concerned about Andrew's venture in Alabama. Clemson and Calhoun had provided the funds for the purchase of land and slaves for Andrew's plantation. Calhoun had lent some of his field hands to assist his son in clearing the land and preparing it for cotton. Andrew sent glowing reports that, aware of his son's disposition to exaggerate, Calhoun tended to discount to some extent. Moreover, he knew how long it would take before any income could be realized from a cotton crop that was being produced from raw land. And, Calhoun noted, there was interest to be paid on the notes as well as on the $17,000 debt to Clemson for the purchase of the plantation, which was already causing trouble between his son and his son-in-law.[9] Calhoun very much wanted to visit his son at Marengo and see for himself how the venture was developing.

After spending a month at Fort Hill, relaxing and working with Clemson and Fredericks, Calhoun left for Alabama. Andrew's plantation exceeded his expectations; it was "the finest place that I saw on my visit," he wrote his brother-in-law. There were 620 acres, "all prime, cleared, of which nearly 400 are in cotton, which, barring accidents, ought to make 400 pounds of clean cotton to the acre." But the strain on Calhoun's finances was severe. Contrary to Calhoun's buoyant expectations about the Alabama plantation, Francis Pickens, a highly successful planter, was skeptical of its success. He remarked: "I am perfectly satisfied that his Alabama investment will prove a failure. . . . He is under a profound delusion as to the contrary."[10]

At the same time that Andrew's Alabama venture was draining away Calhoun's capital, his second son, Patrick, was constantly in need of

8. *Ibid.*, 391, 411, 397.
9. *Ibid.*, 393, 114, 115.
10. *Ibid.*, 542, XVI, 247.

funds, which Calhoun arranged to be paid by Floride's merchant-banker cousin in New York, James Edward Boisseau. Patrick was always a year behind in his payments on the notes he gave Boisseau, but there was at least some hope that Patrick would be self-sufficient. After four difficult years at West Point, during which he ran up heavy debts on sprees in New York and contracted a venereal disease, he was about to be commissioned an officer in the army. "You must not think you have finished your education," Calhoun wrote, "but on the contrary, that you have not more than begun. We ought to consider life itself, but as a school, and that our education terminates only with our life."[11]

With both of his grown sons apparently settled and his plantation in good shape, Calhoun turned his attention to interesting developments in politics. He was with Andrew in Marengo when President Harrison died after one month in office. Calhoun had noticed that the old man was in failing health, but the news was nevertheless startling because this was the first time in the history of the Republic that a vice-president would succeed a president. What would happen to this heterogeneous administration? What was the future of the Whig party? Would Tyler, given the punctilio of Virginia politics, be an acting president and defer to his cabinet, headed by the masterful Webster? Would Tyler adhere to the Clay program, which included another central bank, in view of the fact that he had always opposed the Bank of the United States? But he had also opposed Jackson's removal of the government deposits from the bank and the subtreasury system as well. What would point to Tyler's course as president? Calhoun knew many things for certain about the man, most favorable, some unfavorable. Tyler considered nullification to be an absurd abstraction, but he had been the only senator who had voted against the force bill after Calhoun and other opponents of the measure walked out of the chamber. He was, however, a good friend of Clay, and he at one time sought to abolish the slave trade in the District of Columbia. On the right of petition, he did not subscribe to Calhoun's extreme views. He seemed sound on the tariff and states' rights, but he was a strong advocate of Clay's distribution plan.[12] There were enough inconsistencies in Tyler's political behavior to raise serious questions in Calhoun's mind. Calhoun, an acute analyst of men and measures, wondered whether Tyler would go against his party and its strong-minded leaders.

Before his death, Harrison had called for a special session of Con-

11. *Ibid.,* 558, 559.

12. Lyon G. Tyler, *The Letters and Times of the Tylers* (2 vols.; Richmond, Va., 1884), I, 440–41, 461, 570, 579–82, II, 155–84.

gress to meet on May 31, 1841. Clay was ready to implement the Whig program. Soon after Congress assembled and organized itself, he moved that the subtreasury law be repealed. He followed this up with another motion for a resolution that directed the secretary of the treasury, Thomas Ewing, to submit a plan for a bank "to be incorporated by Congress, as in his opinion, is best adapted for public service." President Tyler in his message to the special session had recommended that Congress create "a fiscal agent" but had not elaborated on the form it should take. Calhoun was certain that Ewing would present a bill for a third Bank of the United States along lines Clay staked out and that the Whigs, who held a majority in both houses, would support the measure.

Despite the hybrid mixture of the Whig party, Clay, Webster, and their lieutenants managed to exercise a tight organization and discipline over its members in Congress. Tyler's closest associates, however, thought the president would veto Clay's bank bill. Calhoun was not so sure. "I have no doubt," he wrote Orestes Brownson, the egalitarian editor of the *Boston Quarterly Review,* "if left to his own inclination, he [Tyler] would be thoroughly State rights, but he has voluntar[i]ly accepted office at the hands of those, who differ in toto from him. It remains to be seen, whether he will have the virtue and courage to extricate himself from this Embarrassing position. I am not without hope. . . . Much, very Much is in his power."[13]

With his customary confidence, Clay drove ahead with the Whig program. The Democrats, Calhoun among them, acted as a unit in opposition. The Whigs, though there was much grumbling and many threats to defy Clay's leadership, eventually came to his support. Calhoun's doubts about Tyler increased. "He is no doubt deeply opposed to Clay, but he is essentially a man for the middle ground, and will attempt to take a mid[d]le position now when there is none. . . . If he should he will be lost."[14]

Secretary Ewing's report, which was received in the Senate in mid-June, gave a gloomy assessment of finances. For the government to meet what he declared was a near-desperate situation, he recommended Clay's entire program. First, there must be an issue of treasury notes or a loan to meet the government's pressing obligations, four million dollars of which would be deposited in a national bank as an interest-free loan. He further recommended that the government sub-

13. *Calhoun Papers,* XV, 550.
14. *Ibid.,* 574.

scribe six million dollars for stock in the new bank. The compromise tariff rates should be raised sharply to provide additional revenue. Turning his attention to the continuing financial distress of the states, Ewing boldly supported Clay's distribution scheme. The finance committee of the Senate and the House ways and means committee dutifully reported the bills that embodied the secretary's recommendations.[15]

Democratic orators were ready. Calhoun led the opposition with a series of well-researched speeches in which he portrayed the Clay-Ewing program as fiscally irresponsible and as an engine of centralization. Although they probed special interest and sectional blocs within the Whig delegations, the Democrats were unable to detach a sizable number of votes from the majority. Clay had also used his majorities in both houses to tighten the rules on debate and on parliamentary maneuver. Even the sultry June days helped wear down the opposition. A weary, debilitated Calhoun complained to his daughter that the Senate stayed in session every day for six to seven hours—"so intent are the Whigs on publick plunder." And, he should have added, so intent were the Democrats on defeating the Whig program. "I hope," he continued, "our labour will not be in vain. The very existence of our institution[s] is at stake."[16] The Whig loan bill, which exceeded Secretary Ewing's recommendation, passed both houses and was signed into law by President Tyler on July 19.

Ten days later, Calhoun had the acute embarrassment of seeing the bank bill, which had already been carried in the House, pass the Senate by the one vote his colleague William C. Preston cast. There was hope among Democrats, however, that Tyler would veto the measure. Everyone on Capitol Hill knew that Tyler and Clay were at odds over the direction of the Whig program. The split, Calhoun ventured, could not be healed. "They are both asperants [sic] for the next term, and it is now, or never for both. Neither will yield."[17]

His prophecy proved to be correct. The president went against his party and vetoed the bank bill. He would not accept it even in an amended form that met most of his objections. Calhoun thought that this defeat would break the fragile Whig consensus, but Tyler did approve the repeal of the subtreasury system and a distribution bill that Calhoun regarded "as the very worst ever passed by Congress."[18]

By then the entire Whig cabinet had resigned with the exception of

15. *Congressional Globe*, 27th Cong., 1st Sess., 39, 48–49, 79–81.
16. *Calhoun Papers*, XV, 598.
17. *Ibid.*, 659.
18. *Congressional Globe*, 27th Cong., 1st Sess., 339; *Calhoun Papers*, XV, 769.

246

Daniel Webster, who was in the midst of negotiations with Lord Ashburton over the nation's northern border with Canada. In effect, Tyler was read out of the Whig party. His actions on distribution, the subtreasury, and the loan measures made him unacceptable to the Democrats, however. As Calhoun surveyed the political muddle, Tyler's "position is in many respects exceedingly weak. He will be in a minority—a small minority in both Houses. The only strength he will have is, that he will stand between the two parties."[19]

247

Whatever Tyler's problems, and they surely were severe, the Whig party was in far more serious straits. Only Clay's almost superhuman efforts seemed to be holding it together as a national organization. The Democrats, on the other hand, had emerged from the special session more unified than they had been since Andrew Jackson's second term. Their long, bitter controversy with the Whig majority in Congress had refined the objectives of their leadership group and had immensely strengthened their sense of kinship and dedication to a cause. Thomas Hart Benton exultingly commented: "To the Democracy it was a triumphant session. Triumphant in everything that constitutes moral and durable triumph. They had broken down the Whig party before the session was over—crushed it upon its own measures, and were ready for the elections which were to reverse the party positions."[20]

From Capitol Hill, this ambience was communicated throughout the country. If there was ever a party cohesion, it was present among the Democrats after the special session. Differences over slavery were still a menace to party solidarity, but the temporary expedients of the Van Buren administration seemed to be holding them in check. Free soil was a disturbing issue that had not yet gained any momentum. The Van Buren administration had also managed to stifle sentiment for Texas annexation, which would have opened anew the slavery issue. Disputes with Great Britain were being settled amicably. The depression showed no signs of lifting, giving the lie to the Whigs' campaign promises that they would provide a quick solution to the nation's economic difficulties. Currency and credit were still in a disorganized state, which bore heavily on business transactions in the commodity markets and in the commercial and manufacturing sections of the North.

To Calhoun, who spent the fall of 1841 at Fort Hill, the time seemed

19. *Calhoun Papers*, XV, 773. Hopkins Turney, a Tennessee Democratic congressman and friend of Polk, wrote that Tyler was "a Judas and renegade from all parties. Our party will not toutch [*sic*] him with a ten foot pole" (*Polk Correspondence*, V, 722).

20. Cooper, *The South and the Politics of Slavery*, 152, 153; Thomas Hart Benton, *Thirty Years' View* (2 vols.; New York, 1854–56), II, 373.

appropriate for his presidential candidacy to be made known nationwide. Letters he received from political leaders and newspaper editors
confirmed his judgment. Francis Pickens urged a letter campaign in
Calhoun's behalf. "While the whigs are reeling and falling under panic
and dissolution, and the adm[inistration] with imbecility," he said, "now
is the time to strike boldly for strong men." As he prepared to leave for
Washington, D.C., in late November, 1841, Calhoun wrote Armistead
Burt, a relative by marriage and an influential member of the South
Carolina legislature, "If my friends should think my services ever will
be of importance at the head of the Executive, now is the time." He of
course disclaimed any personal ambition while pointing out that he
had spent thirty years in the public service, devoted to "safety, liberty
and prosperity."[21]

Calhoun's friends, who had organized themselves in a campaign
committee, had already sounded out Silas Wright and Levi Woodbury
on the possibility of running for vice-president on a Calhoun ticket.
Both men politely deflected these feelers. I. G. M. Ramsey, one of
Calhoun's North Carolina supporters, queried Polk on whether he
would consider running with Calhoun, but the wary Tennessean would
not be pinned down at this stage in the campaign.[22] These moves
alerted Van Buren to be more positive about his own candidacy for
reelection. Other would-be candidates were stirring. James Buchanan,
the shifty, wry-necked senator from Pennsylvania, began to line up
local support. And far away in Paris, Lewis Cass, the American minister
to France, was corresponding with friends in the West over his possible
candidacy.

While Calhoun was en route to Washington, D.C., Van Buren wrote
a public letter to Henry Horn, a Philadelphia Democrat and one of his
partisans, that clarified his Missouri letter of a year earlier in which he
seemed to have taken himself out of the presidential contest. This was
another of Van Buren's carefully crafted public pronouncements, denying that his Missouri letter meant he would refuse a mandate from
the party. "Whilst such are the lights in which the subject is regarded by
me," he wrote in his prolix style, "and whilst I shall most assuredly
never take a single step with a view to be made a candidate, I have not
said that I would decline the performance of any public duty."[23]

News of the publication of Van Buren's letter, of his plans for a
southern trip, and of the complete triumph of the Democrats in the

21. *Calhoun Papers*, XV, 782, 828.
22. *Polk Correspondence*, V, 779, 785.
23. Van Buren to Henry Horn, November 13, 1841, VBLC.

New York state election greeted Calhoun when he arrived in Washington. He now knew that his old rival would be his principal competitor for the Democratic nomination, even though the *Globe* and Ritchie's *Enquirer* were not mentioning even the possibility of Van Buren's candidacy in their editorial columns. The cautious Van Buren movement made it all the more important for Calhoun to bolster further the reputation he had gained in the special session for his trenchant attacks on the Whig program. He began preparing himself for speeches and debates, organizing the points he wanted to make on an anticipated renewal of the Whig agenda.

Calhoun seemed not to realize that his practice of lecturing his audience opened him to the charge of patronizing his colleagues. But if some senators wearied at the sight of the lean figure constantly on his feet discoursing learnedly on any subject that might come before the Senate, few dared to challenge him in debate. Calhoun's careful research and immense learning expressed in plain language made complicated issues clear to the educated public when printed in pamphlet form and distributed through the land, or condensed into editorials for those who did not study the *Congressional Globe*.

Calhoun meant to build upon the themes he had already enunciated in the special session and, indeed, had reiterated throughout his senatorial career—retrenchment, economy, and reform in government. These were all sound propositions for a presidential candidate to put forth, but from a party point of view, Calhoun had already damaged his credibility with his stand on nullification and his sensitivity to the slightest criticism of slavery. Another weakness in Calhoun the candidate was that his position on minority rights could and often did clash with popular causes in a country with so many diverse interests, some of which inevitably would take on a majority coloration.

Calhoun's speeches on the treasury note bill and the presidential veto made politically persuasive documents even if they did condescend to his audience. His insistence on injecting his attitudes on slavery and race in his remarks on the navy bill and the *Creole* affair grated on northern sensibilities. His refusal to support the majority will in Rhode Island against an undemocratic elite standing behind a charter granted by King Charles II threatened to fix him with an undemocratic image.

But like that of many powerful minds, Calhoun's capacity for self-delusion was considerable. His latent insecurity frequently led him to overcompensate in his public comments when questions of morality were raised. As he grew older, Calhoun became increasingly defensive about his section and its institutions. His position had moved from a stand against a presumed class interest that sought to subordinate the South to its own economic and social forms to protection of the government and society from anarchical tendencies that he found present in the abolition movement. In a bitter comment on New York governor William H. Seward's refusal to return fugitive slaves to Virginia, he said there could be no doubt that the abolitionist movement aimed to overthrow the government. If the movement was not speedily arrested, it would destroy the social order, northern as well as southern.[24] Calhoun's constant rejoinders to any remarks remotely critical of the South and on the slightest provocation opened him to the charge of being an agitator in the same class as the abolitionists.[25]

Another political weakness that influential northern critics like his sometime colleague John M. Niles, the Jacksonian senator from Connecticut, exploited was Calhoun's alleged inconsistency on public policy issues.[26] But Clay and the Whigs were his most penetrating critics. Whenever the opportunities afforded, they taunted Calhoun on his changing positions, particularly his onetime support of the national bank and federally sponsored internal improvements.

Calhoun was a skillful debater, perhaps the best in Congress. He was also one of the keenest rationalizers in the nation. As he saw it, his position had never changed. Even his stand on a national bank, he argued, had been purely a matter of national security after wartime derangement of finances. He had never thought of the bank as a permanent institution. But there were those congressmen, politicians, and editors whom Calhoun could not confound with his special readings of history and his self-serving justifications, however plausible. And whether or not they oversimplified his remarks in the heat of debate or quoted his carefully reasoned speeches out of context, they managed to convey to their publics that Calhoun's position on matters of moment was so convoluted as not to be trusted. There was considerable truth in their contentions, though Calhoun to the end of his days regarded himself as the most consistent of all public servants. As an astute contemporary observer said of him, "No one doubts his sincerity when most in fault, for he has the faculty of persuading himself that his thoughts are right in whatever channel they may run."[27]

24. *Niles' Register*, LXI, 372.
25. For a harshly critical assessment by a slave-state senator, see Benton, *Thirty Years' View*, II, 698, 699.
26. John Niven, *Gideon Welles, Lincoln's Secretary of the Navy* (New York, 1973), 226.
27. Gideon Welles Diary, May–June, 1848, pp. 37, 38 (MS in Gideon Welles Papers, Huntington Library, San Marino, California).

Like all national figures who attracted publicity to themselves, Calhoun was already a highly controversial statesman when he prepared to make his big push for the presidency. Even in his own section he was distrusted for his presumed arrogance—his stiff, unaccommodating stance on public issues and personal relations. Calhoun never understood, as Van Buren did, that politics was the leaven that compromised differences.[28]

But as he settled down in a Washington mess that he found most agreeable, with board that suited his tastes and "a warm, convenient room on the ground floor," Calhoun viewed his future in a confident mood. He was being especially careful of his health and had thus far in this session of Congress avoided those enervating colds that had worn down his slender frame. Every morning he stripped naked and sponged his entire body with cold water, and then massaged himself with coarse hair gloves, which he thought far superior to stiff brushes. He even brought himself to participate in Washington's social life, which always reached a high point of entertainment during the holiday season. He went to an eggnog party given by Asbury Dickens, secretary of the Senate and the capital's most durable bureaucrat—"everlasting Dickens" Calhoun dubbed him. Then he was off to a family dinner at the home of Stephen Pleasonton, another Washington fixture. On Christmas Day he dined with President Tyler, who, now that he was chief executive, had spruced up his hitherto careless appearance.[29]

At this time Calhoun was studying the president's annual message and reports of the new cabinet chiefs, among whom was a secret collaborator, Abel P. Upshur of Virginia, the secretary of the navy. The Whigs in Congress, under the driving energy of Clay, were again formulating a strategy to devise a program that would escape a presidential veto. The wretched condition of the treasury inspired them with the hope that rather than face the prospect of bankruptcy, the obdurate Tyler might accept a significant boost in tariff schedules, including the protective feature, and even the possibility of a central bank.

Before any part of the Whig program could be considered, Congress was faced with the urgent problem of additional deficit financing. The administration requested authority to raise another five million dollars in treasury notes. The House had already passed the necessary legislation with the provision that the amount asked would replace funds approved the previous session for a long-term loan.

28. Cooper, *The South and the Politics of Slavery,* 103, 104; Robert Woodward Barnwell to Robert Barnwell Rhett, January 23, 1841, in *South Carolina Historical Magazine,* LXXVII, No. 4 (October, 1976), 241.

29. *Calhoun Papers,* XVI, 19, XV, 825.

On January 22, 1842, Calhoun rose to deliver a speech on the subject. He had chosen the treasury note bill not just because he was opposed to additional loans but because it gave him a chance to elaborate on his campaign themes—retrenchment, economy, and reform. He spoke for over three hours, taking up each of the executive departments in turn and comparing their estimates for appropriations with those of the Monroe administration on a unitary basis.

Naturally, Calhoun was able to demonstrate that during his tenure as secretary of war with a comparable military establishment, his reforms and his economical management had operated at a rate over 40 percent less than current estimates for the War Department. This was simply a prelude to the main thrust of his argument—that a weak administration and the Whig party were permitting expenses to rise in order to keep the treasury bare and provide a pretext for the final enactment of Henry Clay's American system. Tyler may not have accepted all of Clay's long-range plans, but he had approved of distribution. The condition of the treasury was such that if there were no significant retrenchment of expenses, the president would be compelled to raise tariff rates and accomplish most of Clay's special interest program, whatever his former position might have been. Calhoun's speech, bristling with statistics, was not fair to Clay or Tyler. It was, however, a good campaign document, as he had meant it to be.[30]

With his eye on the Whig-inclined public outside of Washington, D.C., the stubborn man in the White House, and the almost bankrupt condition of the treasury, Clay wanted to fix responsibility on the president for thwarting a program that he felt would move the economy out of depression. In late February, he offered a resolution for a constitutional amendment that would limit the president's veto powers. Instead of a two-thirds majority in each house, a simple majority would override. Clay's amendment, besides having immediate political motivation, was in line with the old Whig tradition that had always stressed the legislative branch over the executive. Although Calhoun had argued heatedly and repeatedly for years against Jackson's executive tyranny, he would not let Clay's political grandstanding go unnoticed. He found no difficulty in reversing the arguments of his longtime adversary and at the same time reading his colleagues and his constituents another lecture on political theory.

In a speech that lasted several hours, Calhoun utilized historical precedent to demonstrate that what he called the false doctrine of the numerical majority did not elect a president, nor had election by the majority been the aim of the framers of the Constitution. The Constitution was the product of compromise and consensus. If the veto over the years added to the executive power, the fault lay not with the president but with a Congress that, in responding to unwarranted numerical majorities, had ignored the rights of states and passed bad legislation. In tariff, banking, and internal improvements legislation, presidents had refrained from using the veto power. The result had been that Congress had vastly increased with its legislation the patronage of the executive branch. The president "has grown great and powerful," Calhoun solemnly proclaimed, "not because *he used* his veto, but because *he abstained* from using it."[31] Calhoun's argument, which was certainly a tightly constructed and ingenious mode of special pleading, turned the tables on Clay by virtually accusing him and his entire Whig contingent of being responsible for the spoils system in piling up special interest legislation. Calhoun did not mention that the mirror image of the Whig program—his doctrine of state sovereignty, minority rights, and the maintenance of the slave-plantation system—was just as much a special interest initiative as numerical majorities, protective tariffs, or national banks.

Calhoun's address was instantly perceived as an effective campaign document not just by his supporters but by all Democratic aspirants, who were anxious to give the lie to the oft-repeated accusation, which had originated with Calhoun himself, that Jackson had used the veto to enhance his power and protect his patronage machine. Calhoun reported enthusiastically that 46,000 copies of his speech had been purchased and broadcast over the land.[32]

Calhoun was active in debates wherein the Whigs were seeking to make the president accept a tariff bill with distribution that would negate the 20 percent *ad valorem* schedules of the compromise tariff and restore the principle of protection. Silas Wright and James Buchanan, both from large states with strong industrial communities, the one representing Calhoun's leading opponent in the Senate, the other a candidate for the presidency, were placed in a most uncomfortable position. Tyler would accept a high tariff bill only if distribution was not connected with it. Yet distribution was a popular measure in western states, whose economies were either bankrupt or nearly so.

On August 26, 1842, the final version of the tariff bill that met the

31. *Ibid.,* 154.

32. Appendix, *Congressional Globe*, 27th Cong., 2nd Sess., 164–68; *Calhoun Papers,* XVI, 204.

president's objections came up in the Senate. Wright had decided that he must vote for it, despite the damage his action might inflict on Van Buren's candidacy. Buchanan was in the same quandary; and in fact his vote for the tariff helped uproot his budding campaign. Wright voiced his plight to a political associate at home. "We are now upon the third tariff of the House," he said, "a horrible bill, I am miserably perplexed to know how to vote myself, but as we ought to pass some bill and this one will kill distribution, I shall vote for it and produce great dissatisfaction both in the city of New York and at the South." Calhoun would have enlarged upon this statement. In a letter to Duff Green that he wrote after Tyler signed the tariff bill, he said: "It prostrates Mr. Van Buren in the South. The whole is much like what occurred in 1828."[33]

Calhoun's single-issue prognosis was entirely too optimistic. Van Buren was just concluding a triumphant tour through the South and the Northwest. One of Calhoun's trusted lieutenants, Dixon Lewis, conceded that the Van Buren movement had gained such momentum that it was becoming increasingly difficult to deflect it.[34] Numerical majorities, Calhoun's bête noire, were beginning to make themselves felt in mass meetings even within southern states. But it was in the populous, bellwether states of New York, Pennsylvania, and Virginia that the winning trend would be established. Calhoun was certainly aware of this fact of political life. Efforts had been made early in 1842 to establish a communication network in these states. They had been most successful in Virginia and New York, where a combination of extreme states' rights men like Littleton Tazewell and Robert M. T. Hunter made common cause with the free traders and workingmen groups in New York City and a scattering of old Clintonians like Jabez Hammond and Calhoun's college friend Micah Sterling upstate.

The Locofoco element in New York City and radical activists like Michael Walsh, John Commerford, and Levi Slamm had long been dissatisfied with the political dictation of the Van Buren–dominated Tammany Hall. Many, if not most, of the mechanics and clerks in their midst gained their livelihood from shipbuilding and associated commercial industries of the great port. Frequently at odds with their employers over labor problems, they formed a solid phalanx with management over the tariff issue, believing that Whig tariff policies favored

33. Silas Wright to Azariah Flagg, August 26, 29, 1842, FNYPL; *Calhoun Papers*, XVI, 437–38.

34. *Calhoun Papers*, XVI, 262, 263.

254

upstate and New England textile manufacturers at their expense.[35] Van Buren's apparent equivocation on this measure of economic importance to them helped Calhoun's cause immeasurably among the Democrats of the city.

Calhoun's attacks on banks, and his advocacy of a sound currency in either specie or notes fully backed by the government, were also popular issues among the restive, radical Democrats. His forthright defense of slavery in the South was likewise applauded, because he coupled his argument with a spirited attack on the lowly conditions of free white labor in the North. Slavery may have been essentially immoral, but unemployed or underemployed workingmen in New York were much more concerned with what Calhoun had to say about the exploitative instincts of factory owners and their allies, the bankers, than with his defense of slavery.

After Van Buren's defeat and the unfolding of the Whig program in Congress during 1841, and particularly because of the continuation of economic distress, the party organization in New York City, unstable at best, threatened to break down completely. This situation invited would-be party leaders within Democratic ranks to bid for control if they could plead a cause and a candidate. The Calhoun candidacy seemed to fit all contingencies. Joseph Scoville, an ambitious merchant who combined a bit of journalism with some bad fiction and a taste for politics, sensed the political opportunity in New York. He made contact with Calhoun's organization and eventually with Calhoun himself. Calhoun's managers were somewhat skeptical of the young man's professional qualifications, but the Carolinian accepted his services uncritically, and he became the leader of the campaign in New York City. Scoville was on good terms with the old Locofoco leaders like Fitzwilliam Byrdsall and Levi Slamm. He also enjoyed a working relationship with Parke Godwin—William Cullen Bryant's son-in-law and the editor of several city publications—and with Bryant himself.

Slamm began a new Democratic daily, the *Plebeian,* in June, 1842. Calhoun's group initially subsidized the paper, but neither its policies

---

35. Chauncey S. Boucher and Robert P. Brooks (eds.), *Correspondence Addressed to John C. Calhoun, 1837–1849: Sixteenth Report of the Historical Manuscripts Commission* (Washington, D.C., 1930), 174–78. See James Auchincloss to Calhoun, September 20, 22, October 1, 1842, for the views of the New York commercial community. See also Sean Wilentz, *Chants Democratic: New York City and the Rise of the American Working Class* (New York, 1984), 333. Wilentz does not develop the political relationship of the New York merchants and the radical activists with Calhoun.

nor its circulation met expectations. After two months of publication, Byrdsall complained that Slamm "yields frequently to the pressure of the intelligent working men and puts in a Calhoun article now and then, but it is to please the radical democracy, and it will go J.C.C. if it be policy, or profitable so to do." Godwin's *Morning Post* was a far more consistent supporter.[36]

During the summer of 1842, Calhoun's supporters made efforts to enlist postmasters and customs collectors in his cause. There seems to have been some willingness on the part of the Tyler administration to encourage this move, but after the pragmatic politicians David Henshaw and Caleb Cushing briefly became members of Tyler's cabinet, the effort to swing officeholders behind Calhoun came to naught. Although Calhoun had denounced frequently in speeches beginning in the early 1830s the use of government patronage for partisan purposes, he had come to adopt what might be euphemistically called a realistic attitude. He certainly knew and presumably approved the policies of Rhett, Hunter, and Scoville in attempting to enlist federal employees in his campaign.[37]

Calhoun's campaign was making some headway in New York and in Connecticut, where his Yale connections and his free trade doctrines appealed to those in the coastal counties, but Pennsylvania seemed a lost cause from the outset. Buchanan was still the major Democratic candidate, but Van Buren had so balanced the party factions in Pennsylvania that his organization appeared impenetrable. Francis Pickens had tried without success to cut through the thicket of party loyalties during the summer of 1842. "I would be glad for you to inform me candidly," he wrote Samuel Ingham, "whether you think the prejudices enlisted ag[ain]st Mr. Calhoun amongst the great masses in Penn[sylvania] are of such a nature as to render it impossible for him to run . . . with any prospect of success."[38] Ingham's reply must not have been favorable, because the Calhoun committee practically ignored Pennsylvania in its organizing efforts.

Calhoun's prospects were best in Virginia, where he held a reservoir of support for his antitariff, states' rights stand and where he had able political workers like Hunter, Thomas W. Gilmer, and Tazewell. But again he had to face veteran party organization, the Richmond junto. This in turn meant facing Thomas Ritchie, older and more dogmatic than he had been in the days of the first Jackson coalition but still the

36. *Calhoun Papers,* XVI, 422, XV, 280, 281.
37. *Ibid.,* XVI, 485, 486.
38. *Ibid.,* 278, 279.

commanding figure in the Democratic party politics of the Old Dominion. Calhoun had corresponded with Ritchie before any Democratic
candidate had surfaced. Although he had left several openings without
of course mentioning that he was considering a run for the presidency,
Ritchie had been just as delicately noncommittal. In the fall, Ritchie
threw off all pretense and advised Hunter that he was for Van Buren.
"He speaks of you in the highest terms and would go for you heart and
hand if nominated," Hunter reported to Calhoun, adding, "there's the
rub. We shall have to abide the decision of the convention. . . . You
know what that means."[39]

Calhoun's managers had already accurately assessed the power of
Van Buren's organization not just in Virginia but in all the states save
South Carolina and possibly Georgia. Even in Dixon Lewis' Alabama,
Van Buren's partisans controlled most of the populous northern coun-
ties.[40] Jackson's influence was still a factor with local politicians in the
West, and Jackson was squarely behind Van Buren, as was one of his
protégés, James K. Polk, the quiet, calculating ex-governor of Ten-
nessee and former Speaker of the House.

As Calhoun's managers saw it, their candidate's strength was scattered throughout the Union, wherever free trade and his orthodox
views on government prevailed. His vehement defense of slavery cost
Calhoun some support in the free states, but this was more than balanced by southern and border state backing for his views. He was a
more outspoken opponent of distribution than Van Buren's partisans,
which again probably added to his popularity in various areas of the
Northeast. But if state conventions controlled by professional politicians should determine the nominations, Calhoun would most likely
lose. His managers were inexperienced at organization politics. They
were short of funds, lacked government patronage, and were just
beginning to develop newspaper support. Moreover, there was rivalry
and mistrust between Pickens and Rhett, both ambitious, strong-willed
men. And when Rhett and Elmore visited the North in the fall of 1842,
they gained an unfavorable view of Scoville, whom they decided was
indiscreet.[41]

Calhoun's followers needed time to strengthen their organization,
raise funds, and, if possible, draw Tyler with his control of government
patronage into their ranks. They also recognized that if they were to

39. *Ibid.*, 531, 532.
40. *Ibid.*, 526.
41. John Boyd Edmunds, "Francis W. Pickens: A Political Biography" (Ph.D. dissertation, University of South Carolina, 1967), 82; *Calhoun Papers*, XVI, 522–24.

concentrate Calhoun's strength, they must convince party leaders that delegates to the nominating convention at Baltimore should be chosen by districts, not by state legislatures or too easily manipulated state conventions. Thus they proposed that the national party convention be held in the summer of 1844—as late as possible before the election, not, as formerly, eighteen months before the polling. When Rhett made this proposition to Blair, he was unable to convince that wily editor, who was secretly a Van Buren partisan.[42]

During December, 1842, Rhett drafted a lengthy exposition of these views, which no doubt he shared with Calhoun and the other members of what might now be considered a campaign committee. Rhett's paper was published in the *Mercury* on January 25, 1843, and run off in pamphlet form, which was given wide distribution. The document stressed democratic and popular procedures in what amounted to a demand for proportional representation. Its argument for delay, also made in a democratic context, was that the people needed sufficient time to acquaint themselves with the principles involved as well as the positions of the candidates so that they could make a reasoned choice. Unfortunately, in its argument for the popular nomination of presidential candidates, Rhett's pamphlet conflicted with Calhoun's view on concurrent majorities. The inconsistency would prove a minor source of difficulty for the campaign. This sort of blunder, however, epitomized the communication problems that bedeviled the committee.[43]

Meanwhile, Scoville in New York had made arrangements with the Harpers' publishing house to print and distribute a campaign biography of Calhoun along with a separate volume of his speeches. Calhoun and Robert M. T. Hunter wrote the text, which was completed at the end of 1842. Both volumes were published in February, 1843.

Rhett's pamphlet and the preparation of the campaign biography were followed by Calhoun's resignation from the Senate, to take effect on March 4, 1843. Calhoun was emulating Clay, who had resigned his seat some months before so that he could present himself as a candidate for the presidency in the guise of a private citizen without any encroachments on his time or any connection with political office. Calhoun followed his letter of resignation with a brief laudatory sketch of

42. Silas Wright to Van Buren, January 27, February 19, 1843, VBLC; Joseph H. Scoville to Levy Woodbury, January 13, 1843; Scoville to Calhoun, January 15, 1843, in Dixon Lewis Papers, University of Texas at Austin; Franklin Elmore to Fitzwilliam Byrdsall, September 9, 1843, JHLC; William H. Roane to Silas Wright, February 9, 1843, VBLC.

43. Laura A. White, *Robert Barnwell Rhett: Father of Secession* (New York, 1931), 61, 62.

his public career, which he sent to Hammond for publication in the *Carolinian.*[44]

Calhoun's resignation precipitated a struggle in the South Carolina legislature. Hammond, who longed for political advancement but had **259** been forced to defer his ambition for the governorship, was finally elected to that office by a close vote that reflected deep-seated personal divisions in state politics. For years Calhoun had acted as peacemaker, but when he removed himself from office, the restraints he had imposed were relaxed. There were two Senate seats up for election, his own and that of William C. Preston, who had resigned earlier. Calhoun, striving for unity in his own state, managed to sidetrack the Pickens-Rhett dispute by having McDuffie elected in his place and the former Unionist Daniel E. Huger chosen for the other seat.

In the closings days of 1842, the South Carolina legislature nominated Calhoun for the presidency.[45] At the same time, in a series of resolutions, the legislature made a concise campaign statement that advocated a late convention date and the election of delegates by district. Calhoun was unable to restrain that body from passing another series of resolutions harshly condemning the tariff and raising the specter of nullification, which placed him in just the position that Van Buren wanted.

Although Calhoun was still holding back, maintaining the posture that he would accept only a draft, the legislature had made him appear to be grasping avidly for the prize, despite his high-flown rhetoric about acting only from principle. The legislature's tariff resolutions reinforced the false yet plausible assumption in the Van Buren press that Calhoun was not a national or even a sectional candidate but simply the chosen creature of a planter oligarchy. This charge seemed to gain credence when, over considerable opposition and highly vocal recrimination, the Georgia legislature a few days later also nominated Calhoun.[46]

Calhoun's committee had been slow to establish a Washington, D.C., newspaper. His partisans had made the decision in August, 1842, in Washington with Calhoun's concurrence. It was not until March, 1843, however, that they raised enough money to purchase a struggling Washington weekly, the *Spectator.* There was confusion about the editorship of the paper from the very beginning. Virgil Maxcy, Calhoun's

44. *Calhoun Papers,* XVI, 554–57.
45. *Ibid.,* 574–76.
46. Niven, *Martin Van Buren,* 504, 505; Washington *Globe,* December 19, 1842; *Polk Papers,* VI, 141, 142.

devoted friend and a person of considerable editorial experience and knowledge of the ways of Washington, was one of the three individuals who negotiated the purchase of the *Spectator*. He should have assumed the editorship, but Scoville, who had arrived on the scene from New York and made a strong personal impression on Calhoun, elbowed Maxcy out of the way. He brought a New York journalistic flavor and bias to the *Spectator*'s editorial columns, which the campaign committee soon came to resent. Scoville was forced out, and a series of part-time editors, Maxcy, Rhett, and Hunter, followed. As a result, the paper never wielded the influence in Washington it should have, or set the proper tone for Calhoun newspapers in other states.[47]

Another problem that faced the Calhoun campaign was President Tyler. It was tempting to Calhoun's managers to make a deal with Tyler that would bring all the federal officeholders and their widespread political organization behind Calhoun. But the president, stubborn where his own image was concerned and ambitious for a full term on his own, was not ready to play a subordinate role. Furthermore, Tyler, anathema to the Whigs, was a figure of scorn to orthodox Democrats. Any alliance, even on Calhoun's terms, could be more expensive than it was worth. Calhoun and McDuffie in the Senate, however, did make a gesture toward Tyler by voting twice to confirm the Virginia lawyer Henry A. Wise, a high-strung, tobacco-chewing extrovert, as minister to France and Caleb Cushing, the highly intelligent political pariah from Massachusetts, as secretary of the treasury.[48]

Tyler subsequently sought to launch his candidacy at a mass meeting in New York City, where it failed to generate any groundswell of support. Still, the fiction of a Tyler party was maintained. His supporters, especially the officeholders whom Cushing and Henshaw had selected to replace the Whig incumbents, moved cautiously behind Calhoun. The Carolinian scored an important advance in the administration when his ally Abel P. Upshur became secretary of state. Through Upshur and Thomas W. Gilmer, another Virginian who had long been Calhoun's supporter and who was finally confirmed as Upshur's successor in the Navy Department, Calhoun exercised significant influence over the policies of the weak, faltering administration.[49]

If Tyler's mass meeting was a failure, the meetings that Van Buren's lieutenants organized in Philadelphia and elsewhere in the country were resounding successes. Van Buren's management in Washington,

47. *Calhoun Correspondence*, 535, 540.
48. *Senate Executive Journal*, 27th Cong., 3rd Sess., 175–90.
49. *Calhoun Correspondence*, 526.

D.C., maintained a low profile—too low for Thomas Hart Benton, who fretted about Van Buren's continued diffidence. In the insulated society of Washington, Calhoun seemed a stronger candidate than he was. "He has been going on without balk of any kind," Benton wrote to Van Buren. "You will soon find yourself what Crawford was in 1824 and it behooves your friends here to begin in time to counteract the schemes against you."[50]

261

Van Buren refused to be rushed. He was still determined to make his candidacy appear to be a draft without his own direct involvement or obvious organization. After another "spontaneous" nomination in Indiana, Van Buren had Silas Wright, his only avowed representative in Washington, sound out the Virginians. Wright adopted just the right tone in a letter to William H. Roane. No "clique of busy electioneers here," he said. "The truth is we have not made a motion and any results which are seen are not of our production, but, as we believe, proceed from the deep prevailing sense of justice and principle of the democracy of the country."[51]

Calhoun had made such progress in Virginia that Ritchie refused at first to take a stand. When Van Buren made clear his position on the tariff and other public issues in his reply to the Indiana nomination, Ritchie and his associates decided that the time for direct action was at hand. On March 2 the first trial of strength between the two candidates occurred. Despite the best efforts of Hunter, Gilmer, Tazewell, and former governor David Campbell, the Virginia convention decisively repudiated the district plan. Calhoun, who had been supremely confident of his success, was bitterly disappointed. He singled out Ritchie as the marplot, who, since 1824, had been determined to remove Virginia from her natural southern brethren and make the state a satellite of New York.

As usual when his plans went awry and his hopes were blasted, Calhoun saw a sinister conspiracy in the making that would subjugate the South to the "great central non slave holding states . . . [that] would centralize the powers of the union, and establish the most intolerable despotism." Calhoun had only his organization to blame for the Virginia debacle. It was still riven with jealousies and short of funds. Moreover, Calhoun's personal stance created problems for the committee. His followers could cope with his impulsive actions, but they found it difficult to agree with his plan to stand on principle and refuse

50. Thomas Hart Benton to Van Buren, August 16, 1842, VBLC.
51. Silas Wright to Roane, February 25, 1843, in Silas Wright Miscellaneous Papers, New York Historical Society.

to campaign outside of his home state. Green, Hunter, and other members of the committee pleaded with Calhoun to travel through the country. Had he been present at the Virginia convention, they claimed, he may well have won the day. But Calhoun would not listen. "It may be pride, it may be fastediousness [*sic*] or a sense of propriety, or the whole combined," he wrote Hunter, "but so it is, and I cannot help it . . . I am averse to being made a spectacle." His family kept his spirits up. Anna Maria thought her father's prospects were "fair." As the summer wore on, excitement increased at Fort Hill. "I don't know whether you are a politician," Anna Maria wrote her brother Patrick, "but we here are all in line, even Mr. Clemson talks and writes politics."[52]

In August, 1843, while Calhoun was at home in Fort Hill, his supporters nearly captured the New York City convention that would name delegates to the state nominating convention at Syracuse. Had not Benjamin Butler, Van Buren's agile-minded associate, been present, Calhoun's district plan would have carried, and Calhoun delegates would have been elected to the state convention. Butler managed to have the district plan defeated. The Van Buren slate was carried by a one-vote margin.[53]

The New York state convention, which met in September, 1843, composed the tensions that had threatened to disrupt the party in the state over the past six years, since the subtreasury was first made a party test. The convention selected Van Buren delegates and turned down by a decided majority the district plan. In its one concession to Calhoun's forces, it ratified a prior agreement Van Buren had made to hold the national convention in May, 1844, but its attempt to compromise on the tariff issue resulted in a resolution that maintained the principle of protection and was completely unsatisfactory to the South.[54]

The Virginia and New York defeats, preceded by evidence of Van Buren's strength in Pennsylvania and the Northwest, were discouraging. Still, the Calhoun campaign committee determined to make a final test against Van Buren in the organization of the House of Representatives for the Twenty-eighth Congress. The Democrats had won sweeping victories in the fall of 1843 and would be in control. If Calhoun's men could elect the House officers, they would dominate the committees and the party caucus. They calculated that this turn of events would enhance Calhoun's political chances throughout the country

52. *Calhoun Correspondence,* 528, 541; Lander, *Calhoun Family,* 71.
53. *Calhoun Correspondence,* 510.
54. *Ibid.,* 553.

because he would be perceived as a winning candidate. Election of his adherents as officers would give him a position of leadership in Congress, where partisan initiative was made and maintained. Calhoun's candidates were decisively beaten, however, by more than a two-thirds majority. Van Buren's candidate for Speaker, John W. Jones of Virginia, was elected handily. Every House officer, elected or appointed, was on the Van Buren slate.[55]

After this reverse, Calhoun decided to withhold his name from consideration at the Baltimore convention, though he had not by any means given up his candidacy. When the Charleston *Mercury* published the statement in January, 1844, that Calhoun had personally withdrawn from the contest, he was quick to emphasize that he had done no such thing. He explained that he had withheld his name only from convention consideration, and he had the *Mercury* correct its statement. But clearly Calhoun was planning to bolt the party if Van Buren were nominated and the platform did not support his views on the tariff and slavery. "A split between us and the Northern Democracy is inevitable," he wrote his brother-in-law. "Unless . . . they should reverse their course . . . which I do not expect."[56]

In December, Calhoun prepared an address announcing his decision, which included a scathing attack on Van Buren and party regulars who supported the New Yorker. Calhoun's committee in Charleston and Washington deleted specific references to Van Buren before publication, but to the wary candidate in Kinderhook, the address bespoke a party division if he were nominated at the Baltimore convention.[57]

55. *Ibid.*, 898, 899, 907.
56. *Ibid.*, 548, 549, 566, 567.
57. *Ibid.*, 552–56.

XIV

Texas

Calhoun's anger at Van Buren and his anguish at the collapse of his campaign were surely heightened by serious family and financial problems that came to a head in the fall of 1843. His son-in-law Thomas Clemson would no longer postpone repayment of the large loan he had made to Andrew five years earlier to purchase a plantation in Alabama. The quarrel between the two had caused Calhoun much distress over the years. Some months earlier, Clemson had threatened to institute legal proceedings against Andrew. Calhoun appealed to Clemson's good judgment, remarking that such an action would simply throw all the Alabama land on the market at the low prices then prevailing. "To see you and him and all my children prosperous and happy is the great object of my desire," he wrote Clemson. "I would not for all I am worth see them, including of course yourself, embroiled in feuds and conflicts to their mutual disgrace and mine."[1]

Clemson's renewed insistence on full repayment came as much from his own desperate need for ready cash as from his rankling irritation at Andrew's casual way of doing business. Clemson had just purchased the plantation known as Cane Brake from Arthur Simkins. Outlays for the property, the slaves to work it, and essential farming equipment surpassed his ready capital. Calhoun made arrangements to settle Andrew's debt on his own credit. He borrowed $18,000 from James Barbour, one of his Democratic supporters from Culpepper County, Virginia, and $4,500 from Franklin Elmore's South Carolina state bank. Legal complications forced Barbour to cancel the loan, so Calhoun borrowed the sum from other sources. Raising the money left him strapped financially. Fort Hill was fully mortgaged, and there was now an additional debt of about $25,000. For the payment of the interest on these notes, he pledged the cotton crop he expected in the fall from his own fields and those of Andrew's plantation.

Calhoun was less concerned about money matters than about the

---

1. *Calhoun Papers*, XVI, 597.

break between his son and son-in-law. He conceded that Andrew was not as punctual as he might be in meeting his business obligations. Yet he felt that Clemson did not understand the problems plantation owners faced in raising, moving, and marketing a crop, which in the best of circumstances created a time lag of at least nine months before any cash was realized. Clemson was simply not doing Andrew justice. "Few things have grieved me as much," Calhoun remarked.[2]

Acute financial problems were only one source of Calhoun's anxiety during these years. His large family had been the source of constant strain and heartache. His three brothers, William, Patrick, and James, all of whom were very close to him, died within the space of three years.[3] Floride was more critical than ever of the behavior of the house servants, suspicious of their intentions, and capricious in the handling of discipline. She believed Calhoun's boyhood companion, now known as Old Sawney, was responsible for what she perceived as unrest among the household slaves, particularly the independent attitude of his son Young Sawney. She was certain that Young Sawney meant to attack Fredericks, the overseer, with a dirk he carried, and she wrote Margaret, Andrew's wife, that he had thrown a stone at Clemson.

Clemson did not mention this incident in his correspondence with Calhoun. In the many letters he devoted to plantation affairs, the methodical Clemson never commented on unrest among the slaves at Fort Hill or at the gold mine in Georgia. Young Sawney may have been rebellious, and probably the lash or threat of the lash prompted him to run away. When he was apprehended in Georgia, Calhoun ordered that he be sent in chains to Andrew. Floride thought that he ought to be sold. As for his father, she said, "Old Sawney, is at the bot[t]om of all, he has done. I think him a dangerous old negro, but cannot convince his Master of it."[4]

Another of Old Sawney's children, Issey, a favorite of Calhoun's crippled daughter, Cornelia, attempted to burn down Fort Hill, apparently in a fit of rage. The fire was detected before any damage was done, and Issey confessed to the arson. The penalty for slave-committed arson was death by hanging. Although Floride did not insist on informing the authorities of Issey's crime, she demanded that Issey be sold, and again denounced Old Sawney, who disappeared temporarily. In deference to Cornelia's wish, Calhoun refused. And he would take

2. *Ibid.*, 660.
3. *Ibid.*, I, 433, XV, 315, 317.
4. *Ibid.*, XVI, 117.

no drastic steps against Old Sawney, who was still living on the Calhoun estate in 1865.[5]

Floride's disposition, which had become increasingly erratic as she grew older, was probably affected by the hypertension from which she suffered. She had gained weight despite her frequent labor in the gardens, her overseeing of household chores, her acting as hostess for the stream of visitors that came when her husband was at home, and her constant reception of relatives and friends. In the summer of 1842, she suffered a stroke, from which she slowly recovered, subjecting the family to great strain. Calhoun, who was battling the Whig tariff bill and launching his presidential candidacy in hot, humid Washington, was most apprehensive. Anna Maria described her mother's recovery as "tedious and retarded by her great nervousness and the great fear she labored under." She wrote her brother Patrick, "All this was painful and distressing especially as she was very querulous and I was almost worn down by constant nursing night and day."[6]

Anna Maria herself was far from well when her mother was stricken. Five months pregnant, she had been living at the O'Barr gold mine with Clemson and her year-old son John Calhoun under extremely primitive conditions. Anna Maria's pregnancies, which were invariably difficult, always alarmed Calhoun. After her first son, Calhoun, as they called him, was born in July, 1841, he was much relieved at her safe delivery, only to be deeply concerned when she became seriously ill with a breast infection, from which she made a slow and painful recovery. Soon after, Clemson accepted an offer to inspect a mining operation in Cuba. He expected to remain there only a few weeks, but when he found that his stay had to be extended, he asked Anna Maria to join him. She was disposed to do so. Calhoun was upset at the thought of his beloved daughter, who had just regained her health, subjecting herself and her infant son to the perils of a sea voyage and the tropical climate of Cuba. He wrote Floride that she must by no means permit Anna Maria to go if she thought there would be "any hazard either to her, or the child." He also wrote Anna Maria, expressing his "decided dissent." A combination of his daughter's insistence and the fact that her brother Patrick, who was on leave, would accompany her eased his fears. But he continued to worry about the Clemsons and Patrick until their safe arrival home in the spring.[7]

5. Lander, *Calhoun Family,* 69.

6. *Calhoun Papers,* XVI, 415.

7. Lander, *Calhoun Family,* 39; *Calhoun Papers,* XVI, 26, 31, 32, 37, 46, 87, 91, 107, 203, 238, 261.

Soon after their return from Cuba, Clemson left Anna Maria, who was again pregnant, to go to Dahlonega, where his mining expertise and his capable management soon put Calhoun's gold mine in order. He also expanded mining operations, which he hoped would result in a profitable production. His letters to Calhoun alternated between confidence when a rich pocket was discovered and pessimism when the vein tailed out.

Despite her pregnancy, Anna Maria was determined to be with her husband, even though she knew that roads to Dahlonega were little better than wilderness trails over the mountains, on which stumps and boulders made carriage travel jolting and occasionally dangerous from an upset. She had scarcely settled herself and the baby, Calhoun, in the log dwelling Clemson had the slaves construct when she received word of Floride's stroke. Anna Maria immediately returned to Fort Hill.

As soon as her mother became convalescent, Anna Maria returned to Dahlonega in the stage, which proved, as she remarked, "a good deal worse than the carriage and we arrived here the second time too with whole bones so bruised that we were absolutely sore to the touch from the tossing about and thumping we had received." Calhoun must have been uneasy about the condition of his pregnant daughter and his grandson, who were living far from any medical help in a hut that Anna Maria described as having "bark on the logs—the floor not planed and daylight, wind, and rain coming in on all sides of the single room."[8]

Fortunately, these primitive living conditions had no adverse effect, but Anna Maria paid for her indiscretion after she returned to Fort Hill in the fall. She was threatened with a miscarriage and had to remain in bed for the remainder of her pregnancy. On December 29, 1842, her daughter Floride Elizabeth was born. Four days later, Anna Maria became desperately ill. "She was in agony and almost frantic," wrote Clemson to Calhoun. "The physicians were all absent from Pendleton . . . I never saw one with higher fever or quicker pulse. She was in the most imminent danger for forty eight hours and as you may suppose we were all in the greatest anxiety of mind." Anna Maria was out of immediate danger when Calhoun read Clemson's letter, but it was most disquieting for him to learn that her health was still precarious. He was not completely relieved from anxiety until the latter part of January, when Clemson wrote that she was so much better that he felt he could leave for the mine in Georgia.[9]

8. *Calhoun Papers,* XVI, 415.
9. *Ibid.,* 589–91, 611.

268

Anna Maria, Andrew, and Floride were not the only members of the family who were a source of constant concern. Patrick continued to live beyond his army salary. He was on furlough, which his father had managed to extend since his graduation from West Point six months earlier, and showed no disposition to plan for his future, though he made it clear that he did not want a military career. Calhoun wrote frequent, long letters of concern and advice. Patrick finally agreed to stay in the army and was ordered to Fort Towson in the Arkansas Territory, far from the fleshpots of Charleston, New Orleans, and Havana. He would nevertheless be subject to the temptations of drink and gambling in the isolated frontier post.

On the eve of Patrick's departure for Fort Towson, Calhoun expressed his fatherly concern. "You will be liable to many errors and exposed to many temptations," he wrote. "Plausible men may captivate you, artful impose on you and profligate attempt to seduce you. . . . Associate with the honest and honorable . . . be too proud to sacrifice your independence; and to preserve it resolve to live within your means, and never owe a cent of debt."[10]

Calhoun's younger sons, William Lowndes, John C., Jr., and James Edward, were either at home or at schools to which their parents sent them in an effort to give them a sound secondary education difficult to obtain in the South at the time. Cornelia remained at home, indulging her passion for reading. She seems to have been an unassuming, introverted member of the family that James Edward Colhoun's wife, Maria, said had the "gift of the gab."[11]

Despite all his family tensions, business reverses, and political defeats, Calhoun had not given up on his candidacy and was still hoping that enough pressure would be brought upon Van Buren to force him out of the race. An issue had been developing for some time that could make grave difficulties for the New Yorker. That issue was the possible annexation of Texas, which Van Buren had managed to skirt during his administration.

Texas had been independent since its successful revolt against Mexico in 1836. The United States and the major nations of western Europe had recognized it as an independent state, but there was a growing political force on both sides of the Louisiana-Arkansas border that separated the two nations in favor of the annexation of the republic by

10. *Ibid.*, 202. This was typical of the more than a dozen letters of advice that Calhoun wrote Patrick over an eighteen-month period. See also *ibid.*, 37, 106, 107, 201, 202, 502, 503.

11. *Ibid.*, 327.

the United States. Andrew Jackson was a powerful and outspoken advocate of annexation. And within the Democratic party, sizable elements, stimulated by the clamor of American immigrants in Texas and expansionists in the United States, began to urge that Texas become a state in the Union. Calhoun had always recognized the importance of Texas not just as another slave state, or as a region of great size and natural resources, but as a bastion of defense for the Union against the possible incursion of strong foreign powers. Writing to George McDuffie in early December, 1843, Calhoun said, "I think no alternative is left us, and that if the Executive should take a stand for it, he ought to be unanimously and decidedly supported by the South."[12] Calhoun was aware that annexation was becoming a popular issue in the South and the West.

Thomas W. Gilmer had urged immediate annexation in a public address he gave in Richmond during the fall of 1842. Calhoun's committee sent a copy of Gilmer's speech to Jackson along with a letter asking him if he favored annexation. Jackson responded with an emphatic affirmative. Plans were then made to publish Gilmer's address and the Jackson correspondence before the Baltimore convention. As yet, Calhoun's organization had remained silent on the question. In October, 1843, however, after the setbacks in Virginia and New York, Hunter openly identified Calhoun with annexation at another public dinner in Richmond. But what really gave momentum to Texas annexation was a long public letter written by the short, bald senator from Mississippi, Robert John Walker. A Pennsylvanian by birth, connected by marriage with George M. Dallas, Walker represented the speculative, entrepreneurial interests of the West and Southwest. He ranged over all aspects of annexation, arguing that the admission of Texas would benefit every section of the Union. It would, he suggested, help solve the slavery question, too, by drawing the slaves from the Southeast and dispersing them throughout the immense new territory. Walker's background and party affiliations, as much as his arguments, made the annexation of Texas a major campaign issue.[13]

In January, 1844, Gilmer had become secretary of the navy, and more importantly for Calhoun's fortunes, Upshur had earlier moved up to the State Department. Through these allies, Calhoun learned that Tyler was anxious to promote annexation. It would, the president

12. *Calhoun Correspondence,* 555.
13. Andrew Stevenson to Van Buren, October 8, 1843, William H. Roane to Van Buren, October 17, 1843, VBLC; *Calhoun Correspondence,* 521; Frederick Merk, *Fruits of Propaganda in the Tyler Administration* (Cambridge, Mass., 1971), 97–104.

hoped, refurbish his public and political image, which was still very negative, despite the settlement of the northern boundary with Canada from Maine to the Rocky Mountains in the Webster-Ashburton Treaty. No sooner had Upshur been confirmed as secretary of state than Maxcy and Rhett called upon him to discuss annexation. A week later, Calhoun wrote the first of his letters on Texas to Upshur. Their correspondence laid the basis for the Tyler administration's policy on annexation.[14]

All of the principals involved knew that Great Britain was taking a decided interest in Texas. Dispatches from Edward Everett, United States minister to Great Britain, were freighted with examples of Whitehall's policies on trade with the republic and its efforts to mediate between Texas and Mexico. In addition, Duff Green, who was then in London as a confidential agent, kept both Tyler and Calhoun supplied with information he picked up in parliamentary debates and conversations with knowledgeable Britons, which tended to confirm American suspicions about British objectives.

Green's thesis, which agreed with Calhoun's long-held views, was that Britain was seeking to monopolize world trade at the expense of the United States. An important part of this ongoing process was to make the empire self-sufficient in raw materials, which would maintain its manufacturing and commercial hegemony, and at the same time provide expanding markets for its goods. Calhoun's view of Britain's aims fit the classical definition of imperialism.

One of the direct means for achieving these objectives was the elimination of the slave labor supply in the two most important slave nations of the world, the United States and Brazil. If Texas were to remain independent and abolish slavery, Calhoun thought, as he analyzed Britain's motives from Green's information, this circumstance would weaken the institution in the United States. With Texas a free nation, it would be but a matter of time before the American slave-plantation system was destroyed. The cost of American cotton would then rise sufficiently in the world market to make British India the prime source for the staple. Calhoun's view of Britain's imperial trade policies coincided with what he knew about the progress of abolitionist sentiment in the British government. He set forth his conspiracy thesis in the early fall of 1843.

> In the advanced state of commerce and the arts, the great point of policy, for the older and more advanced nations is to command the trade of the newer

14. John A. Upshur, "Letters of A. P. Upshur to J. C. Calhoun," *William and Mary Quarterly*, 2nd Ser., XVI, October 1, 1937, pp. 554–57.

and less advanced. . . . But, if force is resorted to, the blow will first be struck at the United States, Brazil and other slave holding countries. . . . The abolition of slavery would transfer the production of cotton, rice and sugar etc. etc. to her colonial possessions, and would consummate the system of commercial monopoly, which she has been so long and systematically pursuing. Hence the movements in Texas and elsewhere on abolition subject at this time.[15]

Green was not the only foreign correspondent who deepened the administration's and Calhoun's suspicions of British intent. The American chargé in Texas, William S. Murphy, was an untrustworthy but prolific source of information on the British. In his vivid imagination, Murphy saw British intrigue everywhere and abolitionist plots against annexation hatching in dark corners of Galveston, the major port of Texas.[16]

Lord Aberdeen, the foreign minister in the Peel government, contributed, perhaps unwittingly, to the administration's fears about Texas and abolition. A Scottish peer of liberal sentiments, Aberdeen was a dedicated philanthropist who had early embraced the ideas of William Wilberforce and Thomas Clarkson in the world abolition movement. Considering his position in the government, Aberdeen was apt to be indiscreet in informal conversation. His comments to a committee of the General Anti-Slavery Convention in 1842 were reported to the State Department.

But what really caught the ear of the suspicious Americans was remarks of Aberdeen and Lord Brougham in the House of Lords in August, 1843. Brougham said that he was "irresistibly anxious for the abolishment of slavery in Texas, for if it were abolished there, not only would that country be cultivated by free and white labor, but it would put a stop to the habit of breeding slaves for the Texian market." In answer to questions Brougham put, Aberdeen stated that Britain had arranged an armistice between Texas and Mexico, which he hoped would lead to a permanent peace. On the slavery question, he said that "no one was more anxious than he to see abolition of slavery in Texas," but he could not give any comment on that matter because doing so might injure peace negotiations between Texas and Mexico.[17]

Brougham's comments on slave breeding struck an acutely sensitive nerve in the seaboard slave states, which were the major suppliers of

15. *Calhoun Correspondence*, 546.

16. William R. Manning (ed.), *Texas and Venezuela*, vol. XII of *Diplomatic Correspondence of the United States, Inter-American Affairs* (12 vols.; Washington, D.C., 1932–39). See, for instance, 299, 327.

17. Manning (ed.), *Great Britain*, vol. VII of *Diplomatic Correspondence*, 249, 6–11.

slaves to Texas and the rich cotton region of the Mississippi delta. Aberdeen's reply, while vague, did convey the impression that if Mexico and Texas signed a peace treaty, the abolition of slavery would be a part of it.

Upshur sent two strongly worded notes to Everett, the second of which propounded Calhoun's thesis on the connection between British imperialism and abolition in Texas. Upshur also commented broadly on what he perceived to be the adverse effects of abolition in the United States. His major arguments could have been taken directly from Calhoun's speeches in the Senate against abolition petitions. Emancipation would degrade white labor while stimulating animosity against the blacks, which would inevitably lead to their extermination. He requested that Everett present these views to Aberdeen.[18]

Upshur kept Calhoun fully informed of the administration's policy towards Britain, Texas, and Mexico. There the matter stood until the explosion of the "peacemaker" cannon on the new warship *Princeton* killed Upshur, Gilmer, and Maxcy. They were observing the firing of the gun on a junket that the *Princeton*'s captain had arranged for the president and members of the Washington establishment. The president, who had gone below the deck for another glass of champagne with the beautiful and shapely Julia Gardiner, soon to be his bride, was unhurt but badly shaken by the event. Patrick Calhoun, who was one of the guests aboard the *Princeton* and who only by a chance encounter with a young female friend escaped death or serious injury, penned a graphic account of the accident to his father.[19]

President Tyler had scarcely composed himself at the White House when numerous politicians and congressmen appeared to press their candidates for the two vacant cabinet posts. Tyler, however, had already made up his mind to offer the post of secretary of state to Calhoun if he had good reason to expect the Carolinian would accept. The Texas negotiations were at a critical stage; talks were under way with Great Britain over a settlement of the long-disputed Oregon boundary. Tyler had need of Calhoun's prestige and ability to push these negotiations through to a successful conclusion. He had twice before offered Calhoun the post, but each time the Carolinian had refused.

Before Tyler made his third offer, he consulted McDuffie and the entire South Carolina congressional delegation. They thought that Calhoun would accept as a matter of duty. Still in shock over the acci-

18. *Ibid.*, 6–17.
19. Thomas Hart Benton, *Thirty Years' View* (2 vols.; New York, 1854–56), II, 567, 568; Lander, *Calhoun Family,* 77.

dent, Tyler decided that he would nominate Calhoun and risk the possibility of refusal. With Benton absent, the Senate voted unanimously to confirm him. It had been just a week since the *Princeton* explosion.[20]

At Fort Hill, Calhoun had already learned of the tragedy that killed two of his close allies in the administration and perhaps his closest personal friend, Virgil Maxcy. Calhoun, too, was badly shaken when he wrote a letter of condolence to Maxcy's widow. In the same package of mail was a letter from McDuffie stating that he had had an interview with the president and that Calhoun would probably be offered the State Department. McDuffie urged him to accept on both idealistic and practical grounds. "The Texas question is in such a state, that in ten days after your arrival the Treaty of annexation, would be signed, and from poor Upshur's count 40 Senators would vote for it," he wrote. "It is a great occasion involving the peace of the country and the salvation of the South."[21]

Calhoun certainly agreed with McDuffie's view of the Texas situation, but he was hesitant to accept a post in the Tyler administration. He was still unsure whether Tyler intended to be a candidate in the upcoming election, and he was dubious about lending his prestige to a possible competitor. Moreover, associating himself with an administration that was both weak and discredited in public and party opinion could subject Calhoun to the same sort of criticism that had wrecked Tyler's position before the country. He also had to consider his personal affairs. Calhoun was anxious to begin an essay on government he had long contemplated writing. Floride under no circumstances would accompany him to Washington.[22]

Except for the Texas negotiations, Calhoun was unfamiliar with policy measures of the State Department. And except for two brief periods, one as long ago as 1812, when he was chairman of the House foreign relations committee, the other during the Webster-Ashburton negotiations, he had not been in touch with the day-to-day operations of foreign policy. Yet Calhoun was disposed to accept the post, especially after pondering a letter from Dixon Lewis that arrived in the

20. Lyon G. Tyler, *The Letters and Times of the Tylers* (2 vols.; Richmond, Va., 1884), II, 294, 295; Charles Wiltse, *John C. Calhoun, Sectionalist: 1840–1850* (Indianapolis, 1951), 161–63. Henry Wise, the Virginia congressman, claims credit for the Calhoun nomination, but considering Tyler's personality, this seems most unlikely. I agree with Wiltse that the president took the initiative.

21. *Calhoun Correspondence*, 934.

22. *Ibid.*, 574.

same package of mail as McDuffie's. Lewis reinforced McDuffie's argument about duty and held out tempting bait: "A ground swell from the people themselves growing out of the Texas question may roll you into the position of a candidate."[23]

Calhoun did not receive Tyler's offer until March 15. The president echoed the sentiments of McDuffie and Lewis. He put the nomination in the highest possible context of duty, patriotism, and necessity. "We have reached a great crisis in the condition of public affairs," Tyler said. "The annexation of Texas to the Union, and the settlement of the Oregon question on a satisfactory basis, are the great ends to be accomplished. . . . Do I expect too much of you when I, along with others, anticipate at your hands, a ready acquiescence in meeting my wishes, by coming to the aid of the Country at this important period?"[24]

In accepting Tyler's offer, Calhoun wanted to make sure that his many supporters as well as the president understood his reluctance to become a member of a discredited administration. He did not of course express his view explicitly, but the inference was plain. "But as nothing short of the magnitude of the crisis," he wrote Tyler, "occasioned by the pending negotiations, could induce me to leave my retirement, I accept on the condition, that when they are concluded, I shall be at liberty to retire." By taking the turn he had, Calhoun was also ensuring for himself a minimum of presidential interference in settling both the Texas and the Oregon issues.[25]

Calhoun left Fort Hill in late March by stage from Pendleton to Edgefield, and from there he went by carriage to the Clemson plantation, Cane Brake, where he spent one or two days. From Edgefield he traveled by train to Charleston and then by coast packet to Washington, D.C. As soon as he arrived in early April and settled himself at the new United States Hotel, Calhoun plunged into State Department affairs with his accustomed vigor. Although he concentrated on the Texas and Oregon negotiations, he did not neglect the routine business of the department.

Calhoun found that the Texas negotiations were far advanced, with areas of major contention between the two governments already settled. But many sticking points remained, the boundaries of Texas and guarantees of defense if Mexico should resume hostilities being the most significant. Calhoun gave qualified assurances on these issues that satisfied the Texas emissaries. About a week after his arrival in Wash-

23. *Ibid.*, 935.
24. *Ibid.*, 939.
25. *Ibid.*, 577, 932–39; Tyler, *Letters and Times of the Tylers*, II, 295.

ington, a secret treaty was signed, pending, of course, the agreement of the Texas government and the United States Senate.

Calhoun was quick to recognize that ratification would be difficult. President Houston and President-elect Anson Jones of Texas headed a faction that was interested in Texas continuing as an independent nation. Both had ideas of imperial expansion in the Southwest, and both were intrigued with the possibility of exploiting the economic potential of the British Empire—a position that coincided with Whitehall's policies on commercial expansion.

Calhoun had some data on British involvement in Texas affairs before he became secretary of state. But even if there were no solid evidence, he was suspicious of British policies in the Western Hemisphere. The mentality he had assumed after the war hawk Congress, it seems, remained after thirty years. He had based his policy as secretary of war squarely on countering presumed British efforts to strangle the United States commercially, since they had failed in the military sphere. As vice-president and senator, Calhoun had betrayed a continuous alarm at the dependence of American cotton production, banking, and manufacturing on the transient interests of Manchester, Birmingham, and London. Skewed information that he received from Green, Upshur, and other sources, coupled with what he read in the British press and Hansard's, convinced him that Whitehall was directing the abolition movement in Europe to further its imperialist policies. British interest in Texas was, Calhoun believed, but a prelude to the destruction of the American economy, northern as well as southern; and abolition was one of the principal instruments of that destruction. Many other informed southerners felt the same way, but few with the intensity of Calhoun.

As he pondered the fate of the treaty with Texas, Calhoun cast about for a means to dramatize what he considered to be the desperate need for annexation. Among Upshur's papers was a dispatch of Lord Aberdeen's on Texas to the new minister, Richard Pakenham. Pakenham had read the note to Upshur and then had a copy made for the secretary, who had been killed before he could make a reply. Aberdeen's dispatch sought to dispel any suspicion the United States might have that Great Britain had designs on acquiring Texas or interfering in its internal affairs. Texas' independence and normal commercial relations were all that Britain sought. Aberdeen disavowed any surreptitious effort to abolish slavery in Texas, while openly declaring that Britain was opposed to slavery and would continue to promote openly and peacefully its abolition wherever it existed, including Texas. What especially caught Calhoun's eye was the hope that Mexican recognition of the Texas republic "should be accompanied by an engagement on the part of Texas to abolish Slavery eventually and under proper conditions in the Republic."[26]

Had Calhoun sent into the Senate Aberdeen's dispatch with the draft treaty and merely called attention to British activities in Texas, he would have strengthened his case. He knew that public opinion on annexation was sharply divided both by party and by section. But Calhoun wanted to do more. He had not given up all hope of a presidential candidacy, and he was anxious to check Van Buren. More importantly, he wanted to serve notice on Europe and the North that the institution of slavery was beneficial and that its abolition was not negotiable.[27]

Relying on a selective use of census statistics, Calhoun argued that when blacks were freed the incidence of physical and mental disease among them rose dramatically. He made invidious comparisons in this regard between free blacks in the North and slaves in the South. The two races, he concluded, could only coexist in the United States when the blacks were held in bondage. Slavery, he held, "is consistent with the peace and safety of both [races], with the great improvement to the inferior, while the same experience proves that . . . the abolition of slavery would (if it did not destroy the inferior by conflict to which it would lead) reduce it to extremes of vice and wretchedness."[28]

Pakenham replied in careful diplomatic language which nevertheless made the point that Calhoun's statistics and proslavery arguments were not germane to Aberdeen's dispatch or to British policy on Texas. Calhoun had hoped to draw out the debate in diplomatic discourse, but Pakenham had closed the argument.[29]

Presumably, Calhoun thought that in educating the British he was also providing support for the treaty in the Senate. He was wrong on both counts. Democratic senators from the North and Northwest, where sentiment against the expansion of slave territory was a growing force in politics, reacted unfavorably to what amounted to libels on Maine and Massachusetts, the states Calhoun chose for his statistical analyses. More significantly, the close connection between annexation and slavery, which Calhoun made clear, dampened the expansionist

26. Manning (ed.), *Texas and Venezuela*, 252.

27. See W. J. Cooper's discussion of Calhoun's motives in Appendix A of his *The South and the Politics of Slavery*, 375, 376.

28. Manning (ed.), *Great Britain*, 18–22.

29. *Ibid.*, 256–58.

sentiment that existed among some northern senators. Benton bitterly denounced Calhoun for concocting what he declared to be a conspiracy "with a double aspect—one looking to the presidency, the other to disunion." The Washington *Globe* that had hitherto treated Calhoun gently became splenetic in its attacks. If Calhoun's use of the Pakenham correspondence was meant to draw the party lines on Texas, it certainly did accomplish its purpose. It made no impression, however, on British policy.[30]

While the Senate was digesting the Texas treaty and the Pakenham correspondence in executive session, Calhoun and the other members of the Washington community were startled when they read in the *Globe*'s Saturday evening edition letters from Clay and Van Buren opposing immediate annexation. Clay's was a short and seemingly forthright rejection. Van Buren's was lengthy and characteristically hedged his opposition with various contingencies.

Calhoun may have exaggerated when he said that "V.B.'s letter has completely prostrated him," but it did seriously weaken if not eliminate the New Yorker's chances for nomination in the South and the Southwest. Clay, too, felt the instant impact of his letter on expansionist elements in the Whig party and began issuing statements that qualified his rejection of annexation. The Texas issue gave new hope to minor candidates—Buchanan, Cass, Richard M. Johnson, and Commodore Charles Stewart—and it moved Tyler to declare that he would seek the Democratic nomination. To this end, his supporters made preparations to have a convention of their own, which would meet in Baltimore at the same time as that of the Democrats. The movement turned out to be a complete failure, however.

Calhoun still held himself in readiness for a draft, but by now he realized there was little chance for the nomination. Annexation to him had become the vital question, the defeat of Van Buren a personal goal. His preferred candidate at this time was Tyler. "I think," he wrote Anna Maria, "the South will be safer in his hands." Despite his partiality for Tyler, Calhoun must have reluctantly agreed with his friend Francis Wharton, the Philadelphia authority on criminal law, that the chances for Tyler's nomination were remote. Wharton had written that in Pennsylvania "so great is the distrust felt here towards him, that nominated or not nominated anti-Texas or pro-Texas, he will not collect a thousand votes in the state." The treaty itself remained in abeyance until the

30. Benton, *Thirty Years' View*, II, 590; *Calhoun Correspondence*, 588, 599; Manning (ed.), *Great Britain*, 256–58.

party conventions met and made their nominations. Division in the Senate over annexation was replicated in Baltimore on May 27, when the Democrats met for their nominating convention.[31]

South Carolina was not represented officially, but its influence was certainly felt on the Texas, tariff, and abolition issues, which were debated in the platform committee and among the various delegations. Walker and Romulus Saunders, a gregarious wire-puller from North Carolina, directed the anti–Van Buren annexation forces. Both men were partial to Calhoun's views and were ready to lead the southern delegations out of the convention if Van Buren received the nomination. Francis Pickens and Robert M. T. Hunter were Calhoun's representatives. "Walker I have been with much," Pickens wrote Calhoun. "He fights nobly, but does not see the end of his own nose." Pickens underestimated Walker's logrolling ability; even as he was writing his critical evaluation to Calhoun, Walker was scoring a decisive victory. He and Saunders managed to drive through the convention a two-thirds rule for nomination. On the first ballot, Van Buren had a majority of the convention votes. He might well have achieved two-thirds on the next ballot had not the word been passed that most of the delegates from the slave states would bolt the convention if Van Buren were nominated. Lewis Cass was next tried as a compromise candidate, but he could not gain a two-thirds majority. "I began to doubt any nomination being made," wrote Pickens, his tense language underscoring his excitement. "It is best for us to break up without agreeing. Van Buren is dead forever. They begin to see the consequences of things."[32]

Evidently, Pickens was unaware of a clever plan that was emerging to break the deadlock. The neophyte politician George Bancroft, working with the Tennesseans, Cave Johnson, Gideon Pillow, and Andrew Jackson's nephew, A. J. Donelson, promoted James K. Polk as the only candidate who could stop Cass's nomination and who could be supported by both free and slave state delegates. Bancroft's strategy succeeded when he convinced Van Buren's manager, Benjamin Butler, to support Polk. Before the agreement was sealed, Calhoun's supporters wrung a one-term pledge from the Tennessee delegates "as we mean to run him [Calhoun] in 1848, if alive."[33] On the ninth ballot Polk was

31. *Calhoun Correspondence*, 586, 957.

32. *Ibid.;* John Boyd Edmunds, "Francis W. Pickens: A Political Biography" (Ph.D. dissertation, University of South Carolina, 1967), 101, 102; James E. Winston, "The Lost Commission," *Mississippi Valley Historical Review*, V, No. 2 (September, 1918), 164–66.

33. Charles G. Sellers, *James K. Polk, Continentalist: 1843–1846* (Princeton, N.J., 1966), 113.

nominated. The next day, in an effort to appease New York and other states loyal to Van Buren, Walker, Saunders, Bancroft, and other leading spirits had Silas Wright nominated for vice-president. Wright, however, declined the nomination, and George M. Dallas, once Calhoun's Pennsylvania campaign manager, was named in his place.   **279**

If Calhoun was disappointed that the delegates did not turn to him after the Van Buren-Cass deadlock, he gave no sign. Rather, he seemed satisfied that the convention had made a good choice. He was especially grateful for Van Buren's defeat. "It has done much by freeing the party of the dangerous control of what may be called the New York Dynasty," he wrote Francis Wharton. "Another four years of its control, after a restoration, would well near have ruined the party and the country. A more heartless and selfish body of politicians have rarely ever been associated together."[34]

And Calhoun could not quarrel with the platform, which was substantially the same one that he and South Carolina had supported in 1840. On the issues of slavery and the tariff, he wished that it was more specific. But he approved of its call for the "reannexation" of Texas and its assertion of American claims to all of the Oregon Territory up to latitude 54°40'. He must have been critical, however, of a platform that was not more direct in condemning abolitionism and in maintaining the twenty-first rule of the House—the "gag rule" that had stifled John Quincy Adams' antislavery petitions.

There was no doubt that the Democratic party was in tenuous condition after the Baltimore convention. The so-called mandate on Texas was promptly disavowed when Van Buren's partisans in the Senate joined with the Whigs to defeat the annexation treaty on June 18 by a vote of thirty-five to sixteen. And many southern Democrats were much more dissatisfied than Calhoun that the platform was not forthright on tariff revision for revenue only. Their alienation stemmed from what they felt was the betrayal of northern Democrats in the first session of the Twenty-eighth Congress.

In the House, a number of disaffected Van Buren partisans near the close of the session had joined with the Whigs and very nearly repealed the "gag rule." The same combination defeated the McKay tariff bill, which scaled down key schedules in the tariff of 1842 and had southern support.[35] Robert Barnwell Rhett, hot-tempered and impulsive, had denounced the northern Democrats unsparingly on the floor of the

34. *Calhoun Correspondence*, 601.
35. *Senate Journal*, 28th Cong., 1st Sess., 436–38.

House for their "betrayal." His colleagues in the South Carolina delegation were less outspoken than Rhett but just as angry. Rhett brought the delegation together and secured its approval of an address he had prepared that came close to nullifying the 1842 tariff. Although the prose was extravagant and abounding in threats, McDuffie signed the proposal. Calhoun was unaware of the address until, at Senator Huger's insistence, Rhett brought it to his attention.

Calhoun was not well at the time and was overworked preparing the American position on Oregon while trying to put Texas' annexation back on course in the aftermath of the treaty defeat. But he took the measure of the inflammatory proposal immediately and recognized its danger to the Polk campaign. One can picture the South Carolina delegates headed by Rhett, a handsome, self-assured journalist-planter, facing the tired, painfully thin old man, his penetrating eyes deep in their sockets, his iron-gray hair falling to his shoulders. In firm but modulated tones, Calhoun insisted that the address be suppressed. His reasons convinced the members of the delegation except Rhett, who, however, kept his own counsel during the meeting.[36]

Afterwards, Rhett revised the address so that it conformed with his own more extravagant opinions and broadened it to include a denunciation of the party members in Congress who had defeated the Texas treaty and seemed about to repeal the twenty-first rule. He threatened secession if Congress and the party did not mend their ways. Published in the *Mercury* on June 27, Rhett's address was as politically indiscreet as it was appealing to the young hotheads in the state. While the Whigs attacked Rhett as a disunionist, meetings around the state and public letters in the press began to demand action. Polk, seeking to conciliate the two major factions within the Democratic party, wrote a public letter to John K. Kane of Philadelphia, who had inquired about his position on the tariff. Polk's letter endorsed a tariff for revenue but also provided protection through discriminating duties. The letter was general, smacking of the old Jacksonian formula, "a judicious tariff." It was just the kind of pronouncement that many southerners, Calhoun among them, had charged Van Buren with concocting in 1828.[37]

36. White, *Robert Barnwell Rhett*, 72, 73; Sellers, *James K. Polk, Continentalist*, 124–26.

37. White, *Robert Barnwell Rhett*, 74, 75; Charleston *Mercury*, June 27–29, 1844; Chauncy S. Boucher, "The Annexation of Texas and the Bluffton Movement in South Carolina," *Mississippi Valley Historical Review*, VI, No. 1 (June, 1919), 17–25; Chauncy S. Boucher and Robert P. Brooks (eds.), *Correspondence Addressed to John C. Calhoun, 1837–1849: Sixteenth Report of the Historical Manuscripts Commission* (Washington, D.C., 1930), 241–49.

Calhoun could not have been happy about the letter to Kane, though the situation was very different from what it had been sixteen years before. Polk had a long antitariff record in Congress. There were no organized parties then; now there were two national political organizations. With the prospect of annexation, on which Polk was solidly committed, the South would be less exposed to economic and social penetration from the free states. Texas could in time provide for the South that equality in resources, population, and representation that Calhoun had yearned for since the Missouri crisis had revealed northern superiority in these vital areas. Polk, he believed, was infinitely more acceptable than Clay. Calhoun realized, however, that he had felt the same way about Jackson and Adams.

Yet Polk was no Jackson, and there would be no Van Buren around to manipulate power for his own selfish ends. Calhoun hoped to play a major role in shaping the policies of a man whom he considered inexperienced and bound to take his advice on foreign policy, economic affairs, and internal adjustments. Polk had already announced that he would serve but one term if elected. As Beverly Tucker, the acidulous commentator on current politics, observed, "Mr. Calhoun's misfortune is a fixed idea concerning the presidency."[38] Neither old age nor chronic illness would restrain his ambition for the glittering prize in 1848 after four years as the controlling power in the new Polk administration.

Rhett did not share Calhoun's vision. Nor did many other South Carolinians, who had neither Calhoun's personal aspirations at stake nor his single-minded view of the overwhelming importance of Texas to the South. Polk's letter to Kane touched off the necessary spark to the combustible materials Rhett had assembled in his address. On July 31, at a dinner his admirers gave him in Bluffton, South Carolina, Rhett enlarged upon his theme of treachery on the part of the northern Democrats and charged Polk of being their catspaw. At Orangeburg, a market town south of Columbia, on August 5, Rhett was even more emphatic in his denunciation. He then trod more dangerous grounds, calling for a state convention whereby those who advocated nullification, whether by the legislature or the courts, and those who advised immediate secession from the Union might confer together. "The controversy," he told an excited crowd, "is not to be avoided, the issue is submission or resistance, and we only weaken ourselves by delay."[39]

38. Tucker to James H. Hammond, March 13, 1847, JHLC.
39. *Niles' Register*, LXVI, 410. See also White, *Robert Barnwell Rhett*, 72–76; Sellers, *James K. Polk, Continentalist*, 126.

Both Polk and Calhoun reacted swiftly to the challenge from South Carolina. Polk sent out a call for a Democratic mass meeting at Nashville on August 15, where leading party figures could discuss campaign strategy and iron out conflicting issues. The convention accomplished little except to calm the anxieties of southern politicians on the tariff and on Texas, but it did tend to isolate Rhett politically from the southern Democrats. The convention also furnished Calhoun with a pretext for sounding out Polk on his policies if elected. Francis Pickens journeyed to Nashville as Calhoun's personal representative. Although he arrived too late for the meeting, he went from Nashville to Polk's home at Columbia, where the candidate outdid himself in expressing his hospitality and his cordiality towards Calhoun. Pickens wanted assurances from Polk that Blair's *Globe* would cease to command executive patronage, that the candidate would support a revenue tariff, and that he would retain Calhoun as secretary of state with controlling influence in his administration.[40]

Polk convinced Pickens on all these points, but he had other thoughts about Calhoun's future in his administration. In the present state of the Democratic party, Polk could bow neither to its southern nor its northern wing. This trim little man who had presided over several tempestuous sessions of the House was determined not to become a captive of either Calhoun or Van Buren. Nevertheless, Pickens' confident report reassured Calhoun about the candidate, and it helped Elmore and others of Calhoun's organization to put down the Rhett revolt. Calhoun dismissed the movement in his correspondence except to mention that he had "to act with great delicacy, but at the same time firmness."[41]

Yet Calhoun could not dismiss the fact that the abolitionists had organized themselves in a political movement, the Liberty party, and had nominated James G. Birney for president. More alarming than the unrest in his home state was the division over slavery in the Methodist church, which had occurred during the fateful summer of 1844. These events aroused again Calhoun's defensiveness and his apprehension about the stability of a Union which was part slave and part free. Ominous, indeed, were editorials in the *Mercury* that proclaimed the Methodist schism "the first dissolution of the Union."[42]

40. Sellers, *James K. Polk, Continentalist*, 127, 128; Edmunds, "Francis W. Pickens," 106, 107; Chauncy S. Boucher, "The Annexation of Texas and the Bluffton Movement in South Carolina" *passim.*

41. Sellers, *James K. Polk, Continentalist*, 127, 128; *Calhoun Correspondence*, 616, 624; Edmunds, "Francis W. Pickens," 110, 111.

42. Charleston *Mercury,* June 14, 20, 1844.

XV

Oregon and Mexico

I regard the defeat of Clay and the election of Polk, under all circumstances," said a rested and hopeful Calhoun on November 20, 1844, "as a great political revolution. Great events may grow out of [it], if the victory be used with prudence and moderation."[1] He had only been able to leave Washington, D.C., for a month at Fort Hill, where he found the plantation in good shape, but the brief absence from his labors at the State Department had eased his respiratory problems. An important aspect of Calhoun's improved physical condition and mental outlook were his living conditions when he returned to his office. This time he would be with his family; Floride, Cornelia, James, and his niece Eugenia made up the household.

After the family settled itself in hotel lodgings, Calhoun's domestic arrangements in Washington were more comfortable than they had been for years. James would not be with them long as he was about to attend the University of Virginia at Charlottesville. William had remained at Fort Hill under the care of the housekeeper, Mrs. Margaret Rion, and her son James.[2] Patrick and John, Jr., were at Fort Bent in the Far West, whither Patrick had gone to join a company of dragoons. John, Jr., who had contracted tuberculosis, had accompanied him in the hope that the trip would improve his health. Andrew was in Alabama, still struggling to pay off his debts. The one person who would have really brightened Calhoun's domestic circle in Washington, his daughter Anna Maria, was far away in Belgium. One of the first patronage favors that President Tyler had bestowed on Calhoun was the appointment of Clemson as chargé of the American legation at Brussels. The family kept in touch with letters, which, however, were always delayed two to three months. Calhoun's brother-in-law, the dependable James, and Francis Pickens did as much as what two unusually busy men could do to look after Clemson's plantation.

Calhoun's political affairs seemed in good order. The tensions he had experienced during the past election year had eased with the

1. *Calhoun Correspondence,* 629–30.
2. *Ibid.,* 626, 627.

Democratic victory. His negotiations with Pakenham over the Oregon border were at a standstill that favored the United States. American settlers were pushing into the Oregon Territory in considerable numbers, and politicians had begun to clamor for territorial expansion into the far Northwest. Moreover, the fur trade had diminished in that area so that pressure from the Hudson's Bay Company and other British interests had lessened considerably over the past ten years.

The British government was now more receptive to a generous settlement—though not on the extravagant terms that some American newspapers were demanding, primarily those journals published in the North and in the interests of the Democratic party. Lord Aberdeen instructed Pakenham to reopen negotiations on Oregon. Britain was willing to establish the forty-ninth parallel—the present border between Washington and British Columbia—as the boundary between the two nations, reserving, however, all of Vancouver Island, a portion of which lay south of the parallel.

But the British negotiating position as Pakenham outlined it in his first meeting with Calhoun was far less favorable than this. He proposed the Columbia River as a boundary, roughly along the present-day border between Oregon and Washington. Calhoun recognized the tactic, and though he did not insist on the most extreme American claim, which included much of present-day British Columbia, he reserved this point for future discussion. Five subsequent sessions were held, with some give and take on both sides, until Pakenham called a halt pending further instructions from home. Calhoun was well satisfied that Britain would settle on the forty-ninth parallel at the very least, and believed that further delay would improve the American case.[3]

Delay, however, was having the opposite effect on the cause for Texas' annexation. Calhoun had been prepared for the defeat of the treaty. He had had Senator McDuffie offer a joint resolution that, when Texas ratified the rejected treaty, would become binding on both nations.[4] There were enough supporters of annexation in both Houses, he calculated, to assure a simple majority.

When the Senate refused to confirm William Murphy, who was holding a recess appointment as Tyler's envoy to Texas, Calhoun had the president replace the grandiloquent and excitable Murphy with the steady, well-experienced Indiana lawyer Tilghman Howard. A South

3. *Ibid.*, 653, 654; *Calhoun Works*, V, 419–26.
4. William R. Manning (ed.), *Texas and Venezuela*, vol. XII of *Diplomatic Correspondence of the United States, Inter-American Affairs* (12 vols.; Washington, D.C., 1932–39), 73, 74.

Carolinian by birth, Howard had important political connections in the Southwest and in the Texas government. Calhoun counted on him to keep the wavering Houston and Jones behind the annexation supporters in the republic.

Just before Calhoun left for his short visit home, Howard reported that Mexico was about to break the armistice and renew hostilities. He added that Houston was insisting on military assistance from the United States as a condition for his support of annexation. Without making any specific commitment, Calhoun advised Howard that the United States would protect Texas from any hostile incursion. He also sent through the American minister to Mexico, Wilson Shannon, a warning that the United States would resist an invasion of Texas. He had no sooner taken these actions than he learned that Howard had died of yellow fever. At this stage of affairs, urgent action was necessary. Cool in the crisis, Calhoun again combined political necessity with sound judgment. He easily convinced the worried president to appoint Andrew J. Donelson, Jackson's nephew and a prime mover in the Polk nomination, to replace Howard. Donelson was close to Houston and still maintained cordial relations with the Van Buren wing of the party.[5] He was, besides, a calm, deliberative person who, like his predecessor, could be counted on to maintain the momentum for annexation in Texas. Donelson's appointment was put on such a basis of national urgency that he had little choice but to accept.

Two weeks earlier, before he learned of Howard's death, Calhoun had sent Duff Green, who had just returned from England, to Texas and Mexico as a confidential agent, under the cover of American consul at Galveston.[6] Green's son Benjamin was chargé at the American embassy in Mexico City. The assignment certainly showed some favoritism, but Calhoun had great respect for Green's reportorial abilities. The appointment was not entirely a patronage favor.

Shannon, who had replaced Waddy Thompson, Jr., as American minister to Mexico, had shown little finesse in dealing with the Mexican government. An Ohio politician whose farthest vistas had been the low hills of St. Clairsville, his home town, and the statehouse at Columbus, Shannon had scarcely the vision required to handle what had suddenly become the nation's most sensitive foreign post. A self-important courthouse lawyer, he regarded Mexicans in much the same light as he did blacks and Indians—a lesser breed of humans. Where subtlety and

5. *Ibid.*, 362–64; Manning (ed.), *Mexico*, vol. VIII of *Diplomatic Correspondence*, 155–61; *Calhoun Correspondence*, 964, 965.

6. *Ibid.*, 612.

delicacy were a necessity, he relied on bluster and threats. Yet with the two Greens in Mexico City and Donelson in Texas, Calhoun had felt secure enough about annexation to take his short home leave.

Calhoun's optimism over the election when he returned to Washington, D.C., in mid-November was soon dispelled by news from both Texas and Mexico. Two long dispatches from Duff Green justified Calhoun's appointment of him as a special agent, even if they painted a gloomy picture of Mexican policy towards Texas and the United States. Green found Mexican politics in chaos but all parties in agreement that war with the United States was inevitable. Shannon had delivered Calhoun's warning in a note to Manuel Rejon, the Mexican foreign minister, only to receive a lengthy and indignant protest charging the American government with seeking to dismember Mexico in gross violation of international law and "against public opinion by the northern part of the United States itself."[7]

From Texas, Calhoun learned that Anson Jones, president-elect, was moving towards a position against annexation and that if there was further delay on the part of the United States, the current majority for annexation in the Texas congress might disappear. After considering Green's letters, Shannon's dispatches, and the Mexican notes, Calhoun felt that the chaotic conditions in Mexico would prevent the war against Texas from being prosecuted with any vigor for the time being. "A very angry correspondence has taken place between our Minister in Mexico and her government," he wrote Clemson. "It will end in words. She is on the eve of anarchy and revolution and is destitute of the means of waging war."[8]

Calhoun was more concerned with public opinion in Texas and in the United States against annexation. Dispatches from Donelson, who had finally reached his post, reinforced previous information that delay could defeat annexation. As the second session of the Twenty-eighth Congress convened on December 2, 1844, the division over Texas was deeper than it had ever been. McDuffie's joint resolution, which had lapsed in the previous session, was reintroduced in both houses. Thomas Hart Benton took the lead in denouncing it and was supported by the *Globe*, which launched a furious attack on the Tyler administration.

For over a month, debate raged in the Congress. Finally, on January 25, 1845, the House narrowly approved a mofidied joint resolution

7. *Ibid.*, 975–80, 991–95; Manning (ed.), *Mexico*, 654–75.
8. *Calhoun Correspondence*, 634.

that would admit Texas as a state rather than have it go through the forms of a territorial government. In the Senate, however, it appeared that the resolution would never muster enough votes. The Senate committee on foreign relations reported unfavorably; and on the floor itself, a combination of Whigs and Van Buren Democrats controlled the majority of votes. But President-elect Polk arrived in Washington on February 13 and brought pressure to bear on the recalcitrant Democratic senators. On February 27, Robert John Walker offered a compromise amendment to the House version, which gave the president the option of accepting immediate statehood or appointing a commission to negotiate annexation with Texas. The following day, the Senate approved the amended resolution by a bare, two-vote majority, with the Van Buren senators Benton and John A. Dix from New York voting for it. The House followed suit, accepting the Senate resolution. President Tyler signed the measure on March 1, 1845.

During this tempestuous debate, in which sectional as well as partisan lines were sharply drawn, Calhoun became seriously ill with pneumonia. With his wife, daughter, and niece in constant attendance, he passed the crisis and slowly began to convalesce. Francis Wharton, who visited the sick man on February 18, was shocked at Calhoun's appearance. "As he rose to meet me, on my entering the room," said Wharton, "I was much struck with the emaciation of his frame, and the feebleness of his gait . . . his eye was glazed, his cheek hectic, and his voice broken by cough."[9] After a month, during which he was frequently wracked with fits of coughing and had difficulty in breathing, Calhoun was finally well enough to pay a brief visit on President Tyler and President-elect Polk. There is no doubt that the stormy reception of the joint resolution in Congress and Calhoun's efforts to resolve the disagreements had contributed to his illness and his slow recovery.

Calhoun also felt anxiety, though he would not admit it even to himself, over whether he would continue as secretary of state in the Polk cabinet and what influence he would command in the new administration. Despite his fragile health and his age (he was now sixty-three), he was looking ahead to a run for the presidency in 1848. His campaign committee had not disbanded. The *Spectator,* his Washington paper, was still publishing a daily edition. His supporters were making plans to take over the administration's press, the *Madisonian,* and combine it with the *Constitution,* which was about to replace the *Spectator.* Much of this advance work was contingent upon whether Calhoun remained in

9. *Ibid.,* 644.

conspicuous public and political view as secretary of state. Beyond the power and prestige of the position was, of course, Calhoun's overriding sense that he, and he alone, could save the South and the Union from destruction. A first and most important step in that direction was achieving southern unity on matters vitally affecting the domestic institutions and economic well-being of the slave states. This objective could be realized, he thought, through the policies of the new administration and its successors.

Repeal of the "gag rule" in the House soon after Congress organized gave renewed impetus to Calhoun's plans. The fact that most of the Democrats from the Northeast and the Northwest voted together in this instance was upsetting. "It was, with few exceptions, the votes of the two sections, slave holding and non slave holding arrayed against each other," he wrote Hunter. "They appear to me to be coming daily, more and more, into deadly conflict." To William H. Roane he said a few days later: "We have, indeed, at last reached a crisis. It has been long coming, but come it has. It remains to be seen whether our institutions and liberty will survive it."[10]

Unknown to Calhoun, Polk had already decided the Carolinian's fate. At a conference with the critically ill but still alert Jackson, it was tentatively decided that Buchanan, presumed acceptable to both wings of the Democratic party, would be secretary of state. Calhoun would be offered the British mission as a consolation. That the mission would remove Calhoun from the political scene was certainly an important motive of the president-elect.

Polk was determined that neither the pressure group led by Van Buren and Benton nor the Calhoun influence would control him. But he leaned towards the Van Buren group, sharing Jackson's deep suspicion of Calhoun's motives and especially of what he regarded as Calhoun's constant, disruptive agitation on slavery. Aaron Brown, a Tennessee congressman, former messmate of Calhoun's, and a member of Polk's inner circle, was charged with sounding him out on the diplomatic post. Brown was to stress the importance the post would have in bringing about an Oregon settlement and to promise that Calhoun would have a free hand in his negotiations with Whitehall. Brown was slow in making the approach, if indeed he ever broached the subject before all cabinet positions were filled. Three days after Polk's arrival in Washington, Calhoun wrote Hunter that "nothing is yet known of Mr. Polk's Cabinet arrangements. I think the probability is that he will form

10. *Ibid.*, 636, 637.

one of entirely new members."[11] On February 16, Calhoun paid a courtesy call on Polk, but neither mentioned the cabinet makeup. He was kept in suspense until Feburary 26, when a summons arrived from Polk's headquarters at Coleman's Hotel.

An emaciated Calhoun, showing signs of the ravages of his recent illness but still intimidating as he stood before the president-elect, was received with all the marks of care and respect. Polk may have presented a chilly exterior to the outside world, but he could be most charming and thoughtful if the occasion demanded. This occasion was eminently one that required all of Polk's political finesse. After the formal niceties were concluded, he told Calhoun that he was forming an entirely new cabinet and gave plausible reasons for doing so. His decision made political sense though it did not, in Calhoun's opinion, resolve the problems the nation was facing.[12] Polk then offered Calhoun the British mission, urging him to accept for the good of the country. Calhoun politely declined on the grounds of poor health and his doubt whether the Oregon negotiations would be better carried on in London than in Washington.

Since Polk had brought up the Oregon question, Calhoun gave the president-elect his advice on the subject. He believed Britain was anxious to settle the dispute without war. But she would resist forcibly if the United States took unilateral action by denouncing the joint occupation agreement that had been effective since 1818. In time, "the whole territory must become ours by the natural progress of our population," he said. Polk listened with seeming interest, but his reply was noncommittal.

The president-elect was insistent. After the meeting was over, he had Brown renew the offer, but to no avail. Buchanan, now designated secretary of state at Polk's direct request, made a final desperate effort to have Calhoun change his mind through Calhoun's close friend, the South Carolina congressman Isaac Holmes. Calhoun resisted all blandishments. His pride was hurt, but more importantly, he saw the beginnings of a betrayal similar to the one Jackson had dealt him and the South on the tariff. The assurances he had received from Pickens months earlier, after the Nashville meeting, seemed so much political persiflage aimed selfishly at ensuring Calhoun's support for a difficult

11. *Polk Correspondence*, V, 317, 330, 331; Charles Henry Ambler (ed.), *Correspondence of Robert M. T. Hunter, 1826–1876* (2 vols.; Washington, D.C., 1918), II, 75. See also George M. Dallas to Polk, December 15, 1844, *Pennsylvania Magazine of History and Biography*, LXXIII, No. 3 (July, 1949), 357–59.

12. *Calhoun Correspondence*, 647, 648; *Congressional Globe*, 31st Cong., 1st Sess., 621.

campaign. Although he parted from Polk in a friendly, cooperative manner and made sure that the *Constitution* continued to support the new administration, Calhoun was bitterly disappointed, his fears about the future intensified. He gave vent to his feelings in a long letter to Hunter. "It seems, indeed, strange," he wrote, "that one who had been forced into office in reference to two important negotiations, by the united voice of both parties, and who brought one to a satisfactory close as far as it depended on him, and made satisfactory progress in the other, should without the slightest objection be superceded."[13]

The inaugural address would indicate Polk's position on the tariff. Calhoun had risked his political supremacy in South Carolina less than six months before in putting down Rhett and fellow extremists on the tariff issue. Would Polk now give the lie to all of Calhoun's professions that if the Democrats won, their candidate would seek a return to compromise tariff levels? Would the new president, who had just rejected him, prove that Rhett had been right all along?

Calhoun, though still not completely recovered, braved a downpour when he joined other members of the outgoing administration and rode in an open carriage to the inauguration ceremonies, held at the east portico of the Capitol. As he listened to Polk restate the party platform and the generalities of his letter to Kane on the tariff, Calhoun felt that he had been deceived again. Here was a balancing act that offered little or no protection to the South. Even on slavery in Texas the new president was equivocal, to Calhoun's highly sensitive ear. "Whatever is good or evil in the local institutions for Texas will remain her own whether annexed to the United States or not," Polk said. On abolition in the District of Columbia and in the territories he was silent. Even the despised Van Buren had been explicit on that subject in his inaugural address. "The ground taken in the inaugural," Calhoun remarked, "is but a repetition of Jackson's judicious tariff in different language."[14]

At Buchanan's request, Calhoun remained in his office until March 10. Shortly thereafter, he left Washington, D.C. He made a brief stopover in Richmond, where the Virginia Democratic politicians feted him. His old nemesis Ritchie presided at a dinner in his honor and joined with others when they proposed toasts expressly naming Calhoun to be the party's candidate in 1848.[15] At another stopover in

13. Ambler (ed.), *Correspondence of Hunter*, 76; *Calhoun Correspondence*, 645, 647.

14. James D. Richardson, *A Compilation of the Messages and State Papers of the Presidents, 1789–1897* (20 vols.; Washington, D.C., 1900), IV, 373–82.

15. *Calhoun Correspondence*, 650.

Charleston, he received similar expressions of respect and enthusiasm. His belief that Polk's cabinet appointments and inaugural address would prove unpopular in South Carolina was confirmed in his conversation with leading figures in the city. From correspondence that awaited him at home, which he reached on March 21, he concluded somewhat rashly that the new administration was already being viewed with distrust throughout the entire South.

Calhoun had not been home long when he learned that Polk had offered the British mission to Pickens, who had declined, and then to Elmore, who also refused.[16] If the president could not placate the Calhoun wing of the party, he would attempt to soothe the Van Buren group, which was deeply upset over the New York appointments that favored the conservative, Hunker, or anti-Van Buren faction. Polk offered the post, which had now been thrice refused, to former president Van Buren, who declined. Finally, he turned to Louis McLane, who had been minister to Britain, then secretary of the treasury and secretary of state in the Jackson administration. To Polk's evident relief, he accepted.

Calhoun must have been pleased at McLane's appointment. Although the two had been political adversaries in the past, they were now on cordial terms. Calhoun respected McLane's abilities and his experience as a seasoned diplomat. He felt certain that McLane would keep him informed on the Oregon negotiations, a favor that he did not expect from the guarded Polk or the supple Buchanan. For reasons of state as well as his own aspirations, Calhoun wanted also to be informed about the Texas question, which was not yet resolved. He could expect informal communications from Donelson, who stayed on in Texas until annexation was completed.

Buoyed up by the enthusiastic receptions at Richmond and Charleston and by letters he received from all over the Union, Calhoun dismissed for the time being his worries about challenges to his leadership in South Carolina. He was eager to begin his campaign for the presidency. Members of his campaign committee shared his premature optimism when they met in Charleston on May 9 to consider the direction he should take. They advised Calhoun to follow a conciliatory course towards the administration. They also recommended a program of publicity through correspondence and loyal presses that featured opposition to future nominating conventions controlled by officeholders and office seekers. This campaign was to be carefully monitored so that

16. *Ibid.*, 653, 654, 1029.

there would be no reference to Calhoun himself. All the committee members felt that Calhoun was in a strong position.[17] Finally, they suggested that Calhoun travel north in a month or so as a private citizen, making no public comments on the policies of the administration.

Calhoun agreed with all the recommendations except the northern tour, which he thought should be deferred for a year. For once, he shrewdly analyzed the partisan politics involved. "If we are resolute and determined, the office holders and office seekers will succumb," he wrote Lewis. "They are a compromising race. With them a half a loaf is better than none; and prospect of success is better than no prospect. The mercenary corps . . . had rather see me elected than an opponent from whom they can have nothing to hope. . . . We can only succeed by showing them that I am the only man who can be elected . . . without it, establishing newspapers, travelling and every other thing is in vain."[18]

When Calhoun wrote these words, the *Constitution* had just ceased publication, along with Blair's *Globe*, which for so many years had opposed him with such ruthless vigor. Ritchie had been persuaded to edit a new administration paper, the *Union*. Clearly the situation in Washington, D.C., was in a state of flux. Calhoun had enough political sense to bide his time before he took a definite stand on public policies. "Retirement for me at present, is the proper position," he said, but he did not rule out a return to the Senate.[19]

This position, however, would not go unprotested in South Carolina. Although Robert Barnwell Rhett and his brother James had been included in the Charleston meeting of the campaign committee, neither was satisfied with a posture of neutrality towards the Polk administration. Cotton prices were hovering around four to five cents a pound, and the hard times that had begun in 1837 still persisted in much of the plantation South. The Charleston *Mercury*, now under the editorship of J. Milton Clapp, Ohio born, Yale educated, but closely identified with the radical views of the Rhetts, began a public letter

17. Dixon Lewis expressed the committee's feelings in awkward language: "[You] commanded so much sympathy of the Party, while at the same time you were not only exempt from the responsibility of any failure on the part of Polk and his administration, but for every such failure the public would give you the credit of saying and believing that if you were in his Cabinet, it might by your prudence have been averted" (Chauncey S. Boucher and Robert P. Brooks [eds.], *Correspondence Addressed to John C. Calhoun, 1837–1849: Sixteenth Report of the Historical Manuscripts Commission* [Washington, D.C., 1930], 293).

18. Ambler, *Correspondence of Hunter*, 78.

19. *Ibid.*, 79.

campaign that echoed the antitariff mood of the Bluffton rebels. As the summer wore on, antitariff sentiment evolved into a movement against Calhoun, with Rhett as usual in the vanguard, but also including such formerly devoted Calhoun partisans as Pickens and Hammond. Despite a cogent, well-reasoned defense of Calhoun by McDuffie, which was given wide currency, meetings throughout the state passed resolutions that condemned Calhoun's silence on the administration's presumed tariff policy.[20]

Attacks became more pointed after the Memphis convention on transportation in the fall of 1845. The prospect of Texas' annexation and sharp rises in the cotton market had stimulated latent entrepreneurial interests in the South and the Southwest and again focused attention on the lower Mississippi valley as the channel of trade that would compete with the Erie Canal and the Baltimore and Ohio railroad, pushing farther west from Wheeling, Virginia. Calhoun's friend and associate James Gadsden, who had worked with him on the ill-fated Louisville, Cincinnati, and Charleston railroad project, was a prime mover in the Memphis convention. Gadsden had little difficulty in converting Calhoun to a grand scheme for the development of a system of canals, railroads, and turnpikes extending south and east of the vast Mississippi river system to the Gulf of Mexico. Calhoun's actual participation in the convention required more careful thought, however.

Obviously, a project of this scale was beyond the resources of the states affected—if indeed all their individual interests could be satisfied, which Calhoun knew from experience was virtually impossible. Federal support was indispensable. To a rationalizer like Calhoun, his doctrine of states' rights and a weak central government posed no problem of inconsistency. He had always, as he claimed, favored federally financed internal improvements that were clearly interstate in nature and were essential for defense of the nation. Most recently, he had favored distribution of the treasury surplus and of federally owned lands to the states under certain conditions. So long as the federal government only supplied the funds necessary, leaving to the states control and direction of expenditures, development could proceed without any violation of his political doctrine.

Calhoun's overriding concern, as it had been for years, was the added protection this project, if brought to a successful conclusion,

20. *Calhoun Correspondence*, 1038, 1041, 1049, 1050; John Boyd Edmunds, "Francis W. Pickens: A Political Biography" (Ph.D. dissertation, University of South Carolina, 1967), 122, 123.

would give the South. Such a transportation system could be the political and economic corollary to Texas. Not only would his dream of binding together the West and the South, which Hayne had advanced years before in his debate with Webster, be consummated, but the economic potential for both sections would be enormous. The transportation web thus created would go a long way towards creating the unity of the slave states that Calhoun had striven to attain over the past twenty years.

Yet, attractive as the scheme was to a man of Calhoun's vision, he knew that his participation in the convention would spark already smoldering hostility to him in his own state. Elsewhere, he would be accused of inconsistency by members of his party with their own interests to protect and, of course, by the opposition Whigs on a partisan basis. The proposed system might also awaken sectional opposition, unless a similar program of public largesse was allocated to the North. What of the expense? Would this be such a burden on the treasury that current tariff rates would have to be maintained or even raised?

When Gadsden and others urged him to attend the transportation convention and publicly express his support, Calhoun weighed all the ponderables before deciding that he would attend. He was at his son Andrew's plantation in Alabama at the time, within convenient striking distance of Memphis. Andrew and Patrick accompanied him on the trip west to New Orleans and then by steamboat up the Mississippi River to Memphis. At all stopping places on the journey, large crowds gathered to honor Calhoun. As soon as he reached Memphis, he was almost overwhelmed by a concourse of citizens who met his vessel at the wharf and escorted his carriage to the Gayoso House, where he was to stay.

The next day, Calhoun electrified the convention with a speech that emphasized the imperial scope of a project that bound the Mississippi river system to the South Atlantic and the Gulf states, including Texas, which had just joined the Union. He bid also for the northern tier of states and territories by suggesting a canal connection from the Mississippi River to the Great Lakes and the St. Lawrence waterway. He avoided the politically sensitive topic of direct financial aid from the federal government but repeated his well-known position on land policy when he outlined a program whereby the government would bestow alternate sections of public lands to the states along railroad and canal routes as a construction subsidy. Defense was an important argument that he used effectively. The Gulf of Mexico was of vital interest to American security. With the economic development of the Mississippi

Valley that he envisaged, the federal government would have to move ahead with the fortification program on the gulf that had been abandoned to his intense regret at the end of the Monroe administration.[21]

Well before Calhoun went to Memphis, he had decided that he must return to the Senate. The incipient tuberculosis from which he was suffering had subsided, and he was feeling quite well for his sixty-three years. Family affairs, too, seemed to be no particular cause for anxiety. McDuffie had suffered a stroke, which, combined with his other ailments, had completely reduced his effectiveness as a senator. Daniel Huger, South Carolina's other senator, had repeatedly offered to resign his seat in favor of Calhoun. There was persistent concern from within the state and other areas of the Union that the free trade cause in the Senate was losing ground because of the death or resignation of some of its keenest advocates. The growth of the abolition movement worried others in the South, who wanted assurance that there would be an advocate of stature in Congress to defend slavery. "The pressure on me to accept," Calhoun said, "came from all parts of the Union, and every party urging me, as I regarded the peace and safety of the country, not to decline, if the place were offered me." Apart from the timing, which he thought would best suit his presidential campaign, Calhoun made his decision primarily because of what he believed to be a foreign crisis in the making over the Oregon and the Texas boundaries.[22] On September 17, 1845, he wrote Armistead Burt, his relative by marriage, that he would be willing to serve. Burt was to take soundings among members of the legislature and make whatever arrangements he deemed necessary. Three weeks later, Calhoun accepted Huger's standing offer of resignation.

He had feared that his stand at Memphis might have injured his chances; hence Calhoun was gratified to learn that the legislature had elected him to serve Huger's unexpired term with only four abstentions. But there was an undercurrent of opposition to his stand, which surfaced in the *Southern Quarterly Review.* An unsigned article charging Calhoun with inconsistency on internal improvements was clearly aimed at undermining his political leadership. Because of similarities in style and its resemblance to speeches Pickens had made, Calhoun decided his longtime associate and relative was the author. Pickens denied the charge, but the break between the two men was never closed. Calhoun received news of his election along with a copy of

21. *Calhoun Works,* VI, 273–84.
22. *Calhoun Correspondence,* 665, 675, 671, 672, 673.

Polk's annual message to Congress while he was resting from his trip at his son's plantation. He found Polk's statements on Oregon and Mexico so alarming that he left at once for Fort Hill, where he remained a few days, and then proceeded north with Floride and Cornelia for company.[23]

On Saturday, December 20, they reached Washington, D.C. Calhoun had no sooner arrived and was still weary and travel-stained when two members of his campaign committee, Isaac Holmes and Robert M. T. Hunter, called upon him for a conference. They wanted to know if he would follow the president's lead in demanding all of the Oregon Territory. When Calhoun replied with an emphatic negative, they both argued that if he should take such a stand he would fail in Congress, which would eventually injure his reputation throughout the country. Calhoun insisted that Polk's Oregon policy, which included notice of terminating the joint occupation of the territory, was courting a war with Britain at a time when war threatened in Mexico. Exerting his customary powers of argument and persuasion, he convinced both men that compromise was the best course for American interests and that it was achievable, given the political and economic situation in Britain and the problems that country faced on the Continent. The three talked for several hours. By midnight, when Holmes and Hunter took their leave, both men had agreed to rally as many Democrats and antiexpansionist Whigs as they could behind Calhoun's position. On Monday morning, Calhoun had word that he could expect substantial bipartisan support.[24]

With this assurance, the Carolinian hurried over to the White House to call on the president.[25] To Polk he certainly looked healthier and in better humor than when they last met. But the president was not pleased with what Calhoun had to say. Calhoun opened the conversation by expressing himself completely in favor of asserting American rights to the Oregon Territory. He was opposed, however, to Polk's recommendation in his recent message that Congress give notice to Great Britain that joint occupation be terminated in one year's time as provided by the treaty of 1827. Calhoun repeated succinctly his previous argument that "masterly inactivity," as he phrased it, would achieve the territorial ends of the United States through peaceful

23. Edmunds, "Francis W. Pickens," 122–27, 674, 675.

24. Appendix, *Congressional Globe*, 30th Cong., 1st Sess., 806, 807; Isaac Holmes to Calhoun, October 6, 1848, Calhoun-Clemson Papers, Clemson University.

25. Milo M. Quaife (ed.), *The Diary of James K. Polk During His Presidency, 1845–1849* (4 vols.; Chicago, 1910), I, 131.

means. Polk disagreed, insisting that a more forceful policy would bring Britain to terms. Calhoun "expressed a strong desire for delay of action on the subject," Polk wrote in his diary, "and said the Executive should confer with the proper committees of Congress and restrain them from rash or warlike measures." Before Calhoun left, he also said a few words about the administration's tariff policy, which he claimed did not go far enough in scaling down the 1842 levels.

Polk assessed Calhoun's position quite accurately when he observed, "Mr. Calhoun will be very soon in opposition to my administration."[26] On January 10, Calhoun again called on the president and repeated his conviction that Polk should not push termination of joint occupation because it might bring on a war with Britain, which the United States was in no position to wage. While they were speaking, Buchanan came into the president's office, and shortly after, other cabinet members appeared. Calhoun asked if it was cabinet day, and when Polk replied in the affirmative, he made ready to leave.

But the president wanted to show Calhoun that the cabinet was solidly behind his policy. He invited Calhoun to remain. Polk sat silently at the cabinet table while Calhoun restated his conviction that the United States should reopen negotiations with Britain on settlement of the boundary along the forty-ninth parallel, giving up all claims to Vancouver Island and agreeing to free navigation rights on the Columbia River for a fixed period. Buchanan and others defended the administration's position, pointing out, as Calhoun well knew, that Pakenham had recently rebuffed a proposal for just such a settlement.[27] The president said nothing during the discussion. When Calhoun left the White House, he knew that he had been unable to move the administration towards a more conciliatory policy, which would gain the time he felt was needed for an amicable settlement. A period of quiet diplomacy was essential to save the faces of key participants in Britain and the United States whom he believed had mismanaged the negotiations. Delay, he realized, would be difficult to achieve on what had become an emotionally charged issue.

In the Senate, Calhoun had to face the administration supporters of his own party, who were convinced that forceful action must be taken, and spread-eagle imperialists like the bibulous Edward Hannegan of Indiana and the voluble William Allen of Ohio. Both individuals were noisy proclaimers of American rights to all of the disputed territory.

26. *Ibid.*, 132.
27. *Ibid.*, 158–60.

And their slogan of "fifty-four forty or fight" was being sounded in the Democratic press.

Although the Polk administration kept Calhoun in the dark about its formulation of policy and its sources of information, the obliging McLane provided him with unofficial reports on British politics and cabinet opinion. The potato famine had made the Tory ministry of Sir Robert Peel more immediately receptive to a repeal of the Corn Laws, which would throw open the British home market to American grain. Should the United States move towards free trade, which seemed likely, it would improve further the chances of a peaceful solution to the Oregon dispute. So Calhoun assumed from McLane's correspondence.[28]

Calhoun had resigned himself to the passage of the notice terminating joint occupation, but in the interest of demonstrating American willingness to renegotiate on the forty-ninth parallel, he decided on amending the notice to that end. Putting together an unlikely coalition of free trade and protectionist Democrats, he managed to have the amendment passed in the House. It was now up to the Senate to approve the measure. Again acting on a communication from McLane that stressed British willingness to reopen negotiations, Calhoun considered moving a resolution in executive session that would advise the president to take the first step in a boundary settlement along the forty-ninth parallel. Calhoun's tactic gained considerable support even from Benton, who feared he was being upstaged by the extreme expansionists. Polk got wind of the move from Senator Hayward of North Carolina, a close friend, and from Allen, who cast it in its worst shape as an attempt on Calhoun's part to make political capital at Polk's expense. When Calhoun called to sound out the president on the proposition, he was greeted with a chilly negative.[29]

After his failure with the president, Calhoun decided to make a public exposition of his views. To packed galleries on March 16, 1846, he delivered one of his most eloquent speeches, in which he traced the course of the boundary dispute and alluded to changes in the British attitude. Since Pakenham had rejected the American offer to negotiate and the president had called for a termination of joint occupancy, events involving both nations, he said, had changed the diplomatic environment significantly. The British, he was certain, were ready to compromise, but Polk remained unconvinced. Calhoun pointed out

28. Boucher and Brooks (eds.), *Correspondence Addressed to Calhoun*, 311–15, 323, 324; *Calhoun Correspondence*, 1076–79, 1081–83.

29. Quaife (ed.), *Diary of James K. Polk*, I, 240–52.

that "measures of policy are necessarily controlled by circumstances . . . to persist in acting the same way under circumstances essentially different would be folly and obstinacy, and not consistency." Falling back on a familiar metaphor, he likened consistency in diplomacy
or in politics to the administering of the same medicine at every stage of
a disease. This kind of consistency he branded the false remedy "of a
quack, which would be sure to kill the patient." As there were medical
quacks, so there were political quacks, who in dangerous cases caused
similarly fatal results. Despite Polk's strong language, should he now
opt for compromise, he ought not to be charged with inconsistency.[30]
Calhoun was seeking public support for a common ground to resolve
the dangerous impasse and not humiliate the president. Without any
awareness on his part, his speech had taken on a tone of lofty condescension towards Polk.

Although it was not received favorably in the White House, Calhoun's address was a resounding success and surely marked a turning
point in the resolution of the Oregon dispute. Even the ardent expansionists applauded the reasoning that supported Calhoun's assertions.
Polk, sensitive, suspicious, and under heavy pressure on his policies
towards Mexico, made no comment except to admit at a later date that
"Calhoun has embarrassed the administration on the Oregon question." The embittered Polk further commented, "He is playing a game
to make himself President, and his motives of action are wholly selfish."[31] Polk made these caustic remarks shortly after the termination
notice amended in accordance with Calhoun's pacific language passed
the Senate.

By then, the Corn Laws had been repealed in the House of Commons, and debate in Congress was in full swing on the administration's
tariff bill. Secretary of the Treasury Walker had gone over the schedules of the 1842 tariff and had reclassified them in a descending scale of
duties. In his report, the secretary sought to give the impression that
the administration was advocating a free trade bill. In reality, the bill
that North Carolina congressman James J. McKay introduced still retained moderate protectionist features, though it did reduce rates to 30
percent *ad valorem* on those items of special interest to the South.[32] The
McKay bill was not all Calhoun had hoped for—a general reduction in

---

30. *Calhoun Works*, IV, 268.

31. Quaife (ed.), *Diary of James K. Polk*, I, 344.

32. Frank W. Taussig, *The Tariff History of the United States* (New York, 1931), 114.
Cotton cloth was rated at 25 percent.

compromise tariff rates. As he expected, there was an outcry from the *Mercury* and other captious free trade advocates in South Carolina.

After heavy pressure from the Polk administration, the bill weathered the House with its schedules substantially intact. Dixon Lewis, now in the Senate, led the free trade forces in an effort to modify the schedules in the House bill while he sought to hold off protectionists headed by Webster. After much debate, in which Calhoun took a conspicuous part on the free trade side, and parliamentary maneuvers directed by administration leaders, the Senate forced acceptance of the House version. Polk signed the measure, which became known as the Walker Tariff, on July 30, 1846.

Calhoun agreed with his friend James Gadsden, who wrote from Charleston that the tariff "has pleased, but not satisfied us." Calhoun was relieved that his stand on the tariff against the *Mercury* and the Rhetts had proven to be a sound one. The Bluffton people continued to oppose his position on internal improvements, but when he produced his masterful "Report on the Memphis Memorial," the *Mercury* capitulated and praised it extravagantly. Polk vetoed a rivers and harbors bill that resulted from the report, but Calhoun had made his point. Even Rhett came to understand the importance to the South of the Western connection and the rapid economic development of the Mississippi river system.[33]

Meanwhile, the Oregon boundary settlement was jeopardized by British politics and American intransigence. The Peel ministry, which had been reinstated briefly, was about to fall for good. With only a few days remaining to it before the Liberals and the bellicose Lord Palmerston took over the government, Lord Aberdeen wrote out the British agreement to settle on the forty-ninth parallel, utilizing Calhoun's amendment to the notice as his pretext for reopening negotiations and instructing Pakenham to take the initiative. The Polk administration had no choice but to present the treaty to the Senate. On June 18, 1846, the Senate ratified the treaty over the last-ditch efforts of extreme expansionists to defeat it. There is no doubt that Calhoun's efforts in Congress and his clear understanding of the positions involved made the peaceful settlement possible. Nor is there any doubt that both Polk and Buchanan were chagrined at the role the Carolinian played, which in effect moved the diplomatic initiative away from the White House.[34]

33. *Calhoun Correspondence*, 1085; Charleston *Mercury*, July 4, 1846; *Calhoun Correspondence*, 704; White, *Robert Barnwell Rhett*, 90.
34. Quaife (ed.), *Diary of James K. Polk*, I, 474–78.

Aberdeen's draft treaty and instructions to Pakenham were sent just before the ministry resigned and just before word reached London of war between the United States and Mexico. Calhoun claimed that if the British government had learned of this event, it would have ended all negotiations on the assumption that the Polk administration would eventually settle on the Columbia River boundary rather than risk a two-front war.[35] His analysis may have been drawn, but it seems reasonable that the British government would have delayed further negotiations until it could assess the implications of the war.

Calhoun had risked his political future on the Oregon question, pitting himself against the administration, his own party in Congress, and public opinion. As he remarked to Clemson, "When I arrived here, it was dangerous to wisper [*sic*] 49, and I was thought to have taken a hazardous step in asserting that Mr. Polk had not disgraced his country in offering it."[36] The risk had paid off, and Calhoun was not modest in claiming credit for the settlement. His stand opposing the Mexican war, however, entailed a much greater risk. Initially, it appeared that he would suffer the consequences of his position.

As soon as Polk had word that the Texas convention had approved annexation on July 4, 1845, he ordered General Zachary Taylor to move his troops to Corpus Christi on the Texas Gulf Coast at the mouth of the Neuces River. During the fall, Polk sought to establish the southwest border of Texas at the Rio Grande. In addition, he was anxious to purchase territory westward to California along the thirty-second parallel. The purchase would include California and the New Mexico Territory—present-day New Mexico, Arizona, and a part of Colorado. He sent John Slidell, a Louisiana politician from a New York family, to Mexico City to treat with the Mexican government over the Texas boundary and the land purchases. Slidell's mission failed utterly, and there were new threats of war from the Mexican government. Reacting impulsively to the news, Polk directed General Taylor to move his troops westward to the Rio Grande. The president was ordering an occupation of territory that even Texas was reluctant to claim.[37]

As soon as Calhoun learned of the aggressive move, he feared war with Mexico would result, just when the Oregon question had reached a critical point. Yet he felt that if he clashed with the administration over its hostile move, he would jeopardize his effectiveness on the Oregon issue. He explained his predicament to the Whig leaders and

35. *Calhoun Correspondence*, 698.
36. *Ibid.*, 697.
37. Sellers, *James K. Polk, Continentalist*, 227–29.

asked them to take the lead in condemning Polk's course. Suspecting ulterior motives, they refused to comply. "The position, which our army in Texas had been ordered to take on the del Norte, below Metamoras [*sic*], and far in advance of our settlement," he wrote Clemson, "[is] without any apparent reason, as far as I can see."[38]

The day after Calhoun wrote this letter, Polk asked him to call, if convenient, at 7:00 P.M. The two men met in the president's study. Polk opened the conversation by asking Calhoun's opinion on the feasibility of an appropriation to bribe Mexican president Parades to agree to a treaty that would cede all territories westward to the Pacific along the thirty-second parallel. Polk also asked if Calhoun would support an additional appropriation of $25 million for such a cession of territory. Calhoun said that he would support the purchase, adding that "the amount was no object," but that he was opposed to the bribe appropriation. "Should Congress agree and the information become public," he thought, "it would embarrass the settlement of the Oregon question."[39] Other Democratic leaders Polk consulted were more positive, though Benton shared Calhoun's fears that the policy would result in war.

The Mexican government had now ordered its army to take position on the southwestern bank of the Rio Grande opposite Taylor's force. Polk convened his cabinet to consider what response to make. The cabinet advised him to ask Congress for a declaration of war if the Mexicans attacked. Polk decided on his own, however, that the administration would ask for the declaration even if there were no overt action. Fortunately for the peace of mind of all concerned, the administration received news that very evening that Mexican troops had crossed the Rio Grande and ambushed a party of American dragoons, killing or capturing the entire force of sixty-five men. The cabinet reconvened at once and began drafting a war message that was presented to Congress the next day, May 11, 1846. A select group of congressional leaders were informed of the war message beforehand, among them Benton, Allen, and Cass of the Senate, but not Calhoun.

The administration had little difficulty in the House, where opposition was confined to the South Carolinians, John Quincy Adams, and Joshua Giddings, the abolitionist congressman from Ohio—an odd alignment. In the Senate, Calhoun, among others, demanded more information on Mexican aggression. He was also deeply concerned

38. *Calhoun Correspondence*, 693, 687.
39. Quaife (ed.), *Diary of James K. Polk*, I, 313.

whether the Rio Grande was actually American territory, thus implying that the administration was waging a war of aggression.

Calhoun was willing to vote for needed supplies, but he noted a constitutional objection in the war message and pleaded for more time to consider whether war was necessary. Heading what he called a peace party, he succeeded in splitting the message in two parts, the declaration itself going to the foreign relations committee, whose chairman was the hawkish expansionist William Allen, and the request for men and supplies going to Benton's committee on military affairs. Initially, Benton had been dubious about the war, but enough pressure was brought to bear on him to induce him to vote with a majority of his committee in reporting favorably on the administration's message. Calhoun had hoped that his tactic would gain more time for a careful consideration of the message. "But in this I was disappointed," he said. "Contrary to the order of the Senate, the Committee on Military Affairs reported a bill including both the raising of forces and a declaration of War." The Democratic majority overrode protests and amendments in accepting the committee reports. When the bill itself was voted on, all but two of the Whig senators joined the Democrats in sustaining the message. Calhoun and two Whig senators abstained.[40]

In taking this stance on a popular, emotional issue, Calhoun was risking far more than merely the opposition of his party and the administration. He remained silent for several months and was not ready to comment until Congress met in December, 1846. Then he spoke out against the war policy after Taylor's victories at Palo Alto, Resaca de la Palma, and Monterrey had raised the spirit of nationalism and public enthusiasm to a high pitch. Calhoun persisted even after Winfield Scott's successful engagements as the American army moved toward Mexico City, in the face of advice from trusted counselors and overtures from Polk himself that they resume their working relationship.[41] Yet the South Carolina legislature reelected Calhoun to the United States Senate, and he enjoyed considerable bipartisan support in his home state from such political leaders as Waddy Thompson, Jr., and Joel Poinsett.

Calhoun's reasons for opposing the war were complex. At first, he was concerned about the effect of the war on the Oregon negotiations; the latest British offer was not yet known in Washington. When this

40. *Calhoun Correspondence*, 691; *Congressional Globe*, 29th Cong., 1st Sess., 791–95.
41. Ernest M. Lander, Jr., *Reluctant Imperialists: Calhoun, the South Carolinians, and the Mexican War* (Baton Rouge, 1980), 61, 77, 110, 111.

question was resolved, he continued to worry about European intervention, which he thought a distinct possibility if the war degenerated into a long-term guerrilla affair. The clamor of the expansionist press for American seizure of all of Mexico and evidence that some members of Polk's cabinet favored such a land grab were most disturbing. He saw the prospect of the war continuing indefinitely at ruinous cost to the American economy and American lives for the conquest of a people who were alien to American culture and whose ruling classes opposed slavery.

Calhoun's position was at once a purely defensive one that concerned itself with outside forces breaking down through war or assimilation the fragile and divided social order of the Union, and one of high-minded idealism that frowned on an aggressive, plundering war against a weak, distracted neighboring nation. As a politician, Calhoun may have offered as many reasons for his opposition as there were political constituencies. But for him personally there seems to have been a controlling motivation: a profound insecurity about his section and the future of the Union. Calhoun recognized more clearly than most the frailty of the antebellum power structure and the potential for a big land grab that would jeopardize this precarious balance. Underlying all were a profound distrust of Polk and a deep-seated apprehension of what Calhoun deemed to be a rampant executive power riding roughshod over constitutional barriers. But he also consistently misread volatile public opinion—a fatal flaw for any aspiring politician. Calhoun confessed that his abstention on the war vote "has for the present, weakened me with the party and the unthinking portion of the Community. . . . My present position is to wait quietly for a good opportunity, and the subsiding of the existing excitement, to put myself right before [the] country and the world."[42]

Calhoun lost even more than his remote chance for the presidency by his stand. His closest friend and kinsman and one of his most astute political advisors, Francis Pickens, criticized Calhoun's opposition to the war at a public meeting in Edgefield. This reproach, which came at a time when the Democratic press was abusing him roundly, was too much for the old, sick man. "He is full of emulation," Calhoun railed, "and has a strong infusion of envy, jealousy and vanity in his composition." Pickens tried to heal the breach but never succeeded. And of his old associates, Pickens was not alone in condemning Calhoun. James H.

42. *Calhoun Correspondence*, 695.

Hammond, former governor of South Carolina, was unsparing in his criticism.[43]

Calhoun persisted in thinking that the war would prove unpopular in the country. "Many now begin to see," he wrote his daughter Anna Maria, "that it is like to prove a very troublesome and embarrassing affair. . . . There is no seeing when or how it is to be ended. It is like to turn out, as the war in Algeria has—a war between races and creeds, which can only end in complete subjection of the weaker power—a thing not easily effected in either case."[44]

Unfortunately, if Calhoun's prediction proved accurate, only the Whigs would profit in the next presidential election. Calhoun had hoped that his leadership in opposition to what he regarded as a disgraceful war would bring out the best and the most honorable in his section and would contribute to southern unity. This view, to which he clung so stubbornly, soon proved to be politically naïve. On the consequences of the war, however, Calhoun was more insightful. The conflict was only in its third month when on a hot, humid August night, a stout, perspiring young man of thirty-two stood up in the House and proposed an amendment to a $2 million appropriation bill that would provide funds for a secret negotiation with Santa Anna, now president of Mexico. The young man's name was David Wilmot. His amendment, which passed in the House but was defeated in the Senate, would exclude slavery from any territories acquired from Mexico.

43. *Ibid.*, 696, 705; Lander, *Reluctant Imperialists*, 74.
44. *Calhoun Correspondence*, 715.

XVI

A Southern Man and a Slaveholder

On Friday, February 19, 1847, Calhoun rose in the Senate to offer a series of resolutions on the Wilmot Proviso, which Preston King, a Van Buren Democrat from northern New York, had attached to a House appropriation bill. After pointing out that the territories' were the common property of free and slave states, Calhoun uttered what his colleagues rightly took to be his credo. He spoke, he said, as an individual from the South. "There is my family and connections," he said gravely. "There I drew my first breath; there are all my hopes. I am a planter—a cotton planter. I am a Southern man and a slaveholder—a kind and merciful one, I trust and none the worse for being a slaveholder. I say, for one, I would rather meet any extremity upon earth than give up one inch of our equality—one inch of what belongs to us as members of this great republic!"[1] Calhoun then offered six resolutions reasserting his by now familiar argument that the federal government was the agent of the states and that Congress had no right to discriminate against citizens of any state who wished to take their property into the territories.

Since the early debates over the abolition petitions in 1835, Calhoun had seen the antislavery movement gain strength and alter its tactics to meet constitutional objections. The effort to abolish slavery in the District of Columbia clearly foreshadowed in Calhoun's mind abolition in the territories—those already held, like Nebraska, as well as those like Texas that might be gained—for the Constitution gave Congress powers that might be construed as regulating the internal affairs of the territories. And as Calhoun had assumed on December 19, 1837, Benjamin Swift, a Whig senator from Vermont, presented a memorial not from private citizens but from the state legislature against the annexation of Texas or the admittance of any slave territory to the Union. The memorial also declared that Congress had the power to abolish slavery in the territories.[2]

1. *Calhoun Works,* IV, 347–48.
2. *Calhoun Papers,* XIV, 13, 14.

In response, Calhoun had moved resolutions for the Senate's consideration only, which he hoped would forestall the abolitionist strategy. He was unsuccessful in having the Senate go on record as construing attempts to abolish slavery in the District of Columbia as aimed directly at abolishing slavery in the states.[3] The Senate did agree with Calhoun's contention that the Union was the result of a compact between the states and that the Constitution did indeed protect slavery where it legally existed.[4] At the time, Calhoun said that if the abolitionist agitation was not stopped, he feared disunion would result.

Calhoun's misgivings grew in intensity after the abolitionists joined political action with their pressure tactics on Congress to legislate against slavery in the District of Columbia and the territories. The admission of three slave states, Arkansas in 1836 and Florida and Texas in 1845, did nothing to allay Calhoun's concerns about the territorial problem. Sooner or later, he was certain, northern politicians in the two major parties would settle on exclusion of slavery from the territories as a political device that skirted constitutional limitations.

In the election campaign of 1844, the abolitionist Liberty party, which had grown significantly in strength over a four-year period, had all but adopted the territorial approach as its major plank. The remainder of the Louisiana Purchase territory north of the Missouri Compromise line was rapidly gaining in population. Iowa was about to enter the Union as a free state; Wisconsin would soon follow. And the vast Oregon Territory, whose northern boundary had just been settled, was experiencing a population boom that was outstripping immigration to Texas.

The Wilmot Proviso was the signal to Calhoun that the major parties would soon split over the extension of slavery. His worries about the future became immediately focused on the new territories that would be added to the Union—Oregon, already acquired, and a probable huge cession from Mexico. He saw in their population growth a destabilizing factor that would seriously compound divisive forces that threatened the Union. For this reason and because of the costs in

3. *Senate Journal*, 25th Cong., 2nd Sess., 106–107, 117, 122, 126, 132.

4. Calhoun's resolution, however, which the Senate approved by a vote of 31 to 11, neither stated nor implied compact theory. It declared that "this government is bound so to exercise its powers as to give as far as practicable, increased stability and security to the domestic institutions of the states that compose the Union and that it is the solemn duty of the government to resist all attempts by one portion of the Union to use it as an instrument to attack the domestic institutions of another" (*Congressional Globe*, 25th Cong., 2nd Sess., 98).

human and material resources, he had objected strenuously to Scott's invasion of Mexico proper, and while he understood Polk's dilemma of having two politically minded Whig generals in charge of the American military effort, he refused twice to back the president on the appointment of a Democratic lieutenant general to overall command.

Calhoun surely detested Polk's choice for the supreme command, Thomas Hart Benton, but personal grounds were only a small part of his opposition to the administration's conduct of the war. What he was striving for during the winter of 1847 was the establishment of a defensive line of military posts. The government would then negotiate for a settlement that offered liberal terms. If Mexico refused, the United States would simply hold the line indefinitely. He explained his plan to Polk during a private conference after a Christmas Eve dinner party at the White House. Polk made no comment other than to say that their conversation was pleasant and friendly. When the president sought to expand the army by ten regiments of volunteers in January, 1847, Calhoun saw in the move a covert attempt to enlarge the war. On the other side of the political spectrum, the fat, clever congressman Preston King succeeded in attaching the Wilmot Proviso to the administration's ten-regiment bill.

The embattled president was faced with the stubborn opposition of Calhoun and his small but influential group of southern Democrats, and now with an increasing number of northern Democrats who were backing the proviso. Polk's reaction to King's move was predictably explosive. The practical-minded president felt that a debate on slavery had no place in the conduct of the war. And territorial cession was an abstract issue because slavery could not exist in the arid Far Southwest. King's amendment was a mischievous one, Polk thought, and extremely dangerous to the nation. "If persevered in," he confided to his diary, "[it] will be attended with terrible consequences to the country, and can not fail to destroy the Democratic party."[5]

For once, Calhoun would have agreed with the president. To his mind, the administration's policy on beginning the war and widening the conflict was providing the climate of opinion in which antislavery sentiment could grow and extend itself. Thus, Calhoun and his associates in the Senate, or as Polk acidly called them, "his peculiar friends," voted with the Whigs to reject the ten-regiment bill. "I now regard Mr. Calhoun," said Polk, "to be in opposition to my administration."[6]

5. Milo M. Quaife (ed.), *The Diary of James K. Polk During His Presidency, 1845–1849* (4 vols.; Chicago, 1910), I, 305.

6. *Calhoun Works*, IV, 323, 324, 425–43; Quaife (ed.), *Diary of James K. Polk*, I, 371.

Calhoun's risk in opposing the war at the outset seemed finally to be lessening as public opinion began to shift away from the president's policies. The election of two close supporters from Virginia, Robert M. T. Hunter and James M. Mason, to the Senate in January was most **309** heartening to Calhoun, whose ambition again kindled.[7] But he read the portents with only partial accuracy. He was wrong when he said that now "there will be no more Baltimore nominations"; his further comment, "or if there should be, the nominee will assuredly be defeated," was right but for the wrong reason. However Calhoun might set himself against conventions and wire-pullers and placemen, they were all now solidly established on the political scene.

Nevertheless, his optimism again on the rise, Calhoun decided that he would analyze the administration's presumed aims as well as the conduct of the Mexican war. In a speech lasting over two hours on the $3 million appropriation bill, he subjected the administration to a merciless criticism. "What can be gained, if success should finally crown our efforts, by subduing the country?" he asked. "What would we do with it? Shall we annex the States of Mexico to our Union? Can we incorporate a people so dissimilar in every respect—so little qualified for free and popular government—without certain destruction to our political institutions?"[8] Calhoun's opposition to the war and the administration's policy finally broke the president's patience. Although Calhoun and his small group held a balance of power in the Senate, Polk decided to read him out of the Democratic party.

The *Union,* which had been less than enthusiastic about Calhoun since his abstention on the war bill, became bitingly critical in an article it published after his speech on the $3 million bill. Ritchie virtually accused Calhoun and his followers of treason during wartime. After an acrimonious debate, Calhoun and his supporters voted with the Whigs and succeeded in expelling Ritchie from the Senate floor. In terms of his future political course, Calhoun had acted unwisely. Ritchie, with all his faults, was an institution in Virginia. There were other ways to trade blows with Polk than through censuring his editor. Wilson Lumpkin, a member of Calhoun's Georgia contingent wise in the ways of partisan upheavals, wrote that it would have been better to ignore "the old hack. His libels would never have injured the Senate, and their proceedings have only served, to give him a consequence."[9]

7. *Calhoun Correspondence,* 717.
8. *Calhoun Works,* IV, 325.
9. *Congressional Globe,* 29th Cong., 2nd Sess., 408–17; Chauncey S. Boucher and Robert P. Brooks (eds.), *Correspondence Addressed to John C. Calhoun, 1837–1849: Sixteenth Report of the Historical Manuscripts Commission* (Washington, D.C., 1930), 370.

True to his initial conviction when he objected to Polk's war bill, Calhoun voted for the $3 million bill after it was shorn of the Wilmot Proviso, shortly before the end of the session. The Twenty-ninth Congress adjourned on March 3, 1847. Attenuated in body but buoyant in outlook, Calhoun made his way south. Although plagued with what was now a chronic cough, he agreed to address a mass meeting at the New Theatre in Charleston on March 9. To a hall that was packed with enthusiastic citizens, Calhoun spoke in a hoarse voice for over an hour, an effort that placed a heavy drain on his dwindling energy.[10]

Calhoun devoted himself exclusively to the Wilmot Proviso and drew up a conspiracy indictment against both major parties. The abolitionists, he said, were a tiny fraction of the northern public; but the parties were so evenly balanced in most of the free states that abolitionists held the balance of power. With a majority of the voting public in the North opposed to slavery though respecting the constitutional protection of the institution, the abolitionists were able to sway the professional politicians, especially on issues like the restriction of slavery in the territories, where prohibition was not explicitly stated in the Constitution but could be interpreted. Calhoun did not mention this aspect of the controversy beyond alluding to the Wilmot Proviso and the prospect of large territorial cessions from the Mexican war.[11] Surely he had in mind the opinions of Webster and those expressed in Justice Joseph Story's learned three-volume commentary on the Constitution. Both of these constitutional theorists held that Congress had the power to shape the domestic institutions in the territories. Rather, Calhoun emphasized the need for southern unity in the political process, especially in the campaigns for the nomination and election of presidents. He felt this unity would be best achieved by the organization of a new party representing the united opinion of the slave states in their demand for what he called "equality" in the settlement of the territories, including those that might be acquired from Mexico.

The southern party would then, Calhoun stated, unite with sympathetic voters in the free states to form a majority that would oppose national nominating conventions and defend southern interests. "Our object," he said, "is to preserve the Union of these states, if it can be done consistently with our rights, safety, and perfect equality with other members of the Union."[12] His theme was consistent with his views of the nation since he had first entered Congress in 1811.

10. *Senate Journal*, 29th Cong., 2nd Sess., 252, 253; *Calhoun Correspondence*, 720.
11. *Calhoun Works*, IV, 389.
12. *Ibid.*, 395.

First in his order of priorities were the rights of the individual, then those of the local community, then those of the state, and then those of the nation. The Union existed because it was essential to the protection and the advancement of its parts. When a numerical majority centered in one section arrogated to itself its own definition of the national will through well-organized political parties and sought to impose its will throughout the country, Calhoun regarded this as a distortion of the original compact that bound the states together.

The federal Union, he believed, was founded not to promote conformity but to permit diversity within the orderly confines of any socialized community. "I acted on my conception uninfluenced by any others," he wrote from Fort Hill on March 28, 1847. "Even in early manhood, when I felt their impulse stronger, than I now do, they could never overrule my sense of right." This rationale extended to slavery, which Calhoun regarded as the cornerstone of a social order that protected individual liberty and equality for the white population in the South.[13]

Calhoun was heartened by the enthusiasm for him personally among the citizens of Charleston and the ovation that greeted his speech. He immediately turned his thoughts to the more mundane aspects of political organization. Since the termination of the *Spectator* and its successor the *Constitution,* Calhoun had had no press in Washington. Green was again available as a prospective editor, but money was needed and as Calhoun mentioned to Green: "The fate of the *Constitutionalist* [*sic*] has cast a damp. Ten thousand dollars was raised here to support it. The whole has been lost without doing any good."[14] He did speak, however, to a group of wealthy Charleston residents who agreed to consider raising $25,000 to establish another Calhoun paper in Washington.

For a time, Calhoun had high hopes of mounting a vigorous campaign, and the Washington paper was to be its spearhead. But the Charleston capitalists insisted that they not bear the entire cost of the project—that funds be forthcoming from other southern states. Calhoun, sadly though realistically, concluded that monetary support from outside South Carolina was difficult if not impossible. "Their attention is so much absorbed in the events of the Mexican War," he wrote Green, "and . . . they are so much entangled by their party connections, that nothing will be done."[15] He made this comment in April,

13. *Calhoun Correspondence,* 724; *Calhoun Works,* IV, 385–96.
14. *Calhoun Correspondence,* 718, 719.
15. *Ibid.,* 722–25.

a month after his Charleston address. By then, he realized that his call for a new party based on his conception of southern rights was still an idea that had not taken on substance.

312   Refreshed by a spring and summer spent at Fort Hill and its immediate vicinity, Calhoun threw off his persistent cough and seemed to have regained his physical vigor. He was only experiencing a reprieve, however, since the tuberculosis from which he suffered was in temporary remission and a serious heart condition was developing. Yet Calhoun felt fit and looked better than he had for some time when he took his Senate seat on December 7, 1847. As soon as he read Polk's long message to Congress, he began to plan a speech that he hoped would restrain the policy that implied a conquest of Mexico and its incorporation into the Union. "Either will overthrow our system of government," he wrote his son Andrew.[16]

On January 8, 1848, Calhoun moved two resolutions opposing a war of conquest and supported them with a lengthy speech. Although he again put forward his plan for a defensive line and inveighed against the cost of the war, he made his concern about the possibility of absorbing all of Mexico into the Union the major thrust of his remarks. His argument followed racial and cultural lines. He claimed that more than half of Mexico's population was "pure Indians and by far the larger portion of the residue mixed blood."[17]

"I protest against the incorporation of such a people," Calhoun said defiantly. "Ours is the government of the white man," whom he held superior socially and culturally to other races. Indians, he freely admitted, had achieved democracy and indeed had many noble qualities, but these qualities were "much more easily sustained among a savage than a civilized people." He asked: "Are we to overlook this great fact? Are we to associate with ourselves, as equals, companions, and fellow citizens, the Indians and the mixed races of Mexico?" Calhoun answered his own question by declaring flatly that such an association would degrade American whites and destroy American institutions. The alternative to a war of conquest, occupation of Mexico as a military province, he found equally repugnant in that it made a mockery of American law and the Constitution. Calhoun's ethnic and racist arguments found receptive ears among his colleagues and even among northern congressmen, who were beginning to respond to nativist

16. Charles Wiltse, *John C. Calhoun, Sectionalist: 1840–1850* (Indianapolis, 1951), 456, 475, 740, 741.
17. *Calhoun Works*, IV, 410, 411.

sentiment as a wave of Irish immigrants driven by the potato famine from their homes was inundating northern cities.[18]

Apart from its ethnic and racist bias, Calhoun's speech had probed again the administration's policy on the Mexican war—this time with a more sensitive instrument—and had found no policy other than territorial aggrandizement. Polk seemed to be engulfed with perplexities. Bitter feuds among his generals had resulted in a flurry of courts-martial, all of which had serious political ramifications. His party was equally rent with factionalism, which Calhoun's expulsion had only aggravated. Polk's envoy to Mexico, who was charged with negotiating a peace treaty, had exceeded his instructions and refused to obey a direct presidential order for his recall. Looming over all these problems was the rapidly escalating tension over slavery, to which the Wilmot Proviso had given renewed impetus. Under unbearable pressure, Polk overruled his secretaries of state and war and presented to the Senate the treaty of peace that his disavowed agent Nicholas Trist had negotiated. Calhoun gave the treaty his full support against some Democrats and many Whigs who wanted to delay any settlement for partisan advantage. The treaty passed the Senate with votes to spare— "a fortunate deliverance," Calhoun remarked. In this instance, the president would have agreed with him.

The Treaty of Guadalupe Hidalgo simply replaced one set of serious problems with another, as Calhoun recognized. "The Slave question will soon come up, and be the subject of deep agitation," he wrote Andrew. "The South will be in the crisis of its fate. If it yields now, all will be lost."[19] "Free soil" was already entering the jargon of Capitol Hill and cropping up in both northern and southern newspaper editorials and public letters. An avowed abolitionist, John P. Hale, was now a colleague of Calhoun's in the Senate, while in the House, Joshua Giddings of Ohio, John Gorham Palfrey of Massachusetts, and Amos Tuck of New Hampshire, all able speakers and parliamentarians, were goading slaveholding members to outbursts of rhetorical indignation. More ominous to those who would defend slavery were senators like John A. Dix of New York and John M. Niles of Connecticut, Van Buren Democrats, or Tom Corwin of Ohio, a Whig regular, all of whom were swinging over to free soil. A growing number of Whigs and Democrats

18. See Robert W. Johannsen, *To the Halls of the Montezumas: The Mexican War in the American Imagination* (New York, 1985), 288–92, for a perceptive analysis of racist opinion of Mexicans during the war.

19. *Calhoun Correspondence*, 744.

was joining them, including Abraham Lincoln, who could always be counted on to vote for the Wilmot Proviso amendment, Preston King, Hannibal Hamlin of Maine, and Wilmot himself. Free-soilers and abolitionists held a balance of power in both houses, even though the Whigs had gained substantially in the elections to the Thirtieth Congress.

Inspiring the antislavery movement in the United States were the liberal revolutions that swept over Europe early in 1848. Calhoun did not at first equate the rise in reform sentiment with the slavery issue. Kept well-informed of European events by McLane and Clemson, he was, like other Americans, enthusiastic about the political changes that were being implemented in Germany and Austria-Hungary, and less impressed by the revolution in France.[20]

The impending conventions of the two major parties soon directed Calhoun's attention away from the convulsions in Europe. For some time, Calhoun had thought that Zachary Taylor would be the Whig candidate. The fact that the general was a southern man and a slaveholder held some appeal, but Taylor's two public letters setting forth his position Calhoun found unimpressive. Adhering to Calhoun's mandate, the party in South Carolina boycotted the Democratic convention in Baltimore. An unauthorized planter from Georgetown, South Carolina, with the unlikely name of J. M. Commander did attend, was accepted by the credentials committee, and cast all of the state's nine votes for Cass, the nominee. "What a farce!" the disgusted Calhoun expostulated.[21]

At least South Carolina's votes were recorded; New York's were not. When the credentials committee attempted the fatuous compromise of awarding a half vote to each member of the two contending delegations, Van Buren's Barnburners and the Marcy-Dickinson Hunkers, both delegations were silent on the roll calls. Cass achieved nomination and a temporary unity within the party through his acceptance of a doctrine that Dickinson, the Hunker senator from New York, had first adumbrated. Called squatter, or popular, sovereignty, it proposed to have the inhabitants of a given territory determine for themselves whether to admit or prohibit slavery.

Moderate Democrats on both sides of the Mason-Dixon line accepted this solution, which, if carried out, would remove the power of Congress over the territories. Free-soilers and extreme southern states'

---

20. *Calhoun Works*, IV, 451–54; *Calhoun Correspondence*, 748, 751.
21. *Calhoun Correspondence*, 757.

rights men alike condemned popular sovereignty as handing over to a transient, socially and politically irresponsible group the power to shape the destinies of what would eventually become states in the Union. Ahead of his compatriots, Calhoun perceived that the Cass-Dickinson formula would exclude slavery from the territories, because planters who might be willing to immigrate would never venture with their slaves to a region where local law did not protect their property beforehand.[22]

Although the division in the Democratic party posed by the Barnburners' withdrawal and the formation of the Free Soil party at Buffalo practically guaranteed Cass's defeat, Calhoun would not support him. Nor would he back Taylor, who had received the Whig nomination. Van Buren's acceptance of the Free Soil nomination after a political career in which he made party regularity a fetish further confirmed in Calhoun's mind that the former president had never been a trustworthy person. Beyond his personal convictions, Calhoun predicted accurately enough that the Free Soil party would lead "to the formation of two great sectional parties."[23]

News of the Van Buren nomination coincided with the passage of the Oregon territorial bill, whose twelfth section contained the Wilmot Proviso, after extended and heated debate. At the administration's behest, Senator Jesse Bright, a southern-leaning Democrat from Indiana, had moved an amendment to the bill that, if passed in both houses, would have settled the forms of government for Oregon, California, and New Mexico as well. It would have extended the Missouri Compromise line to the Pacific. As a concession to the South, the amendment contained a fugitive slave clause. John A. Dix, once one of Calhoun's protégés in New York, but now a Van Buren man and a vigorous antislavery senator, attacked the amendment and, relying on a broad interpretation of "the rules and regulations" clause of Article IV of the Constitution, argued for the Wilmot Proviso.

Calhoun rose to answer Dix and to oppose the Bright amendment. He repeated his argument that the territories were the property of all the states and that southerners must be free to settle in them with their slave property. He went into the history of the Ordinance of 1787, the so-called Jefferson Ordinance, which was the basis for the Wilmot Proviso. The ordinance was, he maintained, a compromise to which the slave states agreed on condition that it have a fugitive slave clause.

22. *Calhoun Works*, IV, 498, 500.
23. *Calhoun Correspondence*, 760–61.

Since that clause had been very generally evaded, Calhoun charged that the North had broken the compact; and thus he regarded the ordinance as having no effect as a precedent. Then he claimed that the Missouri Compromise was not a precedent, either, for the powers of Congress over the territories. To a hushed audience in the crowded galleries, and with the close attention of his colleagues, Calhoun read Jefferson's letter to John Holmes wherein the former president referred to the Missouri Compromise debates as a "fire bell in the night . . . the knell of the Union." The most interesting aspect of Calhoun's address was his rebuttal of Van Buren's 15,000-word essay that, among other things, charged that free workers would never work side by side with black slaves. This essay, published the previous April, had quickly furnished the theoretical underpinnings of the free soil movement.[24]

Calhoun denied Van Buren's argument as contrary to the facts and explained the position of slavery in the southern class structure, reasserting the comments he had made to John Quincy Adams during the Missouri debates twenty-eight years before.

> There is no part of the world where agricultural, mechanical, and other descriptions of labor are more respected than in the South with the exception . . . of menial and body servants. No Southern man—not the poorest or the lowest—will, under any circumstances, submit to perform either of them. He has too much pride for that, and I rejoice that he has. They are unsuited to the spirit of a freeman. But the man who would spurn them feels not the least degradation to work in the same field as his slave; or to be employed to work with them in the same field or in any mechanical operation. . . . With us the two great divisions of society are not the rich and poor, but white and black; and all the former the poor as well as the rich, belong to the upper class, and are respected and treated as equals, if honest and industrious; and hence have a position and pride of character of which neither poverty nor misfortune can deprive them.[25]

Moving on to the present crisis in political affairs, Calhoun found its roots in what he called the false and dangerous proposition in the Declaration of Independence that "all men are created equal." He declared that this assertion had its origin in the writings of Locke and of Algernon Sidney, which assumed hypothetical states of nature that had no bearing on the actual conditions of society. In his discussion of power, liberty, and anarchy, Calhoun drew freely on the essay he was then writing on government.

24. *Calhoun Works*, IV, 479–512; Niven, *Martin Van Buren*, 568–70.
25. *Calhoun Works*, IV, 505–506.

Calhoun gave an impressive lecture, and his audience, even those who disagreed, marveled at the force of his basic contentions and at his command of logic as he spoke in his usual measured tone of voice without notes. In the process of demolishing to his own satisfaction Jefferson's "glittering generalities," Calhoun swept aside the popular sovereignty formula that presidential nominee Cass had underwritten in the widely publicized letter he had written to the Tennessee politician and journalist A. O. P. Nicholson. When the first half-dozen squatters entered any given territory, it would cease to be a territory of the United States, Calhoun claimed. Sovereignty would reside in the residents, however few, however transient. In the case of New Mexico and California, he said, the conquered would have the power to exclude the conquerors. "How can sovereignty—the ultimate and supreme power of a state—be divided?" he asked. "The exercise of the powers of sovereignty may be divided," he said, "but how can there be two supreme powers?"[26]

The original bill was tabled after heated debate. Calhoun had presented extreme views on the territorial question, but he was willing to compromise. He joined with Whigs and Democrats on a select committee chaired by Senator John M. Clayton of Delaware. The committee worked out a new arrangement, combining territorial governance of Oregon, California, and New Mexico in one bill. Under its provisions, a government would be established in Oregon but without the Wilmot Proviso, and temporary governments would be set up in California and New Mexico with a judicial settlement on slavery. The Clayton bill, which partook largely of Calhoun's thinking on the territorial question, passed the Senate not as a sectional measure but rather as a partisan adjustment that the White House had managed. In part because of its political bias and in part because of Calhoun's involvement, the Clayton compromise failed in the House.[27]

However heated the oratory in Congress over the territorial bills, it was but a prelude to the perfect storm of debate that greeted the House bill on Oregon. The bill was similar to its original Senate counterpart that contained the Wilmot Proviso. Calhoun again made a mighty effort to defeat it, but his major speech was reserved for an amendment sponsored by the administration that would extend the Missouri Compromise line to the Pacific. "It is not for us who are assailed, but for those who assail us," he said looking directly at Benton, who was

26. *Ibid.*, 479–512.
27. *Congressional Globe*, 30th Cong., 1st Sess., 950, Appendix, 1139–1204; Quaife (ed.), *Diary of James K. Polk*, IV, 31; *Calhoun Correspondence*, 760.

marshalling the administration forces, "to count the value of the Union."[28]

Calhoun was answered first by the short, red-faced, red-haired senator from Connecticut, John M. Niles. In a speech that lasted four hours, Niles turned Calhoun's defensive position on itself by pointing out that protection of property was a state concern subject to local police power, but that recognition of property was not uniform. Slaves were property in some states, but what is property in one state is certainly not property in another. He accused Calhoun of seeking to make the federal government the promoter and protector of slavery everywhere in the nation—states and territories alike. Popular sovereignty was, he said, "not so extravagant, but would have the same end. In the one case, we are called upon to incorporate the principle of slavery; in the other, to permit it to be done—to leave it to introduce itself if it can either with or against the will of the people of the territory."[29] In Niles's speech and the speeches of other northerners, one can see a fear of an aggressive slave power every bit as pervasive as the fear Calhoun and his associates felt at the growing pressure for emancipation.

And so the debate raged, with Benton hurling epithets at Calhoun's dignified colleague Andrew Butler, who so far lost his self-control as to challenge the burly Missourian to a duel. Fortunately, tempers calmed down when a sultry August dawn began to lighten the hot, stuffy Senate chamber. Eventually, the Senate by a very narrow margin agreed to the House bill. After President Polk signed it, Oregon was granted a territorial government free of slavery. The bills organizing territorial governments for California and New Mexico were both postponed to the next session of Congress. Gideon Welles summed up Calhoun's stand during the debate from a northern viewpoint. "Mr. Calhoun has a singularly constituted mind," said the sometime journalist and tacit free-soiler. "It is comprehensive yet erratic, profound but impulsive, reflective yet inconsistent . . . often correct but often widely mistaken."[30]

Calhoun had lost his battle on the Oregon question for what he regarded as a principle, because he never for a moment believed that

28. *Calhoun Works,* IV, 513–35.

29. Appendix, *Congressional Globe,* 30th Cong., 1st Sess., 1197–1201; John A. Dix to Azariah Flagg, June 5, 1848, Azariah Cutting Flagg Papers, Butler Library, Columbia University.

30. *Congressional Globe,* 30th Cong., 1st Sess., 1061, 1074–78; Gideon Welles Diary, May–June, 1848, p. 45 (MS in Gideon Welles Papers, Huntington Library, San Marino, California).

slavery would exist in the Far Northwest. He had, however, moved the South closer to unity on the slavery issue and at the same time had driven disparate segments of northern opinion into a more cohesive, antislavery frame of mind. Calhoun was resolved to make a final stand on coexistence for California and New Mexico in the second session of the Thirtieth Congress. He left for home shortly after Congress adjourned, hoping to enjoy a brief respite from the grueling speeches, the rancorous debates, and the wearing conferences, as well as the protracted hot spell in Washington during July and August that had made life itself at times seem unbearable. But family problems intruded and robbed him of needed relaxation.

Calhoun's greatest personal worry was financial, involving primarily his son's plantation in Alabama. Scarcely any of the debt to his son-in-law, Clemson, had been paid off, and what had been paid was still on account from borrowed money. Calhoun and Andrew kept hoping for a rise in cotton prices, but season after season, prices remained at a low point between four and five cents a pound. Andrew followed the wasteful course of many planters by expanding his holdings and his field force to make up what he had lost the previous year—all from borrowed money on which his father had signed the notes. Misfortune seemed to plague Andrew. When cotton prices finally rose in 1846, an insect blight reduced his plantation's output by two-thirds. And Andrew was not a good judge of market conditions, usually holding back too long for a higher price and then being forced to sell when the market collapsed. By the summer of 1848, Calhoun's debts from Andrew's plantation alone were in excess of $25,000. Compounding his financial plight were the personal and physical problems of his four younger sons.

They had, of course, gone through the painful stages of adolescence and young manhood with the typical distress associated with approaching maturity. James, John, Jr., and William all had problems adjusting to their schools, which caused Calhoun anxiety. Coping with their difficulties cut deeply into his overcrowded schedule. Eventually the two youngest boys, responding to the tutelage of their uncle James Edward Colhoun, developed sound work habits. Both young men had good scholastic records at South Carolina College. John, Jr., graduated from South Carolina College and then attended medical school in Philadelphia. He was back at Fort Hill with a medical degree when his father returned from Washington, D.C., in August, 1848. Unfortunately he, like his father, was by now seriously ill with tuberculosis.

Unlike his brothers, Patrick, the army officer, never seemed to have outgrown his youthful waywardness. He continued to put a severe financial drain on his father, who was deeply concerned about his passion for gambling, as well as his penchant for indulging himself fully in other frivolous pastimes. Calhoun had just paid off a $600 debt Patrick had incurred when, in October, 1848, he was compelled to pay out another large sum. This time Patrick had borrowed from Andrew's factors without permission or notice. In two years, Patrick had gambled away over $4,000, which Calhoun had to make good through more notes. By now his financial affairs had become desperate, and as debts mounted, so his health declined appreciably.

Anna Maria and her children returned from Europe in April, 1848, for a brief period on funds advanced by her father. The Clemsons saw from Calhoun's appearance that his health had declined significantly since they had last seen him, more than four years before. Calhoun made light of his illness and seemed to bear up well on his return trip to Washington, D.C., for the short session of Congress in December, 1848. Yet Anna Maria remained concerned about his physical condition. "Do, my dear father, take care of yourself," she wrote in January, 1849. "How I wish I were there to nurse you." She urged him not to work so hard and to delegate more of his responsibilities to others. Still, neither Anna Maria nor any other member of his immediate family knew how serious Calhoun's condition was when the Clemsons returned to Europe in May, 1849. He had been, as always, cheered by Anna Maria's presence; her departure with her family for Brussels was painful to all, but especially to him.[31]

Calhoun's worries about his personal affairs and his debilitating chronic illnesses bore down on him physically and mentally, and certainly contributed to the heightening of his concern for the fate of the Union. The presidential campaign had resulted in the election of the Whig candidate Zachary Taylor in a close vote over Lewis Cass. Martin Van Buren's Free Soil ticket had provided the edge of victory for the Whigs in key northern states. Neither the major candidates nor the platforms had impressed Calhoun, though South Carolina had given Cass a majority. The election of Taylor simply reinforced prejudices Calhoun had formed years before about the dangers military heroes posed to democracies. He had always felt that ignorant masses susceptible to the wiles of professional politicians were too easily seduced by

31. Lander, *Calhoun Family*, 115; Anna Maria Calhoun to Patrick Calhoun, June 24, 1850, in John C. Calhoun Papers, South Caroliniana Library; *Calhoun Correspondence*, 766, 767.

vulgar messages that proclaimed the common touch writ large in the military hero. Once the hero was in office, he became a threat to individual liberty, either engrossing power for its own sake, like Jackson, or like Harrison, being manipulated by designing power brokers and placemen. Calhoun strongly suspected that Taylor would be manipulated. Either way, Calhoun saw in Taylor's election the potential for demagoguery and corruption.

But it was the Van Buren campaign, with its slogans, its fervor, and the votes it gained, that represented the ultimate danger to the South and to its "peculiar institution." Although the Free Soil ticket had not received one electoral vote, it had attracted over 10 percent of the popular vote, which guaranteed a sharp increase in antislavery sentiment during the second session of the Thirtieth Congress. The fact that Van Buren headed the Free Soil ticket made a decided impression on Calhoun. He detested the man and all he stood for; but he gave Van Buren full credit for that rare political talent of sensing accurately a popular mood in his own region.

Calhoun knew now that Benton and other senators would renew their efforts to secure the Wilmot Proviso in the territorial organization of California and New Mexico. He believed that among the Whigs, the newly elected senator from New York, William H. Seward, would be just as forceful in his antislavery convictions. Only 200,000 people cast their votes for the Free Soil ticket, but those sympathetic to the movement who voted for the two major parties counted at least five times as many. Northern politicians in Congress were sure to consider their views, especially when the territorial bills for California and New Mexico were taken up.

XVII

The Price of Union

On his way to the capital, Calhoun stopped for a few days in Columbia, South Carolina, to give the governor and select members of the legislature his advice on national matters. Largely through his efforts, the governor called for a convention of representatives from the slave states to consider the implications of the Wilmot Proviso. A move for unilateral action, which some of the extremists in the legislature proposed, was defeated, and a resolution couched in general terms was passed, calling for resistance should slave owners be excluded from California or New Mexico.[1]

Calhoun arrived in Washington, D.C., on December 11, the very day Stephen A. Douglas, the young senator from Illinois and chairman of the committee on territories, reported a bill that would organize all of the Mexican cession into one state. One section of the bill gave Congress the power to draw the eastern boundaries of California and to create additional states or territories from this huge land mass. The matter was urgent because the gold strike on California's American River was attracting people from all over the world. It was essential that a form of government be set up to establish law and order in the region. Polk discussed Douglas' bill with his cabinet on December 12, 1848. They decided that the territory was too large and sparsely settled to be admitted as a state. Douglas would be asked to alter his bill so as to admit California as a state without going through the intermediate stage of territorial organization. A separate bill would be drawn that would organize the territory of New Mexico. The cabinet was unanimous in its agreement that there be no mention of slavery in the New Mexico bill, the implication being that popular sovereignty would determine that issue when states were carved out of the region.

Polk conferred with Douglas the next day and secured his approval of the modification of the California-New Mexico bill. Soon after the short, dark-visaged senator left, Calhoun called to discuss the ter-

---

1. Charles Wiltse, *John C. Calhoun, Sectionalist: 1840–1850* (Indianapolis, 1951), 374, 375.

ritorial problems. Polk expressed his fear that if Congress postponed the extension of government to California for another session, the region might declare its independence and, together with Oregon, form a separate nation on the West Coast. With this rather startling prelude, he informed Calhoun of the modifications the administration thought necessary in Douglas' bill. Calhoun refused to commit himself on these measures, though he said he was anxious to settle the problem.[2]

While Douglas' new bills were under discussion, the Whig-dominated House committee on territories reported a California bill that organized a territorial government and included the Wilmot Proviso. Southern members of Congress, both Whig and Democrat, were preparing themselves for opposition when a resolution instructing the committee on the District of Columbia to report a bill that would abolish the slave trade there passed the House by a close vote. This show of free soil strength briefly united most of the congressmen of the slave states, regardless of party. It gave renewed impetus to a move already under way among slave state senators to denounce the proviso in a bipartisan address to the southern people.

Calhoun was an enthusiastic backer of the address, which he thought would provide a major step towards achieving southern unity. He was present at a caucus of eighty-eight southern congressmen held in the Senate chamber on the evening of December 22. The first order of business was a series of resolutions offered by a young Virginian member of the House, Thomas H. Bayley. The resolutions followed the oft-repeated contention of states' rights advocates who denied the power of Congress to interfere with slavery in the District of Columbia, the territories, or the states. No sooner had Bayley completed reading his resolutions than discussion and argument, as would be expected from a chamber filled with lawyers, began. The debates went on far into the evening.

Calhoun spoke at length, urging a speedy consensus but warning against any ill-formed decision. He insisted that the South must not retreat from opposition to the Wilmot Proviso. In an obvious reference to the territorial issue, he advised his colleagues to use their collective strength as a bargaining chip with the North on California and the proviso. The caucus then appointed a committee of fifteen Whigs and

2. Milo M. Quaife (ed.), *The Diary of James K. Polk During His Presidency, 1845–1849* (4 vols.; Chicago, 1910), IV, 233; Robert W. Johannsen, *Stephen A. Douglas* (New York, 1973), 249.

Democrats to prepare an address. Calhoun was made a member with the understanding that he would prepare the draft.

After this show of southern unity, which had considerable impact on the Polk administration and the free soil contingent in Congress, the House resolution on abolition of the slave trade in the District of Columbia was recalled and voted down. Thereafter, the Whig members of the newly appointed committee became far less zealous in their demands for southern rights. The appearance of President-elect Zachary Taylor in Washington had much to do with their change in attitude. In the face of rapidly declining Whig participation, Calhoun completed his draft. Some alterations were made in the original document, but none of a material nature. Calhoun, however, was extremely defensive about the address after the Whigs withdrew their support.[3] He had been counting on bipartisan support from southern congressmen, and the refusal of the Whigs to back the address robbed it of much impact.

The address itself was an unusual document. It was a harsh indictment not just of free-soilers and abolitionists but of the entire North. After giving what he called a narrative of "aggressions and encroachments on our rights," Calhoun outlined a conspiracy that, if not stopped through concerted action, would transform the South into a region where the emancipated blacks in political alliance with northern politicians would rule the whites. He criticized especially the refusal of northern states to observe the constitutional provision that required return of fugitives. Although he normally utilized statistics to bolster his arguments, Calhoun provided none in this address, perhaps because he had available the figures from the Seventh Census, which clearly demonstrated how few fugitive slaves there were. Only 1,011 slaves were counted as fugitives over a 10-year period, or .0315 percent of the almost 4 million slaves in the South. His own state of South Carolina had lost 16 fugitives, or an average of 1.6 a year, between 1840 and 1850. And the number of fugitives, aided by northern abolitionists, would not increase, as Calhoun predicted, but actually decline to 803 during the next ten years.[4]

Calhoun's treatment of the fugitive slave issue, like the rest of the address, was written for maximum shock value. Step by step, as he outlined it, the North would eventually subjugate the South and destroy its slave-based society after encircling it though a planned territorial policy. In his grim scenario, the federal government under the

3. See his letter to A. W. Venable, February 2, 1849, in *Calhoun Works*, VI, 288, 289.
4. *House Executive Documents*, 37th Cong., 3rd Sess., No. 116, p. 137.

control of antislavery forces would emancipate all the slaves. Once this had been achieved, it would "raise them to a political and social equality with their former owners, by giving them the right of voting and hold- ing public offices under the Federal Government." Northern politi- **325** cians and their willing black allies would then complete the social revo- lution not for any idealistic ends but simply for patronage and the benefit of economic exploitation. In words that must have chilled his southern audience, Calhoun gave vent to his own extreme defen- siveness as he pictured the South reduced to a poverty-stricken, all- black region, which would happen if united action were not taken to halt the designs of northern spoilsmen, exploiters, and fanatics.

> The blacks and the profligate whites that might unite with them, would become the principal recipients of federal offices and patronage, and would, in consequence, be raised above the whites in the political and social scale. We would, in a word, change conditions with them—a degradation greater than has ever yet fallen to the lot of a free and enlightened people, and one from which we could not escape, should emancipation take place (which it certainly will if not prevented), but by fleeing the homes of our- selves and ancestors, and by abandoning our country to our former slaves, to become the permanent abode of disorder, anarchy, poverty, misery and wretchedness.[5]

Calhoun's bitterness and his personal frustration at the blasting of all his hopes are marked throughout the address. His fears seem far greater than any he had ever experienced, even in the darkest days of the War of 1812 or at the prospect of Jackson's military invasion of his state during the nullification crisis. He was overreacting to the assault on slavery, which he saw as the result of purely selfish actions on the part of political freebooters in league with moral fanatics. The address was an incendiary document every bit as destructive of the Union as any abolitionist tract, however intemperate. It is no wonder that mod- erate southerners, including the southern Whigs on the original con- gressional committee, refused to sign the document. But in part it served its purpose, by moving the southern states closer to a sectional consensus on slavery in the territories, which many still considered an abstract threat.

Calhoun's bargaining chip had expanded into a declaration whose shrill message warned northerners as well as southerners that the seeds of disunion were planted in the controversial ground of the territorial issue. Fitzwilliam Byrdsall, the old Locofoco leader in New York,

5. *Calhoun Works*, VI, 310, 311.

praised Calhoun's address extravagantly. It was a timely reminder, he wrote, that "the history of all democracies, aristocracies and even of our own country, all prove that those who know they have the power will exercise it justly or unjustly, as it appears advantageous to themselves." From Kentucky came agreement of the former Democratic party chief, Robert Wickliffe. "Without union," he said, "the South is to be used up in the next six years." And from Calhoun's own state, the poet and novelist William Gilmore Simms commented tersely, "It will lessen the insolence of our enemies, in alarming their fears."[6]

Unquestionably, a long letter he had received from Henry Workman Connor, a Charleston banker and a person whose judgment he respected, had added a tone of stridency to Calhoun's address. Connor had just returned to Charleston from an extended visit to Georgia, Alabama, Louisiana, and Florida. He found leaders of both parties in Georgia ready to follow Calhoun's lead. Elsewhere, the situation was less clear, and even in Georgia, opinion was divided in Savannah and Augusta. Only eastern Alabama could be counted on as firm. Mobile, like the Georgia cities, was opposed to any strong measure. Louisiana, Connor decided, was the most hostile to Calhoun's leadership. "New Orleans," he reported, "is almost Free Soil in their opinions. The population is one half Northern agents another one quarter or one third are Foreigners. The remnant are creoles who cannot comprehend their dangers until the negroes are being taken out of the fields. . . . Louisiana will be the last if at all to strike for the defense of the South." Connor attributed much of this laissez-faire attitude on the territorial issue to "Northerners and Foreigners." Draymen and laborers in New Orleans were either white or foreign. They would not permit slave competition. Captains of the river steamers, stewards, and other members of their crews, were all white and for the most part northerners. Connor's conclusion was especially upsetting to Calhoun. The banker said that slave owners everywhere were desponding and were beginning to believe that slavery was doomed—"that all the world is opposed to it and that we ourselves will not or cannot do anything to avert it." Prompt and decided action he considered absolutely vital.[7]

Before he completed the address, Calhoun suffered a fainting attack in the lobby of the Senate. Several colleagues rushed to his as-

6. Chauncey S. Boucher and Robert P. Brooks (eds.), *Correspondence Addressed to John C. Calhoun, 1837–1849: Sixteenth Report of the Historical Manuscripts Commission* (Washington, D.C., 1930), 498–501.

7. *Calhoun Correspondence*, 1188–90. Hammond, in a letter to Calhoun praising his address, refers to Augusta, Georgia, as "a Yankee town you know" (*Ibid.*, 1193).

sistance and, after he regained consciousness, helped him to the vice-president's room. Calhoun made little of his seizure, attributing it to the change in his routine when he began sponging his body with cold water as soon as he arose in the morning. For some days, he suffered from a high fever and showed obvious signs of physical exhaustion.[8] Ever since he had arrived in Washington, D.C., in mid-December, he had pushed himself beyond the limits of his now frail and disease-ridden body. Yet he recovered rapidly, heartened to some extent by the reception of the address in the South.

Meetings were held and resolutions of support were written in most southern states, despite the vigorous, combined opposition of administration Democrats and Whig party leaders in Washington and the southern states.[9] The address commanded enough strength in Congress to postpone again the vital question of statehood for California and the future of the New Mexico Territory.

Calhoun was not impressed with Taylor's inaugural, which was brief and general on the problems besetting the government and the people of the Union. But when he paid Taylor a courtesy visit, the president convinced him of his earnest wish for a settlement of the slavery issue on terms that would not injure southern interests. Still, Calhoun had the same qualms about the Taylor administration that he had had about the Harrison-Tyler administration. He doubted that the Whigs could generate a cohesive program, and he distrusted Taylor's advisors, free soil Whigs like William H. Seward.[10]

Shortly after the inauguration, Calhoun left behind him the cold rain and slush of the capital for his journey home. As his train lurched over the uneven roadbed that wound through the deep Virginia and North Carolina woods, he appreciated the appearance of an early spring along cleared stretches of the route. "The contrast was great," he said, "between being pent up in a boarding house in Washington and breathing the pure fresh air of the country, made fragrant by the blossoms of Spring."[11]

Calhoun found Fort Hill in good shape, which further raised his spirits, though his physical condition remained at a low ebb. The improved appearance of his son John, who had recently taken what was called the water cure, seemed to offer the possibility of recovery for himself. Under John Jr.'s instruction, Calhoun began the treatment on

8. Wiltse, *Calhoun, Sectionalist,* 387; *Calhoun Correspondence,* 761.
9. *Calhoun Correspondence,* 761, 762.
10. Glyndon G. Van Deusen, *William Henry Seward* (New York, 1967), 109, 114.
11. *Calhoun Correspondence,* 763.

the morning of April 10. After he stripped himself, his servants wrapped his emaciated body tightly in a damp sheet. As he lay trussed up on his bed, his black body servant piled eight or nine heavy woolen blankets on him. After an hour and a half in this state, during which he sweated heavily, Calhoun took a warm bath, which was followed by a rubdown. "The process was soothing and pleasant," he said. He would give the water cure a fair trial, and if it improved his health, he intended to "fix up a complete bathing establishment." But Calhoun begrudged the two hours each day the cure required, for he was determined to finish the two projects he had begun six years earlier, the treatise on government and a commentary on the Constitution. In addition, there was always correspondence, which consumed at least one day a week, and the entertainment of friends and visitors who flocked to Fort Hill. Somehow he made time to ride, or walk if the weather permitted, twice a day over the plantation—"for the double purpose," he explained, "of exercise and superintendence."[12]

All these activities took a heavy toll on his slender physical resources, but Calhoun persisted in his composition almost with a sense of desperation. By June 14, he had finished the rough draft of what would be called "The Disquisition on Government," 125 manuscript pages. He described this work as an essay on "the elementary principles of the Science of Government." He felt he had explored new territory and hoped that he had provided a "solid foundation for political science." After a few days away from his study and his desk, Calhoun began his commentary on the Constitution, which he planned to be a much longer work than "The Disquisition on Government" but did not expect to be so difficult to compose.

By October 14, Calhoun had written between three and four hundred manuscript pages, and estimated that forty to fifty pages more would complete the work. He had had some assistance with his labors. Joseph Scoville, the novelist and newspaperman who had been the unsuccessful organizer of Calhoun's New York campaign for the presidency in 1843 and briefly the editor of his Washington paper, the *Spectator,* had appeared at Fort Hill. He acted as a foil for Calhoun's ideas, a researcher, and a copyist.[13]

Calhoun thought that he was writing a scientific explanation of government complete with irrefutable laws of human behavior, in the style of the great political theorists of the past. "The Disquisition on Govern-

12. *Ibid.,* 767, 772.
13. *Ibid.,* 768, 772; New York *Herald,* February 5, 1854; *Calhoun Correspondence,* 767–70.

ment" is deliberately couched in philosophical propositions of a general nature and presumably universal application. There is no allusion to contemporary problems, such as slavery or territorial imperatives. There is no mention of tariffs, of abolitionists, of individuals living or dead, American or European. Yet suffusing the text, invading the premises, shaping the conclusions, determining problems studied, explained, and solved are Calhoun's views on the contemporary scene and his frustrations after a lifetime of disappointments, of ambitions unrealized, of individuals scorned, of a political system challenged, and especially of fears for the future of his class, his society, and his region.

"The Disquisition on Government," then, with all its close reasoning and intellectual force, was a rationale for his political and social position and a defense of a lifetime of uncertainty wherein events in rapid succession seemed always to threaten the security of the established order in which he passionately believed. The essay's sense of immediacy gave the assumptions, their corollaries, and their proofs credibility for a generation of southern planters who were measuring the worth of the Union against the perpetuation of a social order based on slavery. The inconsistencies that have been noted in the work between the idea of interests and that of political corruption bear out its contemporary thrust.[14]

"The Disquisition on Government" also reveals a palpable tension between Calhoun's defense of geographic minorities and his belief in the divinity of government, as if he would balance anarchy with tyranny in a given social setting. In his efforts to accommodate philosophically the Union of his youth with the sectionalism of his old age and at the same time protect and defend a system of human exploitation that the modern world condemned, Calhoun impaled himself on conclusions unwarranted by his premises. Even his notion of concurrent majorities simply split popular majorities into many parts, each of which would be subject to the same majority-rule, minority-right problem he had faced in the first place. The paradox should have concerned Calhoun because he had in his own state observed it when the majority nullifiers trampled on the rights of the minority Unionists in the crisis of 1832. Yet so involved had he become in the defense of his admittedly weaker section, with its morally indefensible system of domestic slavery based on race, that he avoided any precise definition of majorities. There is no doubt that Calhoun was desperately seeking to

14. See William W. Freehling, "Spoilsmen and Interests in the Thought and Career of John C. Calhoun," *Journal of American History*, LII, No. 1 (June, 1965), 25–42.

reconcile the opposing ideas of freedom and slavery within the context of Union and nation. Unfortunately, his theory failed to reckon with the transient, flexible nature of human institutions, which, even as he wrote, were changing with time and circumstance. And Calhoun did not realize how much the current political and social scene guided his thoughts.[15]

Clearly the image of Martin Van Buren glides through the pages of "The Disquisition on Government" as the epitome of the spoilsman, the manipulator who would betray the promise of the founders for personal power, profit, and prestige, and as one who not a year earlier had seized upon the free soil idea to mount a partisan attack on the Union for his own political benefit. This assumption was far from the truth, but it suited Calhoun's state of mind and guided his pen. Thus he scored Van Buren much as his Virginia compatriot Beverly Tucker had a decade before in his novel, *The Partisan Leader.*

In Calhoun's condemnation of the numerical majority, the example of Van Buren is everywhere implied and deprecated. Commenting acidly on partisan conflict, Calhoun insisted that it was inevitably a struggle wherein each party "must be alternately forced, in order to ensure victory, to resort to measures to concentrate the control over its movements in fewer and fewer hands, as the struggle became more and more violent."[16] Completely absent in Calhoun's equation is any trust in mass political participation. His compound of incipient Calvinism and elitist Federalism recalls the lamentations of John Knox and the contemptuous acrimony of Gouverneur Morris.

Calhoun's notion that inequality, not equality, is a settled condition

15. See Louis Hartz, *The Liberal Tradition in America* (New York, 1955), 158–66, for a stimulating discussion of Calhoun's dilemma. As Hartz points out, "The idea of state sovereignty shatters a meaningful American union, and yet, he [Calhoun] insists this alone can serve as a national 'perservative.'" Richard Current and Richard Hofstadter have also noted a series of logical inconsistencies in Calhoun's thought, where he confused his conclusions with his premises (Richard Current, *John C. Calhoun* [New York, 1963], 114–20; Richard Hofstadter, *The American Political Tradition* [New York, 1948], 75). But August O. Spain, in his careful analysis, argues that Calhoun's political theory "was internally consistent and universally valid." Certainly from the perspective of an endangered minority, Spain's argument makes sense. It still remains difficult, if not impossible, to settle the problem of sovereignty, which Calhoun himself raises. See August O. Spain, *The Political Theory of John C. Calhoun* (1951; rpr. New York, 1968), 101–22, 164–70, 265.

16. John C. Calhoun, *Disquisition on Government and Selections from the Discourse,* ed. G. Gordon Post (Indianapolis, 1953), 32; Crallé, *Calhoun Works,* I, 86–88. See also Ralph Lerner, "Calhoun's New Science of Politics," in Morton Frisch and Richard G. Stevens (eds.), *American Political Thought* (2nd ed.; Itasca, Ill., 1983), 162, 163.

of mankind (though emphatically not of states in the Union) derives in part from his close reading of Aristotle's *Politics* and *Nicomachean Ethics* and his imbibing of the political skepticism of Machiavelli, Hobbes, and Hume. The belief also derives in part from his own embattled position in a world where the nineteenth-century state was overwhelming a mind set in the presumed sureties of established order found in its readings of classical history, British constitutional development, and Jeffersonian notions of republican virtue.[17]

Yet Calhoun was no antiquarian, nor was he a pagan suckled in a creed outworn. He was intensely realistic about the political process and rightly fearful of the position of the agrarian South with its slave-owning elite in an environment in which the industrial revolution was radically altering traditional social and economic relationships. His reasoning may have resembled that of John Taylor's in *Construction Construed and Constitutions Vindicated,* a notable defense of the agrarian order that provided an ideological link between republican virtue and liberty, but Calhoun's argument does not, like Taylor's, rule out modernization. All those aspects of an industrializing society that Jefferson in his old age feared, and Taylor condemned, Calhoun accepted, provided that they remain ancillary to and supportive of the slave-plantation social system. In this respect, Calhoun differed from English critics of the emerging industrial order. His defense of rural values may have been as vehement as that of any contemporary Tory thinker, but he did not oppose industrial development in the sense that Thomas Carlyle and John Ruskin did.[18]

While discussing the roles of public opinion and social change, Calhoun spoke admiringly of the profound alterations that were taking place in travel and transportation, and in the diffusion of information and intelligence by electrical wires "rivalling in rapidity even thought itself." Yet he could not and would not escape from the habits, the instinctive acculturation, of his heritage. An inbred conservative, Calhoun cherished the values of his home, his people, his section. The slave system was of course the adhesive that held the southern way of life together in Calhoun's mind, and any trifling with this basic institution in the name of freedom, of equality of opportunity, of morality, or of human worth and dignity not only destroyed the economy of his section but demolished its social order. Anarchy would surely result.

17. "A Few Thoughts on the Death of John C. Calhoun," *Southern Literary Messenger,* XVI (June, 1850), 378.

18. Robert Shalhope, "Thomas Jefferson's Republicanism and Antebellum Southern Thought," *Journal of Southern History,* XLII, No. 4 (November, 1976), 529–56.

And to Calhoun, who believed government and society were divinely ordained, anarchy was the worst of all possible conditions.[19]

In reaching this end, Calhoun came down hard against the natural rights theory as expressed in the Declaration of Independence. That all men are created equal, he declared, was a completely erroneous statement. "It never did nor can exist," he wrote, "as it is inconsistent with the preservation and perpetuation of the race." Man's natural state was social and political; men were therefore created unequal. It followed that some men were inferior to others, and in conformance with much, but not all, of the learned opinion of his day, Calhoun claimed that blacks were the most inferior of all, best suited by providence and the immutable laws of society to be held in a condition of servitude when they were brought in contact with the superior whites. Throughout "The Disquisition on Government," there is an inherent, though never expressed, argument for the perpetuation of slavery, concealed behind the façade of minority rights or that of geographic distinctions.

Calhoun's attack on natural rights was supplemented by his attacks on nationalist interpretations of the Constitution, beginning with *The Federalist Papers*. Madison's ingenious formulation that distributed the powers of sovereignty between the states and the central government Calhoun regarded as absurd. Sovereignty was absolute or it was nothing—a doctrine found in Hobbes, but whose implications most European political theorists had rejected for several generations. Yet Calhoun's argument was self-serving. His recognition of indivisible sovereignty supported his stand on the shifting of power from the center to the periphery—his ardent defense of minority rights.

Calhoun was also debating Hamilton, Marshall, Webster, and particularly Story, whose three-volume *Commentaries on the Constitution of the United States* was both encyclopedic and seminal. Using many of Calhoun's sources—Aristotle, Burke, Blackstone, and the common-law theorists Coke and Lord Mansfield—Story's vast work articulated the northern position with authority, if not always with clarity. Its central theme reiterated Hamilton's arguments for a strong central government in *The Federalist Papers* but retained Madison's notion that the powers of sovereignty could be divided. Story's version of state power, however, is more limited than Madison's definition in his *Federalist* 39 and 45. As such, *Commentaries* supported the major contention of the

---

19. Calhoun, *Disquisition on Government and Selections from the Discourse*, 67, 6.

free-soilers, that Congress possessed plenary authority over the territories.[20]

Calhoun's assault on numerical majorities and his consequent argument for concurrent majorities challenged Story's basic assumptions on several levels of inquiry. In a withering comment, Calhoun likened majority rule, which Story upheld, to "the subversion of the constitution, either by the undermining process of construction . . . or by substituting in practice what is called party-usage in place of its provisions, or finally, when no other contrivance would subserve the purpose, by openly and boldly setting them aside."[21] Calhoun's concept of concurrent majority, then, was his final constitutional defense of a minority that found itself in an isolated geographic, social, and moral position. His argument was meant to offer not only a means of constitutional protection but a basic instrument of government that would recapture the promise of an early republic in which a supposed disinterested elite shaped the course of society. In this respect, for a brief time Calhoun's thinking, of which "The Disquisition on Government" is but a part, permeated the thought of southern political leaders almost as persuasively and far more perversely than the ideas of Thomas Jefferson a generation before.

"The Discourse on the Constitution," which Calhoun found much easier to write and which he began drafting soon after he completed "The Disquisition on Government," is a familiar recitation of his arguments in his speeches and writings over a twenty-year period. He develops more precisely and with examples drawn from ancient and modern history his idea of state sovereignty and the notion of the national government as agent for the people in the states. In his emphasis upon the federal character of the United States, Calhoun maintains throughout this work that the states did not lose their sovereignty when a majority of them ratified the Constitution. The only novel aspect of "The Discourse on the Constitution" is the proposal of a dual executive—an idea that Calhoun drew from his reading of Barthold Niebuhr's *History of Rome*. Where Niebuhr emphasized ethnological distinctions in the evolution of Roman government and law, Calhoun substituted geographical distinctions.[22]

20. See Van Buren's reliance on Story in his free soil statement (Niven, *Martin Van Buren*, 568); see also R. Kent Newmeyer, *Supreme Court Justice Joseph Story: Statesman of the Old Republic* (Chapel Hill, 1985), 84–195.

21. Calhoun, *Disquisition on Government and Selections from the Discourse*, 27.

22. *Calhoun Works*, I, 392–95.

Although both essays were written during the intense heat of political and sectional contest and were shaped by contemporary issues, they bespeak an originality in American political thought that remains unequaled. Calhoun's comments on political parties, numerical majorities, and the abuses of power are as appropriate today as they were in 1850. American political and social history from the mid-nineteenth century on reflects a periodic flux of public morals and their intimate connection with political corruption. Calhoun's caustic observation on this point is worth noticing. "That which corrupts and debases the community, politically," he wrote, "must also corrupt and debase it morally."[23] His analysis of the imperfections and the dangers of majority rule has never been refuted in practice or in theoretical explanation. His proposal that the sense of the various interests of a complex society be taken in making up a government influenced the political thought and practice of the progressive movement at the turn of the twentieth century. Progressive political mechanisms such as the direct primary and especially the initiative, the referendum, and the recall, which are embodied in some state constitutions today, have their genesis in Calhoun's political thought.

While drafting "The Disquisition on Government" and "The Discourse on the Constitution," Calhoun must at times have wondered about living standards even for the well-to-do in southern plantation society, which may have led him to question his all-encompassing praise of southern institutions. His son Andrew, scarcely a social prophet, had speculated about the effect of cotton culture on the region. In a long letter to his father from his Alabama plantation he wrote:

> But I am beginning to believe that the culture of cotton is incompatable [*sic*] with any improvement which renders a country attractive to the eye, and which generally indicates prosperity elsewhere, but the absence of which, does not with us. I mean neatness, buildings—good roads—minute attention to stock, improved breeds[;] and we have not the time for these things no matter what our taste may be. And hence the slovenly appearance of our section in contrast with others . . . the cultivation of cotton requires such incessant application to business that neither the planter, or his slave, has time to attend to anything else than the preperation [*sic*], the culture and the gathering of it.

Andrew went on to deplore the mining of the soil and "the dilapidated and ruinous condition of many sections." And he predicted that plant-

23. *Ibid.*, 49.

ers' carelessness and indifference to the land would eventually ruin the South.[24]

Although Fort Hill was neat and well tended and Calhoun spent much of his time at home directing the contour plowing of the hills to prevent erosion, he had certainly noted the run-down condition of the countryside and the straggling villages, and he had certainly observed the results of neglect in gullied fields and silt-laden, sluggish streams. There were few planters in the South who spent more time than he in keeping up with the latest technical and scientific advances in agriculture. There was no more enthusiastic member of the Pendleton Agricultural Society than he in proselytizing his neighbors about the virtues of Edmund Ruffin's experiments in scientific agriculture. Calhoun was like a child who had just learned to read when he received a packet of imported melon seeds or a new strain of grapevines, a thoroughbred sow or seed grain for rust-resistant wheat. But in the last analysis, Calhoun's life as a planter revolved around cotton, with its uncertain world market, its susceptibility to insect blight, its thralldom to the vagaries of the weather, and the care, or more often lack of it, in picking, ginning, and pressing the crop into bales.

Trained as he was in observation, Calhoun could not fail to notice that the road from Pendleton to his own plantation was poorly laid down and badly maintained, and that the nearby rutted, eroded, and abandoned acreage known locally as the Seneca Cowgrounds was a dismal testimonial to nature ravaged by the feckless planter of the recent past. There is evidence in his correspondence with his daughter Anna Maria when she and Clemson were living in Brussels that Calhoun was sensitive to the rustic environment of the agricultural South—"the vexations of housekeeping where supplies are so limited and little diversified." He must certainly have compared the neat towns and villages in the New England of his youth with the ramshackle houses and barns and the poorly tended fields in the South of his old age.[25]

What of slavery, which he was insistent on protecting? What of the purchase and sale of human beings as chattels? What of the slave owners who slept with their female slaves, who treated them as concubines like any despot of ancient or modern times? Calhoun must have known about instances of this conduct in his own family. Francis Pickens, for instance, his cousin and for many years his devoted politi-

24. *Calhoun Papers*, XV, 319, 320.
25. *Ibid.*, 342, 343; Calhoun to Anna Maria Clemson, January 24, 1849, in Calhoun-Clemson Papers, Clemson University.

cal follower, had several black mistresses and children by all of them. James Hammond, another close associate, was notorious for his sexual conduct with his female slaves.[26] Yet as Calhoun grew older, he rejected the criticism that the slave system of the South was an immoral anachronism.

In doing so, Calhoun rejected the evidence of his own senses and became more and more enmeshed in abstract rationalizations of a status quo; morality, economic well-being, and the appearance and very structure of the red clay hills all became subordinated to a desperate quest for social stability. He could say with a confidence bred from his close study of Aristotle and without admitting any paradox that freedom was based on slavery and that therefore the right of petition was unnecessary in a democracy. Discounting the slaves and most of the free blacks, who together accounted for one-third of the South's population, everyone enjoyed freedom. What political grievances existed, he asked, that required petitions? The only real political grievance in Calhoun's mind was majority rule that discriminated against a slave-owning minority. Petitions were useless in this sort of struggle. "The truth is," he said on February 13, 1840, "that the right of petition could scarcely be said to be the right of a freeman. It belongs to despotic Governments more properly and might be said to be the last right of slaves."[27] Fortunately, as he saw it, a proper balance of state power in the constitutional arrangement protected the property and the customs of the slave-plantation system and was extended to social, political, and economic minorities everywhere.

These were the guiding principles that underlay "The Disquisition on Government" and "The Discourse on the Constitution." He wrote Edmund Ruffin, "The great object is to impress the united South, or rather the slave holding states of the paramount importance of maint[ain]ing their peculiar institutions above any other consideration." But the essays must be "able, philosophical and aloof from politics," he added. Unfortunately, he lost sight of this objective when he came to the actual writing.

Calhoun had completed and edited "The Disquisition on Government" before he left for Washington, D.C., in December, 1849. "The Discourse on the Constitution," however, was not quite finished and would not be completed before Calhoun's death. He had been delayed

26. Orville Vernon Burton, *In My Father's House Are Many Mansions* (Chapel Hill, 1985), 185–89; Faust, *James Henry Hammond,* 86, 87.
27. *Calhoun Papers,* XV, 99.

in editing it to his own satisfaction during the summer and fall by the gathering political storm on California.[28]

In the spring of 1848, Democratic party conventions in Virginia, Alabama, and Florida had passed resolutions denying that Congress had the power to prohibit slavery in the territories. During the next year, the movement towards organizing a convention of the slave states gained considerable momentum. Calhoun was in the forefront of those who were counseling joint action. From the detached, one-room structure he used as a study, letters in his scrawling hand went out to political leaders all over the South, urging his oft-repeated theme of southern unity, now with more urgency than ever before. Calhoun was still hopeful that in the face of concerted southern pressure, the North would give way. It might be too late, he warned, for any concession that would guarantee slave property in the territories, but further delay would be fatal. "The prospect is as things now stand," he wrote in April, 1849, "that before four years have elapsed, the Union will be divided into two great hostile sectional parties."[29]

337

In the midst of the Carolinian's efforts to organize a convention of the slaveholding states, Thomas Hart Benton made a furious attack on Calhoun, whom he charged was a disunionist. Benton's speech at Jefferson City, Missouri, was aimed at arresting proslavery sentiment in this important border state and associating in the public mind any southern convention on the territorial issue with a conspiracy to destroy the Union.[30]

Calhoun, of course, saw the danger Benton's remarks posed for united action by the slave states. Drawing on his draft of "The Discourse on the Constitution," Calhoun rejected Benton's charges of disunion and conspiracy. He restated his compact theory of state sovereignty and insisted that since the territories were jointly owned by all the states, slaveholders had just as much right as citizens of free states to take their property into these regions and just as much a claim on the national government for its protection. Calhoun's reply was published in the Pendleton *Messenger* on July 13, 1849. It was republished in full, together with Benton's speech and speeches of other southern leaders, in Ritchie's Washington *Union*, the Washington *Daily Intelligencer*, and the New York *Herald*, and was noticed in editorial columns throughout the nation.[31] The editorial affray, as Benton had intended, deepened

28. *Calhoun Correspondence*, 777.
29. *Ibid.*, 765.
30. See Benton's speech in *Niles' Register*, LXXV, 390–96.
31. New York *Herald*, July 21, 1849; *Calhoun Correspondence*, 768, 769.

the controversy over concerted southern action. But for Benton himself, the incident had disastrous consequences. After forty ballots in the Missouri legislature, he was defeated for reelection, thus bringing to an end his colorful career of thirty years in the Senate.

Calhoun could scarcely conceal his satisfaction at Benton's defeat, which he regarded as a definite setback for those in the South who still sought to temporize. Of far more importance to his plans, however, was the posture of the Taylor administration. By late summer of 1849, Calhoun had learned that the president was following the lead of northern antislavery Whigs. The news was exaggerated, but there was no doubt that Senators William H. Seward of New York and Truman Smith of Connecticut, along with the cabinet members Thomas Ewing of Ohio and Jacob Collamer of Vermont, were exercising a good deal of influence over the policies of the old general.[32]

An apparent antislavery turn to the administration's policy on California had a decided impact on the Deep South. Before Calhoun left for Washington, D.C., in December, 1849, a bipartisan convention met in Jackson, Mississippi. With almost no opposition, the meeting called for a convention of all southern states in Nashville in June, 1850. In addition to the call, the Mississippi convention passed resolutions roundly condemning the Wilmot Proviso in terms that espoused Calhoun's theory of state sovereignty. Calhoun was highly gratified at this action, which began the movement he had been planning for more than a decade. The South Carolina legislature, whose regular session met in late November, chose delegates to the convention. The governors of Alabama, Georgia, and Virginia all endorsed the Mississippi proposal. The idea of southern unity was near realization by the time Calhoun had settled himself in H. V. Hill's Washington boardinghouse on December 1, 1849.[33]

President Taylor had thrown southern members of Congress into a turmoil with his message, urging that California be admitted into the Union without delay in accordance with the sense of its residents. Since the inhabitants of California had met and formed a free soil constitution, Calhoun regarded the president's recommendation as proof that the free soil interest had captured the administration. "I regard it as worse than the Wilmot proviso," he said. "What the latter proposes to do openly the former is intended to do covertly and fraudulently." Calhoun was also highly critical of Howell Cobb's election as Speaker of

32. *Calhoun Correspondence*, 771.
33. *Ibid.*, 773.

the House after more than three weeks of deadlock. A Georgia Democrat, Cobb had refused to go along with Calhoun's southern address. For this he was to be excommunicated—"the least true of all Southern members, of the South, to the South . . . false to his section," Calhoun said.[34]

For the first two weeks of the session, an ill and overwrought Calhoun attended the Senate every day and participated as usual in debate as the lines between the pro- and anti-California forces were more clearly drawn. Compromise was in the air, however. Henry Clay, now in his seventy-third year, had returned to the Senate after an absence of seven years. But before any proposals were made, Calhoun became seriously ill with pneumonia. For two weeks he was confined to his quarters and for most of that time to his bed, where, under the careful ministering of his cousin Martha; her husband, Armistead Burt; and Joseph Scoville, who was now acting as Calhoun's full-time secretary, he slowly regained his strength. By February 18, he felt well enough to resume his attendance in the Senate. He even planned to deliver a speech on the California question but was again stricken with complications of tuberculosis.[35]

Meanwhile, Clay had presented his compromise resolutions, which in some respects resembled the Clayton resolutions Calhoun had supported two years before but went substantially beyond what he would accept in concessions to the North. The abolition of the slave trade in the District of Columbia and the admission of California as a free state were not negotiable as far as he was concerned. Despite his differences with Clay, Calhoun did see the possibility of compromise if he could make northern congressmen realize how serious the situation had become—how separation of the South from the Union was a real alternative, not simply a bluff. Accordingly, he carefully prepared a lengthy speech in which his warning to the North was clear and in which his arguments for southern unity were compelling enough, he hoped, to galvanize hitherto uncommitted slave states into concerted action.

In the late morning of March 4, there was a pause in the usual proceedings of the Senate as visitors in the galleries and the senators themselves watched the slow and painful progress of John C. Calhoun to his desk. Emaciated and pallid, he was so weak that he had to be supported on his way by Senator James M. Mason. Most members of the audience were convinced that they were watching the final moves

34. *Ibid.*, 779, 783. See also R. P. Brooks, "Howell Cobb and the Crisis of 1850," *Mississippi Valley Historical Review*, IV, No. 3 (December, 1917), 282–84.
35. *Calhoun Correspondence*, 780–83.

of a dying man. When Mason settled Calhoun in his chair and, addressing Vice-President Fillmore, declared that he would read Calhoun's speech for him, it seemed apparent that this would be his last comment on a public question. The address began with the remark that unimpeded abolitionist agitation would surely lead to disunion. Calhoun then made a closely reasoned argument that represented the two sections as separate nations in all but name, held together by the thin, frayed strand of political parties.

This tenuous relationship had resulted, Calhoun claimed, from policy decisions that worked against southern interests and were derived from a wrongful interpretation of the necessary and proper clause in Article I, Section 8, of the Constitution. In restating Jefferson's strict interpretation of the implied powers of Congress, as opposed to Hamilton's, Marshall's, and Story's concepts of broad construction, Calhoun derived all of the alleged crimes against the South—the Northwest Ordinance, the Missouri Compromise, tariff legislation, the Wilmot Proviso, and now the Taylor administration's proposal to bypass customary procedures and admit California as a free state, which he stigmatized as the "Executive Proviso." Under its aegis an unlawful group of individuals, he charged, had usurped the sovereignty of the states and arrogated to themselves the right to form a constitution. Calhoun's argument was based on the fact that all the states acting together in the Union had conquered California, not a group of indigenous rebels or outside adventurers. His distinction between individuals and inhabitants as the governing principle over the powers of Congress to legislate for the territories could be taken, and surely was by many at the time, as a blatant example of special pleading. His temporary solution to the California problem was to return the region to the territorial condition.[36]

It was not Calhoun's constitutional and legalistic arguments or his demographic analysis of the relative positions of the two sections but his forthright discussion of the slavery question that commanded the closest attention of his listeners. Bluntly, he accused the North of being wholly opposed to slavery. There were those who regarded the institution to be sin, others a crime, and the remainder a stain on the national character.[37] Calhoun employed a striking metaphor that likened the Union to a fabric of which almost all of the binding cords that held the cloth together had already snapped over irreconcilable differences on

36. *Calhoun Works,* IV, 560, 570, 571.
37. *Ibid.,* 552.

the question of slavery. Calhoun closed his remarks by offering terms that he declared must be met if the Union was to be preserved. He demanded a fugitive slave law, which Clay had already proposed, a cessation of all agitation on slavery, and a constitutional amendment that would establish and guarantee what Calhoun called an equilibrium between the free and the slave states.

How agitation was to be curtailed without censorship and the enhancement of the centralizing powers of the national government, which he so greatly feared, Calhoun did not address. Nor did he give any specific plan for his constitutional amendment, though his listeners could infer that it would partition California and the New Mexico Territory into free and slave states and provide some sort of automatic division of territories in the future so as to preserve the sectional balance. It seems safe to say that Calhoun would never have relied on any amendment that embodied popular sovereignty, nor upon any statutory enlargement of the powers of the federal government to protect slavery within the territories or the free states. Probably the amendment would have included some variation of state veto and possibly the dual executive scheme he outlined in his "Discourse on the Constitution." It seems evident that any terms of final settlement would make the South virtually an autonomous region within the Union. In the last analysis, Calhoun said, the fate of the Union lay not in the hands of the South, the weaker partner, but in those of the North. "If you, who represent the stronger portion, cannot agree to settle them [the differences] on the broad principle of justice and duty, say so; and let the States we both represent agree to separate and part in peace."[38]

When Mason finished reading, there was a brief silence in the chamber. Many of the senators present from the North as well as from the South were deeply disturbed by Calhoun's comments, particularly his demand for a constitutional amendment. Among them were Daniel Webster and Henry S. Foote, the Whig-Unionist senator from Mississippi.

Webster had visited Calhoun's sickroom several times before his speech. As they talked over the present crisis, Webster concluded that Calhoun would not accept Clay's compromise resolutions and, further, that he spoke for a region on the brink of separation from the Union. After listening carefully to Calhoun's speech, he decided that a conciliatory approach was essential when it was his turn to respond.[39]

38. *Ibid.*, 573; *Calhoun Correspondence*, 775–84.
39. Baxter, *One and Inseparable*, 412.

Foote, too, had resolved to speak for those southern moderates who would attempt to soften, in the interests of compromise, the sectional animus he detected in Calhoun's remarks. He feared that the speech would encourage disunionist elements, who would soon meet at Nashville to make formal demands on the North that it could not accept and that, once made, could not be rescinded. One day after Mason read Calhoun's address, Foote gained the floor and criticized various points the Carolinian had made. Calhoun's colleague Butler was seeking to clarify Calhoun's remarks when the senator himself, this time unaided, entered the chamber and took his seat. A brief exchange followed, in which Calhoun asked whether Foote thought the territorial questions before Congress could be solved without a constitutional amendment. Foote replied that he thought they could. Calhoun again insisted that public opinion in the North was hostile to the South. Foote disagreed. Calhoun closed the argument by declaring that he supported the Union but only on his own terms, which included an interpretation of the Constitution that would preserve and perpetuate the slave republic.[40]

Calhoun was well enough to attend the Senate on March 7 when Webster rose to make his reply, presumably for the North. The great Massachusetts statesman, well fortified with brandy, said that he spoke for the Union. He condemned extremists on both sides and declared that in practical terms slavery would be excluded from California and New Mexico not by any fiat but by geography. In glowing language, Webster recalled the glories of the Union, moving his audience as he had moved it years before when he replied to Hayne. Calhoun had been vice-president of the United States then and had listened to the magnificent rolling tones and inspirational rhetoric from his seat beneath the flying eagle above the rostrum. He had disagreed with Webster then; he disagreed with him now, though Calhoun found some basis for compromise in Webster's remarks that would be more favorable to the South than Clay's resolutions. But he saw only a temporary arrangement. "Nothing short of the terms I propose," he said, "can settle it finally and permanently. Indeed, it is difficult to see how two peoples so different and hostile can exist together in a common Union."[41]

Calhoun had just three weeks to live when he listened to Webster's

40. Henry S. Foote, *War of the Rebellion; or, Scylla and Charybdis* (New York, 1866), 141, 142, 574–76.
41. George W. Julian, *Political Recollections, 1840 to 1872* (rpr. Westport, Conn., 1970), 86; Baxter, *One and Inseparable*, 413–15; *Calhoun Correspondence*, 784.

speech. He returned to the Senate on March 13, once more to argue with the persistent Foote, but after that he did not leave his chamber. The scene at Hill's boardinghouse during the last days of his illness was of one of those atavistic ceremonies that memorialized in almost feudal fashion the passing of a great man. A constant stream of visitors came to observe Calhoun on his deathbed and to catch the last bit of wisdom he might impart.

Fully conscious of his condition and of his importance in the history of his section and his nation, Calhoun acted out the role expected of him. His son and namesake, John, Jr., who was one of the medical men attending him, recorded his last words early in the morning of March 31, 1850, after he had refused all medicine and had given instructions about his papers and personal effects. He said, "I am now perfectly comfortable."[42]

Calhoun's anguish about the fate of the South in the Union was but dimly perceived by those around his deathbed. Abraham Venable, the North Carolina congressman, lawyer, and physician, one of the many who watched at his bedside and the one who closed his eyes, came nearest to understanding the mental turmoil of the dying man. Venable said, "He loved the truth, for the truth's sake, and believed that to temporize is but to increase the evil which we seek to remove." In this instance, the truth for Calhoun, of course, was the perpetuation of the slave republic on a permanent, constitutional, legal, and territorial basis. He still hoped that somehow the Union would remain intact with appropriate concessions from the free states to ensure the "peculiar institution" of slavery. But in his darker moments, Calhoun despaired of any solution and in fact anticipated that the Union would break up. Six weeks before his death, he wrote Hammond that compromises and concessions to the slave states were of no avail unless the free states accepted his sweeping terms. Calhoun did not think they would agree to any such settlement. "The impression," he said, "is now very general, and is on the increase, that disunion is the only alternative, that is left to us."[43]

Yet Webster's concessions in his March 7 speech and the evidence of southern disunity that Foote displayed shook Calhoun's confidence in demanding a permanent solution. His doubts about his course deepened, and the future security of the slave states appeared uncertain unless by their united action they could become an autonomous region

42. Margaret Coit, in her biography of Calhoun, gives a slightly different phrasing, as his last words appeared in the Charleston *Mercury*, April 1, 1850.
43. *Calhoun Correspondence*, 781.

within the Union. Shortly before his death, Calhoun indicated a retreat from his insistence on a general arrangement and dictated to Scoville a series of resolutions that dealt specifically with slavery in the Mexican cession and the admission of California.[44]

Neither Venable nor Burt nor Scoville nor even John, Jr., understood the depth of Calhoun's allegiance to the concept of the Union and his near certainty that the Union would be destroyed. Among his contemporaries, only Webster sensed Calhoun's despair. In a brief eulogy delivered before a solemn audience in the Senate chamber on April 5, Webster spoke of the principles that Calhoun espoused, "the measures that he defended . . . the purity of his exalted patriotism." The great Massachusetts orator and statesman, however, took care to distance himself from Calhoun's views on the nature of the Union. He confined his comments to Calhoun's personal qualities. When he was urged to attend the funeral ceremonies in Charleston, Webster was assailed with an agony of indecision that was quite uncharacteristic of him on such occasions. He finally agreed to show his respect by accompanying the body with the official mourners as far as the Virginia landing.[45]

Calhoun's death brought a sense of loss that was nationwide. Even those who disagreed with the southern statesman, who considered his defense of slavery a dangerous obsession, mourned the passing of a national institution. During the lifetime of most living Americans, Calhoun had been a conspicuous member of the government. Visitors to the capital had invariably commented on his striking appearance, his speeches, and his mode of debate and associated him with Clay and Webster as the paragons of American statesmanship, the living embodiments of American nationhood. He had indeed on occasion shown a chilly, impersonal public demeanour—"the cast iron man," as Harriet Martineau, the British traveler and social critic, once described him. But in relaxed, informal surroundings, he had been warm and compelling in conversation, utterly without pretense, and especially impressive to the young.[46]

At Fort Hill, Calhoun had been a kindly, even indulgent husband and father who overlooked Floride's temperamental outbursts and

44. *Ibid.*, 783, 785–87.

45. Fletcher Webster (ed.), *Letters Hitherto Uncollected* (Boston, 1903), 538, vol. XVI of J. W. McIntyre (ed.), *The Writings and Speeches of Daniel Webster* (18 vols.; Boston, 1903); Wiltse, *Calhoun, Sectionalist*, 478.

46. John S. Jenkins, *The Life of John Caldwell Calhoun* (Auburn, N.Y., 1851), 447–53; *Congressional Globe*, 31st Congress, 1st Sess., 625.

Patrick's feckless ways, and sought constantly to ease the friction between Andrew and Clemson. After his death, grief-stricken Anna Maria wrote her brother Patrick. "Can we ever forget his sweet smile and his ready sympathy in all our pleasures and pains? He was our friend our guide our head and he is gone."[47]

Some, of course, who knew nothing of Calhoun's private life, felt that in his public career he had squandered his undoubted talents on an ignoble cause. His old teacher and former friend, Benjamin Silliman, on learning of his death paid tribute to his great mind, only regretting that it had become morbidly sensitive and narrow on slavery. He held Calhoun largely responsible for presenting to the world "the disgraceful spectacle of a great republic—and the only real republic in the world—standing forth in vindication of slavery; without prospect of, or wish for its extinction." Francis Lieber, another vigorous though at the time private critic of slavery and a professor of philosophy at South Carolina College, echoed these sentiments. He felt that Calhoun's death would "be healing rather than otherwise." Lieber was not alone among citizens of Calhoun's own state in looking forward to a period of easing tension between the sections. Such Carolinians as James Petigru, Joel Poinsett, and Benjamin Perry were relieved that Calhoun's formidable presence in South Carolina would no longer be a barrier to political agreement. They felt that with his death, compromise in Congress was now a possibility.[48]

Many southern newspapers and opinion leaders held otherwise. Not long after the bells of St. Michael's and St. Phillip's churches in Charleston had tolled for Calhoun's elaborate funeral procession, the *Southern Literary Messenger* articulated this view in an editorial on Calhoun's life and his passing. "Doubted and denied as it may honestly be by many," the magazine declared, "Calhoun has been for a long series of years, the great and almost sole bulwark between the Union and its dissolution. He stood between the living and the dead, and for a time arrested the plague."[49]

47. Anna Maria Clemson to Patrick Calhoun, June 24, 1850, in John C. Calhoun Papers, South Caroliniana Library.

48. George P. Fisher, *Life of Benjamin Silliman, MD. LL.D.* (2 vols.; New York, 1866), II, 98; Thomas Sergeant Perry, *The Life and Letters of Francis Lieber* (Boston, 1882), 228–44; James Petigru Carson, *Life, Letters and Speeches of James Louis Petigru* (Washington, D.C., 1920), 347, 348; Benjamin F. Perry, *Reminiscences of Public Men* (Philadelphia, 1883), 49.

49. Frederika Bremer, *America of the Fifties* (London, 1924), 112, 113; J. P. Thomas (ed.), *The Carolina Tribute to Calhoun* (Columbia, S.C., 1857), 73; "John C. Calhoun," *Southern Literary Messenger*, XVI (May, 1850), 302.

On the Sources

A Note on the Literature and Primary Sources

If one considers the eminence of John C. Calhoun in the politics and the public policy of his state, his region, and the nation, spanning over forty years of dramatic and often tempestuous change, it seems unusual that his life and career have not attracted more attention from historians and biographers. Apart from a campaign biography, *Life of John C. Calhoun* (New York, 1843), which Calhoun certainly reviewed and probably wrote, no scholarly biography appeared until thirty-two years after his death. His death in 1850 at the very height of the sectional conflict over the Mexican cession produced a flurry of literature about the southern statesman, including a popular biography, John S. Jenkins, *The Life of John Caldwell Calhoun* (Auburn, N.Y., 1850). Obviously capitalizing on the publicity Calhoun's death had generated, Jenkins' biography cannot be taken seriously, though it contains some useful contemporary data. Eulogies by members of Congress and those in his native state fill a volume that contains some significant biographical data, J. P. Thomas (ed.), *The Carolina Tribute to Calhoun* (Columbia, S.C., 1857). Between 1854 and 1857, Richard Crallé published *The Works of John C. Calhoun* (6 vols.; New York), which elicited mixed reviews. Northern writers were generally unfavorable, while southern critics were enthusiastic in their praise. There were no contemporary reviews in significant foreign periodicals. But the Crallé edition is a reasonably accurate and fairly comprehensive collection of Calhoun's public papers, major speeches, and essays.

The first full-scale biography of Calhoun by a trained historian was Herman Von Holst's *John C. Calhoun* (Boston, 1882). A volume in the highly successful American Statesman series, Von Holst's work, unfortunately, is an overly critical treatment of Calhoun's career. Written at the high tide of northern nationalism, it pictures Calhoun as one of the principal originators of a southern conspiracy to destroy the Union for the sake of perpetuating slavery. Von Holst's interpretation of Calhoun is even harsher than that of the Massachusetts radical politician Henry

Wilson, whose polemical work *The Rise and Fall of the Slave Power* (2 vols.; Boston, 1872–77) is the fullest expression of the conspiracy thesis.

J. Franklin Jameson renewed scholarly interest in Calhoun when he published a select edition of Calhoun's correspondence as the fourth annual report of the Historical Manuscripts Commission, *Correspondence of John C. Calhoun* (Washington, D.C., 1900). Prefaced by a brief account of Calhoun's family and early life that a near contemporary, Colonel W. Pinckney Starke, had written, this valuable work—together with Chauncey S. Boucher and Robert P. Brooks (eds.), *Correspondence Addressed to John C. Calhoun, 1837–1849: Sixteenth Report of the Historical Manuscripts Commission* (Washington, D.C., 1930) and the Crallé (ed.) *Works*—became a major source for all subsequent work on Calhoun.

Until the late 1950s, scholars had to depend on the often-unreliable published editions of the papers of Calhoun's contemporaries or study the actual manuscripts themselves for comments about Calhoun. Now, however, fine editions of many nineteenth-century statesmen have been published, making research on Calhoun less time-consuming, much more convenient, and probably more accurate. Among these editions, James F. Hopkins *et al.* (eds.), *The Papers of Henry Clay* (8 vols; Lexington, Ky, 1959–84); Herbert Weaver *et al.* (eds.), *The Correspondence of James K. Polk* (6 vols.; Nashville, 1969–83); and Charles M. Wiltse (ed.), *The Papers of Daniel Webster: Correspondence* (7 vols.; Hanover, N.H., 1974–86) are essential to Calhoun's biographers. For Calhoun's other great contemporary, Andrew Jackson, the venerable edition of his letters, John S. Bassett (ed.), *Correspondence of Andrew Jackson* (7 vols.; Washington, D.C., 1926–35), is accurate and quite comprehensive. The superb, modern, multivolume edition *The Papers of John C. Calhoun* (Columbia, S.C., 1959–   ), under the editorship of W. Edwin Hemphill, Robert L. Meriwether, and later Clyde Wilson, is indispensable. To date, seventeen volumes of Calhoun's papers have been published, carrying Calhoun's career through March, 1844.

Early correctives to Von Holst's biography are Gaillard Hunt, *John C. Calhoun* (Philadelphia, 1908), and William M. Meigs, *The Life of John C. Calhoun* (2 vols.; New York, 1917). In seeking to restore Calhoun's reputation, however, both of these biographers overemphasized Calhoun's contributions to government and to political theory while deemphasizing his role as a passionate defender of slavery. Another thirty years passed before other scholars attempted major biographies. Charles M. Wiltse published his first volume of a projected three-volume work in 1944, *John C. Calhoun, Nationalist: 1782–1828* (Indianapolis). The second volume, *John C. Calhoun, Nullifier: 1829–1839* (Indianapolis, 1949), was followed by *John C. Calhoun, Sectionalist: 1840–1850* (Indianapolis, 1951). In 1950, Margaret L. Coit published *John C. Calhoun: An American Portrait* (New York), for which she received the Pulitzer Prize. Both of these works were highly favorable to Calhoun, but despite Coit's dramatic style, Wiltse's biography remains the standard work on Calhoun. Two other book-length treatments of Calhoun's life are worthy of notice: Gerald M. Capers, *John C. Calhoun, Opportunist: A Re-appraisal* (Gainesville, Fla., 1960), and Richard Current, *John C. Calhoun* (New York, 1963). Capers' work seeks to modify the image of Calhoun as a great theorist detached from the roil of Jacksonian politics, who stood forth as a lonely, tragic figure in defense of the slave-plantation culture. Capers' work makes too much of Calhoun as a politician driven primarily by ambition. Current is also highly critical of Calhoun, though his sharpest thrusts are aimed at Calhoun's political theory and also incidentally at those conservative essayists of the early 1960s who found a justification in his thought for states' rights and racial segregation. Calhoun's essays on political theory, "The Discourse on the Constitution" and "The Disquisition on Government," enjoyed a brief vogue during the civil rights agitation following the desegregation of the Little Rock, Arkansas, school system after the Supreme Court's decision in *Brown* vs. *Board of Education.* Calhoun's carefully constructed argument in defense of minority rights appealed not only to conservatives and white supremacists but also to liberal political theorists who saw in his logic and his ideas a compelling argument for a pluralistic approach to government in a representative democracy.

Such an interpretation of Calhoun's thought was first suggested many years earlier by Vernon Parrington in Volume II of his *Main Currents in American Thought* (New York, 1926). Arthur Schlesinger, Jr., argued along similar lines in *The Age of Jackson* (Boston, 1945). More recently and from a wholly different viewpoint, Peter Drucker, in his article "A Key to American Politics: Calhoun's Pluralism," *Review of Politics,* X (October, 1948), 412–26, made an interesting statement on Calhoun's contribution to political theory and practice. But by far the most insightful analyses of Calhoun's political thought are those of Louis Hartz, *The Liberal Tradition in America* (New York, 1955), Richard Hofstadter, *The American Political Tradition* (New York, 1948), and William W. Freehling, "Spoilsmen and Interests in the Thought and Career of John C. Calhoun," *Journal of American History,* LII, No. 1 (June, 1965), 25–42. August O. Spain has made the most comprehensive assessment of Calhoun's thought to date—*The Political Theory of John C. Calhoun* (1951; rpr. New York, 1968)—but his judgments rarely consider the specific political and social milieu and their impact on Calhoun's writings.

Memoirs and diaries that are essential to an understanding of Calhoun's career are Charles Francis Adams (ed.), *Memoirs of John Quincy Adams* (12 vols.; Philadelphia, 1874–77); Thomas Hart Benton, *Thirty Years' View* (2 vols.; New York, 1854–56); Henry S. Foote, *Casket of Reminiscences* (Washington, D.C., 1874) and *War of the Rebellion; or, Scylla and Charybdis* (New York, 1866); James A. Hamilton, *Reminiscences of James A. Hamilton during Three Quarters of a Century* (New York, 1869); Milo M. Quaife (ed.), *The Diary of James K. Polk During His Presidency, 1845–1849* (4 vols.; Chicago, 1910); John C. Fitzpatrick (ed.), *The Autobiography of Martin Van Buren* (Washington, D.C., 1920); and Charles Henry Ambler (ed.), *Correspondence of Robert M. T. Hunter, 1826–1876* (2 vols.; Washington, D.C., 1918) and *The Life and Diary of John Floyd* (Richmond, Va., 1918). The two most compelling contemporary vignettes of Calhoun are found in Volume II of George William Featherstonhaugh, *A Canoe Voyage Up the Minnay Sotor* (2 vols.; London, 1847), and in Volume I of Harriet Martineau, *Retrospect of Western Travel* (London, 1838).

The debates and the documents of the Twelfth Congress through the first session of the Thirty-first Congress cover Calhoun's public career. The editors of *Calhoun Papers* have included most of the important material relating to Calhoun, including all of his reports, his speeches, and even the debates he participated in. But the *Register of Debates*, the *Annals of Congress*, the *Congressional Globe*, and *American State Papers: Documents, Legislative and Executive, of the Congress of the United States* (38 vols.; Washington, D.C., 1832–61) must also be consulted for references to Calhoun and important background material. *Niles' Register*, the *Washington Daily Intelligencer*, the *Richmond Enquirer*, the Pendleton *Messenger*, the Charleston *Courier*, and the Charleston *Mercury*, and Calhoun's short-lived Washington journals, the *Washington Republican and Congressional Examiner*, the *Spectator*, and the *Constitution*, are among the more important newspapers that concern themselves with Calhoun as a public man.

A Listing of Secondary Sources

Agar, Herbert, ed. *Formative Years: A History of the United States During the Administrations of Jefferson and Madison, by Henry Adams.* 2 vols. Boston, 1947.

Ambler, Charles H. *Thomas Ritchie: A Study in Virginia Politics.* Richmond, Va., 1913.

Ammon, Harry. *James Monroe: The Quest for National Identity.* New York, 1971.

Bancroft, Frederic. *Calhoun and the South Carolina Nullification Movement.* Baltimore, 1928.

Banner, James M., Jr. "The Problem of South Carolina." In *The Hofstadter Aegis,* edited by Stanley Elkins and Eric McKitrick. New York, 1974.

Bates, Mary. *The Private Life of John C. Calhoun.* Charleston, S.C., 1852.

Baxter, Maurice G. *One and Inseparable: Daniel Webster and the Union.* Cambridge, Mass., 1984.

Bleser, Carol, ed. *The Hammonds of Redcliff.* New York, 1981.

Boucher, Chauncy S. *The Nullification Controversy in South Carolina.* Chicago, 1916.

Burton, Orville Vernon. *In My Father's House Are Many Mansions.* Chapel Hill, 1985.

Cash, Wilbur J. *The Mind of the South.* New York, 1957.

Clark, Victor S. *History of Manufactures in the United States, 1607–1860.* 3 vols. New York, 1929.

Cooper, William J. *The South and the Politics of Slavery, 1828–1856.* Baton Rouge, 1978.

Cunningham, Charles E. *Timothy Dwight, 1752–1817.* New York, 1942.

Dodd, William E. *Statesmen of the Old South; or, From Radicalism to Conservative Revolt.* New York, 1929.

Donald, David Herbert. *Charles Sumner and the Coming of the Civil War.* New York, 1960.

Dwight, Timothy. *Travels in New England and New York.* 4 vols. New Haven, 1821–22.

Eaton, Clement. *Henry Clay and the Art of American Politics.* Boston, 1937.

Edmunds, John B. *Francis W. Pickens & the Politics of Destruction.* Chapel Hill, 1986.

Ellis, Richard E. *The Union at Risk, Jacksonian Democracy, State Rights, and the Nullification Crisis.* New York, 1987.

Faust, Drew Gilpin. *James Henry Hammond and the Old South.* Baton Rouge, 1982.

———. "The Rhetoric and Ritual of Agriculture in Antebellum South Carolina." *Journal of Southern History,* XLV, No. 4 (November, 1979).

Franklin, John Hope. *The Militant South, 1800–1861.* Cambridge, Mass., 1970.

Freehling, William W. *Prelude to Civil War: The Nullification Controversy in South Carolina, 1816–1836.* New York, 1966.

Goodrich, Samuel G. *Recollections of a Lifetime.* New York, 1856.

Gray, Lewis C. *History of Agriculture in the Southern United States.* 2 vols. Washington, D.C., 1935.

Hillard, Sam Bowers. *Atlas of Antebellum Southern Agriculture.* Baton Rouge, 1984.

Ingersoll, Lurton D. *A History of the War Department of the United States.* Washington, D.C., 1879.

Jaffa, Harry V. "Defenders of the Constitution: Calhoun Versus Madison." Bicentennial Project of the University of Dallas. Dallas, 1987.

Johannsen, Robert W. *Stephen A. Douglas.* New York, 1973.

———. *To the Halls of the Montezumas: The Mexican War in the American Imagination.* New York, 1985.

Lander, Ernest M., Jr. *Reluctant Imperialists: Calhoun, the South Carolinians, and the Mexican War.* Baton Rouge, 1980.

———. *The Calhoun Family and Thomas Green Clemson: The Decline of a Southern Patriarchy.* Columbia, S.C., 1983.

Lerner, Ralph. "John C. Calhoun." In *American Political Thought,* edited by Morton Frisch and Richard G. Stevens. 2nd ed. Itasca, Ill., 1983.

Maier, Pauline. "The Road Not Taken: Nullification, John C. Calhoun, and the Revolutionary Tradition in South Carolina." *South Carolina Historical Magazine,* LXXXII, No. 1 (January, 1981).

Malone, Dumas. *The Public Life of Thomas Cooper, 1783–1839.* New Haven, 1926.

Mayo, Bernard. *Henry Clay.* Boston, 1937.

Nevins, Allan. *Ordeal of the Union.* 2 vols. New York, 1947.

Niven, John. *Gideon Welles, Lincoln's Secretary of the Navy.* New York, 1973.

———. *Martin Van Buren: The Romantic Age of American Politics.* New York, 1983.

O'Brien, Michael. *A Character of Hugh Legaré.* Knoxville, 1986.

Peterson, Merrill D. *Olive Branch and Sword—The Compromise of 1833.* Baton Rouge, 1982.

———. *The Great Triumvirate: Webster, Clay and Calhoun.* New York, 1987.

Prucha, Francis J. *Sword of the Republic.* New York, 1969.

————. *American Indian Policy in the Formative Years: The Indian Trade and Intercourse Acts.* Cambridge, Mass., 1962.

Ravenel, Harriott Horry. *Life and Times of William Lowndes of South Carolina.* Boston, 1901.

Remini, Robert V. *Martin Van Buren and the Making of the Democratic Party.* New York, 1959.

————. *Andrew Jackson and the Course of American Empire, 1767–1821.* Vol. I, New York, 1977.

————. *Andrew Jackson and the Course of American Freedom, 1822–1832.* Vol. 2, New York, 1981.

————. *Andrew Jackson and the Course of American Democracy, 1833–1845.* Vol. 3, New York, 1984.

Schaper, William A. *Sectionalism and Representation in South Carolina.* Chicago, 1916; rpr. New York, 1968.

Sellers, Charles G. *James K. Polk, Jacksonian: 1795–1843.* Princeton, N.J., 1957.

————. *James K. Polk, Continentalist: 1843–1846.* Princeton, N.J., 1966.

Shore, Laurence. *Southern Capitalists: The Ideological Leaderships of an Elite, 1832–1885.* Chapel Hill, 1986.

Stewart, James Brewer. "'A Great Talking and Eating Machine': Patriarchy, Mobilization and the Dynamic of Nullification in South Carolina." *Civil War History,* XXVII, No. 3 (September, 1981).

Van Deusen, Glyndon. *William Henry Seward.* New York, 1967.

————. *The Life of Henry Clay.* Boston, 1937.

————. *The Jacksonian Era.* New York, 1959.

Viola, Herman J. *Thomas L. McKenney: Architect of America's Early Indian Policy, 1816–1830.* Chicago, 1974.

Wallace, David Duncan. *South Carolina: A Short History.* Columbia, S.C., 1961.

White, Laura A. *Robert Barnwell Rhett: Father of Secession.* New York, 1931.

Woodward, C. Vann. *The Burden of Southern History.* Rev. ed. Baton Rouge, 1960.

Index

A.B. affair, 98
Abbeville, 7, 13, 16, 27, 30, 31, 33, 105, 111, 183
Aberdeen, George Hamilton Gordon, earl of, 271–73, 284, 300, 301
Abert, Major John, 65
Abolition of slavery: 83, 218, 239, 270, 271, 290, 295, 304, 306, 313, 314, 326, 341; in the District of Columbia, 118, 200, 201, 203, 204, 206, 244; abolitionists, 183, 197, 200, 201, 210, 211, 244, 250; and slave trade, 201, 206; in Texas, 270, 272
Adams, Charles Francis, xvii
Adams, John, 24
Adams, John Quincy: memoirs of, xvii; as classical scholar, 35; as secretary of state, 58, 59, 67, 69; defends Jackson, 70, 77; presidential campaign, 80, 92, 93, 96, 99; and Missouri debates, 83; and free-soil argument, 84, 85, 100, 103, 104; and election of 1824, pp. 108, 109, 111, 113; first annual message, 113, 118, 129, 130; campaign rhetoric of, 131, 162; presents abolitionist petitions, 200, 204; gagged, 205, 279; gag rule repealed, 218, 281, 288, 302, 317
Alabama, 71, 208, 243, 257, 264
Albany, N.Y., 45, 49, 88
Albany *Argus*, 97
Albany Regency, 166
Alec, 183
Algeria, 305
Alexandria, Va., 124, 198
Alien and Sedition acts, 136
Allen, William, 297, 302, 303
Ambrister, Robert, 68, 71, 81

Amelia Island, 65, 69
American Colonization Society, 35, 200, 208
American Fur Company, 73, 96
American Revolution, 4. *See also* Revolutionary war
American River, 322
American system, 108, 113, 118, 130, 136, 162, 176, 191, 192, 229, 252
Antislavery movement, 314, 316, 326
Appling, Ga., 15, 16
Arbuthnot, Alexander, 68, 71, 81
Argus of Western America, 173–74
Aristotle, 333, 337
Arizona, 301
Arkansas Territory, 72, 268
Ashburton, Alexander Baring, Lord, 247
Astor, John Jacob, 73, 96
Atkinson, General Henry, 76, 79
Augusta, Ga., 9, 128, 157, 327
Austria-Hungary, 314

Bacon, Ezekiel, 36, 43
Balch, Alfred, 176
Baldwin, Henry, 100
Baltimore, Md.: commercial community of, 45, 221; Democratic convention of 1835, p. 225; Democratic convention of 1844, pp. 258, 263, 269, 277; Democratic convention of 1848, pp. 309, 314
Baltimore and Ohio railroad, 216, 293
Baltimore *Merchant*, 228
Bancroft, George, 222, 278, 279
Bank of South Carolina, 234
Bank of the United States, 185, 187; recharter, veto of, 209; deposits, 209, 227, 230, 239, 249; recharter bill, 244–46, 250

356

Barbour, James, 264
Barbour, Philip P., 94–96
Barry, William T., 166, 174
Barstow, Zedekiah, 16
Bath plantation, 33, 46, 49, 52, 60, 61, 67, 78, 110, 112, 122, 219
Battles: Chippewa, 47, 62; Horseshoe Bend, 49; New Orleans, 51, 52, 165; Lundy's Lane, 62
Bayley, Thomas H., 324
Beaufort County, S.C., 11
Bell, John, 235
Benton, Thomas Hart, 73; attacks JCC, 79, 97, 277; and Webster-Hayne debate, 170; and Jefferson dinner, 172, 211, 226, 230, 242; quoted, 247, 261, 286–88, 302, 303, 308, 318, 319, 322, 338, 339
Berrien, John M., 166, 177
Bibb, George M., 211
Bibb, William, 35
Biddle, Nicholas, 209
Birney, James G., 282
Blackstone, Sir William, 333
Bladensburg, Md., 49
Blair, Francis Preston, 174, 175, 209, 241, 258, 282, 292
Blue Ridge Mountains, 216
Bluffton, S.C., movement, 281, 293, 300
Boisseau, James E., 222, 244
Bonaparte, Napoleon, 28, 37, 43, 46
Bonneau, John C., 105
Bonneau Ferry plantation, 26, 33
Boston, Mass., 45, 105, 228
Boston Quarterly Review, 245
Bowie, George, 27
Branch, John, 166, 177
Bright, Jesse, 316
British Columbia, 284
British Northwest Fur Company, 76
Brooke, Francis, 186
Brough, Mr., 123
Brougham and Vaux, Henry Peter, Lord, 271
Brown, Aaron, 288, 289
Brown, Major General Jacob, 62; and army reorganization, 65, 75, 88; and army reduction, 90, 91
Brown vs. *Board of Education*, 349

Brown's Indian Queen Hotel, 172, 173
Brownson, Orestes, 245
Brussels, Belgium, 283, 321, 336
Bryant, William Cullen, 254
Buchanan, James, 248, 253, 254, 256, 277, 288, 290, 291, 297, 300
Buffalo convention, 315
Burke, Edmund, 332
Burr, Aaron, 18
Burt, Armistead, 1, 248, 295, 339
Burt, Martha, 339
Butler, Andrew, 318
Butler, Benjamin F., 262, 278
Butler, Pierce, 231
Byrdsall, Fitzwilliam, 255, 256, 325

Caldwell, Major John, 10
Calhoun, Andrew Pickins (eldest son of JCC), 34, 52, 123, 157, 184, 215, 220, 221, 243, 244, 264, 265, 268, 283, 294, 312, 320, 334, 345
Calhoun, Anna Maria. *See* Clemson, Anna Maria Calhoun (daughter of JCC)
Calhoun, Catherine Montgomery (grandmother of JCC), 8, 9
Calhoun, Eugenia Chappell (daughter-in-law of JCC), 220, 221, 283
Calhoun, Floride (daughter of JCC), 48, 52
Calhoun, Floride Bonneau (wife of JCC), 1, 21, 32, 283, 296, 344; described, 32, 220; marries JCC, 33; pregnancies of, 34, 46, 52, 122, 155, 156; snubs Peggy Eaton, 167, 168, 183, 184, 193, 219, 221, 244, 265; stroke of, 266–68, 273
Calhoun, James (older brother of JCC), 15, 265
Calhoun, James (uncle of JCC), 9
Calhoun, James Edward (son of JCC), 122, 158, 168, 220, 283, 320
Calhoun, John C.
—early life: birth, 6; at Waddel's school, 13; at Yale, 16–20; influence on, of Dwight and Silliman, 19; at Tapping Reeve's law school, 22–24; studies law with Henry W. DeSaussure, 25, 27; apprenticeship in Abbeville, 27; admitted

to S.C. bar and chancery court, 27; as a lawyer, 28, 34
—family life: illnesses, 20, 49, 102, 154, 251, 287, 295, 312, 319, 320, 326, 327, 339; visits Floride Bonneau Colhoun, 20, 26; courts cousin Floride, 32; marriage, 33, 220; purchases Bath plantation, 33; wife and children, 34, 48, 52, 103, 121–23; love of farming, 48, 49; loss of crops, 68, 121–23; Washington residence, 102–104, 122, 223, 224, 283; at Oakly, 103, 122, 123; religion, 104; at Pendleton, 110, 123; hospitality, 124; at Fort Hill, 155–57, 242, 243, 264, 265; Dahlonega gold mine, 215, 242, 267; financial condition, 219, 264, 320; brothers-in-law, 219, 220
—political beliefs: 2–5; "The Discourse on the Constitution," 3, 333–35, 337, 341, 342; concerning Chesapeake-Leopard incident, 29; upon election to S.C. legislature, 30; opposes caucus nomination for vice-president, 31; on slavery, 84–86; "Exposition" and "Protest," 137, 158, 162, 168, 170; Fort Hill address, 181, 182, 184, 188, 193; Memphis memorial, 298, 299; southern address, 324, 325, 328–34, 336, 340–45
—in Twelfth Congress: elected to, 31; attends first session, 34; spars with Randolph, 37, 38, 40, 41; finds Madison indecisive, 39; chairman, foreign relations committee, 42
—in Thirteenth Congress: 43; attacks Federalists, 44; opposes Gallatin tax policy, 45; and War of 1812 loan bill, 47, 48; defends the administration, 50; proposes military preparedness, 51, 52, 54
—in Fourteenth Congress: proposes bank bill, 53; favors tariff of 1816, p. 54; pushes internal improvements, 55; defends compensation law, 55; and bonus bill, 56, 57
—presidential campaigns: of 1844, pp. 238, 241, 247–64, 268, 269, 276; of 1848, pp. 291, 292; Memphis convention, 293, 294

—as secretary of war: accepts appointment, 60; reasserts civilian control, 62; reorganizes army, 64–67; and Seminole War affair, 68–71; Indian policy, 71–75; partisan assault on, 78–81, 86–88; and Mix contract, 86, 87; northern trip, 88, 89; army reduction, 90–92; appropriations cut, 92; presidential campaign, 93, 94, 96–101; factory system abolished, 96, 97; surveying trip in Pennsylvania, 106; Lafayette visit, 107
—as vice-president: elected, 101, 102; appoints Senate committees, 114; construes role, 116; Patrick Henry–Onslow exchange, 116, 117, 123; on Randolph, 117; alliance with Jackson, 118, 119; *United States Telegraph* promotes presidential candidacy of, 119, 120; and Mix contract investigation, 124, 125; tables woolens bill, 127; Jackson-JCC ticket, 129, 130, 158; and tariff of 1828, pp. 133–37; "Exposition" and "Protest," 137, 158–62, 164, 168–70; and nullification controversy, 158, 162, 170, 179–82, 189, 190, 197–99; Peggy Eaton affair, 167, 168, 174; break with Jackson, 168, 174–77; at Jefferson dinner, 172, 173; conversation with Hammond, 177, 178; Fort Hill address, 181, 182; breaks tie against Van Buren confirmation, 185, 186; resigns, 193; and compromise tariff, 193, 194
—as secretary of state: appointment, 272–74; and British imperialism, 270, 271; and Texas annexation, 272, 280, 284–86; and Oregon boundary, 272, 274, 277, 280, 284, 286, 287, 296, 298, 299, 301; and Pakenham correspondence, 275–77; and Bluffton movement, 280–82; and Polk, 282
—in U.S. Senate: elected, 192; and compromise tariff, 193, 194; and force bill, 194–97, 199; at nullification convention, 198; abolition petitions, 201, 203, 204; debate with Rives, 203; and First and Fifth amendments, 204–206; abolition literature in mails, 205, 206; and Pendleton resolutions, 206; votes to censure Jackson, 210; and select com-

mittee on executive patronage, 211, 212–14; characterizes Clay, 226; characterizes Webster, 226; anticipates panic of 1837, pp. 227, 228; supports Van Buren administration, 229–37; and specie clause, 230, 231, 233; rapprochement with Van Buren, 236; on Tyler, 244, 245; resignation, 258; Polk, 288–90, 296–305, 308, 312, 313, 322–24; reelected, 295; and Mexican-American War, 301–305, 308–13; and Wilmot Proviso, 305, 306, 308, 310, 317, 318, 321, 323; and Taylor, 320, 327, 338, 340; southern address, 320–24; "The Disquisition on Government," 328–33, 334; last speech, 340, 341; and southern moderates, 342, 343; on Webster's March 7, 1850, speech, 342; death, 343–45

Calhoun, John C., Jr. (son of JCC), 121, 122, 158, 268, 283, 319, 327, 344

Calhoun, Margaret Green (daughter-in-law of JCC), 221, 265

Calhoun, Martha Caldwell (mother of JCC), 10, 15

Calhoun, Martha Cornelia (younger daughter of JCC), 158, 168, 221–23, 265, 268, 283, 296

Calhoun, Patrick (father of JCC), 7, 8, 9, 11, 13, 15

Calhoun, Patrick (grandfather of JCC), 6

Calhoun, Patrick (son of JCC), 121, 157, 222, 223, 243, 262, 266, 268, 268*n*, 272, 283, 294, 320, 321, 345

Calhoun, Patrick (younger brother of JCC), 15, 265

Calhoun, William (older brother of JCC), 15, 265

Calhoun, William Lowndes (youngest son of JCC), 168, 221, 222, 268, 283, 319

California–New Mexico admission bill, 322, 323

California Territory, 301, 316, 317, 319, 321–23, 327, 340, 342

Cambreleng, Churchill C., 120, 128, 172, 230, 235

Campbell, David, 261

Campbell, John, 166

Canada, 4, 49, 50, 67

Cane Brake plantation, 264, 274

Capers, Gerald M., 349

Carlyle, Thomas, 332

Casey, Dr. Thomas, 46

Cass, Lewis, 74, 179, 190, 191, 248, 277, 278, 302, 315, 317, 320

Castle Hill plantation, 203

Castle Pinckney, 191

Chappell, John Joel, 221

Charleston, S.C.: 9, 11, 26, 52, 124, 128, 157, 179, 180, 189, 190, 219, 263, 291, 292, 300, 311, 312, 326, 344, 345; JCC's opinion of, 27, 32; merchants, 45; harbor of, 191, 195

Charleston *Courier*, 218

Charleston *Gazette*, 15

Charleston *Mercury*, 163, 231, 234, 241, 242, 258, 263, 280, 292, 300

Chesapeake and Ohio canal, 106

Chesapeake Bay, 67, 86

Cheves, Langdon: 34, 36; navy bill of, defeated, 41, 44, 47, 166; and Pendleton resolution, 206

Chitty, Thomas, 21

Cincinnati, Ohio, 217

Clapp, J. Milton, 292

Clarkson, Thomas, 271

Clay, Henry: 34, 52; committee assignments, 36, 38–43, 47, 52, 53, 56, 58–60, 75; partisan attack on JCC, 79–81; Missouri Compromise, 85, 89, 101; and election of 1824, pp. 108, 109, 114–20, 125, 129, 130; and tariff of 1828, pp. 133, 134, 161, 162, 184–87, 191; and compromise tariff, 193, 194, 208; censure of Jackson, 209, 226, 227, 229, 236, 239–41; and legislative program of 1841, pp. 244–47, 250–53; and Texas annexation, 277, 283, 339, 342, 344

Clayton, John M., 317

Clemson, Anna Maria Calhoun (daughter of JCC), 2, 26, 157, 220, 223, 235, 239, 240, 243, 262, 266–68, 277, 283, 305, 320, 335, 345

Clemson, Floride Elizabeth, 267

Clemson, John Calhoun, 266

Clemson, Thomas Green, 224, 242, 243, 262, 264–67, 283, 301, 314, 320, 335, 345

Clergy Hall, 95, 110, 124

Clinton, De Witt, 31, 82, 89, 100, 112, 130
Clinton, George, 30, 31
Coast defense program, 66, 67
Cobb, Howell, 339
Coit, Margaret L., 349
Coke, Sir Edward, 332
Colhoun, Floride Bonneau (mother-in-law of JCC), 20–22, 24, 25, 32, 103, 104, 219
Colhoun, James Edward (brother-in-law of JCC), 21, 219, 229, 283, 319
Colhoun, John Ewing, Jr. (brother-in-law of JCC), 21, 104, 155, 156, 215, 216, 219
Colhoun, John Ewing, Sr. (cousin of JCC), 20, 25
Colhoun, Colonel Joseph E. (cousin of JCC), 29, 31, 55
Colhoun, Maria, 268
Collamer, Jacob, 338
Colorado, 301
Columbia, S.C., 11, 27, 193, 195, 223, 232, 284, 297, 301, 322
Columbus, Ohio, 285
Commander, J. M., 314
Commerford, John, 254
Concord (N.H.) *Patriot,* 174
Condorcet, Marquis de, 18
Congress: Thirty-first, 2; Twenty-fifth, special session of, 228–32; Twenty-sixth, 235, 241; Twenty-seventh, special session of, 244, 245; Twenty-eighth, 262, 279, 286, 306; Twenty-ninth, 310; Thirtieth, 312, 314, 319, 321; Thirty-first, 339
Connecticut, 22, 250, 256
Connor, Henry Workman, 326
Constitution, U.S.: Bill of Rights, 2, 12, 206; Article IV, 85, 158–60, 162; commerce clause, 176; Fifth Amendment, 204, 206, 207; and executive veto power, 253, 306, 307; fugitive slave clause, 315, 328, 332, 340
Construction Construed and Constitutions Vindicated, 331
Conventions: Nashville, 2, 3; S.C. constitutional (1790), 11; Democratic, 338
Cooper, Thomas, 129, 134, 159, 162, 170
Corn Laws, 298, 299

Corpus Christi, Tex., 301
Corwin, Thomas, 313
Cotton market, 105, 128, 156
Council Bluffs, Iowa, 77
Crallé, Richard, 184, 228, 347
Crawford, William Harris: 31, 96, 120, 125, 126, 131, 165, 174, 207, 261; seeks presidency, 58; as treasury secretary, 59; and army reorganization plan, 64, 65, 75; partisan attack on JCC, 79–81, 89, 90, 92; Van Buren supports, 97; illness, 99, 100; caucus nomination, 99, 101; and election of 1824, pp. 108, 111
Crittenden, John J., 240
Crowninshield, Benjamin, 59
Cumming, Colonel William, 95
Current, Richard, 349
Cushing, Caleb, 256, 260

Dahlonega, Ga., 215, 220, 265–67
Dallas, Alexander J., 51
Dallas, George M., 100, 101, 269, 279
Dawson, William C., 237
Day, Jeremiah, 20
Declaration of Independence, 35, 84, 183, 316, 332
Delaware, 94, 193
Deposit banks, 232
Depression of 1819, p. 78
DeSaussure, Henry William, 21, 25–27
Detroit, Mich., 43, 55
Dickens, Asbury, 229
Dickerson, Mahlon, 157
Dickinson, Daniel, 314, 315
"Discourse on the Constitution, The," xv, 3, 333, 334, 335, 337, 341, 342
"Disquisition on Government, The," 328–33, 337
Dix, John A., 287, 313, 315
Donegal, 6
Donelson, Andrew J., 166, 168, 172, 278, 285, 286, 291
Douglas, Stephen A., 322, 323
Drayton, Colonel William, 128, 179, 207
Drucker, Peter, 349
Dwight, Timothy, 16, 17, 18, 19, 36, 39

Eaton, John H., 136, 165, 166, 168, 174, 175, 177

Eaton, Peggy O'Neil, 165, 167–69, 174
Edgefield, S.C., district of, 22, 95, 110, 217, 223, 231, 274, 304
Edgefield letter, 232
Edwards, Ninian, 98, 119
Elizabeth City, N.C., 67
Elliot, Jonathan, 136
Elmore, Franklin H., 234, 235, 257, 264, 282, 291
Embargo Act, 45
Eppes, John W., 51
Erie Canal, 106, 169, 176, 216, 293
Everett, Edward, 270, 272
Ewing, Thomas, 245, 338
Expedition, 77
"Exposition" and "Protest," 137, 158, 162, 168, 170

Fairfax County, Va., 119
Farmer's Hall, 206
Featherstonhaugh, George, 215
Federalist Papers, The, 37, 47, 333
Felder, John, 20, 22
Fillmore, Millard, 340
Florida: Spanish, 64, 65; East and West, 67–71, 174; territory of, 92; state of, 154
Floyd, John, 177, 182, 183, 184, 186
Foote, Henry S., 1, 342, 343
Foote Resolution, 164
Force bill, 194, 199, 237, 244
Forsyth, John, 174, 175, 196, 197
Fort Barrancas, 68
Fort Bent, 283
Fort Hill address, 181, 182, 184, 188, 193
Fort Hill plantation, 154, 155, 177, 214, 215, 219, 231, 242, 243, 247, 262, 264, 267, 273, 274, 283, 296, 311, 312, 319, 328, 335
Fort Moultrie, 191
Fort Niagara, 67
Fort Towson, 268
Forty-ninth parallel, 284, 297, 298
France: 18, 37, 38, 42, 43, 227, 228, 260, 314; and Berlin and Milan decrees, 28; spoliation of, 213; settlement of, 214
Frankfort, Ky., 173
Fredericks, Mr., 156, 242, 243, 265
Freehling, William W., 349

Free soil: 84, 218, 247; convention of 1848, p. 316
Free-soilers, 313–16, 321, 323, 324, 326
French and Indian War, 9
French Revolution, 4, 38
Furber, Frederick, 222
Fur trade, 73, 74, 96, 97

Gadsby Hotel, 165
Gadsden, Christopher, 17
Gadsden, James, 293, 300
Gag rule, 288
Gaillard, John, 120
Gaines, Leonard Edmund, 63, 65, 69, 91
Gales, Joseph, 171
Gallatin, Albert, 45, 51, 91, 213
Gardiner, Julia, 272
General antislavery convention (1842), 271
Georgia: colony of, 9; state of, 13, 15, 31, 58, 64, 65, 67, 110, 111, 126, 154, 176, 216, 220, 237, 257; and Cherokees, 187, 188
Gibbon, Edward, 48
Gibson, David C., 215
Gibson, George, 78
Giddings, Joshua, 302, 313
Gilmer, Thomas W., 234, 256, 260, 261, 269, 272
Glorious Revolution, 4
Godwin, Parke, 255, 256
Gold rush, California, 323
Gould, James, 22, 23, 24, 39
Gouverneur, Samuel, 112, 182
Graniteville, S.C., 218
Great Britain: 2, 18, 54, 59, 68, 70, 202, 227, 228, 247, 270, 271, 272, 275, 276, 284, 291, 296–98, 301; trade policies, 28; and impressment, 29, 41, 42; in North America, 35, 37–39; orders-in-council, 38, 41, 42
Great Dismal Swamp, 67
Green, Benjamin, 285, 286
Green, Duff, 116, 119, 131, 136, 165, 175, 180, 206, 208, 221, 237, 254, 262, 270, 275, 285, 286, 311
Greenville District, S.C., 110, 234
Gregg, William, 217, 218
Grosvenor, Thomas P., 44, 46, 47

Grundy, Felix, 35, 44, 212
Guadalupe Hidalgo, Treaty of, 313

Hackett, James Henry, 223
Hagner, Peter, 88
Haiti, 115, 118
Hale, John P., 313
Hamilton, Alexander, 53, 159, 165, 197, 239, 332, 340
Hamilton, James, Jr., 128, 163, 165, 166, 168, 179, 180, 182, 188, 189, 192, 193, 231, 234
Hamlin, Hannibal, 314
Hammond, Jabez, 254
Hammond, James H., xvii, 177–79, 218, 234, 237, 259, 293, 304, 305, 343
Hampton-Sydney College, 13
Hannegan, Edward, 297
Harper, Chancellor William, 163
Harpers Ferry, Va., 216
Harrisburg, Pa., 101, 129, 236
Harrison, William Henry, 227, 236, 237, 240, 244, 321, 327
Hartz, Louis, 349
Hayne, Robert Y.: 108, 118, 179, 191–93, 196, 198, 216, 217, 231, 294; and tariff of 1828, pp. 134, 135, 166; reply to Foote, 170; to Webster, 171
Hayward, William Henry, 298
Hector, 61
Henshaw, David, 256
Hill, Isaac, 174
Hill's boardinghouse, 1, 338, 343
Hobbes, Thomas, 136, 332
Hofstadter, Richard, 347
Holmes, Isaac, 289, 296
Holmes, John, 316
Horn, Henry, 248
House of Representatives, U.S.: v, 5, 107, 112, 234, 235, 286, 300, 302, 313, 318, 319, 324, 325, 340; abolition petitions in, 200; gag rule in, 200, 204, 205, 279, 286; organization in Twentieth Congress, 263
Houston, Samuel, 275, 285
Howard, Tilghman, 284, 285
Hudson's Bay Company, 284
Huger, Daniel, 179, 259, 295
Hume, David, 331

Hunter, Robert M. T., 234, 235, 254, 256–58, 260, 261, 278, 288, 296, 309

Illinois, 82, 83
Indiana, 82, 200
Indians: Six Nations, 6, 75; Cherokee nation, 7, 8, 72, 73; Creek nation, 9, 49, 73, 187, 188; War Department policies on, 64, 71; land of, 72; emigration of, 72; and Georgia, 111
Ingersoll, Charles J., 64, 65
Ingham, Samuel, 81, 111, 164, 166, 186, 208, 226, 256
Internal improvements, 3, 55, 253
Ireland, 6
Issey, 265

Jackson, Andrew: 51, 52, 61–65, 67, 177, 185, 213, 225, 229, 232, 244, 252; correspondence of, xvii; and invasion of Florida, 68, 69, 70, 71, 78, 80, 81; nominated for president, 100, 102; and election of 1824, pp. 108, 111, 112, 118, 119, 121; campaign rhetoric, 131, 166, 167, 171; and Jefferson dinner, 172, 173; break with JCC, 174–76; and Bank of the United States, 187, 209–10; and nullification, 190, 191, 193, 202; and Texas annexation, 269, 288, 321
Jackson, Rachel, 165
Jameson, J. Franklin, 348
Jefferson, Thomas, 12, 35, 82, 110, 137, 159, 160, 162, 188, 317, 318, 333, 340
Jenkins, John S., 347
Jesup, Thomas Sidney, 78
Johnson, Cave, 278
Johnson, James, 76, 78
Johnson, Richard M., 36, 43, 59, 76, 78, 277
Jones, Anson, 275, 286
Jones, John Winston, 235, 263

Kane, John K., 280, 290
Kendall, Amos, 173, 175, 209
Kentuckian in New York, The, 224
Kentucky, 34, 98, 108, 176, 185, 240
Kinderhook, N.Y., 263
King Charles II, 249

King, John P., 204, 211
King, Preston, 306, 314
King, Rufus, 82, 83
Knox, John, 330
Knoxville, Tenn., 217

Lafayette, Marquis de, 107
Lakes: Erie, 43, 47, 56; Ontario, 43, 56, 67, 88; Champlain, 49, 67; Sakakawea, 76
Langdon, John, 31
Laurens County, S.C., 7
Legaré, Hugh, 163, 179, 205, 207, 234
Leigh, Benjamin W., 195, 198
Lewis, Dixon, 208, 234, 235, 254, 257, 273, 292, 300
Lewis, William B., 166, 168
Liberal party, 300
Lieber, Francis, 345
Lincoln, Abraham, 314
Linn, Dr. Lewis Fields, 224, 228
Litchfield, Conn., 22, 23, 24
Livingston, Edward, 190
Locke, John, 14, 15, 39, 316
Locofocos, 254, 255, 325–26
London, 105
Long Canes Creek, 7, 9
Long Island Sound, 45
Long, Major Stephen H., 76, 79, 216
Louisiana, 190, 191, 307
Louis Philippe, King, 213, 224
Louisville, Cincinnati, and Charleston Railroad Company, 217, 218, 293
Lowndes, William, 34, 35, 36, 45, 47, 52, 53, 56, 59, 67, 89, 93, 99
Lumpkin, Wilson, 309
Lynchburg Jeffersonian and Virginia Times, 184
Lyttelton, William Henry, 7

MacBride, Dr. James, 20, 52
McClintock, H. W., 123, 222
McCulloch case, 171
Macdonough, Thomas, 49
McDow, William P., 232
McDuffie, George: 95, 96, 108, 125, 129, 130; on tariff of 1828, pp. 135, 136, 161, 163, 293; radical nullifier, 179; extremist speech of, 180; supports

Bank of the United States, 187, 208, 234, 259, 260, 269, 272, 273; and Texas annexation, 284, 286, 293, 295
McKay, James J., 299
McKenney, Thomas, 72, 73, 74, 97–99, 102
McLane, Louis, 94, 185, 291, 298, 314
McLean, John, 101, 136, 164, 166, 182
Macomb, General Alexander, 63
Macon, Nathaniel, 114
Madison, James: 22, 30, 36, 332, 333; war message of, 42, 43, 50, 53; vetoes bonus bill, 56, 57; report on Alien and Sedition Acts, 159, 160, 181, 196
Maine: district of, 49, 67; separates from Massachusetts, 83; state of, 276
Mallary, Rollin C., 132
Manchester economics, 162
Mandan Villages (Bismarck, N.D.), 76
Mangum, Willie, 225
Marcy, William L., 202
Marengo County, Ala., 220, 243, 244
Marshall, John, 171, 190, 196, 332, 333, 340, 341
Martineau, Harriet, 344, 345
Marx, Karl, 3
Maryland, 59, 81, 94, 98, 176
Mason-Dixon line, 314, 315
Mason, James M., 1, 309, 340, 341, 342
Massachusetts, 36, 130, 171, 196, 208, 225, 276
Matamoros incident, 302
Maxcy, Virgil, 42, 81, 100, 102, 166, 259, 260, 270, 272, 273
Maysville veto, 176
Meigs, Return J., 73, 101
Memphis, 294–95
Memphis convention, 293
Memphis memorial, 300
Mexican-American War, 303, 309–13
Mexico, 285, 286, 296, 301–13
Mexico City, 285, 301
Mill, John Stuart, 3
Millwood plantation, 219
Mine La Motte, 224
Miner, Charles, 118
Mississippi, 208
Missouri: territory of, 73, 81; debates over slavery in, 82, 83–85, 89, 184,

191, 201, 218, 307, 317, 318, 322, 323, 328, 340, 343; state of, 108, 228, 242, 248
Missouri Compromise, 307, 315–18, 340
Missouri Fur Company, 73, 96
Mitchell, David, 73
Mix, Elijah, 86, 87, 124, 125, 126, 130
Mobile, Ala., 67, 326
Monroe, James: and war hawks, 39, 40; elected president, 58; cabinet appointments of, 58–60, 62, 68, 69; and Jackson, 70, 71, 75, 78, 79; on Missouri question, 84, 92, 96, 98, 112, 131, 175
Monsieur Townson, 224
Monterrey, battle of, 303
Montreal, 88
Morris, Gouverneur, 330, 331
Morton, Marcus, 168
Murphy, William S., 271, 284

Nashville, Tenn., 289, 338
Nashville *Banner,* 189
Nashville committee, 131, 165
Nashville convention, 2, 3, 338
National Advocate, 97
National Journal, 99, 116, 120
National Theatre, 223
Negroes: 19, 72; free, 85, 136, 276
Netherlands, 59
New England, 20, 24, 45, 47, 96, 98, 107, 124, 170, 183, 188, 255
New Hampshire, 44, 225
New Haven, 17, 18, 20, 45
New Jersey, 157
New Mexico Territory, 315, 317–19, 321, 322, 327, 341, 342
New Orleans, 49, 294, 326, 327
Newport, R.I., 20, 21, 32
New Theatre, 310
New York, 30, 31, 43, 47, 49, 98, 112, 119, 124, 126, 208, 225, 233, 249, 250, 256, 264
New York City, 16, 67, 89, 105, 216, 254, 255, 260
New York *Courier,* 97
New York *Herald,* 338
New York *Morning Post,* 256
New York *Patriot,* 99
New York *Plebeian,* 255

Nicholson, A. O. P., 317, 318
Niebuhr, Barthold, 159, 333, 334
Niles, Hezekiah, 129
Niles, John M., 250, 313, 318
Niles' Register, 80
Ninety-Six, district of, 6, 7, 12, 13
Noah, Mordecai M., 174
Noble, Mary, 8
Nonintercourse Act, 45
Norfolk, Va., 214
North Carolina, 7, 67, 126, 127, 176, 177, 179, 184, 225, 248
Nullification, 160, 161, 179, 181, 187–90, 194, 195, 197–99, 202, 207, 232, 237, 244, 320, 330
Nullification crisis of 1832, pp. 325, 329

Oakly, 113, 154, 155
Ohio, 82, 96, 101, 108, 216, 227
Old Point Comfort, 86
Onís, Luis de, 67
Orangeburg, S.C., 28
Ordinance of 1787, pp. 84, 315, 316, 340, 341
Oregon: boundary of, 272, 279, 297; territory of, 284, 288, 289, 291, 295–97, 299–303, 307, 315, 317–19, 323
Osborne, Selleck, 24

Pakenham, Richard, 175–277, 284, 297, 300, 301
Palfrey, John Gorham, 313
Palmerston, Henry John Temple, Lord, 300
Palo Alto, battle of, 303
Panama mission, 113–115, 121
Panic and depression of 1837, pp. 218, 227, 233
Paredes y Arrillaga, Mariano, 302
Parker, General David, 65
Parrington, Vernon M., 349
Peace of Amiens, 18
Pea Patch, 67
Peel, Sir Robert, 298, 300
Pendleton, S.C., 21, 33, 105, 110, 112, 128, 154, 157, 168, 335
Pendleton Academy, 222
Pendleton Agricultural Society, 157, 335

364

Pendleton (S.C.) *Messenger,* 182, 217, 337, 338
Pennsylvania: colony of, 6, 7, 9, 96; state of, 101, 102, 105, 107, 118, 124, 136, 164, 176, 208, 217, 254, 256
Pensacola, Fla., 68
Perry, Benjamin F., 201, 345, 346
Perry, Oliver Hazard, 47
"Pet" banks, 209
Petersburg, Va., 214
Petigru, James Louis, 16n, 207, 345, 346
Philadelphia, Pa., 45, 221, 248, 319
Phoenix *Gazette,* 124, 125
Pickens, Andrew, 16, 26, 34
Pickens, Andrew, Jr., 16, 20, 21, 24, 39
Pickens, Ezekiel, 26
Pickens, Francis, 179, 198, 208, 235, 243, 248, 256, 257, 259, 278, 282, 283, 289, 291, 293–95, 304, 335
Pickering, Timothy, 44, 48
Pillow, Gideon, 278
Pinckney, Henry L., 205
Pitt, William, the Elder, 39
Pittsburgh, Pa., 100, 106
Pleasonton, Stephen, 251
Poindexter, George, 208, 212
Poinsett, Joel, 157, 179, 190, 191, 207, 303, 345, 346
Political parties: Federalists, 2, 23, 24, 40, 41, 43, 44, 48, 52, 53, 82, 98, 100, 126, 162, 169, 191, 193, 195; Jeffersonian Republicans, 24, 43, 53, 58; Bucktails, 81, 82, 88, 89; Family party, 81, 98, 100, 101; Clintonians, 88, 90, 254; Radicals, 90, 125, 131; People's party, 99, 100; Amalgamators, 100; Democrats, 207, 208, 246–49, 284, 285, 290, 296, 298, 302–304, 308, 309, 313–15, 317, 323, 324, 327; Whigs, 207, 208, 219, 225–37, 239, 244–51, 279, 287, 294, 296, 301, 303, 306–309, 313, 314, 318, 321, 322, 324, 325, 328, 339; Conservatives, 230, 231, 233; Liberty party, 282, 307; Hunkers, 291, 314; Free Soil party, 313–17, 321, 322, 325, 327; Barnburners, 314
Polk, James K.: correspondence of, 176, 198, 230, 234, 248, 257; presidential candidacy of, 278, 280, 281; calls Nashville meeting, 282, 283, 287–91,
296–302, 304, 308–10, 313, 319, 323, 325; and Calhoun, 282, 288, 290, 296–305, 308, 312, 313, 322–24; inaugural message of, 290
Popular sovereignty, 314, 316, 318
Porter, Peter B., 36, 42, 43, 185
Portsmouth, N.H., 130
Preston, William C., 137, 195, 208, 230, 231, 233, 237, 246
Princeton University, 22
Princeton (ship), 272
Providence College (Brown), 16, 222
Prussia, 59
Public lands, 211, 230, 241

Quakers, 200
Quincy, Josiah, 43

Raleigh, N.C., 184
Ramsey, I. G. M., 248
Randolph, John: in Twelfth Congress, 34; coins "war hawk" label, 36, 37, 39, 40, 43, 52; opposes bank bill, 53; described, 114; in U.S. Senate, 115, 116, 124, 130, 191
Rawdon, Francis Lord, 39
Reeve, Tapping: described, 22, 23; law school of, 24; network of, 36, 81
Regulator movement, 10
Rejon, Manuel, 286
Resaca de la Palma, battle of, 303
Revolutionary war, 10, 79
Reynolds, Thomas, 242
Rhett, James, 292, 300
Rhett, Robert Barnwell, 163, 231, 234, 256, 257–60, 270, 279, 280, 281
Rhode Island, 249
Richardson, J. P., 234
Richmond, Va., 128, 166, 177, 236, 290, 291
Richmond (Va.) *Enquirer,* 97, 119, 249
Richmond junto, 119, 120, 126, 128, 166, 184, 234, 256
Rion, James, 283
Rion, Margaret, 283
Ripley, General Eleazer Wheelock, 63
Ritchie, Thomas, 97, 119, 120, 126, 128, 166, 184, 234, 249, 256, 257, 261, 290, 292, 309, 338
Rivers: Savannah, 33, 110; Tallapoosa,

49; Hudson, 49; Delaware, 67; Mississippi, 71; Yellowstone, 76; Missouri, 76; Red River of the North, 76; St. Peters (Minnesota), 76; St. Lawrence, 88; Ohio, 106, 216; Tugaloo, 110, 217; Seneca, 110, 184; Saluda, 217; Keowee, 217; Columbia, 284, 297, 301; Nueces, 301; Rio Grande, 301–303; American, 323
Rives, William C., 203, 207, 213, 230
Roane, John, 172, 173
Roane, William H., 236, 261, 288
Roberdeau, Major Isaac, 88
Rodney, Caesar, 94
Round Hill Academy, 222
Ruffin, Edmund, 336, 337
Rush, Richard, 59
Ruskin, John, 332
Russia, 43, 59

Sackets Harbor, 88
St. Clairsville, Ohio, 285
St. Dennis Parish, S.C., 26
St. Louis *Enquirer,* 79
St. Marks, Fla., 68
St. Thomas Parish, S.C., 26
Salisbury, N.C., 122
Santa Anna, Antonio Lopez de, 305
Saunders, Romulus, 278, 279
Savannah, Ga., 326
Sawney, Old, 3, 265, 266
Sawney, Young, 265
Schlesinger, Arthur M., Jr., 349
Scotch-Irish, 6, 7, 38
Scotland, 6
Scott, Sir Walter, 223
Scott, General Winfield, 47, 62, 63, 91, 191, 303, 308
Scoville, Joseph A., 1, 254, 256, 257, 258, 329, 340, 345
Seaton, William W., 171
Secession, 188, 281
Seminole War, 64, 65, 68–71
Senate, U.S.: 200, 203, 205, 210, 286, 287, 297–300, 303, 305–309, 312, 313, 319, 323, 324, 339, 340, 343
Seven Buildings, 56
Seward, William H., 250, 322, 328, 339
Shaftesbury, Lord, 39
Shannon, Wilson, 285, 286

Shelby, Isaac, 59, 78
Sherman, Roger, 20
Sidney, Algernon, 317
Silliman, Benjamin, Sr., 19, 20, 36, 39, 346
Simkins, Arthur, 222, 264
Simkins, Eldred, 22, 81, 95, 120, 222
Simkins, Emma, 222
Simkins, Maria, 224
Simms, William Gilmore, 326
Sismondi, Jean Charles, 47
Slamm, Levi, 254, 255, 256
Slavery: 2, 3, 295; density of, in S.C., 11; slave revolts, fear of, 38; at Fort Hill, 156, 161; Nat Turner revolt, 181–83, 197; abolished in West Indies, 200; northern opposition to, 200; in District of Columbia, 200, 201, 202, 203, 204; First Amendment and, 204–206; Fifth Amendment and, 206, 218, 238, 247, 255, 276, 279; and Methodism, 282, 290, 295, 305–11, 313, 322, 325, 331, 333–43; and the territories, 290, 305–307, 317–19
Slave states, 191, 207, 231
Slidell, John, 301
Smith, Adam, 4
Smith, Mrs. Margaret Bayard, 103
Smith, Dr. Nathan, 221
Smith, Samuel, 94
Smith, Truman, 339
Smith, William, 34, 60, 120, 164
Southampton County, 179
Southard, Samuel L., 211
South Carolina: colony of, 3, 6, 9; state of, 21, 31, 36, 37, 38, 52, 95, 98, 99, 105, 110, 126, 154, 158, 164, 169–71, 176, 178; extremists in, 179, 182, 187, 189–91, 194–98, 202, 207, 218, 223, 231, 234, 235, 237, 259, 299, 311, 320, 338
South Carolina College, 31, 95, 159, 320, 346
South Carolina Unionists, 179, 189–91, 196, 207, 210
Southern Literary Messenger, 345
Southern Quarterly Review, 295
Southern Review, 136
Southern Times and the State Gazette, 177
Spain, 67, 71

Spain, August O., 349, 350
Spartanburg County, 7
Specie Circular, 227
Spoils system, 211
Starke, W. Pinckney, 348
Sterling, Ansel, 22
Sterling, Micah, 20, 36, 81, 254
Stevens, Green, 242
Stevenson, Andrew, 130
Stewart, Commodore Charles, 277
Story, Joseph, 310, 332, 333, 341
Stuart, John A., 231
Subtreasury system, 210, 229–33, 235, 246
Swartwout, Samuel, 165
Swift, Benjamin, 306
Swift, General Joseph, 65, 67, 86, 108, 113, 124

Tait, Charles, 69
Tallmadge, James, Jr., 82
Tallmadge, Nathaniel, 230
Tammany Hall, 254
Taney, Roger B., 209, 214
Tariffs: of 1816, p. 53; of 1824, p. 5; Minimum valuation of, 53, 107, 108, 121, 127, 129, 159, 180, 202; of 1828, pp. 132–34, 202; opposition to, 133–35, 154, 158, 168, 169, 180, 186; of 1832, p. 187; Verplanck bill, 193; compromise tariff, 193, 194, 197, 232, 244, 246, 251–53; of 1842, pp. 254, 263, 266, 279; McKay bill, 279, 289, 290, 340; Kane letter, 280, 281; and Walker, 297, 299, 300
Tarleton, Banastre, 39
Taylor, John, 60
Taylor, John, of Caroline, 162, 331
Taylor, John W.: attacks slavery, 82; elected speaker, 89, 90; defeated, 94, 95; reelected speaker, 125; defeated, 130
Taylor, Zachary, 301, 303, 314, 320, 321, 324, 327, 338, 340
Tazewell, Littleton, 114, 119, 120, 164, 165, 234, 254, 256, 261
Tennessee, 71, 176, 189, 216, 227, 235
Texas: 285, 307; annexation of, 247, 268–77, 293, 294; treaty defeated, 280, 281, 284; joint resolution approved, 286, 287, 290, 295, 301

Thomas, Jesse B., 83
Thompson, Smith, 59, 96
Thompson, Waddy, Jr., 230, 234, 237, 285, 303
Tipton, John, 200
Tompkins, Daniel D., 114
Tories: in American Revolution, 10; in S.C., 38
Treasury notes, 230, 245, 246, 252
Treasury surplus, 211, 239, 241, 244, 246, 254, 257
Treaties: of Paris in 1763, p. 9; of Ghent, 49, 59; of Guadelupe Hidalgo, 313
Trist, Nicholas, 313
Troup, George M., 111
Tuck, Amos, 313
Tucker, Beverly, 281
Turnbull, Robert, 129, 134, 135, 170
Turner, Nat, 179, 182, 184, 187
Turney, Hopkins, 247n
Tyler, John: 197, 242, 244, 245, 283, 327; vetoes bank bill, 246, 247, 251, 253; signs tariff bill, 254, 256, 257, 260; and Texas annexation, 269, 270, 287; appoints JCC secretary of state, 272, 273; candidacy of, 277

United States Army, 63, 64, 65
United States Telegraph, 116, 119, 120, 131, 173
Upshur, Abel P., 251, 260, 269, 270, 272, 275

Van Buren, Martin: 82, 88, 191, 192, 193, 200, 207, 218, 225, 285, 287, 290, 291, 306, 314, 316, 317, 321, 322, 331; elected U.S. senator, 94; and speakership, 94, 95; backs Crawford, 95–101, 112, 113; joins Jackson coalition, 119, 120, 125; reelected to Senate, 126; proposes alliance to JCC, 126, 127; on woolens bill, 127, 128, 128n; southern trip, 128; and tariff of 1828, pp. 132–34; as secretary of state, 164–67, 169; at Jefferson dinner, 172, 173; resigns from cabinet, 177; rejected as minister to Great Britain, 185, 186, 187; Jackson–Van Buren ticket of 1832, pp. 185, 188; and gag rule, 204, 205, 212, 213, 214; as president, 218, 227, 228,

229, 232, 233; rapprochement with Calhoun, 236, 239; 1840 campaign, 237, 238, 241; 1844 campaign, 248, 249, 254, 256, 257, 260–63; Texas annexation, 268, 277, 280, 281, 282
Vancouver Island, 284, 297
Vandeventer, Major Christopher, 64, 86, 87, 166, 167, 199, 207
Vattel, Emeric De, 47
Venable, Abraham, 344
Verplanck, Gulian, 193
Virginia: colony of, 9; state of, 30, 31, 58, 94, 119, 126, 165, 166, 176, 177, 179, 192, 194, 195, 203, 233, 234, 244, 250, 254, 260; and Democratic convention of 1843, p. 262
Virginia and Kentucky resolutions, 129, 181
Voltaire, François Marie Arouet, 18
Von Holst, Herman, 347

Waddel, Catherine Calhoun, 14
Waddel, Moses: 13, 14; early teacher of JCC, 14, 15; educational philosophy of, 16, 31; school of, 32, 39, 95
Walker, Robert John, 269, 278, 279, 287, 299
Walsh, Michael, 254
War Department, 60, 80, 81, 87, 88, 96, 97, 199, 252
War of 1812, pp. 43, 52, 56, 127, 195, 326
Washington, D.C., 34, 48, 50, 52, 61, 64, 65, 67, 69, 88, 89, 93, 105, 107, 110, 112, 156, 158, 163, 164, 167, 168, 177, 184, 198, 210, 213, 221, 229, 232, 238, 242, 248, 249, 251, 283, 284, 288–90, 292, 296, 303, 306, 307, 313, 320, 321, 323–25, 328, 337–40
Washington, D.C., *Constitution,* 287, 290, 292, 311
Washington, D.C., *Daily National Intelligencer,* 80, 98, 116, 171, 173, 337
Washington, D.C., *Gazette,* 87, 97
Washington, D.C., *Globe,* 175, 187, 249, 277, 282, 286, 292
Washington, D.C., *Madisonian,* 230, 287, 333
Washington, D.C., *Reformer,* 231

Washington, D.C., *Republican and Congressional Examiner,* 97, 98, 102, 236
Washington, D.C., *Spectator,* 259, 287, 311, 328
Washington, D.C., *Union,* 292, 309, 337
Washington, George, 40
Waxhaw, S.C., 7
Wayland, Francis, 222
Wayland, Thomas, 222
Webster, Daniel: March 7, 1850, speech, 1, 44, 48, 50; opposes bank bill, 53; elected U.S. senator, 130; replies to Hayne, 170–72; on nullification, 182, 190, 192, 195, 196, 207, 227, 228, 242, 247, 270, 294, 300, 310, 332, 341–44
Welles, Gideon, 319
Western Engineer, 77
Western expeditions, 75–77, 80
West Indies, 45, 154
West Point, 88, 157, 244
Wharton, Francis, 277, 279, 287
Wheaton, Henry, 136
Whigs: in American Revolution, 10; political ideology, 80, 197, 252
White, Hugh Lawson, 114, 118, 227
White House, 61, 252, 296, 297, 299, 300, 308
Whitney, Reuben, 4, 213
Wickliffe, Robert, 327
Wilberforce, William, 271
Williams, David, 30, 43
Willington, S.C., 33
Wilmot, David, 305
Wilmot proviso, 306–10, 313–16, 318, 322–24, 339, 341
Wilson, Henry, 347, 348
Wiltse, Charles M., 348
Wirt, William, 59, 89, 96
Wise, Henry A., 260, 273n
Wolcott, Oliver, 24
Woodbury, Levi, 248
Wright, Silas, 132, 133, 164, 212, 230, 248, 253, 261, 279
Wyly, James W., 198

Yale College, 17, 18, 22, 32, 36, 50, 157, 256
Yancey, Bartlett, 127
Yates, Robert, 136
Yorktown, Va., 107

DATE DUE
